Chess Olympiad – Skopje 1972

To Elsie, Larry & Nan

Chess Olympiad Skopje 1972

Ray Keene, David Levy

B. T. Batsford Limited London

First published 1973
© Ray Keene, David Levy, 1973
0 1734 0373 X

Printed and bound in Great Britain by
Cox & Wyman Ltd, London, Fakenham and Reading
for the publishers

B. T. Batsford Limited
4 Fitzhardinge Street, London W1H 0AH

Contents

The Illustrations

Symbols

+	Check
+ +	Double check
±	Clear advantage for White
∓	Clear advantage for Black
=	Balanced position
!	Good move
!?	Interesting move
?!	Dubious move
!!	Excellent move
1–0	Black resigned
½–½	Draw agreed
0–1	White resigned

W or *B* by the side of a diagram indicates which side is to move. In the text, a number in brackets refers to the corresponding diagram number.

Preface

The biennial chess Olympiad is the world chess championship for teams. The gigantic tournament at Skopje (lasting a whole month – the last two weeks of September and the first two weeks of October) was the twentieth in the series. A total of 63 teams competed in the men's event and each team comprised four regular players plus two reserves. Skopje saw for the first time the joint staging of the men's and women's team championships. This was the fifth such tournament for the ladies and involved 23 teams of two players plus one reserve. Both the men's and women's events were run on a system with preliminary qualifying groups followed by finals. The town of Skopje is in southern Yugoslavia on the river Vardar about equidistant from the borders of Bulgaria (to the east), Albania (to the west) and Greece (which lies due south). It is in the district of Macedonia which was the home of Alexander the Great.

One might ask why Skopje should be chosen as the site of an Olympiad. The answer lies in the aftermath of the earthquake which destroyed the town in 1963. International aid poured in from all sides to the afflicted inhabitants and a few years later a series of annual chess tournaments was inaugurated to commemorate this aid and the international goodwill shown. This series culminated most fittingly in the staging of the chess olympics, the most lavish possible expression of the FIDE motto: 'Gens una sumus'.

After the most tragic incident at the Munich Olympics in which Arab terrorists murdered Israeli athletes, the organizers at Skopje took great pains to ensure that a repetition of this atrocity did not occur on Yugoslav soil. Since, in addition, the authorities were concerned about the possibly violent activities of Serbian nationalists (a purely internal Yugoslav problem), the security precautions were unusually severe for a chess Olympiad. The hotels housing the players and the playing halls themselves were surrounded by armed police, and players had to pass through several checks each day just to enter the arena. As an extra precaution, the hotel floors of the rooms occupied by the Israeli team and Dr Euwe were guarded by special agents.

A chess Olympiad is an event of many facets. Besides being the contest for the world team championship, it is an excellent opportunity for the host country to display its finery before a multi-national audience. It is also the greatest social event of the chess calendar – old friendships are renewed; hundreds of dollars pass across the poker table. . . .

The Skopje Olympiad was all of these. Housed in shining new hotels and chalets, the 444 contestants were treated to the best that Macedonia has to offer. Competing in a vast, newly finished trio of convention halls some players met opponents with whom they had played a dozen or more times before, while others were making their début in the international arena.

We have tried to make this volume much more than a mere mass of games. We have included a varied collection of material which, we feel, will be of interest to all followers of the royal game. Of the 2964 games played at Skopje we have included 144 of the more interesting and entertaining. Almost all of these have notes, in many instances by those who played them. We also have a few unannotated games which have value, but for which we had no space for notes.

We would especially like to thank ex-World Champion Mikhail Botvinnik and Lt. Col. Ed Edmondson for granting us interviews and Alberic O'Kelly de Galway who acted as interpreter during our interview with Botvinnik. Our thanks are also due to the many players and commentators who supplied us with annotations, to *The Chess Player* for allowing us to make use of analyses contained in its issues 15a, 16 and 16a (volume 3), to Andrew Whiteley and Jana Hartston who translated material from Russian and Czech and to Jacqueline Keene who typed part of our manuscript.

Photographs 6, 7, 12, 13, 23, 25, 41 and 42 are by Gerhardt Bruckner and the remainder by David Levy.

RDK DNLL

London, November 1972

Interview with Mikhail Botvinnik

Ex-World Champion Mikhail Botvinnik was present in Skopje throughout the Olympiad as a spectator. His main interest nowadays is his work on computer chess. My [DNLL] first contact with him in Skopje was when he searched me out during one of my games and presented me with a copy of his new book *Blok-Schema Algoritma Igri v Shakhmati* ('Block-Scheme of an Algorithm for Playing Chess'). On the morning that we interviewed him in his hotel room, Botvinnik's table was covered with his writings on computer chess; he was preparing for a lecture on the subject which was to be filmed by Yugoslav television (see photograph 2). Nevertheless, he still takes an active interest in world chess and has many interesting views and comparisons which have been drawn from almost fifty years of experience.

Q Do you regard the present Olympiad system with qualifying groups and finals as a good one?

A Yes. There is no other possible system. This was decided twenty years ago. Everything was decided depending on the number of teams in such a way that the time of the olympiad cannot be much more than three weeks.

Q How deeply has the Soviet Chess Federation considered entering teams from the separate USSR republics?

A Well, Britain has Scotland and Wales and from the Soviet Union it would be possible to do that because we have a lot of strong teams: Latvia, Estonia, Bielorussia, Ukraine. . . . But you should put this question to the Soviet Federation.

Q The system for holding the individual World Championship has undergone many changes during the past forty years. Originally, the champion could defend his title when and against whom he liked. There is now no right of a return match for the defeated champion as there was in previous years but it seems that Fischer is willing to defend his title against Spassky next year, and then possibly against other players who have not worked their way up through the FIDE qualifying system. What do you think of this possibility that there could be matches outside the FIDE system?

A FIDE can exist only so long as the rules are rightly applied. FIDE has three basic constitutional principles. Firstly, there is the right to play chess. The second is that there should be some parliament-like structure within FIDE. The third is that FIDE should have the right to organize the World Championship. If something is done outside these rules then I think that it will be the first step on the road to the destruction of FIDE. FIDE can do anything she wants including changing the rules but some rules must be there. At the moment there are no rules concerning a return match and no rules which allow the champion to play against a player who didn't go through the qualifying system.

Why does Fischer want to play these additional matches?

Reply Because he likes to play matches with strong players and he wants to make more money.

Aaah – He wants to make chess into a business. If he wants to make money he should do something other than chess. If he absolutely wants to play chess then let him play chess but not for the World Championship.

As you said the rules have often been changed in the past forty years. If you decide something today it does not apply to the past. The champion who won the title according to the rules has to defend the title according to the same rules. Any change in the rules can only be brought in after a three year championship cycle has been finished. Thus, nobody has the right to change the rules before the next world championship. Perhaps you had better ask Euwe this question. Before the war, Euwe was very strict about keeping the rules as they were. Well there were not really any rules at that time because Alekhine and Capablanca were against the idea of rules. Now there are strict rules but Euwe is against them. But if you don't apply the rules then you are following a very dangerous course because these rules guarantee to the young, talented players that they will be sure to play for the World Championship if they really have the talent. The proof of that is what has happened in the past twenty-five years. Fischer got the title just because of these rules. I don't see why, in another six years, Karpov should be in a different position to Fischer.

Q How would you compare the quality of play in the seven matches and one tournament which you played for the World Championship. In which match did you yourself play the best? How do you rate the performances of your opponents?

A The first time, at the 1948 match tournament, I was not yet thirty-seven. Then I was at my best. As for the question of my opponents. They were all different. The difficulty of playing a match for the World Championship is not primarily your opponent but yourself. You have to fight yourself. You feel that this house is my house; this wife is my wife; this shirt is my shirt. It is my property. You feel like the owner of a house, that the title belongs to you. When you have something you consider it as your own, and therefore it seems somehow unlikely that the

challenger would take the title away. And when you feel like that there
seems to be no point to work for the match. This is the main danger for
the champion. Spassky, up to the twentieth game, did not think that
Fischer could take the title away from him. Now he believes it!

Q How do you think the standard of play in the Reykjavik match
compares with the standard in your own matches?

A That is a very difficult question. In a way it is impossible to compare them. I think that the quality of the games were on the normal
level for the World Championship. The first ten games were below
normal. The second half possibly a little higher than the normal
standard. The tenth game was a good one. But it is too little that I can
pick out just one game.

Q You are the only Grandmaster who has clashed with all the World
Champions of the twentieth century; with Lasker, Capablanca, Alekhine and Euwe and with Smyslov, Tal, Petrosian and Spassky. In
addition, we assume that you have studied Fischer's games in depth
as well as the games of all these other players. Do you think that
Fischer has some extra quality that these other great masters did not
possess?

A He has a great capacity for work, just like Alekhine. It is very
difficult to play against him because he works all the time. In the
second half of the recent match Spassky demonstrated a plus in almost
all the games. But when he got to the point where it was necessary to
realize his pressure Spassky was weaker than Fischer.

Q Which games from your own career do you recall with the greatest
pleasure? Do you have one particular favourite, played either by yourself or by another player?

A It is difficult to answer because I had a lot of good games as well
as bad games. Possibly my game against Capablanca which I won with
bishop to a3.*

* The game to which Botvinnik refers was played in the AVRO tournament
in 1938. Botvinnik frequently uses the final combination as an example in his
work on computer chess. White: *Botvinnik* Black: *Capablanca* Nimzo Indian
Defence. 1 P–Q4 N–KB3 2 P–QB4 P–K3 3 N–QB3 B–N5 4 P–K3 P–Q4
5 P–QR3 B×N+ 6 P×B P–B4 7 BP×P KP×P 8 B–Q3 0–0 9 N–K2
P–QN3 10 0–0 B–R3 11 B×B N×B 12 B–N2 Q–Q2 13 P–QR4 KR–K1
14 Q–Q3 P–B5 15 Q–B2 N–N1 16 QR–K1 N–B3 17 N–N3 N–QR4
18 P–B3 N–N6 19 P–K4 Q×P 20 P–K5 N–Q2 21 Q–B2 P–N3 22 P–B4
P–B4 23 P×P ep N×BP 24 P–B5 R×R 25 R×R R–K1 26 R–K6 R×R
27 P×R K–N2 28 Q–B4 Q–K1 29 Q–K5 Q–K2 30 B–R3 Q×B 31 N–R5+
P×N 32 Q–N5+ K–B1 33 Q×N+ K–N1 34 P–K7 Q–B8+ 35 K–B2
Q–B7+ 36 K–N3 Q–Q6+ 37 K–R4 Q–K5+ 38 K×P Q–K7+ 39
K–R4 Q–K5+ 40 P–N4 Q–K8+ 41 K–R5 Resigns.

Q Do you think that interest in chess in the Soviet Union will decline at all because the World Champion is now from another country, or will this stimulate more interest?

A On the contrary. Before the match, chess had become more popular and now after the match it will still be more popular. In the twenties the Soviet people did not play chess well. But then there was a big effort to play chess well and it became more popular. I think that the same sort of thing will happen now.

Q What do you think of the leading, young Western Grandmasters: Browne, Hübner, Ljubojevic, Mecking and Andersson, and how do they compare in their styles with the young Soviet players Karpov, Tukmakov, Balashov etc.?

A I think that Karpov is the strongest of them and I think that he has a bright future.

Q Why do you think it is that women, in general, are much weaker players than men?

A It is a biological phenomenon. The woman is biologically more complex than a man. She is made in such a way that she has to procreate and that is a responsibility but it is also a burden. If you force a computer to work in one direction and then you put in another task it will work with more difficulty. But women think quite differently about this.

Q To most chess lovers the game is like a drug. People fail exams at university because they play too much chess. Or they lose their jobs because they take time off to play in some tournament. Yet you managed to give up the game, apparently without suffering any withdrawal symptoms. Did you find it very easy to make this break? When you come to an event such as an Olympiad are you sorry that you are a spectator rather than a player?

A I was always very disciplined in such matters. Now I consider that my duty is to produce a good chess program.

Q If you are successful in this work and in twenty or thirty years' time there is a computer program which can play Grandmaster chess or maybe even World Championship chess, how do you think this will affect the game?

A This will happen, probably even earlier. And there will be no problem because the game will become more popular. Although it is possible to go everywhere by car, a lot of people still want to walk.

Interview with Ed Edmondson

Ed Edmondson, Executive Director of the United States Chess Federation, was present at Skopje during the meetings of the FIDE congress.

Q Why was the best American team not available for this Olympiad?

A The primary reason of course is that Bobby Fischer, the best
player in the world, was too tired from the Reykjavik match. The
second player, if we had our best team, was Reshevsky, and although
the Yugoslavs knew more than a year in advance that there were
(Jewish) holidays that would prevent Reshevsky playing at that time
they were unable to get the playing hall for another period, and to consider Reshevsky more important than all the teams of all the other
nations. . . . And so Reshevsky couldn't play because of religious holidays.

Lombardy and Evans are the other two strong players who were not
with our team. Lombardy is a teacher in a Catholic school and he had
been all summer in Iceland with Fischer as his second in the championship match. It was impossible for Lombardy to even consider asking for
time off again so quickly from his duties with the Catholic school.
Evans would have played if we had wanted to pay him a sufficient
honorarium but since we felt that the presence of Evans might make
the difference between us finishing ninth and sixth, we saw no reason
to pay the honorarium.

Q How do you think you would have done if you had had your best
team?

A We would have been first.

Q Will future American teams receive sufficient financial sponsorship to enable them to be at full strength in Olympiads?

A I emphasize again that I don't think it was financial sponsorship
which was the problem this time. The problem was primarily that
Fischer was too tired to play, Reshevsky had religious conflicts with the
schedule, Lombardy couldn't get away from school. If those three
players had been available this time then I feel confident that the
financial terms would have been met.

Q But now that chess seems to be big money in the United States
don't you think it likely that for future team tournaments the players
will all want substantial honoraria?

A Yes, and I think they can have it.

Q What do you think would be fair fees for your players?

A It depends on the growth of chess in the next two years. It would be very difficult to speculate on it at the moment. However, we have, in the last couple of Olympiads, paid our Grandmasters (apart from Fischer) $2,000. This is a pretty fair fee, I think, compared with what anyone else in the world gets for coming to an Olympiad. But I would expect that to at least double for the next Olympiad.

Q And what do you think Fischer should get?

A I don't know. That's a very difficult thing to say. I believe that what Fischer gets in the future depends to a great extent on the professional management that I believe he should have now. When I say professional I mean entertainment, legal and accounting professionals who will, I hope, be able to win Bobby's trust, and I hope that Bobby will take their advice in all matters concerning his career. He can make money today beyond the dreams of any chess player by overlapping into the field of entertainment, into the world of education for sale in the form of phonograph records or eventually TV cassettes on chess. In order to continue selling these items he must continue to play in certain chess events to keep his name in front of the public. Therefore I would hope that the financial rewards which Bobby gets in the future come from allied activities and make it unnecessary for him to demand huge fees to play chess.

Q Do you approve of the structure of the Olympiad? Do you think that the present system is the best or are there too many teams?

A It would be unfair of me to answer that because I haven't studied both sides of the question sufficiently. It is obvious from listening to other people that there is a general unhappiness but I do not have a personal opinion as to how to correct what seem to be the problems and I think it unfair to make only destructive criticism.

Q Do you think that the Elo system imposes too much strain on players?

A The ratings have become very important in the United States to even the lower-ranking club players. In a way this is unfortunate because I see too many people now who play for ratings rather than for love of the game, and I think that is unfortunate.

Q How has the Fischer-Spassky match affected interest in chess in the United States?

A Chess in the United States has been on a definite upswing for six years. We have had an average annual growth rate of 24 per cent per year for the six years preceding the match. Since the match we have had a tremendous increase even over that growth rate. I would say that it is going to double our growth rate this year; that we will grow approximately 50 per cent.

Q In the United States most players compete in individual events rather than in club matches or other team competitions as is the case in Europe. Why is this?

A The obvious difference is geography. I have played and still play in team matches. But suppose that we had team contests just in the state of Texas: it is 1,200 miles from Houston to El Paso, one way. This means that if they play each other on a home and away basis they must make a trip of 2,400 miles to play one or two games in a match and that's rather discouraging. It applies to a lesser extent in other states. In California, for example, I was once a member of a team in the Central California Chess League. We used to drive 300 miles on a Sunday to play one game of chess. It is rather demanding, I think, and now that individual tournaments are available quite frequently on weekends in every major metropolitan area of the country, every player can play four or five games without leaving home. It is only human, I think, that they would prefer to do that than drive hundreds of miles just to play one game.

Q Is there any likelihood of the United States organizing a chess Olympiad?

A I would say that it's utterly impossible. In our country it would cost at least two million dollars. We have no Government support and no likelihood of commercial support for that kind of a budget.

Q How do you see the future of international chess in the United States?

A There will be a steady increase in international activity. We have Church's international tournament in November. We are already planning in late June or early July of 1973 for a twelve man international tournament of a much lower FIDE category. We are hopeful that we may have a second 12-man tournament by the end of 1973 and another sponsored 16-man tournament of great importance in 1974. So I believe that in the future we will see at least two international tournaments a year in the United States which is of course much more than we have ever had in the past. There is also a good likelihood that we may be able to host such events as the World Junior Championship from time to time. We definitely will be hosting one or other of the Pan-American championships either the individual or the team championship.

We don't really think we can afford an Olympiad, but short of the Olympiad we do expect a tremendous increase of international activity on USA soil.

B

The Preliminaries

Organization of the Preliminary Groups

For the strongest teams in an Olympiad, the preliminary rounds provide a few days of relaxation. Qualifying for the A-final is accomplished by smashing the weakies 4–0 or 3½–½ and inflicting less crushing defeats on the middling teams. Their nearest rivals are normally content to agree four quick draws if offered them. It is therefore extremely rare for one of the top seeded teams to be in any danger of finishing below the A-final.

At the other end of the scale there is also little tension during the preliminaries. Andorra, Guernsey, the Virgin Islands and Malta never need to fear being promoted above the D-final. They take great delight in their one biennial encounter with one of the very strongest chess nations, one of their number occasionally earning immortality by succumbing to a dashing attack or a brilliant combination perpetrated by a Grandmaster.

It is for the multitude of teams in the middle that the seeding and organization of the preliminary groups is so important. Failing narrowly to qualify for the A-final dooms a team which might have finished anywhere upwards from sixteenth to a struggle in which success is marked by seventeenth place and total failure by thirty second. One might argue that a team only fails to qualify for some particular final group through its own inadequacies but this is not always the case. Take for example the case of Australia in preliminary group VII. When the last round started they looked set to finish in final group B. Their only rivals, Columbia, being paired with the strong Bulgarian team which was destined for the A-final. But Bulgaria and Columbia agreed to a 'package deal' for a 2–2 draw, the games ending in 11, 13, 11 and 10 moves. Had this match really been played the Columbians would have met with certain defeat and thereby finished in group C instead of the luckless Australians.

The method of seeding the teams and arranging them into groups also carries some element of luck. The size of the preliminary and final groups naturally depends on the total number of teams in the Olympiad. A system has been worked out for any number of teams from twenty-one to seventy-two, specifying how many teams play in each preliminary group and how many from each group are allocated to each final group. If there are sixty teams in total, there are five final groups, each of twelve teams. A team seeded thirteenth would thus be expected to qualify for group B where theoretically it would finish first but where it could, if hit by a succession of disasters, finish twenty-fourth. With sixty-one teams instead of sixty, the top three final groups would each have sixteen teams and number thirteen would be seeded for the A-final.

The method used to seed the teams has changed since the last Olympiad at Siegen. Previously it was the practice to arrange a rough seeding order based on the results of the past few Olympiads and then make small adjustments depending on the inclusion or exclusion of various star players in some of the teams. This method worked well. No team could honestly claim to have suffered an injustice through their seeding. In the interim however, we have been blessed with the Elo system for rating international players according to their results. What could be fairer than seeding all teams in the order of the average ratings of their players? Nothing at all, provided that the ratings reflect the true strengths of the players. But when deciding that they actually would use this method, the seeding committee forgot one important factor. Many players whose strength is well above Elo's minimum rating figure of 2200 have no official rating because they have not, within a prescribed period, played sufficient games in international competition. Again we use Australia as an example of the bad luck that can befall a team in this way. At the Lugano Olympiad in 1968, Australia finished 29th. At Siegen, two years later, they were 15th. This time, with a stronger team than ever before, they had hoped to reach the A-final but with only four of their players on the Elo list (the remaining two were assigned ratings of 2200) their average rating was artificial and their seeding position commensurately low.

The disadvantage of a low seeding can be seen from the following table:

Group	I	II	III	IV	V	VI	VII	VIII
Seeding	1	2	3	4	5	6	7	8
positions of	16	15	14	13	12	11	10	9
the teams	17	18	19	20	21	22	23	24
	32	31	30	29	28	27	26	25
	33 . . . etc.							

If your team is seeded 14th, the three strongest remaining teams in your group are those seeded 3rd, 19th and 30th: average seeding just below 17th. If, however, you are seeded 30th, the average seeding of your three rival teams is 12th. You therefore meet substantially stronger opposition in your fight for a place in the A-final simply because your merited seeding place is taken by a team which is much stronger than the one you displace by your artificially low seeding.

So much for the element of luck in the preliminaries. Let us now move on to a detailed analysis of each preliminary group.

PRELIMINARY GROUP I

	U	D	B	C	F	D	L	Total	Final Group
USSR	×	3½	4	2½	4	4	4	22	A
Denmark	½	×	3	2	2½	3	4	15	A
Belgium	0	1	×	3	3	3½	3½	14	B
Cuba	1½	2	1	×	2½	2½	3½	13	B
Finland	0	1½	1	1½	×	4	3½	11½	C
Dominican Republic	0	1	½	1½	0	×	3	6	C
Luxemburg	0	0	½	½	½	1	×	2½	D

Of course the USSR won this group with great ease, but they had some unpleasant moments. The Soviet Champion, Savon, did not seem to be at home with his senior Grandmaster colleagues and was responsible for 1½ of the 2 points missing from a 100 per cent score (½ v Denmark – 0 v Cuba). Korchnoi was also engaged in a dubious battle in the Cuba Match and could well have lost to Silvino Garcia, which would have been a real sensation. Surprisingly enough it was not Cuba (who faltered in some other matches) but Denmark who nosed into Final A with the Russians. The Belgians put up a great fight to take third place, while the performance of Finland – led by Westerinen and Ojanen – must have been a bitter disappointment to them.

1 **Beyen** (Belgium) – **Tal** (USSR)

Modern Benoni Defence

1 P–Q4 N–KB3 2 P–QB4 P–B4
3 P–Q5 P–KN3 4 N–QB3 B–N2
5 P–K4 0–0 6 B–Q3 P–K3 7 KN–
K2 P×P 8 BP×P P–Q3 9 0–0
P–N3 10 B–KN5! This is more active than 10 P–KR3 B–QR3 11 B×B N×B 12 N–N3 N–B2 13 P–QR4 P–QR3 14 Q–Q3 Q–Q2 when the position offers equal chances. 10 . . . P–KR3 11 B–KB4 B–R3 12 P–QR4 R–K1 13 P–R3 Q–K2 14 N–N3 P–B5?! Better is 14 . . . B×B 15 Q×B QN–Q2.

After all, the point of Black's . . . P–QN3 and . . . B–QR3 is to exchange the light squared bishops in order to reduce White's pressure on the K-side. 15 B–B2 QN–Q2 16 Q–Q2 Q–B1 17 B–K3 N–B4 18 P–B3? Unnecessary. The KP already has enough protection. White should continue putting Black's K-side under pressure by 18 P–B4 or 18 B–Q4. 18 . . . N/3–Q2 19 P–B4 N–N6 20 B×N P×B 21 R–B3 QR–B1 22 P–R5? This completely unthematic move throws away White's advantage. Correct was 22 P–K5 P×P 23 P–B5, with good attacking chances to compensate for the sacrificed pawn. **22 . . . P–QN4! 23 B×P R–B5 24 R–K1 P–R4 25 N–B1 P–N5 26 N–Q1 N–B3 27 N–B2 N× KP 28 N×N R/1×N 29 R×R R×R 30 R×P Q–K2 31 B–B2 R–K7 32 Q×P?** 32 Q–Q1 R×P 33 R×R B×R is clearly better for Black, but this was White's best course. **32 . . . R×B 33 K×R Q–K7+ 34 K–N3 Q×N 35 Q×P B–Q5 36 P–B5 Q–K8+ 37 Resigns** the queen is lost: 37 K–B4 B–K4+ 38 Q×B/ 5P–N4+.

Analysis by Gufeld in THE CHESS PLAYER

2 **Estevez** (Cuba) – **Savon** (USSR)

Sicilian Defence

1 P–K4 P–QB4 2 N–KB3 P–Q3 3 P–Q4 P×P 4 Q×P B–Q2 5 P–B4 N–QB3 6 Q–Q2 P–KN3 7 P–QN3 B–N2 8 N–B3 N–B3 9 B–N2 0–0 10 P–KR3 P–QR3? Better is 10 . . . Q–R4 11 B–Q3 N–R4! 12 0–0 N–B5 13 Q×N B×N 14 Q–R6 P–B3 with equal chances. **11 B–Q3 Q–R4 12 P–R3! KR–B1 13 0–0 Q–Q1 14 P–QN4 B–K3 15 KR–K1?** After 15 N–Q5 White would have had a clear advantage. **15 . . . N–Q2! 16 N–Q5 N/3–K4 17 N×N N×N 18 B×N B×B** Black's two bishops provide sufficient compensation for White's well posted knight. The chances are roughly equal. **19 QR–B1 P–QR4 20 P–N5 R–B4 21 P–B4 B– N2 22 K–R1 B–Q2** Too passive. Black should have exchanged on Q4. **23 QR–Q1 P–K3 24 N–K3 Q–B3 25 N–N4 Q–N7?** 25 . . . Q–K2 26 P–K5 P×P 27 N×P

would have kept White's advantage within manageable proportions. But after the text Black should always be lost. **26 Q×Q B×Q**

27 P–K5! Winning a pawn because of the threat of 28 N–B6+. **27 . . . B–K1 28 P×P R–Q1 29 B–B1 B–Q2 30 R–K3 R/4–B1 31 P–QR4 B–N2 32 N–B2** 32 N–K5 was stronger. On KB2 the knight has no big future, but by now Black was so short of time that any move would probably have won. **32 . . . P–B4 33 R/3–K1 P–N3 34 R–K3 R–B4 35 R/3–K1 R/1–QB1 36 B–K2 B–B6 37 R–KB1 Black lost on time**

Analysis by Gufeld in THE CHESS PLAYER

3 **Fernandez** (Cuba) – **Rantanen** (Finland)

King's Indian Defence

1 P–Q4 N–KB3 2 P–QB4 P–KN3 3 N–QB3 B–N2 4 P–K4 P–Q3 5 P–B3 0–0 6 B–K3 QN–Q2 It is more usual to play 6 . . . P–K4 or 6 . . . N–B3. **7 Q–Q2 P–B4 8 KN–K2 P–QR3 9 B–R6?!** Too hasty; 9 0–0–0 is superior. Now Black could have achieved excellent prospects by means of 9 . . . B×B! 10 Q×B Q–R4 11 Q–Q2 P–QN4. **9 . . .**

Q–R4? **10 B×B K×B 11 P–KN4**
P×P it was better to play . . . P–
QN4. **12 N×P N–B4 13 B–K2**
P–QN4? Now this advance is incorrect, since it creates a fatal weakening of QB3. Up to here the play on
both sides has been far from dis-
tinguished, but now White rescues
the game from the oblivion which has
so far been its just destiny by pro-
ducing a most elegant combination
which leads by force to the capture
of Black's queen. **14 P–N5 N–R4**
15 P–N4! Q×NP 16 N–B6 Q–R6
17 N–N1 Q–R5 18 Q–N2+ P–K4
19 N–B3 N–B5 20 N×Q Resigns
Notes by Keene

4 **Sloth** (Denmark) –
  Karpov (USSR)

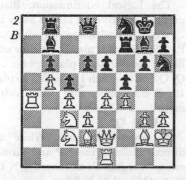

Karpov takes full advantage of the
lack of co-ordination of White's
forces.

28 . . .	**P–K4!**
29 N–Q5	**KP×P**
30 NP×P	

If 30 B×P P–N4 31 B–Q2 B×N
followed by . . . P–B5, or 30 N×BP
P–N4 31 N–R5 B–K4 with excellent
attacking chances in each case. The
text is White's best hope.

30 . . .	**P×P**
31 P×P	**N–K3**
32 Q–Q3	

32 P–B5 P×P 33 P×P fails to
33 . . . B–K4+ and 34 . . . N×P.
The text is the only satisfactory way
to defend the KBP against the threat
of . . . B×N. e.g. 32 R–KB1 B×N
33 KP×B N×P 34 B×N R×B
35 R×R B–K4.

32 . . .	**Q–KB1**

Since on 32 . . . B×N 33 Q×B
Black cannot capture the KBP
because of the pin on the KN1–QR7
diagonal.

33 R–KB1	**K–R1!**

Destroying the potential pin mentioned in the last note.

34 N×P

If 34 Q–KN3 P–N4 35 P–B5
B–K4 36 B–QB3 N–Q5! end of
game. Unable to defend his BP Sloth
embarks on a somewhat irrelevant
Q-side gesture but in any event
his position is collapsing around
him.

34 . . .	**N×P**
35 B×N	**R×B**
36 N–Q7	**R×R!**
37 Q×R	

37 N×Q B–K4+ leaves Black a
rook ahead.

37 . . .	**Q×Q**
38 B×Q	**R–Q1**
39 N–N6	**B×P**
40 N–K3	**B–K4+**
41 K–N1	**B–Q5**
42 Resigns	

Because of 42 K–B2 N–B4 43
R–R3 R–KB1.
Notes by Levy based on analysis in 64

5 **Alvarez** (Dominican Republic) –
  Karpov (USSR)

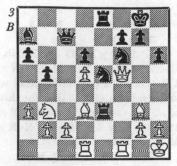

Karpov wins by a neat combination: **25 . . . R×B/N6! 26 P×R N/4–N5 27 QR–K1 R×R 28 R×R N–B7+ 29 K–R2 N/3–N5+ 30 K–N1 N–K5+ 31 Resigns**

6 Karpov (USSR) – **Cobo** (Cuba)

Sicilian Defence

1 P–K4	**P–QB4**
2 N–KB3	**P–Q3**
3 P–Q4	**P×P**
4 N×P	**N–KB3**
5 N–QB3	**P–QR3**
6 P–B4	

6 B–K2 can transpose into the positions arising after the text.

6 . . .	**P–K3**
7 B–K2	**Q–B2**
8 0–0	**N–B3**
9 K–R1	**B–Q2**

We have now reached a position more characteristic of the Scheveningen Variation than the Najdorf Variation with which the game began. Black's position perhaps suffers from the slight disadvantage that the queen has gone to QB2 too soon.

10 P–QR4	**B–K2**
11 N–N3	**0–0**
12 B–K3	

There was no point in trying to tie up the Q-side with 12 P–R5 as Black could break out with 12 . . . P–QN4. But now 13 P–R5 is an unpleasant threat.

12 . . .   **N–QN5**

Black ignores his opponent's plan. He had to play 12 . . . P–QN3 and only then 13 . . . N–QR4 or 13 . . . N–QN5. The alternative 12 . . . N–QR4 would give White a slight advantage after 13 P–K5 N–K1 14 N×N Q×N/R4 15 Q–Q2 and 16 B–Q4.

Now White gets a clear positional advantage.

13 P–R5   **B–B3**

If 13 . . . P–Q4 14 B–N6 Q–B1 15 P–K5 N–K5 16 N×N P×N 17 P–B4.

14 B–N6   **Q–N1**

The logical continuation. Black prepares to drive the bishop away by . . . N–Q2 and follow up with . . . P–QN4. But this plan is too slow and Black should have played 14 . . . Q–Q2 after which I intended to play 15 B–B3, preventing the freeing move . . . P–Q4.

15 Q–Q2

An important move. White indirectly defends the KP and threatens to win Black's advanced QN by 16 N–Q1 and 17 P–B3.

15 . . .   **P–Q4**
16 P–K5   **N–Q2**

16 . . . N–K5 17 N×N P×N 18 P–B4 (threatening 19 N–B5) is horrible for Black.

17 B–Q4   **P–QN4**
18 B–N4

Preparing P–B5 and preventing Black from advancing his BP. White would have achieved nothing concrete with 18 P×P ep N×NP 19

P–B5 because of 19 . . . P×P 20 R×BP N–B5.

18 . . .   **P–N3**

19 QR–K1

Black's pieces are clustered on the Q-side and he takes no steps to transfer them to the defence of his king. He even removes his KR from the vital square KB1 to make room for the knight.

19 . . .   **R–B1**

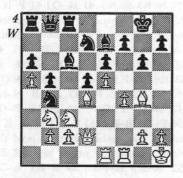

20 P–B5

Decisive.

20 . . .   **NP×P**

If 20 . . . KP×P 21 P–K6.

21 B×P   **N–B1**

Again if 21 . . . P×B, 22 P–K6 wins.

22 Q–R6   **N–N3**

After 22 . . . P×B White breaks open Black's position by 23 P–K6 P–B3 24 R×P N×BP (24 . . . B–K1 25 R×BP and 26 R–B7) 25 R–N5+ N–N3 26 R×N+ P×R 27 Q×P+ K–R1 28 B×P+ B×B 29 Q×B+ K–R2 30 R–K5!

30 N–Q4 (instead of 30 R–K5) is tempting. e.g. 30 . . . N×R (30 . . . N×N 31 R–K3) 31 N–B5 R–R2 32 P–K7 R×P 33 Q×R+ K–N3 34 Q–K6+ K–N4 (34 . . . K–R4 35 Q–R6+ K–N5 36 N–K3 mate) 35 P–R4+ K–N5 (35 . . . K–R4 36 Q–R6+ K–N5 37 Q–N5 mate) 36 N–K3+ K–N6 (36 . . . K–R4 37 Q–N4+ K–R3 38 N–B5+ K–R2 39 Q–N7 mate; or 36 . . . K×P 37 Q–N4 mate) 37 Q–N4+ K–B7 38 NB3–Q1 mate. However, Black can avoid mate by 30 . . . R–B1 when White has to fight to win.

23 B×N   **RP×B**

Eldis Cobo overlooks that after 24 . . . B–B1 he loses control of KR4 and White's major pieces are able to attack his king along the open KR-file. If 24 . . . BP×B the immediate 25 R–B7 does not work because the Black king can escape to the Q-side via K1 and Q2. So I had intended to play 24 Q–R3 B–Q2 25 R–B7 K×R 26 Q×RP+ K–K1 27 Q–N8+ B–B1 28 R–KB1 K–Q1 29 Q×B+ B–K1 (29 . . . K–B2 30 Q–Q6+ K–N2 31 Q–N6 mate) 30 B–N6+ K–Q2 (30 . . . R–B2 31 N–B5) 31 R–B7+ B×R 32 Q×B+ K–B3 33 N–Q4 mate.

24 R–K3   **B–B1**

25 Q–R4   **B–KN2**

26 R–R3   **B–K1**

27 Q–R7+   **K–B1**

28 Q×NP   **P–B3**

If 28 . . . B×P 29 Q×KP with an easy win, and if 28 . . . N×P 29 R–R7 forces mate.

29 R×P+   **Resigns**

Notes by Karpov in 64 translated specially for this volume by Andrew Whiteley

7 **S. Garcia** (Cuba) – **Korchnoy** (USSR)

French Defence

1 P–K4 P–K3   2 P–Q4 P–Q4 3 N–Q2 N–KB3   4 P–K5 KN–Q2 5 P–KB4 P–QB4   6 P–B3 N–QB3

7 QN–B3 Q–R4 On a previous occasion Korchnoi had been successful against Silvino Garcia with 7 . . . P–B5. The text is currently fashionable after Korchnoi's introduction of the move against Matulovic in the 1972 USSR–Yugoslavia match. For a further game with the line see Portisch-Hug (game 82). **8 N–K2 P–QN4 9 B–Q2** Korchnoi intended to meet 9 P×P with 9 . . . P–N5, which leads to obscure complications. **P–N5 10 P–N4** It is more accurate to insert 10 P×NP. After the text White's position becomes a little loose, granting Korchnoi just the kind of counterchances he relishes. **NP×P 11 NP×P N–N3 12 B–R3 N–B5 13 0–0 P–R4 14 B–B1 RP×P 15 B×P P–N3 16 N–N5 N–K2 17 R–B3 R–R5 18 B–KR3 R–N1** Black has excellent play on both sides of the board. **19 Q–K1 R–KR1 20 Q–B1 Q–R5 21 B–N4 R–R5 22 Q–N2 Q–Q8+ 23 R–B1 Q–B7 24 Q–N3 R–KR1 25 B–K3 N–B4 26 B×N NP×B 27 QR–K1 Q×RP**

28 R–B2 R–N8 29 B–B1 Q–R8 30 R–N2 R–R3 31 N×BP A desperation sacrifice, but in acute time pressure Black defends inaccurately and then the fun starts. **K×N 32 Q–N8+ K–K2 32 . . .** K–K1 leaves White with nothing for the piece. **33 R–N7+ B×R 34 Q×B/N7+ K–Q1 35 Q×R P×P 36 Q–B8+ K–B2 37 Q–B5+ K–N2 38 P×P Q–R4 39 Q×Q N×Q 40 N–B3 R–N5 41 R–Q1** 41 P–R4! followed by rushing this pawn forward at top speed, would bring White close to victory. **B–Q2 42 K–B2 R–N6 43 R–Q3 N–B3 44 P–R4 B–K1 45 R–N3 N×QP 46 N–K2 R×R 47 N×R N–N6 48 B–R3 P–Q5 49 P–R5 P–Q6 50 P–R6 B–N3 51 B–N4** 51 K–K3! would still enable White to hold the draw. Now he must lose. **K–B3 52 K–K3 K–N4 53 B–K1 K–B5 54 N–R5 P–R4 55 N–B6 P–R5 56 N–K8 N–B4 57 N–Q6+ K–N6 58 K–Q4 P–R6 59 N–N5 P–R7 60 B–B3 and Resigns**

Notes by Keene

PRELIMINARY GROUP II

	Y	S	P	E	B	J	S	C	Total	Final Group
Yugoslavia	×	2	3½	3	3	4	3	4	22½	A
Switzerland	2	×	2	1½	2½	3½	3½	4	19	A
Peru	½	2	×	2	2½	4	4	4	19	B
England	1	2½	2	×	3	2½	3½	4	18½	B
Brazil	1	1½	1½	1	×	3½	4	3	15½	C
Japan	0	½	0	1½	½	×	2½	3	8	C
Syria	1	½	0	½	0	1½	×	1½	5	D
Cyprus	0	0	0	0	1	1	2½	×	4½	D

Yugoslavia qualified with ease although some of her players were not always so comfortable against the weaker teams (Matanovic put a piece *en prise* against a Syrian and Rukavina was a piece down for nothing against Brazil, but still managed to draw the ending).

The real fight here was for the second place in the A-final. England's chances appeared excellent until she dropped 1½ points against Japan (in final group C Scotland defeated Japan 4–0 and Wales won 3½–½). This left the fight between Switzerland and Peru. When the last round began, Switzerland were two points behind Peru but while Peru were paired against Yugoslavia, the Swiss were playing the weak Brazilian team that lacked their country's one star player, Henrique Mecking. Peru lost by 3½–½. Switzerland drew level with them on game points and the Peruvians were demoted to the B-final on tie split – match points were even, the result of their individual match was a draw but the Swiss team had the better Sonneborn score.

8 Gligoric (Yugoslavia) – Hug (Switzerland)

Dutch Defence

The Yugoslav Grandmaster demolishes the positionally unsound Stonewall version of the Dutch Defence in classic style. First of all he takes control of the dark squares, weakened by Black's very choice of opening, and then he smashes open the centre to clear a path to his opponent's weak pawns. The result of this is that Gligoric emerges with an extra pawn which is sufficient to win the ending. Unchastened by this lesson the effervescent Junior World Champion went on to employ this very line in the Final, against Petrosian of all people (see game Petrosian-Hug, page 93)!

1 P–Q4	P–K3
2 P–QB4	P–KB4
3 N–KB3	N–KB3
4 P–KN3	B–K2
5 B–N2	0–0
6 0–0	P–B3
7 P–N3	P–QR4
8 N–B3	P–Q4
9 B–N2	B–Q2
10 P–K3	B–K1
11 N–K2	B–Q3
12 N–B4	Q–K2
13 Q–B2	N–K5
14 N–K5	N–Q2
15 P–B3	N–N4
16 N/B–Q3	N–B2
17 N× N/d7	B×N
18 P–K4	P–K4

19 P–B5	B–B2
20 KP×QP	BP×P
21 P×P	N–N4
22 P–B4	N–K5
23 B–Q4	R–R3
24 N–B2	R–KN3
25 N×N	BP×N
26 Q–K2	Q–K1
27 Q–K3	P–R4
28 R–B2	P–KR5
29 P×P	B–Q1
30 P–R5	R–KR3
31 B–R3	R×RP
32 B×B	Q×B
33 R–KN2	Q–B4
34 Q–N3	R–B2
35 Q–N4	K–R2
36 R–Q1	P–KN3
37 Q×Q	R/R×Q
38 B–K3	B–K2
39 R–N3	P–Q5
40 R×QP	B×P
41 R×P/e4	R×BP
42 R×R	B×B+
43 R×B	R×R
44 P–K6	R–B1
45 P–K7	R–K1
46 K–B2	K–N2
47 K–K2	K–B2
48 K–Q3	P–R5
49 P×P	R×P and Black Resigned

9 Hartston (England) – Ljubojevic (Yugoslavia)

Sicilian Defence

1 P–K4	P–QB4
2 N–KB3	P–Q3
3 P–Q4	N–KB3

An unusual move-order probably played to avoid the currently fashionable 3 ... P×P 4 Q×P followed by P–QB4. I think that White can keep some advantage with 4 P×P now, but I prefer the positions arising from the main line.

	4 N–B3	P×P
	5 N×P	P–QR3
	6 B–K3	

Robert Byrne's line with which I have had some pleasant experiences recently.

	6 . . .	QN–Q2

6 . . . N–N5 7 B–KN5 seems to waste more of Black's time than White's, but 6 . . . P–K4 is the most critical response.

	7 B–K2	N–B4
	8 B–B3	B–Q2

8 . . . P–K3 may be better, leaving the Q2 square for the knight.

9 P–KN4!

This thrust combined with long castling is one of the thematic ideas of 6 B–K3.

	9 . . .	P–R3
	10 Q–K2	P–KN3
	11 P–N5	

The alternative is 11 0–0–0 followed by P–KR4 and P–N5; it is difficult to say which is better.

	11 . . .	P×P
	12 B×P	B–N2
	13 0–0–0	Q–R4
	14 P–KR4	R–QB1

Black seems to have some queen's side pressure, but it is difficult for him to get his king's rook into play since castling will always allow an instant attack with P–R5. I think White stands better, but I could easily be wrong.

	15 K–N1	N–R5

I had expected 15 . . . N–K3 when 16 B–K3 may be best; I don't believe the exchange sacrifice on c3.

	16 N×N	B×B
	17 B–B1!	

This removes the bishop from attack and renews possibilities of P–R5. I also wanted to have the QNP protected in case Black had ideas of . . . Q–K4 and mating me on the diagonal.

	17 . . .	N–R4
	18 N–N3	Q–B2

18 . . . Q–K4 19 R–Q5 is too strong.

	19 B–K3	B–K4
	20 Q–Q2	Q–B5?

This must be wrong because White now seizes the initiative, but I am not sure what is better. Perhaps 20 . . . BQ–B3 is best.

21 R–QB1!

Both defending the QBP and preparing its advance.

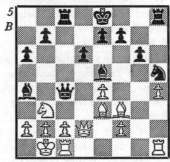

	21 . . .	N–B3
	22 N–R5	Q–B2
	23 P–B4	N–Q2

23 . . . P–N3? is killed by 24 Q–N4!

24 P–R5!

Black's knight cannot hold up breakthroughs on both sides at once; White should win such a position comfortably now.

	24 . . .	P–N3
	25 P×P!	R×R
	26 P×P+	K–Q1!

After 26 . . . K×P? 27 R×R

P×N 28 B–R5+ Black's king is quickly torn to pieces.

27 B×R	**P×N**
28 P–B5!	**N–B1**

For the piece White has two pawns, a strong attack and every prospect of crushing through. Now, however, instead of continuing forcefully I begin a series of dithering second-best plans while my opponent starts playing with great ingenuity.

29 B–Q4?

The simple 29 P–B4 B–N2 30 P–K5 is quite overwhelming. It is difficult even to suggest moves for Black after that.

29 ...	**B×B**
30 Q×B	**B–B3**
31 Q–N7	**K–Q2**
32 B–B3	**B–R1**

Black has now cleverly straightened out his defences.

33 B–N4+	**P–K3**
34 P–K5	**B–K5+!**

All these moves were played with both sides in time trouble, but Ljubojevic continues to find excellent defensive ideas. 34 ... P–Q4 35 P–B4 followed by P–B5 would be very dangerous.

35 K–R1	**P×KP**

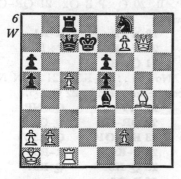

36 R–Q1+

I played this very quickly then suddenly remembered that I had intended 36 P–B6+. Black is then forced to play 36 ... K–Q3 since 36 ... B×P loses to 37 R–Q1+, but after 37 P–B4 White still has at least a draw and perhaps better.

36 ...	**K–B3**
37 R–Q6+	**K–N2**
38 Q×P	**B–N7!**

I had underestimated this and only calculated 38 ... B–B3 39 B×P which is better for White.

39 P–N4?!

This was intended as a bold winning attempt, but I should have been satisfied with 39 B×P N×B 40 R×N Q×QBP 41 Q×Q R×Q 42 P–N4 R–B4 43 R–K7+ K–B3 44 R–K6+ with a draw.

39 ...	**Q×KBP**
40 B–K2?	

Another rotten move! After 40 P–N5! things get interesting again since 40 ... P×P 41 R–N6+ K–R2 42 R×NP is by no means comfortable for Black.

40 ...	**B–B3**
41 P×P??	

A final piece of nonsense – after the time control now – throws away what remained of White's chances. Still 41 P–N5! was correct when after 41 ... P×P 42 B×P the position is still unclear; 42 ... B×B 43 R–N6+ K–R2 44 R×B is not bad for White, while after 42 ... Q–N1 (analysed as best by Ljubojevic) his recommendation of 43 K–N2! avoiding back row checks, makes it difficult still. After the text move Black has no problems.

41 ...	**Q×P**
42 B–B4	**N–Q2**

43 Q×P   Q–N8+
44 K–N2   N×P
45 Resigns
Notes by Hartston specially for this
                                    volume

10 **Markland** (England) –
Bhend (Switzerland)

Caro-Kann Defence

1 P–K4   P–QB3
2 P–QB4   P–Q4
3 KP×P   P×P
4 P×P   N–KB3
5 N–QB3   N×P
6 B–B4   N–N3
If 6 . . . N×N then 7 Q–N3! followed by 8 QP×N gives White a
strong position.

7 B–N3   N–B3
8 N–B3   P–N3
8 . . . P–K4 is a direct attempt to
refute White's opening. After 9 0–0
B–QB4   10 P–Q4! the position is
unclear, but probably in White's
favour.

9 P–QR4
Played so as to take the a5 square
away from the knight. Black's next
move is obligatory since 9 . . . B–N2
10 P–R5 N–Q2 11 B×P+! wins for
White.

9 . . .   P–QR4
10 P–Q4   B–N2
11 B–K3
11 B–KB4 is also possible, since the
pawn sacrifice cannot be accepted on
account of N–QN5.

11 . . .   N–N5
12 P–Q5
The pawn is again unacceptable.
If 12 . . . B×N+ 13 P×B N/5×QP
14 B/K3×N N×B   15 Q×Q+

K×Q 16 N–N5! and White is winning.

12 . . .   0–0
13 0–0   B–B4
If now 13 . . . B×N 14 P×B
N/5×QP 15 B–R6 and then (i) 15
. . . R–K1 16 Q–Q4 N–B3 17
Q–R4 with a very strong attack; or
(ii) 15 . . . N×BP 16 Q–B2 N3–
Q4 17 Q–N2! Q–N3 18 KR–Q1
with a winning position.

14 B–Q4   B–R3?
A poor move by Black. After
14 . . . B–Q6 15 B×B K×B 16
R–K1 and 17 N–K5 White stands a
little better.

15 N–K5!
This time the pawn sacrifice must
be accepted. White has many threats
e.g.: P–KN4, Q–B3 etc.

15 . . .   N/3×QP
16 N×N   N×N
17 Q–B3   N–B3
Overlooking a little combination.
After 17 . . . P–K3 18 P–KN4 N–B3
19 QR–Q1 B–K5 the position is unclear. But 17 . . . B–K3 18 QR–Q1
and 17 . . . N–N3 18 QR–Q1 both
give White a clear plus.

18 N×BP!   Q×B
Forced. If 18 . . . R×N 19 B×N
P×B 20 Q×P B–Q2 21 QR–Q1
wins.

19 N×B++   K–R1
20 N×B   P×N
21 Q×BP
Now 21 . . . N–K5 or 21 . . . N–N5
can be answered by 22 Q–Q5.

21 . . .   Q×NP
22 QR–N1   Q–Q7
23 KR–Q1   Q–R3(7)
24 B–K6   R–R3
25 Q–K5   Q–R5!
26 B–Q5

If 26 R×P R×B! 27 Q×R N–N5.

26 ...	Q×QRP
27 Q×P	R–K1
28 Q×NP	R–Q3
29 B–N3	

And not 29 B–B3?? on account of the back row mate.

29 ...	R×R+
30 R×R	Q–K5
31 Q×Q	N×Q
32 R–K1	R–QB1

If 32 ... N–Q3 33 R–R1!

33 P–B3	N–B6
34 R–K7	P–R5
35 B–B2	N–Q4
36 R×P+	K–N1
37 B–K4	R–B2
38 R×R?	

Better was the simple move 38 R–R6 R–B8+ 39 K–B2 N–B6 40 R–R6 R–QR8 41 B–Q3 P–R6 42 B–B4+ K–N2 43 P–R4 winning easily.

38 ...	N×R
39 B–Q3	P–R6
40 B–B4+	K–N2
41 K–B2	N–N4
42 P–N4	N–B6
43 P–R4	K–B3

Here the game diverges from our adjournment analysis. The key position to the end game is one in which

C

White's pawns are on f4,g5,h6 with Black's king on g6 and knight on f5, White's king on f3 and most important Black to move. If in this position it is White to move then the game is a draw! After 43 ... P–R7 44 B×P N×B 45 P–R5 N–B6 46 P–N5 N–Q4 47 K–N3 K–R2! 48 P–R6! K–N3 49 P–B4 N–K6 50 K–B2! White wins because he can reach the position given above.

44 K–K3	P–R7
45 B×P	N×B
46 K–B4	N–B6
47 P–N5+	K–K3!

If 47 ... K–N3 48 K–N4 N–Q4 49 P–R5+ K–N2 50 K–B5 wins.

48 P–R5	N–Q4+
49 K–K4	N–B6+
50 K–B4	N–Q4+
51 K–N4!	

The right way.

51 ...	N–K6+
52 K–N3	

52 K–R3 also wins since 52 ... K–B4 53 P–R6 N–Q4 (If 53 ... K–N3 54 K–N3 N–Q4 55 P–B4 N–K6 56 K–B2! wins.) 54 P–R7 N–B5+ 55 K–R4 N–N3+ 56 K–R5 N–R1 57 K–R6 N–N3 58 P–B4! wins.

52 ...	K–B4
53 P–R6	K–N3
54 P–B4	N–B4+
55 K–B3!	

55 K–N4? only draws after 55 ... N–Q3 56 K–B3 K–B4 Even with the White king on e4 the position is a draw! Since 1 ... N–Q3+ 2 K–K5 N–B2+ 3 K–K6 N–R1 4 K–K7 K–B4 5 P–R7 (so that 5 ... K×P?? 6 K–B6 wins) 5 ... K–N3 6 K–B8 K×P7 P–B5 N–N3+ etc.

55 ...	N–Q3
56 K–N4	

Now 56 ... N–B4 is answered by
57 P–R7

56 ...	K–R2
57 K–R5	N–K5
58 P–N6+	K–N1
59 P–B5	N–B3+
60 K–N5	N–K5+
61 K–B4	N–B3
62 P–R7+	K–N2
63 K–K5	N–Q2+
64 K–K6	N–B1+
65 K–K7	K–R1
66 P–N7+	K×RP
67 K×N	Resigns

*Notes by Markland specially for this
volume*

11 Ljubojevic (Yugoslavia) –
Honda (Japan)

Sicilian Defence

1 P–K4 P–QB4 2 N–KB3 P–K3 3
P–Q4 P×P 4 N×P N–QB3 5 N–N5
P–Q3 6 P–QB4 N–B3 7 N/N5–B3
B–K2 8 B–K2 0–0 9 0–0 P–QR3
10 P–QN3 B–Q2 11 B–N2 N–R2
12 B–R3 B–B3 13 Q–Q4 Q–B2 14
N–Q2 KR–Q1 15 Q–K3 P–QN4
16 QR–B1 Q–R4 17 B–N2 P–N5 18
N–Q5!! P×N 19 KP×P B–Q2 20
Q×B R–K1 21 Q×QP R×B 22
B×N P×B 23 Q×B R×N 24
Q–N4+ K–R1 25 Q–B4 R×RP 26
Q×P+ K–N1 27 KR–K1 Q–Q1
28 R–K7 Q–KB1 29 R–K3 P–R3 30
R–N3+ K–R2 31 R–K1 N–N4 32
P×N P×P 33 P–R4 R/R1–R3 34
R–K6 Black Resigns

PRELIMINARY GROUP III

	H	P	N	I	S	B	M	L	Total	Final Group
Hungary	×	2	3	3½	3	4	4	4	**23½**	A
Poland	2	×	2½	3	4	3	4	3½	**22**	A
Norway	1	1½	×	3½	3	3½	3½	4	**20**	B
Indonesia	½	1	½	×	3½	3	4	3	**15½**	B
Scotland	1	0	1	½	×	3½	2½	3	**11½**	C
Bolivia	0	1	½	1	½	×	2	3	**8**	C
Morocco	0	0	½	0	1½	2	×	2½	**6½**	D
Lebanon	0	½	0	1	1	1	1½	×	**5**	D

No surprises at all in this group. Each team qualified convincingly for
the group for which it had been seeded, although when the last round
started Norway could have made the A–final by inflicting a heavy
defeat on Poland and Scotland would have reached the B–final had
they beaten Indonesia 2½–1½.

Galeb, the Lebanese captain, threw away half a point against
Indonesia through either not knowing one of the rules or a language
problem. In his game with Sampouw he reached a position in which, by

making a certain move, Galeb could have repeated the position for the third time. He wanted to draw the game and so said 'Draw' to his opponent without making the move. Sampouw replied 'No', which he was quite entitled to do since Galeb's utterance could have been the offer of a draw and not a claim for one. (Ordinarily no claim or interruption is tolerated during an opponent's thinking time. The correct procedure to claim the draw is to announce to the arbiter 'I intend to make the move . . . which will repeat the position for a third time and I claim a draw', but in doing so it is essential that the move is not actually made on the board.)

Upset by his opponent's apparent disregard of the rules (as he thought was the case) Galeb rushed off to find an arbiter to verify his claim but in order not to lose time on his clock Galeb first made the move, thereby invalidating his claim. The arbiters did not know the rules properly and so Kotov, the chief arbiter, was called in. After consulting with Dr Euwe for rather a long time, Kotov gave the ruling that the game must go on, Galeb having made his move on the board. The Lebanese was furious, played badly and lost.

12 **Wibe** (Norway) –
   Bilek (Hungary)

Pirc Defence

1 P–K4	P–KN3
2 P–Q4	B–N2
3 N–QB3	P–Q3
4 B–K3	P–QB3

In this position 4 . . . P–QR3, followed by the expansion of Black's Q–side pawns, is very much in fashion at the moment.

5 B–QB4?!

Premature. I feel that White should delay the development of this piece and retain all his options with 5 Q–Q2.

| 5 . . . | N–B3 |

Threatening . . . P–Q4, neutralizing White's centre.

6 B–N3	N–N5
7 B–B1	0–0
8 P–B3	N–B3
9 B–K3	

As you were!

9 . . .	QN–Q2
10 Q–Q2	P–QN4
11 P–KR4	

Looks very dangerous, but Black has plenty of counterplay – most of it based on the exposed situation of White's KB.

| 11 . . . | P–QR4 |

If his KB were not on QN3 White could ignore this demonstration and get on with the game on the other side of the board.

12 P–R3	N–N3
13 B–R6	P–N5
14 N–Q1	P–R5
15 B–R2	P×P
16 P–R5?	

White is carried away by his own designs. Best is 16 P×P e.g.: B×B 17 Q×B B–K3 – then it would be anybody's game.

16 . . .	RP×P
17 N×P	B×B
18 Q×B	P–N4!

A typical device to prevent the opening of the KR file.

19 Q×NP+	K-R1
20 N-R3	R-KN1
21 Q-Q2	B×N

Eliminating the knight before it can inflict any damage. Black now concentrates on shutting the White KB out of play.

| 22 R×B | P-Q4 |

Closing the diagonal.

| 23 N-Q3 | KN-Q2 |
| 24 K-B2 | P-K3 |

And ensuring that it's kept shut.

25 P-B3	R-N1
26 P-K5	Q-K2
27 N-N4	QR-QB1
28 B-N1	

Seeking new employ, but by now White's position has become so fragile that it cannot stand up to Black's undermining thrusts, which are quite typical for the Pirc Defence.

| 28 ... | P-QB4 |

29 N-B2	P×P
30 P×P	N-B5!
31 Q-R6	P-B3

The second of the typical Pirc demolition thrusts.

| 32 P×P | N×P |
| 33 R×P | |

The passed pawn had to be eliminated, but now White's poor, hounded bishop is out on a limb.

| 33 ... | R-N1! |
| 34 N-N4 | |

34 Or R-QR1 R-KN4! 35 R-N3 R×P winning. Of course 35 Q×R loses the queen.

| 34 ... | KR-KB1 |

Covering the knight and threatening ... N-N5+.

| 35 N-B6 | |

If 35 R-N3 R-B2   36 B-B2 Q-Q3! 37 N-R2 N-N7 threatening the QR and ... N-Q8+ followed by ... N-K5+. A piquant variation. 36 ... R×N? would actually lose to 37 R-R8+ N-K1 38 B×P!

35 ...	N-N5+
36 K-K2	N×Q
37 N×Q	R×B
38 R-R7	R-N7+

White Resigns

A game with a pronounced theme (cf moves 5-37).

Notes by Keene based on analysis by Bilek in THE CHESS PLAYER

13 **Aliaga** (Bolivia) –
   Filipowicz (Poland)

Sicilian Defence (by transposition)

1 P-Q4	N-KB3
2 P-QB4	P-B4
3 N-KB3	P×P
4 N×P	P-K3
5 N-QB3	P-QR3
6 P-K4	

Transposing to the Kan Variation of the Sicilian.

6 ...	B-N5
7 B-Q3	N-B3
8 N×N	

Alternatives are: (i) 8 N-B2 B×N+ 9 P×B P-Q4! with roughly

equal chances; or (ii) 8 B–B2 Q–B2
9 0–0 N×N 10 Q×N N–N5 11
P–K5 N×KP 12 B–B4 P–B3 13 N–
K4 P–QN3 14 B–KN3 B–N2 15
QR–Q1 0–0–0 with a sound position
for Black (Boleslavsky).

8 . . .   QP×N

Not 8 . . . NP×N? 9 P–K5!
Q–R4 10 P×N B×N+ 11 P×B
Q×BP+ 12 Q–Q2 Q×R 13 P×P
Q×NP 14 0–0 with more than ample
compensation for the exchange in
view of the weak position of Black's
king and his sick dark squares.

9 0–0

Possibly stronger is 9 P–K5 N–Q2
10 P–B4. e.g. 10 . . . N–B4 11 B–B2
Q×Q+ 12 K×Q P–QN4 13
N–K4 N×N 14 B×N B–N2 15
B–K3 0–0–0+ 16 K–K2 with a very
slight edge for White.

9 . . .   P–K4

Theory recognizes this position as
offering equal chances after either
10 Q–K2 or 10 N–K2 but Aliaga
finds a different continuation.

10 B–N5	**0–0**
11 K–R1	**B–K2**
12 Q–K2	**N–N5!**
13 B×B	**Q×B**
14 P–B3	

Already White is under some pressure because of the threat of 14 . . .
Q–R5 15 P–R3 N–B3 followed by
. . . N–R4, . . . N–B5 and a piece
sacrifice at KR6 or KN7. The text is
probably the best way to meet this
threat.

14 . . .	**N–B3**
15 N–R4	**B–K3**
16 Q–K3	**QR–Q1**
17 KR–Q1	

On 17 N–B5 Filipowicz had intended 17 . . . R–Q5 when he assesses

the position as being slightly in
Black's favour. After 18 N–N3 however, Black has nothing better than
to repeat the position by 18 . . . R/5–
Q1. In view of the inactive nature of
White's position he would have done
better to have taken this line.

17 . . .   R–Q5

Now there is no time to drive away
the rook.

18 P–QN3	**KR–Q1**
19 N–N2	**Q–R6!**
20 Q–B1	**P–R3**
21 Q–B3	**P–QN4!**
22 P–B5	**N–Q2**
23 R/Q1–QB1	**N×P!**
24 Q×N	**Q×N**
25 Q×KP	**P–QB4!**
26 B–B1	**P–B5!**
27 P×P	**B×P**

28 B×B   P×B!

After 28 . . . R–Q8+ 29 R×R
R×R+ 30 R×R Q×Q 31 B–Q5,
Black still has many technical difficulties to solve. The text results in an
easy win.

29 P–KR3?

In time trouble, White makes it
even easier than necessary. Relatively best was 29 Q–N3 but then
comes 29 . . . Q×R/B8+! 30 R×Q
R–Q8+ 31 Q–K1 R×Q+ 32
R×R P–B6 etc.

29 . . .	R–Q8+
30 R×R	R×R+
31 Resigns	

Analysis by Filipowicz in THE CHESS
PLAYER

14 **Sax** (Hungary) –
Aitken (Scotland)

Two Knights' Defence

1 P–K4 P–K4 2 N–KB3 N–QB3
3 B–B4 N–B3 4 P–Q4 P×P 5
P–K5 P–Q4 6 B–QN5 N–K5 7
N×P B–Q2 8 B×N P×B 9 0–0
B–K2 10 P–KB3 N–B4 11 P–KB4
N–K3? Correct is 11 . . . N–K5 12
P–B5 B–B4! with an equal game.
12 P–B5 N×N 13 Q×N P–B4!?
If 13 . . . Q–N1 14 P–K6! P×P 15
Q×NP with a clear advantage to
White. **14 Q–KN4!** Not 14 Q×QP
B–QN4! 15 R–Q1 (15 Q×Q+ R×Q
16 R–K1 B–Q2   17 P–KN4–*17
P–K6? P×P 18 P×P B×P*–17 . . .
B–KR5!) 15 . . . Q×Q 16 R×Q
B–Q2 and Black can regain his pawn
(17 P–KN4 P–KR4!). **14 . . . K–B1
15 N–B3 P–Q5?** Conceding a valu-
able square to White's knight.
Necessary was 15 . . . P–QB3. **16
N–K4 P–KR4 17 Q–N3 P–R5 18
Q–B4 P–KB3 19 P×P P P×P 20
Q–N4** Threatening to invade at
KN6. **20 . . . Q–K1 21 B–Q2 Q–R4
22 Q–B4 B–B3 23 QR–K1 R–KN1**
Black has no time to defend his
QBP. If 23 . . . R–B1 24 N×KBP!
B×N 25 R–K6. After the text how-
ever, Black gets some swindling
chances. **24 Q×BP**(*10*)
24 . . . R×P+ If 24 . . . Q–N5 25
N–N3! stopping one mate and
threatening another. **25 K×R Q–
N5+ 26 K–B2 B×N 27 R–K2**

R–K1 **28 R–KN1 Q×P+ 29 K–K1
Q–R2** 29 . . . K–B2 fails to 30
R–B1 Q–R2 31 B–N5. **30 Q–B4
B–N3 31 R–N4 P–B4 32 R–N1
P–R6! 33 K–B1 Q–R4 34 R–K6
B–R2** If 34 . . . Q–Q8+ simply 35
B–K1. **35 Q–R6+ Q×Q 36 B×Q+
K–B2 37 R–R6 B–B3 38 R×P+
R–K2 39 R×R+ K×R 40 B–B4
Resigns**

Analysis by Sax in THE CHESS PLAYER

15 **Pritchett** (Scotland) –
Johannessen (Norway)
Caro-Kann Defence

1 P–K4	P–QB3
2 P–Q4	P–Q4
3 N–QB3	P×P
4 N×P	B–B4
5 N–N3	P–KN3?!

An extravagant move. If White
exchanges knight for bishop, the
recapture with the KNP gives Black
an open file and a grip on the central
light squares but, after simple
development, the bishop begins to
look silly. It can only sit and wait to
be exchanged.

6 N–B3	N–Q2
7 B–QB4	N–N3
8 B–N3	Q–B2
9 0–0	P–K3

Afraid of a variety of possible

sacrifices (on his KB2 or K3) which might materialize if he developed his K-side pieces and played for . . . 0–0, Black decided that a blockade in the centre and castling Q–side was his best chance of checking the white pressure.

10 P–B4	0–0–0
11 P–QR4!	

Crude but straight to the point. White wants to smother his opponent before his pieces have a chance to breathe.

11 . . .	B–N2
12 B–K3	P–B4

If 12 . . . N–B3 13 P–R5 QN–Q2 14 P–Q5! with a clear plus for White.

13 P–R5	N–Q2
14 P–Q5!	

Establishing a powerful central wedge. In reply, 14 . . . B×P leads to losing positions: 15 P–Q6 Q–N1 (15 . . . Q–B3? 16 B–R4 Q–R3 17 B–QN5) 16 R–R2 B–B6 17 B–R4! B–QN5 18 R–N2 and now: (i) 18 . . . B×P 19 B×N+ R×B 20 B×P; and (ii) 18 . . . KN–B3 19 R×B P×R 20 P–B5 are both overwhelming for White.

Black also disliked 14 . . . N–K4. The simplest reply is 15 N×B NP×N 16 R–K1 with a clear advantage to White, but this may at least have been a better practical try than the retreat played in the game.

14 . . .	N–N1
15 Q–K2	N–KB3
16 KR–Q1	KR–K1

Perhaps 16 . . . N–K1 was the best chance. Now White develops a winning initiative.

17 Q–Q2!

Threatening 18 P–Q6 Q–Q2 19 B–R4 etc.

17 . . .	Q–Q3
18 B–R4	KN–Q2

If 18 . . . R–K2, maybe even 19 P–N4 immediately.

11
W

19 B–B4	P–K4
20 B–KN5	P–B3
21 B–K3	

Simple chess. Black has no defence against the twin white threats 22 P–QN4 and 22 N–R4. The rest is misery.

21 . . .	P–K5
22 B–B4	Q–B1
23 N×B	NP×N
24 N–R4	R–K4

Why not?

25 B×R	P×B
26 Q–N5	B–B3
27 Q–R5	B×N
28 Q×B	N–KB3
29 Q–N5	Resigns

Notes by Pritchett specially for this volume

16 **Sznapik** (Poland) –
   Ribli (Hungary)

Sicilian Defence

1 P–K4	P–QB4
2 N–KB3	P–Q3
3 B–N5+	N–Q2

This move has always been considered inferior to 3 . . . B–Q2 but recently Ribli has been trying to revive it. The positions arising after 3 . . . B–Q2 are normally lacking in chances for a Black advantage whereas if 3 . . . N–Q2 cannot be refuted the move may actually be the refutation of White's third move since the first player will later be obliged either to waste a tempo with his bishop or concede the advantage of the two bishops by exchanging on Q7.

4 P–Q4   N–B3

The main point of Ribli's idea – Black hopes to force White to defend his KP thereby gaining a tempo for his development. The older 4 . . . P×P 5 Q×P N–B3 puts White's attack a tempo ahead of the game continuation because he has not yet spent a move on the development of his QN and he therefore has an extra move which can be used for other purposes. e.g. 6 0–0 P–QR3 7 B×N+ B×B 8 B–N5 with advantage to White.

5 N–B3

5 P–K5 is possibly a more effective way of taking advantage of Black's poor K-side development: 5 . . . Q–R4+ 6 N–B3 N–K5 7 B–Q2 and now: (i) 7 . . . N×N 8 BN5×N+ B×B 9 B×N Q–R3 10 P–Q5, when Black has problems concerning the development of his KB (Hecht-Ljubojevic, Teeside 1972 continued 10 . . . B–B4 11 N–R4! B–Q2 whereupon 12 Q–R5! would have been very strong); or (ii) 7 . . . N×B? 8 Q×N when Black has a host of losing continuations at his disposal, Browne-Levy, Skopje 1972. After

our game, Browne expressed the opinion that 5 P–K5 completely refutes Ribli's idea.

5 . . .   P×P
6 Q×P   P–K4

A new move, clearly aimed against the thrust P–K5 which has proved successful in the past. e.g. 6 . . . P–KN3 7 P–K5 P×P 8 N×P B–N2 9 B–N5 (even 9 N×N B×N 10 B×B+ Q×B 11 Q×Q+ N×Q 12 B–Q2 N–N3 13 0–0–0 is slightly better for White. Mista-Ribli, Cienfuegos 1972) 9 . . . 0–0 10 0–0–0! with the more active game. Larsen-Csom, Palma 1971.

6 . . . P–K3 is also unsatisfactory after 7 B–N5 B–K2 8 0–0–0 0–0 9 KR–K1.

7 Q–Q3   P–KR3!

Helping to keep some control over his Q4 square by preventing 8 B–N5.

8 0–0

8 B–K3 followed by 0–0–0 would have put Black under more pressure because the freeing move . . . P–Q4 would never be possible.

8 . . .   P–R3
9 B–QB4   P–QN4?!

A very dangerous move which adds further value to White's control of his Q5 square. The safest course would have been 9 . . . B–K2, while 9 . . . N–B4 10 Q–K2 B–K3 was a possible alternative, blunting White's pressure along the QR2–KB7 diagonal.

10 B–Q5   R–QN1
11 B–K3!   P–N5??

A colossal positional blunder, completing White's domination of the light squares. Essential was 11 . . . Q–B2.

12 Q–B4!   N×B

If 12 ... Q–K2 13 B–R7! N–N3!
14 B×N P×N 15 B–B7!! R×P 16
B×QP winning. 12 . . . P×N??
would be good if it didn't allow mate
in two.

13 N×N   **B–N2**

If 13 ... R–N2 simply 14 Q×RP.

14 N–B7+   **K–K2**

12
W

15 B–N5+??

15 N–R4 seals Black's fate at once
because 15 ... P–N3 can be answered by 16 N×NP+. Other moves
fail to stem the force of White's attack.
e.g. 15 ... R–B1 (or 15 ... K–B3 16
P–B4!) 16 N–N6+! K–B3 17
N×R Q–K2 18 N–Q5+ B×N 19
Q×R.

After the sacrifice in the game
however, the position becomes extremely unclear.

15 ...   **P×B**

Forced. If 15 ... N–B3 16 N×KP
P×N 17 QR–Q1 Q–B1 18 Q–B5
mate.

16 N×NP   **P–Q4!**

There is no other move.

17 N×QP+

17 P×P looks more dangerous for
Black. e.g. (i) 17 . . . N–B3 18
P–Q6+ K×P 19 N×BP+; or (ii)
17 ... N–N3 18 P–Q6+ K–B3 19
Q×BP+ K×N 20 N–K6+. But in

fact Black can probably escape by
17 ... K–B3! 18 P–B4 K–N3, when
White's forces do not cooperate well
and he is hard pressed to justify his
piece sacrifice.

17 ...   **B×N**

18 Q×B   **Q–K1**

19 QR–Q1

Possibly too slow, but on 19 P–KB4
Black has 19 ... R–N4 followed by
20 . . . P×P when his defensive
resources should prove adequate and
his extra material decisive.

19 ...   **R–R3**

20 P–KB4   **R–N4!**

21 Q–B4   **P×P**

22 N×P?

In acute time trouble White
misses a better chance in 22 P–K5!
(depriving Black's KR of the important defensive square KB3) and if
22 ... N×P 23 Q–B7+ or 22 ...
R–B4 23 Q×NP with the threat of
24 N–K4.

22 ...   **R–QB4!**

22 ... Q×N is answered by 23
R×N+.

23 Q–N3   **R–KB3**

24 P–K5   **N×P**

25 N–N5

Threatening 26 N–K4.

25 ...   **Q–B3**

26 KR–K1

With the same threat.

26 ...   **R–QB4**

27 P–KR4

If 27 R×N+ R/QB4×R 28
Q×NP+ R–B4 (not 28 ... K–B3??
29 N–R7+!) 29 N–K4 K–B2 and
White has nothing to show for the
rook.

27 ...   **K–B3?**

Much better would have been
27 ... P–QR4 or even possibly 27 ...

R×N!? Now White has a win at his disposal by . . .

28 R×N!

Draw Agreed

In desperate time trouble White did not dare risk everything. After 28 . . . K×R 29 R-K1+ K-Q3 30 R-K6+ K-B2 31 R×Q+ R×R 32 N-K6+ K-B1 33 N×B R×N 34 Q×P R/1-B3 35 Q-K4 followed by the advance of the Q-side pawns, White should win without much difficulty.

Notes by Levy based on analysis by Sznapik (in THE CHESS PLAYER*) and Despotovic*

17 Denman (Scotland) – **Pytel** (Poland)

Alekhine's Defence

1 P-K4	N-KB3
2 P-K5	N-Q4
3 P-Q4	P-Q3
4 P-QB4	N-N3
5 P-B4	B-B4
6 N-QB3	P-K3
7 N-B3	P×P
8 BP×P	N-B3
9 B-K3	B-K2
10 B-K2	

For the modern refutation, 10 P-Q5, see game 40.

10 . . .	0-0
11 0-0	P-B3
12 P×P	B×P
13 Q-Q2	Q-K2
14 QR-Q1	QR-Q1
15 P-B5?	

An unjustifiable positional error, giving Black control of his K5 square and permanently fixing White's hitherto flexible pawn duo (Q and QB–files). Normal and correct is 15 Q-B1.

15 . . .	N-Q4
16 N×N	

Otherwise White's dark squared bishop is exchanged and his Q-side soon collapses, e.g. 16 P-QR3 (to prevent 16 . . . N/3-N5 followed by . . . N×B and . . . N-Q4) 16 . . . K-R1 17 B-QB4 N×B 18 Q×N B-N5 19 N-K2 B×N 20 R×B B×P! 21 R×B N×R 22 N×N Q×P 23 R×R+ R×R 24 B-N3 R-Q1! 25 Resigns (If 25 N-B2 Q×Q 26 N×Q R-Q6! etc.) Naegeli-Muffang, The Hague 1928.

16 . . .	P×N
17 QR-K1	

If 17 P-QN4 QR-K1 18 N-K5 B×N 19 P×B Q×KP 20 R-B3 B-K5! and Black should win. If 17 B-QN5, intending QR-K1, 17 . . . P-KR3 (to prevent N-N5) followed by . . . B-K5 when White has no real play.

17 . . .   P-QR3?

Black's position has become good with such amazing rapidity that he is a little confused and wastes a tempo. There is no need for Black to fear B-QN5 followed by B×N since this manoeuvre only serves to strengthen his grip on the light squares. Correct was 17 . . . P-KR3 (this move must be played at some stage or other in order to keep White's knight away from KN5) 18 B-QN5 B-K5 19 B×N P×B 20 B-B4 R-N1 21 B-K5 K-R2.

17 . . . B-K5 at once however, is only good if followed up by (18 B-QN5) P-KR3 transposing back to the line mentioned above. If instead Black goes pawn hunting he loses a

piece in rather a comical manner:
18 . . . B×N? 19 R×B N×P??
20 R×B N×B 21 R×R+ Q×R 22
P–QR4 and the knight has no
squares.

18 B–Q1   B–K5

18 . . . Q–K5 followed by . . .
Q–Q6 (to exchange queens) is also
plausible but with queens on the
board Black preserves some possibilities of a K-side attack.

19 B–R4

This Bishop manoeuvre has re-
turned the tempo mentioned in the
note to 17 . . . P–QR3.

19 . . .   P–R3

The only difference between this
position and the one arising in the
first note to Black's seventeenth
move is that here Black's QRP is on
QR3 instead of QR2. The consequences of this will become apparent
later.

20 B×N   P×B
21 B–B4   K–R2
22 B–K5

If 22 N–K5 Q–K3 followed by . . .
R–QN1.

22 . . .   R–B2

Intending to double rooks on the
KB-file, . . .

23 B×B?

. . . but now Black is given a better
opportunity – he can double on the
KN-file.

23 . . .   P×B
24 Q–B4?!

Originally White had intended 24
N–R4 but after 24 . . . R–KN1
25 N–B5 Q–B1, Black will drive away
the knight with . . . R–N4 and then
double rooks in peace. Better would
have been 24 Q–R5 and if 24 . . .
R–KN1 25 Q×RP R/1–N2 26

R–B2 and 27 Q–B1. With Black's
QRP on R2 instead of R3 (see note
to Black's 19th move) the white
queen would put herself too much
out of play by going after this pawn.

24 . . .   R–KN1
25 R–K2   R/2–N2
26 R/1–B2   R–N5
27 Q–B5+   K–R1
28 N–K1

Defending KN2 yet again and
threatening something (the KBP) for
the first time in the game.

28 . . .   R/5–N3
29 Q–R3   Q–N2

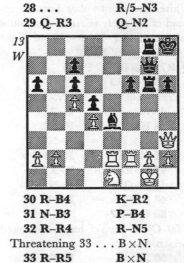

13
W

30 R–B4   K–R2
31 N–B3   P–B4
32 R–R4   R–N5

Threatening 33 . . . B×N.

33 R–R5   B×N

33 . . . P–B5 is also possible,
restricting White still further on the
K-side. But the text is quite convincing and the ensuing complications
provided excellent spectator value.

34 R–K7!   R×NP+
35 K–B1

35 Q×R loses in more ways than
one, the simplest being 35 . . . Q×R
36 R×RP+ K×R 37 Q×R Q–K8
mate.

35 . . .   B–K7+
36 K–K1   Q×R

36 . . . B×R 37 R×Q+ R/1×R
38 Q×B R/7–N4 is also straight-
forward.

37 R×RP+　　K–N2
38 R–R7+　　　K–B3

Not 38 . . . K–B1　39 Q×P+
K–K1　40 Q–QB8+ Q–Q1　41
Q–K6+ and mate next move.

39 Q–R4+　　　R/7–N4
40 R×Q　　　　K×R
41 K×B　　　　K–Q2
42 K–B3　　　　R/1–N2

The immediate 42 . . . K–B1 gives
White less counterplay because in-
stead of his reply move White could
have tried 43 P–N4 R–N8 44 P–R4
R–KB8+　45 K–K2 R/2–N8　46
Q–R7+ K–B1 47 P–N5.

43 P–KR3

Preventing 43 . . . R–N5.

43 . . .　　　　K–B1
44 K–B4　　　　R–N7
45 K×P　　　　K–N2!
46 K–B6　　　　R/2–N6
47 K–K6　　　　R–K7+
48 K–Q7　　　　R–N2+
49 K–Q8　　　　R×P
50 Q–K1?

50 Q–R6 would have prolonged
the struggle.

50 . . .　　　　K–R2
51 Resigns

*Notes by Levy based on analysis by
Pytel in* THE CHESS PLAYER

18 **Bedros** (Lebanon) –
　 Bonner (Scotland)

Centre Counter Game

**1 P–K4 P–Q4　2 P×P N–KB3　3
B–N5+** 3 P–Q4 N×P　4 P–QB4
N–N3　5 N–KB3 and 3 P–QB4
P–B3　4 P–Q4 P×P　5 N–QB3 are
popular alternatives. **3 . . . B–Q2**

4 B–B4 P–B3 Not often seen. 4 . . .
B–N5　5 P–KB3 B–B1 is the main
line. **5 P×P N×P　6 N–KB3** Or 6
P–Q4 P–K4　7 P×P N×P　8
Q–K2 B–QN5+　9 P–QB3 0–0 and if
10 P×B N×B　11 Q×N R–B1　12
Q–B4 R–K1+ with a tremendous
game for Black. **6 . . . P–K4　7 N–N5
B–QB4　8 B×P+** If 8 N×BP
B×P | 9 K×B N–K5+ with an
excellent game for Black. **8 . . . K–K2
9 B–B4** Better is 9 B–N3.

**9 . . . B×P+　10 K×B B–N5　11
B–K2 Q–Q5+　12 K–B1** Or 12
K–K1 B×B and now: (i) 13 Q×B
Q–KR5+　14 K–Q1 Q×N or (ii)
13 K×B Q–KN5+　14 N–KB3
Q×P+　15 K–K3 N–KN5+ and
Black wins. **12 . . . N–K5 13 N×N
KR–KB1+　14 B–B3.** If 14 K–K1
Q×N 15 N–B3 Q×NP　16 R–B1
N–Q5. **14 . . . Q×N** 14 . . . B×B
15 P×B Q×N 16 K–N2 Q–N3+ 17
K–B2 N–Q5 is much more effective.
15 P–Q3. A game Buzek-Kolozeiczik,
1958 went 15 Q–K2 B×B when
Black's position is even better than in
the present game: 16 Q×Q B×Q+
17 K–K1 B×BP, and White's QP
cannot move. **15 . . . B×B 16 P×Q
B×Q+　17 K–K1 B×P 18 B–N5+
K–K3 19 N–B3.** White has managed
to survive the attack without mater-

ial loss but he now faces an uncomfortable task in view of Black's superior development.

19 ... P–KR3 20 B–K3 QR–Q1 21 R–KB1 R×R+ 22 K×R B–Q6+ 23 K–K1 N–Q5 24 R–Q1 Great care is required. 24 R–B1 loses to 24 . . . N–B7+ 25 K–B2 R–KB1+ and 26 . . . N×B. 24 . . . N–B7+ Now the White king is driven into an exposed position where it is subject to mating threats. 25 K–B2. If 25 K–Q2 B×P+ 26 K–K2 R×R 27 N×R N×B 28 N×N B–N8 with a won ending. 25 . . . R–KB1+ 26 K–N3. Not 26 K–N1?? N×B winning a piece because of the back rank mate. 26 . . . N×B 27 R×B N–B8+ 28 K–R3 R–B5 29 R–B3. 29 P–KN3 loses to 29 . . . R–B7. 29 ... P–KN4 30 R×R KP×R 31 K–N4. Or 31 P–KN3 P–B6 32 P–KN4 K–K4. 31 . . . N×P+ 32 K–R5 K–K4 33 K×P P–N5 34 K–N5 P–B6 35 P×P P×P 36 N–Q1 K×P. The rest is easy. 37 K–R4 K–B5 38 K–R3 N–N5 39 P–QR3 P–N4 40 P–N3 P–R4 41 N–B3 Or 41 N–N2 N–B7+ 42 K–R2 K–K6 43 K–N1 K–K7 44 P–R4 N–R6+ etc. 41 ... N–K6 42 K–R2 P–B7 43 N–K2+ K–B6 44

N–N3 P–B8=Q 45 N×Q N×N+ 46 Resigns
Notes by Bonner specially for this volume

19 **Ribli** (Hungary) – **Sampouw** (Indonesia)

Ruy Lopez

1 P–K4 P–K4 2 N–KB3 N–QB3 3 B–N5 P–QR3 4 B–R4 N–B3 5 P–Q4 P×P 6 0–0 B–K2 7 R–K1 More usual is 7 P–K5 N–K5 8 N×P, a variation with a drawish reputation. **7 ... P–R3** The start of a strange strategical plan which involves Black playing almost entirely on the wings while White builds up his centre in a stereotyped manner. I find it difficult to believe that when playing this move Sampouw really intended the manoeuvre ... N–R2–B1–K3. More likely, he thought that from R2 the knight could move to KN4. Well, he was wrong. The normal continuations are 7 . . . P–QN4 8 P–K5 N×P 9 R×N P–Q3! and 7 ... 0–0 8 P–K5 N–K1, both of which should lead to equality. **8 P–K5 N–KR2 9 N×P N×N 10 Q×N P–QN4** 10 ... N–N4? allows 11 B×N B×B 12 P–K6 etc. **11 B–N3** Threatening 12 Q–Q5. **11 ... B–N2 12 P–QB4 N–B1** 12 ... N–N4 13 B×N B×B 14 N–B3 is very good for White. As well as the QNP White threatens 15 N–K4 B×N (or 15 . . . B–K2 16 P–K6 QP×P 17 Q×NP) 16 Q×B, when Black cannot castle K-side because B–B2 would force ... P–N3 and then P–KB4–5 is devastating. **13 Q–Q3 P–N5 14 N–Q2 P–QR4** Continuing his policy of looking after the edges while the centre is left to care for itself.

15 N–K4 N–K3 16 B–K3 P–R5 17
B–B2 R–R4 The point of Black's
recent Q-side gesture. His QR
creeps into play via the R-file.
18 P–B4 Q–R1 Yet another thematic, decentralizing move. 19 QR–Q1
B–QB3

20 P–KB5 R×P If the knight re-
treats, 21 P–B6 is crushing. 21 P×N
R×N 22 P×QP+ K–Q1 23 B–B2
R–N5 Decentralizing again! 24
R×B R×NP+ 25 K–B1 R×B+
26 K×R K×R 27 Q–Q4 Threaten-
ing 28 Q–K5+ K–Q1 29 Q×NP.
27 . . . Q–R4 Or 27 . . . Q–Q1 28
Q–B5+. 28 P–Q8=Q+ Resigns
Notes by Levy

20 **Bednarski** (Poland) –
  Wibe (Norway)

Modern Defence (Hippopotamus?)

1 P–K4 P–KN3 2 P–Q4 B–N2 3
N–QB3 P–N3?! Wibe often does this
sort of thing! Can it really be sound
against 3 N–QB3? I suspect not, but
the testing response is doubtless
4 P–B4. However . . . 4 N–B3 P–Q3
5 B–QB4 P–K3 6 0–0 N–K2 7
P–QR4 P–QR3 8 R–K1 P–R3 9
N–K2 N–Q2 10 P–B3 Maybe
10 N–B4 is more to the point. White
seems anxious to avoid over-exten-
sion against Black's weird set-up,

and, in a sense, this is a moral
triumph for the experimenter. 10 . . .
0–0 11 N–N3 B–N2 12 B–B4 K–R2
13 P–R3 P–KB4?! What's this?
Surely it was time for . . . P–K4

Black has already offended against a
sufficiency of Classical principles and
this weakening of the KP (and e6) is
too much. Avant-gardism can only
support so much strain . . . then it
snaps.

14 P×P 14 B×KP? P×P is less
happy for White. 14 . . . N×P 15
R×P N×P The 'point': 16 N×N
R×B 17 R×NP!! SNAP! If 17 . . .
K×R 18 Q–R5+ is obviously
horrible for Black. 17 . . . B×N 18
P×B K×R 19 Q–Q3+ The pro-
saic win was 19 B–Q3+ K–B2 20
Q–R5+ winning back the rook and
gaining two pawns into the bargain.

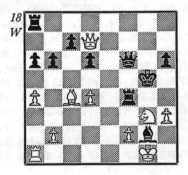

19 ... K–N4 20 Q–R7? missing two clear wins: (i) 20 Q–K3 with unanswerable threats of N–K2 and P–R4+; (ii) 20 P–R4+ K×P 21 N–B5+ K–N4! 22 N–N7! and Black is in a parlous state. Now he fights back. **20 ... Q–B3 21 Q×N B×P! (*18*)**

22 K×B R×BP+ 23 K–N1 Q×P 24 K–R1 Not 24 Q–K7 +

K–N3 25 B–Q3+ R–B4+! **24 ... Q×B?** Missing 24 ... R–R7+! 25 K×R Q–B7+ draw! Or was Black playing for a win? **25 Q–N7+ K–R5 26 Q×RP+ K×N 27 Q–K3+ R–B6 28 R–KN1+ K–R5 29 Q–R6 Mate!**

Amazing.

Notes by Keene based on analysis by Bednarski in THE CHESS PLAYER

PRELIMINARY GROUP IV

	WG	A	I	G	NZ	M	F	G	Total	Final Group
West Germany	×	4	3½	4	3	3½	3	4	**25**	A
Argentina	0	×	3	2½	2	4	3	4	**18½**	A
Iceland	½	1	×	2½	3½	3	3½	3½	**17½**	B
Greece	0	1½	1½	×	3	1½	2½	4	**14**	B
New Zealand	1	2	½	1	×	2	3	4	**13½**	C
Mexico	½	0	1	2½	2	×	2	3	**11**	C
France	1	1	½	1½	1	2	×	3½	**10½**	D
Guernsey	0	0	½	0	0	1	½	×	**2**	D

Argentina were missing their most redoubtable Grandmasters Panno and Najdorf, while Olafsson was not available to represent Iceland. These two relatively inexperienced teams battled for second place, since it was a foregone conclusion that the Germans (1 Hübner, 2 Darga) would run away with the top place. The second qualifying place was decided by their individual match which went 3–1 in favour of the South American Team. France made a supreme effort this year and even obtained the services of Grandmaster Rossolimo – but he was badly out of form and once again the French were doomed to the bottom final group. Guernsey made a brave showing, but were generally outclassed, a drawn game with Iceland being their best achievement. Still, Olympiads are for everyone – and only continual practice at high levels will bring improvement.

21 **Hübner** (W. Germany) –
Sigurjonsson (Iceland)

Neo-Grünfeld/English

1 P–QB4	N–KB3
2 N–QB3	P–Q4

3 P×P	N×P
4 P–KN3	P–KN3
5 B–N2	N–N3

5 ... N×N was popular in many games of the 1958 Botvinnik-Smyslov Match, but modern theory considers

that it lends too much support to White's centre.

6 P–Q3

Here White could have aimed for a genuine Neo-Grünfeld with N–KB3 and P–Q4, but then he would be faced with rapid pressure against his QP after . . . N–QB3.

6 . . .   **B–N2**

7 B–K3!?

Planning to follow with Q–Q2 and B–R6 in order to weaken Black's king's defences.

7 . . .   **N–B3**

8 N–B3

Now 8 Q–Q2 N–Q5 is not so good for White. For Petrosian's mystical interpretation of the position compare his game against Schmidt from the final (game 58).

8 . . .   **N–Q4**

Dubious. Normal was 8 . . . 0–0 9 Q–Q2 P–K4 with a slight White edge, but play for both sides.

9 B–Q2   **0–0**

10 0–0   **P–KR3**

Obviously Black wants to prevent B–KR6 for ever.

11 R–N1

A strange possibility leading to an unclear position was: 11 Q–B1 N×N (11 . . . K–R2? 12 N×N and N–N5+ is an old trap) 12 P×N K–R2 13 R–N1 P–K4 14 B–K3 R–QN1 15 B–B5 R–KR1 16 N–N5+ P×N 17 B×N P–N3 and Black follows up with . . . P–KN5.

11 . . .   **B–K3**

12 N–K4

Striving to reach QB5 – a key square for White in this system.

12 . . .   **Q–B1**

13 Q–B1   **K–R2**

14 P–QN4   **P–R3**

15 P–QR4   **B–N5**

16 P–N5   **P×P**

17 P×P   **N–Q1**

This retreat is obligatory. The attempt to invade the d4 square with a knight fails lamentably: 17 . . . B×N 18 P×N! B×B 19 P×P Q–R6 20 P×R=Q R×Q (or 20 . . . B×R 21 N–N5+! P×N 22 Q×N!) 21 R–K1 and Black's menacing hordes in fact accomplish nothing.

18 R–K1!

It's very useful to have the KP protected in advance.

18 . . .   **R–K1**

Probably . . . P–K4 was an improvement.

19 P–R3   **B×N**

Of course, . . . B×P 20 B×B Q×B loses the queen.

20 B×B   **N–K3?**

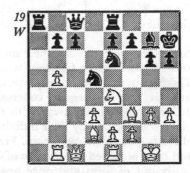

Here it was absolutely imperative for Black to plunge into complications in order to minimize White's advantage: 20 . . . Q×P! 21 Q–B4 P–QB3 22 P×P P×P 23 N–N5+ P×N 24 B–KN4 Q–R3 25 K–N2 P–KB4 26 R–KR1 P×B 27 R×Q+ B×R 28 R–KR1 K–N2 29 P–K4 N–B3 30 P–K5 N–Q4 31 Q×NP N–KB2 32 P–K6 In this position Black even has a material superio-

1 The President of the Macedonian Chess Federation speaking at the opening ceremony

2 Botvinnik lectures on computers using his game *v.* Capablanca, Avro 1938, as an example. Could a computer ever play that well?

3 A general view of the playing hall

4 General view of playing area with Donner towering above the Yugoslavia–Switzerland match

5 Excitement in the crowd

rity, but his pieces are badly lacking in co-ordination.

Such deep and beautiful variations abound in Hübner's games.

21 P–R4	N–Q5
22 B–N2	R–Q1
23 P–K3	N–K3
24 P–Q4	Q–Q2
25 Q–B2	

Now that Black has avoided the challenge White has a massive positional superiority: B-pair, strong centre, superior mobility and chances against Black's QBP. Black's next move makes things worse. He should play . . . P–R4!

25 . . .   **P–KB4?**

Presenting White with new targets on the K-side.

26 N–B3	N×N
27 B×N	R–R2
28 P–R5	N–B1
29 P–K4	P–B5
30 P–Q5	

White is winning now

30 . . .	R/1–QR1
31 B×B	K×B
32 NP×P	P×P
33 P–B5	N–R2
34 R–N3	R–KN1
35 Q–Q1	

Black lost on time. White wins anyway – e.g.: 35 . . . R–R7 36 Q×P Q–Q3 37 P–K5 Q–QN3 38 R–K2.

Notes by Keene based on analysis by Hübner in THE CHESS PLAYER

PRELIMINARY GROUP V

	C	S	M	I	P	I	H	M	Total	Final Group
Czechoslovakia	×	3	3½	3	2	4	4	4	23½	A
Spain	1	×	2½	2½	4	1½	4	4	19½	A
Mongolia	½	1½	×	2	3½	2½	4	3½	17½	B
Israel	1	1½	2	×	2	3	3½	4	17	B
Portugal	2	0	½	2	×	2½	3½	3	13½	C
Ireland	0	2½	1½	1	1½	×	3	3	12½	C
Hong Kong	0	0	0	½	½	1	×	3½	5½	D
Malaysia	0	0	½	0	1	1	½	×	3	D

Once again all teams justified their seedings. Czechoslovakia won every match with the exception of their draw with Portugal when Durao surprisingly beat their newest Grandmaster Jan Smejkal.

22 **Krstic** (Hong Kong) –
    Uitumen (Mongolia)

Two Knights Defence

1 P–K4	P–K4
2 N–KB3	N–QB3

3 P–Q4	P×P
4 B–QB4	N–B3
5 0–0	N×P
6 R–K1	P–Q4
7 B×P	Q×B
8 N–B3	Q–KR4?!

D

8 . . . Q–Q1 and 8 . . . Q–QR4 are both better than the text.

9 N×N	**B–K3**
10 B–N5!	**B-QN5**

If 10 . . . P–KR3 11 B–B6! Q–R4 12 N×P! P×B 13 N×P+ K–K2 and now 14 P–QN4! is just one way for White to continue his attack. e.g. 14 . . . N×P 15 N×B! K×N/B3 16 Q–Q4+ with an excellent game for White. Rossolimo-Prins, Bilbao 1951.

10 . . . B–K2 is also unsatisfactory: 11 B×B N×B 12 N×P B–N5 (or 12 . . . Q×Q 13 QR×Q 0–0–0 14–N KN5!) 13 P–KB3 B–Q2 14 Q–Q2 0–0 15 N–KB6+. Chigorin-Janowski, Paris 1900.

11 P–B3	**P×P**
12 P×P	**B–K2**
13 R–N1!	**0–0**
14 R×P	**B×B**
15 N/4×B	**N–Q1**

15 . . . B–N5 16 R×BP QR–B1 17 Q–Q6 is also better for White. Zhkurovich-Hasin, Leningrad 1968.

16 R×BP	**P–KR3**
17 N–K4	**Q–R4?**

Better would have been 17 . . . B–N5.

18 R–B5	**Q×RP**
19 N–Q4	**R–N1**
20 Q–Q3	**R–N3**

20
W

21 N–KB6+!	**P×N**
22 R–KR5	**P–B4**

Black has no satisfactory defence. If 22 . . . R–K1 23 Q–N3+ K–B1 24 R×P Q–Q4 25 R–R8+ K–K2 26 Q–B7+ Q–Q2 27 N–B5 mate; or 22 . . . K–N2 23 Q–N3+ K–R2 24 Q–B4 and mate in two.

23 R×RP	**K–N2**

23 . . . R–K1 still fails to save Black even though it provides his king with an escape square: 24 Q–N3+ K–B1 25 N×P and mate on the back rank.

24 Q–R3!	**R–KN1**

If 24 . . . Q–Q7 25 R–R7+ K–B3 26 Q–R4+ K–N3 27 N–B3 and 28 Q–R6 mate.

25 Q–R4!

Threatening 26 R–R7+ K–B1 27 Q×N mate.

25 . . .   Q–Q4

25 . . . Q–Q7 loses as before: 26 R–R7+ K–N3 27 N–B3 etc.

26 P–QB4!	**Q–Q2**
27 P–B5!	**R–B3**

Other rook moves are no better. e.g. 27 . . . R–N1 28 R–R7+ K–B1 29 R–R8! P–B3 30 Q×P+ Q–KB2 31 Q–R6+ Q–KN2 32 N×B+ N×N 33 R×R+ K×R 34 Q×N+ etc.

28 R–R7+	**K–B1**
29 Q–R6+?	

After conducting his attack in such exemplary style White is most unlucky to be rushed by the clock into an inferior continuation. 29 R–R8 would have been decisive, Black having no good move. e.g. 29 . . . B–Q4 30 N×R or 29 . . . P–B3 30 Q×P+ B–B2 31 N×R.

29 . . .   K–K1
30 N×P

Now 30 R–R8 can be met by 30 ... Q×N – The positions in which Black has two minor pieces for a rook offer him very good winning chances indeed.

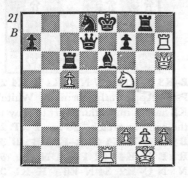

21
B

30 ...   R×NP+!?
30 . . . Q–Q4 may be stronger objectively but the text is extremely difficult to meet when under severe time pressure.
31 K–R1
31 K×R loses to 31 . . . Q–Q4+ 32 P–B3 Q×N 33 R–R8+ K–Q2 34 R–Q1+ B–Q4.
31 ...   R–N1
Not 31 . . . Q–Q4? 32 N–K3 forking queen and rook.
32 P–B3?
32 N–N7+ R×N 33 R–R8+ K–K2 34 Q×R Q–Q4+ 35 K–N1 K–Q2 is probably lost for White but at least he can fight. After the weak text move he is totally lost.
32 ...   Q–Q4
33 Q–R5   Q–Q7
34 Q–R4   Q–KN7 mate
Possibly White should be awarded a special prize for the unluckiest loss of the Olympiad.

Notes by Levy based on analysis by Jansa in THE CHESS PLAYER

23 Kong (Hong Kong) – **Kaldor** (Israel)

Sicilian Defence

1 P–K4 P–QB4 2 N–KB3 N–QB3 3 P–Q4 P×P 4 N×P P–KN3 5 N–QB3 B–N2 6 B–K3 N–B3 7 Q–Q2 7 B–QB4 is better. **7 . . . 0–0 8 B–K2 P–Q3** 8 . . . P–Q4 leads to equality but I wanted more. **9 N–N3 P–QR4 10 P–QR4 N–QN5 11 P–R4?!** It was better for White to castle short. Now he has no safe place for his king. **11 . . . P–R4 12 0–0–0 B–Q2 13 P–B3 R–B1 14 N–Q4?** Better was 14 K–N1. **14 . . . P–K4 15 N/4–N5 P–Q4 16 P×P B–B4 17 N–R3 R×N!** Otherwise White will consolidate his position with 18 K–N1. **18 P×R N/5×QP 19 B–B5?** 19 N–N5 was better. **19 . . . P–N3! 20 B×R Q×B** Now Black threatens 21 . . . B–R3. **21 K–N2 P–K5 22 B–B4?** Losing at once, but if 22 N–N5 P–K6 23 Q–K1 N×P! 24 N×N N–Q4! **22 . . . N×P 23 Q×N N–Q4 24 R×N Q–N5+ 25 B–N3 Q×Q+ 26 Resigns**
Notes by Kaldor specially for this volume

24 Krstic (Hong Kong) – **Foo** (Malaysia)

Sicilian Defence

1 P–K4 P–QB4 2 N–KB3 P–K3 3 P–Q4 P×P 4 N×P P–QR3 5 N–QB3 Q–B2 6 P–KN3 P–QN4 7 B–N2 B–N2 8 0–0 N–B3 9 R–K1 P–Q3 10 B–N5 B–K2? Better 10 . . . QN–Q2. **11 B×N! B×B?** Overlooking a well known idea. **12 N/4×NP! P×N 13 N×P Q–B3 14 N×P+ K–K2 15 N×B B×P** Since 15 . . . Q×N 16 P–K5 is cur-

tains. **16 P–K5 Q–B2 17 Q–Q6+!
Q×Q 18 P×Q+ K–Q2 19 QR–
Q1 R×P 20 N–B5+ K–Q1 21
P–QB4 P–K4 22 R–K2 R–R8 23
R×R B×R 24 R–R2 B–Q5 25
R–R8 Resigns** If 25 . . . K–B1 26
B–N7+ and mate next move.

Notes by Levy

25 **Hort** (Czechoslovakia) –
Kagan (Israel)

King's Indian Defence

**1 P–Q4 N–KB3 2 P–QB4 P–KN3
3 N–QB3 B–N2 4 P–K4 P–Q3 5
B–K2 0–0 6 B–N5 P–B4** An interesting alternative is 6 . . . P–KR3
followed by . . . P–K4. **7 P–Q5 P–
QR3 8 P–QR4 Q–R4?!** And now 8
. . . P–R3 followed by . . . P–K3 is
probably best. **9 B–Q2 Q–B2 10
N–B3 P–K3 11 P–R3 P×P 12
KP×P** The most accurate recapture.
Black's slightly unsophisticated opening play has left him without real
counter-chances to compensate for
White's space plus on the K-side.
12 . . . B–Q2 13 0–0 Also very fair is
13 P–R5 P–N3 14 P×P Q×P 15
P–QN3 and White's pawn structure
is superior. The text grants Black the
opportunity to block the position,
but at the cost of putting one piece
off-side. **13 . . . P–QR4 14 B–Q3
N–R3 15 R–B1 N–QN5 16 B–N1
QR–K1 17 R–K1 R×R+ 18
Q×R R–K1 19 Q–B1 P–R3 20
B–B4 B–KB1 21 N–Q2 Q–Q1 22
P–N4!** White's strategy is, simply
put, to push forwards on the K-side
while ignoring Black's QN which is
temporarily up a gum-tree. (22)
**22 . . . P–N3 23 Q–N2 B–B1 24
Q–R2! N–R2 25 Q–N3 P–KN4 26**

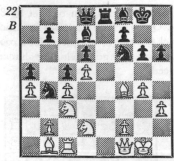

**B–K3 B–KN2 27 N/2–K4 B–K4 28
P–B4** Apparently dormant, White's
KB has an important part to play in
the coming attack. **28 . . . P×P 29
B×KBP N–N4 30 R–KB1 B×B 31
R×B R–K4 32 P–R4 N×N 33
N×N Q–K2 34 N–B6+ K–R1 35
B–K4 N–R7 36 P–N5 N–B8 37
K–B1 P–R4 38 Q–QB3 N–R7 39
Q–B3 N–N5** or 39 . . . B–N5 **40
R×B!** **40 Q×P+ Resigns**

*Notes by Keene based on analysis by
Jansa in* THE CHESS PLAYER

26 **U. Geller** (Israel) –
Durao (Portugal)

English Opening

**1 P–QB4 N–KB3 2 N–QB3 P–KN3
3 P–KN3 B–N2 4 B–N2 0–0 5
N–B3 P–Q3 6 0–0 P–K4 7 P–Q3**
It's a matter of taste whether one
adopts this restrained set-up or goes
into the King's Indian with 7 P–Q4.
**7 . . . N–R4 8 B–N5!? P–KB3 9
B–Q2 P–KB4 10 Q–N3?** White has
formed an over-ambitious plan based
on exploiting the apparent weakness
along the diagonal from White's
QR2 to Black's king, but tactical
circumstances render this strategy
quite impracticable and White should
have contented himself with a normal Q-side advance based on R–

QN1, P–QN4–N5 etc. **10 . . . K–R1
11 P–B5 N–QB3 12 P×P P×P 13
N–KN5** White is carried away by
the thought of a quick win based on
N–KB7+. 13 QR–B1 was more
suited to the needs of the position.
13 . . . Q–Q2 14 B–Q5 Consistent
but disastrous. Black's counter-play
now speaks for itself. **14 . . . N–Q5 15
Q–B4 P–KR3 16 P–K3** Or 16
N–B3 P–QN4. **16 . . . P–QN4! 17
N×P N–K7+ 18 K–R1 R–QN1**
and wins, now it's like an action
replay of the Retreat from Moscow.
**19 N–KB7+ R×N2 20 B×R
R×N 21 B×NP B–N2+ 22 P–B3**

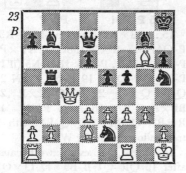

**22 . . . N/R4×P+! 23 P×N P–B5
24 K–R2 R×P 25 QR–Q1 P×KP
26 KR–K1 R×B 27 R×R P×R 28
R–Q1 N–Q5 29 Resigns**
Notes by Keene

27 **Durao** (Portugal) –
Smejkal (Czechoslovakia)
Sicilian Defence

1 P–K4	**P–QB4**
2 N–KB3	**P–Q3**
3 P–Q4	**P×P**
4 N×P	**N–KB3**
5 N–QB3	**P–QR3**
6 P–B4	**Q–B2**
7 P–QR4!?	

Not usually seen at this point. The
idea is simply to prevent . . . P–QN4
which is Black's strongest reply to the
normal 7 B–Q3.

7 . . .	**P–KN3?!**

Durao suggests 7 . . . P–K4 8
N–B3 QN–Q2 9 B–Q3 P–QN3 10
0–0 B–N2 as an equalizing alterna-
tive, but after 11 Q–K1 P–N3 (if 11
. . . B–K2 12 K–R1 0–0 13 N–R4
P–N3 14 P×P P×P 15 B–R6 KR–
K1 16 Q–K2 – intending B–QB4 –
and if 16 . . . N×P 17 N×N
BK2×N 18 B–QB4 R–K2 19
N–N5 is very strong) 12 Q–R4,
White soon develops the traditional
K-side attack associated with this
variation: 12 . . . B–N2 13 P×P
P×P 14 B–R6 0–0 15 N–KN5
KR–Q1 (not 15 . . . N–R4 16 B×B
K×B 17 R×P+! K–N1 18 R–
N7+! winning. Kupper–Olafsson,
Zürich 1959) 16 B–K2, and White,
who has the double threat of QR–Q1
followed by QR×N and B–N4
followed by B×N, retains the advant-
age.

8 B–K2	**B–N2**
9 B–K3	**N–B3**
10 0–0	**0–0**

The opening has developed from a
Najdorf to a Dragon/Najdorf hybrid.
In the Classical Dragon there is a
well known position which can be
set up from the present position by
retreating both QRP's to their
original squares and doing the same
with Black's queen. In that position
it is Black's move. The correct move
(9 . . . Q–N3) guarantees him at
least equality because of the threat of
10 . . . N×KP! but in the present
game his queen has already moved
and this resource is not available

(apart from which it is now White's move).

11 K–R1

A useful precaution, but perhaps 11 N–N3 was more accurate, preparing for P–KN4 which cannot be played at once because of 11 . . . N×NP.

11 . . .   N–QR4

On 11 . . . N–KN5, White does not play 12 N–Q5? N×B 13 N×Q N×Q 14 N×N P×N 15 N×R N–K6 16 R–B3 N×BP 17 R–QB1 N–Q5 18 R–KB2 N×B 19 R×N B–N5 20 R–Q2 R×N with an easy win for Black, but simply 12 B–N1 followed by P–KR3 at an opportune moment.

Possibly more active would have been 11 . . . P–K4 12 N–N3 B–K3.

12 Q–Q3!

Keeping Black out of the QB4 square, although after 12 P–B5 N–B5 13 B×N Q×B 14 Q–Q3 Q×Q 15 P×Q N–N5 16 B–N1 White still has chances of keeping some advantage.

12 . . .   P–K4

13 N–N3!

13 P×P P×P 14 R×N? B×R 15 N–Q5 does not work: 15 . . . Q–Q3 16 N–KB3 N–B3 17 P–B3 (with the idea of 18 P–QN4 and 19 B–B5) 17 . . . P–QR4! with a clear advantage to Black.

13 . . .   N×N

Black would be able to create more play after 13 . . . P–N3! 14 QR–Q1 (14 P×P P×P 15 R×N B×R 16 N–Q5 fails to 16 . . . Q–Q3 as before) 14 . . . N–N2. But 13 . . . B–K3 would be a mistake: 14 N×N Q×N/4 15 Q×QP KR–Q1 16 B–N6! (not 16 Q–R3 B–KB1 nor 16 Q–N6 Q×Q 17 B×Q R–Q7).

14 P×N   B–K3

14 . . . B–Q2 loses material by force, since after 15 P×P P×P 16 R×N B×R 17 N–Q5 Q–Q3, White exchanges on KB6 leaving Black's bishop *en prise*.

15 P–B5!   P×P

15 . . . B×NP is met by 16 R–R3! P–Q4! 17 R×B (not 17 KP×P? P–K5) 17 . . . P–Q5 18 B–N5 (if 18 P–N4 QR–Q1! 19 P–N5 P×N 20 Q–B4 Q×Q 21 B×Q N×P 22 BP×P P–B7) 18 . . . P×N 19 R×BP Q–R4 20 Q–B4 with a tremendous game for White.

15 . . . B–Q2 loses a pawn because after 16 QR–Q1 B–B3 17 Q×QP Q×Q 18 R×Q 18 . . . B×KP? allows 19 R×B and 18 . . . N×P? 19 R×B.

16 P×P   B–Q2

Or 16 . . . B×NP 17 R–R3 P–Q4 18 R×N P–Q5 19 B–N5 as in the note to Black's previous move.

17 R–B3

It is typical of Durao's attacking style that he should prefer this move to the consolidating 17 QR–Q1.

17 . . .   K–R1!

18 R–N3

Not 18 R–KR3? P–K5 19 N×P B×BP winning.

18 . . .   R–KN1

If 18 . . . B–B3 19 R×B K×R 20 B–R6+ K–R1 (20 . . . K×B only draws after 21 Q–K3+ K–N2 22 Q–N5+ etc.) when Black's position is perfectly secure on the K-side and his domination of the centre gives him the advantage. So after 18 . . . B–B3, White should transpose back to the game by 19 R–QB1 R–KN1.

19 R–QB1   B–B3
20 P–N4   P–Q4!
21 N×P

By 21 P–N5 P–Q5 (21 . . . P×P 22 P×P P–Q5 23 P×B P×B allows 24 N–N5, an important difference) 22 P×B P×B 23 P×P Q×P 24 B–B3 Q×P 25 R–QN1 QR–Q1 26 Q×KP Q–QB7! it is Black who gets the advantage of the open QB-file and not White!

21 . . .   N×N?

21 . . . P–K5! would have opened up a hoard of tactical complexities, one of which might well have turned the tables on White. After 22 Q–Q4 N×N 23 Q×N (not 23 R3×B R×R 24 B–R6 P–B3! when Black wins a piece) Black wins by 23 . . . Q×R. So White must reply to 21 . . . P–K5 with 22 N×Q (22 R×B R×R 23 N×Q P×Q 24 N×R P×B 25 B–Q4 R×P 26 B×N+ R–N2+ 27 R×B P–K8=Q mate) 22 . . .

P×Q 23 B×P (23 N×R P×B 24 N–N6 R–Q1 25 R–K1 R–Q8 26 B–B2 N–K5 wins for Black) 23 . . . QR–Q1! (23 . . . QR–QB1 24 P–N5!) with good play for Black. e.g. 24 B–KN5 N–R4! 25 R–R3 B×KNP+ 26 K×B B×P or 24 B–QB4 N–R4 25 R–N5 (probably White should take a draw by 25 B×BP N×R+ 26 P×N B×QNP 27 R×B P×R 28 B×R K×B 29 N×P) 25 . . . B×QNP 26 R×R+ R×R 27 R–KN1 N–B3, when Black has compensation for the sacrificed pawn because White's knight is completely out of play, his BP vulnerable to attack by . . . B–K5 and his K-side under pressure.

22 Q×N   Q–K2

If 22 . . . B×Q 23 R×Q QR–QB1 24 R–B5.

23 Q–B5   Q–B3

On 23 . . . Q×Q 24 R×Q B×RP (24 . . . B–B1 25 R×P) comes 25 R–B7.

24 B–KN5   Q×P
25 B–Q3   Q–K3

25 . . . B–K5 26 R–B1 B×B 27 R×Q B×R 28 Q–KB2 B–N3 29 B–B6 is hopeless for Black.

26 R–B1   Q–Q4

If 26 . . . P–K5 27 B–QB4.

27 Q–QB2

27 Q–B3 would be a technical win since on . . . P–K5 White has the move B–B6 at his disposal.

27 . . .   P–K5
28 B–QB4   Q–K4
29 Q–Q1

Much more convincing was 29 R×P and now: (i) 29 . . . Q×P 30 R×B! Q×R (30 . . . Q×Q 31 R×R+ R×R 32 B–B6+ and mate next move) 31 B–QB1!; or (ii)

29 ... QR–KB1 30 Q–B2 R×R 31 Q×R R–KB1 32 Q×R+ B×Q 33 B–B6+ and mate next move.

29 ...   P–B4

30 Q–R5?

30 B×R R×B 31 B–Q2 Q×P 32 R×P R–Q1   33 R–B2 was the simplest win. Now Black has a chance he doesn't deserve ...

30 ...   B–Q4??

Overlooking a horrible threat. After 30 ... B–K1 31 Q–R4 R–KB1 (31 ... B–N3 is also playable) 32 B–K7 (not 32 B–R6 B×B 33 Q×B B×P 34 R–B4 Q–K2! 32 ... B×P the situation is very unclear.

31 R–KR3   B–R3
32 Q×B   Resigns

Notes by Levy based on analysis by Durao in INFORMATOR and by Zaitsev in 64

28 Pomar (Spain) –
Hort (Czechoslovakia)

King's Indian Defence

1 P–Q4 N–KB3 2 P–QB4 P–KN3 3 N–QB3 B–N2 4 N–B3 0–0 5 P–K4 P–Q3 6 B–K2 QN–Q2 7 0–0 P–K4 8 P×P?! Such exchanges have almost vanished from modern master play since Black gains too

great a grip on White's Q4 square. In fact, having played over Hort's brilliant technical achievement in this game I would imagine that any prospective fancier of 8 P×P would be turned off the move for life – yet Pomar specializes in the byways of combating the King's Indian, and normally he is quite successful. **8 ... P×P 9 P–QN3 R–K1 10 Q–B2 P–B3** Black can protect his own Q4. **11 R–Q1 Q–B2 12 B–R3 B–B1! 13 B–N2** Exchanging on B8 would leave White with the 'bad bishop', hemmed in by the pawns on QB4 and K4. **13 ... N–R4** Normally Black goes for Q5 by means of QN–KB1– K3–Q5, but Hort's method is even more effective (N–KR4–N2–K3) since the black QN still has something left to do on the other wing. **14 P–N3 N–N2 15 P–QR3 P–QR4 16 N–QR4 P–N3!** P–B5 must not be allowed. **17 Q–B3 P–B3 18 P–QN4 P×P 19 P×P P–QB4** Increasing his central influence at the cost of weakening d5, but White is in no position to arrange the manoeuvre N–QB3–Q5 while it can still inflict some damage. **20 Q–Q2 N–K3 21 P×P N/2×P**

22 Q–B2 N×N 23 R×N B–QN2 White's KP is also a weakness.

24 R×R R×R 25 N–Q2 Q–B3 26
B–N4 N–B4 27 B–KB3 Q–R5 In the
resultant ending White will be un-
able to protect all his weak pawns
(QB4/K4/KB2). 28 Q×Q R×Q 29
R–R1 B–KR3! 30 R–Q1 R–R7 31
B–B1 B–KB1 Heading for QB4.

32 N–B1 R–R8 33 N–Q2 B–B3 34
B–QN2 R×R+ 35 B×R N–Q6 36
B–QB3 B–B4 37 B–K2 N×P 38
K–N2 N×KP 39 B–B3 N×B 40
B×B K–B2 41 N–K4 N×N 42
B×N and **White Resigned**

Notes by Keene

PRELIMINARY GROUP VI

	EG	S	C	I	W	T	S	M	Total	Final Group
East Germany	×	3	2½	3	3½	3½	4	4	**23½**	A
Sweden	1	×	2½	2	3½	4	3	4	**20**	A
Canada	1½	1½	×	2½	3½	2½	2½	4	**18**	B
Italy	1	2	1½	×	2½	2½	4	3½	**17**	B
Wales	½	½	½	1½	×	2½	3	3	**11½**	C
Turkey	½	0	1½	1½	1½	×	1½	3½	**10**	C
Singapore	0	1	1½	0	1	2½	×	3	**9**	D
Malta	0	0	0	½	1	½	1	×	**3**	D

The young Canadian school seems to thrive on eccentric opening variations. This makes for entertaining chess but it is a severe hindrance
when competing for high international honours. In contrast to the
Canadians, the young Swedish team, led by Grandmaster Ulf Andersson, exhibited a thorough theoretical knowledge. As a result the
Swedes were much more in command when playing against the weak
countries and it is this which enabled them to finish a convincing second.
Wales was the only newcomer to the FIDE membership list which
finished above the D–final.

29 **Eroezbek** (Turkey) –
   Schöneberg (East Germany)

Benko Gambit
1 P–Q4 N–KB3 2 P–QB4 P–B4 3
P–Q5 P–QN4 4 P×P P–QR3 5
P×P B×P 6 P–KN3 P–Q3 7
B–N2 P–N3 8 N–KR3?! Usual is
8 N–KB3. 8 . . . B–KN2 9 0–0 0–0
10 N–B3 QN–Q2 11 R–K1 Q–N3?
More accurate is 11 . . . Q–R4.
12 Q–B2 KR–N1 13 R–N1 If 13

P–N3 P–B5 with an unclear position.
13 . . . N–K4 14 N–KN5 B–N2?!
Hoping for 15 P–K4 when the
bishop returns to QR3 with a ven-
geance. 15 R–Q1 B–QB1 16 N/5–
K4? Better is 16 P–KR3, depriving
three of Black's minor pieces of the
use of an important square and aiming to meet 16 . . . B–B4 with 17
P–K4. 16 . . . B–B4 17 N×N+
B×N 18 B–K4 B–R6 19 P–N3 19
B–N2 would leave Black with nothing

better than 19 . . . B–B4 and a draw by repetition. **19 . . . N–N5** Now Black threatens 20 . . . P–B5! **20 N–R4 Q–R2 21 P–K3 N–K4 22 P–B4? N–N5 23 R–K1 B–N2 24 B–KN2 B×B 25 K×B Q–N2! 26 Q–B4** If 26 P–K4 R×N! winning as in the game. Or if 26 N–B3 B×N 27 Q×B Q×QP+ followed by 28 . . . R×RP with an easy win.

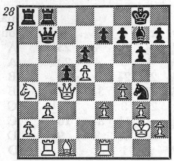

26 . . . R×N! 27 Q×R Q×QP+ 28 P–K4 Q–Q6 29 Q–B4 Q×Q 30 P×Q R×R 31 Resigns
Analysis by Malich in
THE CHESS PLAYER

30 **Choong** (Singapore) – **Day** (Canada)
Sicilian Defence

1 P–K4 P–QB4 2 N–KB3 P–Q3 3 P–Q4 P×P 4 N×P N–KB3 5 N–QB3 P–QR3 6 P–B4 Q–B2 7 B–Q3 P–QN4 8 P–QR3 B–N2 9 0–0 QN–Q2 10 N–B3 P–K4 11 Q–K1 P–N3 12 P×P P×P 13 Q–R4 B–N2 14 B–R6 0–0 15 N–N5 QR–K1 Not 15 . . . N–R4?? 16 B×B K×B 17 R×P+ R×R 1 N–K6+. **16 P–KN4 R–K2** Overprotecting the KBP so that after . . . **17 R–B3!** . . . he can move his KR . . . **17 . . . R/1–K1** . . . so that after

18 QR–KB1 Q–N3+ 19 K–R1 . . . he can retreat the KB . . . **19 . . . B–KR1** . . . so that after . . . **20 R–R3** . . . White will not be threatening to exchange on KN7 and then capture on KR7. **20 . . . N–B4**

21 B–B8!! K×B 22 R×N! N–K3 If 23 . . . B×R 23 N×RP+ K–N2 24 N×B Q×N 25 P–N5 etc. **23 N×RP+ K–N2 24 P–N5 Q–Q5 25 N–B8! N×P 26 Q×B mate**
Notes by Levy

31 **Schöneberg** (E. Germany) – **Day** (Canada)
English Opening

1 P–QB4	**P–K4**
2 N–QB3	**N–QB3**
3 N–B3	**P–Q3**
4 P–Q4	**P–B3**

Better than it looks, but more easily justified psychologically than objectively as White now becomes impatient and over-estimates his chances. The move was played by Riumin against Mazel in 1937 when the modern King's Indian was in it's formative stages and there was much experimentation involving the development of the KN. As one of the leading players in this experimentation, Fyodor Bohatirchuk, later moved to Ottawa (where I learnt my chess) I feel quite at home in such positions. Incidentally another Canadian player, Duncan Suttles, has also questioned the logic of the normal King's Indian development N–KB3 followed later by N–K1, P–KB4 and N–KB3.

5 P–Q5

As Black cannot himself exchange or advance in the centre there is no need to rush this move.

5 . . .   N–N1

5 . . . N–K2?! would lead to a traffic jam on the K-side.

6 P–K4   P–KN3

7 P–KR4

Hoping to take advantage of the absence of the KB3 knight to gain space on the K-side.

7 . . .   P–KR4

Maintaining the frontier! Another possibility is 7 . . . B–R3 exchanging the bad bishop but this leads to a dry, defensive game.

8 B–K2   N–KR3

9 N–Q2   N–Q2

10 P–QN4

Allowing Black to weaken the Q-side pawn structure. After the patient 10 P–R3 P–R4 11 R–QN1 N–N3 12 P–QN4 P×P 13 P×P B–Q2 Black may contest the QB4 square by N–R5.

10 . . .   P–R4!

11 P×P   R×P

12 N–N3   R–R1

13 P–N4

When such ideas work they are referred to as a brilliant conception, playing on both wings simultaneously. When they fail they are simply aimless play. Here it comes very close, but ultimately fails, so the

move is objectively bad. The root of the error may be traced back to the evaluation of the position after 4 . . . P–B3. By under-estimating that move White felt obliged to obtain a great opening advantage. Here he may continue with quiet Q-side play but since Black has evident control of QB4 no break is allowed and at the very most a small advantage is possible. Therefore 13 P–N4 must be the move. All very logical but 4 . . . P–B3 is *not* a bad move, and now Black obtains the advantage.

13 . . .   P×P

14 B×P   P–KB4!

15 P×P   N–B3!

The key move which turns the tables.

16 B–B3   P×P

Now Black has one pawn island to White's four and also controls all the centre squares. White has, however, a strong initiative.

17 B–N5   B–N2

Reptilicus in fianchetto, eager to breathe fire down the dragon diagonal.

18 Q–Q2   K–B1

19 0–0–0   B–Q2

20 P–R5   Q–N1

With the dual ideas . . . P–N4 and . . . Q–R2.

21 QR–N1   B–K1

Preventing 22 B×NB6 B×B 23 R–N6.

22 B–K2   Q–R2

23 B–R4

Threatening 24 R×B.

23 . . .   N/B3–N1!

(That's the QN!–RDK.)

The best move of the game, stabilizing the K-side and unmasking the fianchetto.

24 R–R2	R–R2	
25 R/2–N2	B–R1	

30
W

Vacuum packed development!
26 P–B3

Hoping for 26 ... B×P when the rooks may infiltrate on the KR-file. But White has no more threats and Black now assumes the initiative.

26 ...	Q–R6+
27 K–Q1	Q–N5
28 R–N5	

Now White hopes for 28 ... B–KB3 29 R×N+ creating some play on the K-side, but there is no threat.

28 ...	P–N4
29 N×P	Q×Q+
30 N×Q	B×N
31 P×B	N–K2

A trap in time trouble.
32 B–B4
(but if the QP goes White's position collapses anyway – RDK.)

32 ...	B–B3
33 K–B2	N–B2
34 P–B4	B×R
35 B×B	R×KRP
36 B–N3	N×B
37 P×N	K–B2
38 P–R4	K–N3
39 N–B4	N×P

40 P–R5	R×NP	
41 R×R+	K×R	
42 K–Q2	N–B3	
43 Resigns		

Notes by Day specially for this volume

32 **Yanofsky** (Canada) – **Jansonn** (Sweden)

A classic example of a game won *because* the bishops were on opposite coloured squares.

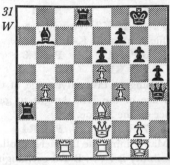

31
W

37 Q–KB2 Q–N5   38 R–B2 38 Q–K2 allows 38 ... R×B. **38 ... P–R5   39 Q–K2 Q–B4   40 R–Q2 R×R 41 Q×R** If 41 B×R R–KN6. **41 ... B–Q4 42 Q–KB2 R–R7 43 R–K2 R–R8+   44 R–K1** If 44 K–R2 Q–N5 (Threat 45 ... P–R6) 45 B–Q4 R–Q8 46 R–Q2? Q–N6+. **44 ... R×R+   45 Q×R Q–N5** With the rooks exchanged Black's attack is all the more deadly because White has only his queen to defend the KN2 square. **46 Q–B2 P–R6! 47 K–R2 P×P 48 Q–N3 Q–R4+ 49 Q–R3 P–N8 =Q+   50 B×Q Q–K7+   51 K–N3 Q–B6+   52 K–R4 Q×P+   53 Q–N4 P–N4+ 54 K–R3 B–N7+ 55 Resigns**

Notes by Nilsson in AFTONBLADET

PRELIMINARY GROUP VII

	B	H	A	C	A	P	I	A	Total	Final Group
Bulgaria	×	1½	3	2	2½	3½	4	4	**20½**	A
Holland	2½	×	2	2½	3	2	4	4	**20**	A
Albania	1	2	×	2½	3½	3½	4	3	**19½**	B
Colombia	2	1½	1½	×	2	3½	2½	3	**16**	B
Australia	1½	1	½	2	×	4	3	4	**16**	C
Puerto Rico	½	2	½	½	0	×	3	3	**9½**	C
Iraq	0	0	0	1½	1	1	×	3	**6½**	D
Andorra	0	0	1	1	0	1	1	×	**4**	D

Colombia (3 wins 2 draws) qualified for B final ahead of Australia (3 wins 1 draw) because of their better match record.

That the honours would fall to Bulgaria and Holland in this group was hardly headline news. But the good showings of Albania and Colombia were a real shock, especially when one realizes that Australia was led by Grandmaster Walter Browne. One cannot cavil at the performance of Albania. Admittedly, they were given a free 2–2 v Holland in the penultimate round (average length of game about 10 moves) to ensure the qualification of the Netherlands team, but it was clear that Albania were destined for the B group anyway. But the Colombian performance requires more explanation – in fact Bulgaria conceded 2–2 against them in the last round without a fight, thus putting the Australians out of the B group on tie-split. It seems anomalous that a team's chances of qualifying should be so considerably enhanced or damaged by the order in which they meet their opponents. There must surely be good arguments for the Olympiad to be run on a Swiss or League system to avoid such injustices. The Australians protested, but what could be done? It seems that chess-diplomatic relations between Australia and Bulgaria have touched a low-point. The Australians must have been doubly furious when the Albanians acted so idiotically in the B-final as to have themselves expelled.

33 **Browne** (Australia) –
   Kaplan (Puerto Rico)

Pirc Defence

1 P–K4	P–Q3
2 P–Q4	N–KB3
3 N–QB3	P–KN3
4 N–B3	B–N2
5 B–K2	0–0
6 0–0	B–N5

After 6 . . . P–B3 7 P–KR3 QN–Q2 8 P–QR4! Q–B2 9 B–K3 P–K4 10 P×P P×P, White is a little better.

7 B–K3	**N–B3**
8 Q–Q2	**P–K4**
9 P×P	

After 9 P–Q5 N–K2, the game takes on the character of a King's Indian Defence.

9 . . .	**P×P**
10 QR–Q1	**Q–K2**

Or 10 . . . Q×Q 11 R×Q KR–Q1 12 KR–Q1 R×R 13 R×R N–K1 14 N–Q5 B×N 15 P×B! N–Q5 16 B–Q1 N–K3 17 P–B3 B–B1 18 B–R4 with a slight advantage to White. Larsen-Ivkov and Reshevsky-Ivkov, Santa Monica 1966.

11 B–KN5	**Q–K3**

A new idea. More usual is 11 . . . B×N 12 B×B N–Q5 13 N–Q5 Q–Q3 14 P–B3 N×B+ 15 P×N N×N 16 Q×N Q–R3 17 R–Q2 (my move) with a superior position for White.

12 B×N	**Q×B**

If 12 . . . B×B 13 N–Q5 B–Q1 and now: (i) 14 Q–R6 (threatening 15 N×BP B/1×N 16 N–N5) 14 . . . B×N 15 B×B N–Q5 16 R–Q3 when White is better; or (ii) 14 P–B3 and if 14 . . . N–K2 15 N–N5 when Black is in dire straits (the threats include 16 B–B4 and 16 Q–R6).

13 N–Q5	**Q–Q3**
14 P–B3	**QR–Q1**

14 . . . KR–Q1 is slightly better.

15 Q–N5!	

A very good move.

15 . . .	**B–K3!**

A very sharp move. If 15 . . . B×N 16 B×B and White has a clear advantage because his bishop is better than Black's and Black's knight has no good moves.

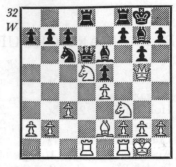

32
W

16 B–N5!

The winning move. If instead 16 N–B4? Black has an incredible counterpunch in 16 . . . N–Q5!! 17 P×N P–KR3! and now: (i) 18 P×P Q×R! 19 R×Q P×Q with an unclear position which probably favours Black; or (ii) 18 Q–R4 P–KN4! 19 N×NP RP×N 20 Q×P P×N 21 P–K5 Q–N5 22 Q×P P–QB4 with a clear plus for Black who is about to win a pawn.

16 . . .	**B×N**

The only move. e.g. 16 . . . K–R1? 17 B×N Q×B (or 17 . . . P×B 18 N–K3!) 18 N×KP winning; or 16 . . . P–B3? 17 N×KBP+! B×N 18 R×Q B×Q 19 R×B.

17 R×B	**Q–K2**
18 B×N	**Q×Q**
19 N×Q	**P×B**
20 R–R5	**R–Q7**
21 P–QN3!	**R–R1**
22 R–R6!	

Trying to force . . . P–QB4 and . . . P–B5 when Black's bishop cannot come to light.

22 . . .	**R–Q3**
23 P–QB4	**B–B1**
24 P–B5?!	

Correct was 24 N–B3 R–K3 25 P–QR3! with the threat of P–QN4 and P–B5. Black's two rooks are then tied down by the single white rook at QR6 and White can take control of the Q-file with his KR.

24 ...   R–Q7
25 R×BP?

25 P–QN4 R–Q5 26 P–QR3 P–R3 27 N–B3 would have left White in command. Now Black equalizes.

25 ...   R–B1!
26 R–R1   P–QR4!
27 N–B3   R–B7

Now Black should draw. 28 N×P B–N2 29 P–B4 B×N 30 P×B R–K1? 30 ... R–Q1! followed by ... R/1–Q7 draws easily. 31 R×BP R×KP 32 R–KB1 R×KP 33 R/7×P R×BP 34 R–B8+ K–N2 35 R/1–B7+ K–R3 36 R–KR8 K–N4 37 R/8×P R–B7! 38 P–KR4+ If 38 R–B2? R–K8+ 39 R–B1 R/8–K7. 38 ... R×KRP 39 R×R K×R 40 R–B2 R–B8+ 41 K–R2 P–N4! 42 R–Q2 R–B6! 43 R–Q8 R–B7 44 R–KR8+ K–N5 45 P–R3 R–R7 46 P–R4 R–QB7? 46 ... R–N7 is more accurate. 47 R–R8 (33)

47 ... K–R5?? Losing the game. 47 ... R–B6 would still draw. 48 R×P P–N5 49 R–KB5 R–N7 50 R–B1 R×QNP 51 R–QR1 R–N3 52 P–R5 R–QR3 53 R–R4 K–N4

54 K–N3 K–B4 55 R–KB4+ K–K3 56 R–R4 K–B4 57 K–B2 K–N4 58 P–N3 Resigns

Notes by Browne specially for this volume

34 **Timman** (Holland) – **Radulov** (Bulgaria)

Queen's Gambit, Delayed Acceptance

Radulov employs a suspect opening variation and soon has an inferior position. On move 16 he fails to exchange White's dangerous KB thus allowing White to inaugurate a dangerous attack which leads to the win of the Black queen for several pieces. Although Black has nominal material parity his pieces are much too disorganized to offer effective resistance to White's queen. A most attractive game by the young Dutch Master.

1 N–KB3 N–KB3 2 P–B4 P–K3 3 N–B3 P–Q4 4 P–Q4 P×P 5 P–K4 P–B4 6 B×P P×P 7 N×P P–QR3 8 P–K5 Q–B2 9 Q–K2 KN–Q2 10 B–B4 B–B4 11 R–Q1 0–0 12 0–0 B×N 13 R×B N–QB3 14 R–K4 P–QN4 15 B–Q3 N–B4 16 R–K3 P–B4? He absolutely had to play 16 ... N×B!

17 P×P ep! Not a particularly difficult combination, but beautiful

nevertheless. **17 . . . Q×B 18 B×RP+! K×B 19 Q–R5+ K–N1** Or 19 . . . Q–R3 20 Q×N threatening the rook on f8 and also R–KR3. **20 P×P K×P 21 R–N3+ Q×R 22 BP×Q** This recapture eliminates Black's only active piece. **22 . . . R×R+ 23 K×R P–K4 24 Q–N5+ K–B2 25 N–Q5 B–K3 26 Q–B6+ K–N1 27 Q–N6+ K–B1 28 N–B7 B–B5+ 29 K–B2 R–Q1 30 Q×N R–Q7+ 31 K–B3 R–Q6+ 32 K–N4 N–Q2 33 P–N3 B–B2 34 Q×RP R–Q5+ 35 K–B5 K–K2 36 N×P Black Resigns**

35 **Cuellar** (Colombia) – **Donner** (Holland)

This, the longest game of the Skopje Olympiad, went past six time controls (moves 40, 56, 72, 88, 104 and 120). Cuellar was under time pressure at all six controls and Donner at five of them. The game lasted for fifteen hours and five minutes, and it was not until move 113 that Cuellar made the decisive mistake, throwing away a win. Here is the position after Cuellar's sealed move (at the end of the third session) 109 B–N6.

Play continued: **109 . . . R–R5+ 110 K–B5 R–Q5 111 Q×R!! P×Q 112 P–Q7 Q–R6+ 113 K–B6??**

Now the game is drawn. Correct was 113 K–Q5 when 113 . . . Q–R1+ can be met by 114 K×P and 113 . . . Q–R7+ by 114 K–Q6! Q–R6+ 115 K–K6 and in each case, with no perpetual check at Black's disposal, White's two pawns and bishop triumph against the queen. **113 . . . Q–R1+ 114 K–B7 P–Q6!** The saving clause. **115 B–K3 P–Q7 116 B×QP Q–R2+ 117 K–B6 Q–R1+ 118 K–B7 Q–R2+ 119 K–B6 Q–R1+ 120 K–Q6 Q–QN1+ 121 K–B6 Q–R1+ Drawn**

Notes by Donner specially for this volume

36 **Browne** (Australia) – **Taha** (Iraq)

French Defence

In the chess olympics it often happens that Grandmasters are paired with unknown players. Normally the Grandmasters win. But sometimes there are surprises as in this game. Browne possibly thought that he would have an easy win against his unknown opponent. He played a very bad opening variation in the hope that his opponent wouldn't know all of its tricks. But . . . **1 P–K4 P–K3 2 P–Q4 P–Q4 3 N–QB3 N–KB3 4 B–KN5 B–K2 5 P–K5 KN–Q2 6 B×B** Very interesting is the Albin-Chatard-Alekhine Attack, 6 P–KR4, and that move would be in keeping with Browne's style. But the young Grandmaster has other ideas. **6 . . . Q×B 7 N–N5?!** An old move, first played by Chigorin in the nineteenth century. Better is 7 P–B4 or 7 Q–Q2. **7 . . . N–N3!** Threatening 8 . . . P–QR3 followed by 9 . . .

АКАДЕМИСТОР
Н. ПАДЕВСКИ
БУГАРИЈА
ВЕЛЕМАЈСТОР
N. PADEVSKI
BULGARIE

3

М. ШОНЕБЕРГ
ДЕМОКРАТСКА РЕПУБЛИКА ГЕРМАНИЈА
M. SCHÖNEBERG
ALLEMAGNE DEMOCRATIQUE

6   N. Padevsky I G M (Bulgaria) playing M. Schöneberg (East Germany)

7   L. Vogt (East Germany) playing P. Peev (Bulgaria)

Л. ФОГТ
ДР ГЕРМАНИЈА
L. VOGT
ДДR

4

П. ПЕЕВ
БУГАРИЈА
P. PEEV
BULGARIE

8   J. Donner I G M (Holland)

9   W. Uhlmann I G M (East Germany)

10   M. Bobotsov I G M (Bulgaria)

11   I. Bilek I G M (Hungary)

Q–N5. **8 P–QR4?** Better is 8 P–
QB3 even though Black would have
a good game after 8 . . . P–QR3
9 N–QR3 P–QB4 10 P–KB4 N–B3
11 N–B2 N–R5 12 R–N1 P–
QN4 13 N–B3 B–Q2 14 Q–Q2
R–QB1 15 B–Q3 P–B5! **8 . . .
P–QR3 9 P–R5 P×N 10 P×N
R×R 11 Q×R** P–QB3 11 . . . 0–0
was also good. e.g. 12 P×P Q×P 13
B–Q3 N–B3 14 P–QB3 P–N5 with a
slight advantage to Black. **12 Q–R8
0–0** (*36*)
**13 Q×N–N Q–N5+ 14 P–QB3
Q×NP 15 N–K2 P–N5 16 P×P
Q×NP+ 17 K–Q1 Q–N6+ 18
K–Q2 Q–N5+ 19 K–Q3?** White
should have gone back to Q1 and
hoped that Black would take a draw.
19 . . . P–QB4! 20 Q–B7 20 P×P
loses to 20 . . . B–Q2 and 21 . . .
B–N4+ with a decisive attack.

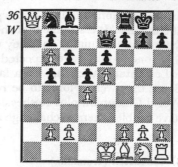

**20 . . . P–B5+ 21 K–K3 Q–N6+ 22
K–B4 Q–Q6** White is completely lost
– he has no good moves. **23 P–B3
Q–Q7+ 24 K–N3 Q–K8+ 25
K–R3 Q–B7 26 K–N4 P–B3 27
P×P P–K4+ 28 K–R5 NP×P 29
P×P P×P 30 Q–K7 R–B4+ 31
Resigns** After 31 K–R6, Q×QNP+
is unpleasant.

*Notes by Despotovic specially for this
volume*

PRELIMINARY GROUP VIII

	U	R	P	A	T	I	F	V	Total	Final Group
USA	×	2	2	3	3½	3	4	4	**21½**	A
Rumania	2	×	2	2	3	3½	4	4	**20½**	A
Philippines	2	2	×	2	3½	2	4	4	**19½**	B
Austria	1	2	2	×	3½	2	2½	3½	**16½**	B
Tunisia	½	1	½	½	×	4	3	4	**13½**	C
Iran	1	½	2	2	0	×	4	3½	**13**	C
Faroe Islands	0	0	0	1½	1	0	×	4	**6½**	D
Virgin Islands	0	0	0	½	0	½	0	×	**1**	D

The close scores at the top here reflected a bitter struggle which was
only resolved at the close of the last round when Rumania defeated the
Faroes by 4–0 and the USA held the Filipinos to 2–2. The Filipinos
played with immense energy and fully held their own with the leading
teams. However, they were badly let down by their score against Iran.
On top board for the Phillipines the youthful Eugenio Torre made a

fine impression, winning a sharp game from Grandmaster Gheorghiu of Rumania. It is strange that the Filipino morale seemed to crack after their failure to qualify and they were much less of a force in the B–final than one would have expected from their preliminary performance.

Lamentably the USA team lacked Fischer. Led by Kavalek and R. Byrne they were a force to be reckoned with, but the inclusion of the World Champion plus Reshevsky, Lombardy and Evans would surely have enabled them to challenge for the gold medals.

37 Ciocaltea (Rumania) –
   Cardoso (Philippines)

Sicilian Defence

1 P–K4 P–QB4 2 N–KB3 P–Q3 3 P–Q4 P×P 4 Q×P P–QR3 4 . . . N–QB3 5 B–QN5 B–Q2 6 B×N B×B 7 P–B4 is considered to be slightly in White's favour but Gheorghiu assesses the line as equal. The usual move is 4 . . . B–Q2. **5 P–B4 N–QB3 6 Q–Q2 P–KN3 7 N–B3 B–N2 8 P–QN3 N–B3 9 B–N2 0–0 10 P–KR3! R–N1** 10 . . . B–Q2 transposes to game 2. **11 B–Q3 Q–R4 12 P–R3 R–Q1 13 P–QN4 Q–B2 14 0–0 N–K4!? 15 N×N P×N 16 Q–K3 P–K3** Otherwise 17 N–Q5. **17 KR–Q1 P–N3 18 QR–B1 B–N2**

*37
W*

19 P–B5 Much stronger is 19 N–R4 N–Q2 20 P–B5! By playing the moves in the wrong order Cio-

caltea gives his opponent an unde-served opportunity. **19 . . . P×P 20 N–R4 P–B5!! 21 R×P Q×R 22 B×Q R×R+ 23 K–R2 N×P 24 B–Q3?!** N×P **25 B–B2! R–KR8+ 26 K–N3 R–KB8?** 26 . . . R–KN8 is simple and strong: 27 Q×N R R×P+ 28 Q×R B×Q 29 K×B R–QB1! and now 30 B–Q3? loses to 30 . . . P–K5! 31 B×KP B×B 32 N×B P–B4 33 B–N1 R–B6 etc., while the endings after 30 B–K4 P–B4 and 30 N–B5 B–B1 are very much in Black's favour. Now White wins a piece. **27 Q–R7 R–Q1 28 Q×B P–B4 29 Q–K7 P–B5+ 30 K–R4 R–KB1 31 Q×P+ K–R1 32 B×KP R–B8 33 Q–K7 R–KN1 34 B–N3 R/8–B1 35 B×R R R×B 36 B×B+ R×B 37 Q–K8+ R–N1 38 Q–K5+ R–N2 39 N–B5 K–N1 40 Q–K8 mate**

Analysis by Gheorghiu in THE CHESS
PLAYER

38 Torre (Philippines) –
   Harandi (Iran)

Ruy Lopez

1 P–K4 P–K4 2 N–KB3 N–QB3 3 B–N5 P–QR3 4 B–R4 N–B3 5 0–0 P–QN4 6 B–N3 B–N2 7 R–K1 Regarded by theory as best. For 7

P–Q4 see game 133. **7 . . . B–B4 8 P–B3 P–Q3 9 P–QR4** Probably stronger is 9 P–Q4 B–N3 10 B–N5! P–R3 11 B–KR4 though the whole system is so complicated that no-one really knows! **9 . . . P–R3 10 P–Q4 B–N3 11 RP×P RP×P 12 R×R Q×R 13 N–R3 0–0** 13 . . . P×P! 14 N×NP 0–0 15 N/5×P/4 N×N 16 N×N B×P is possibly slightly better for Black, Kostro-Tseshkovsky, Varna 1969. But the text is not without a latent sting. **14 P–Q5 N–QR4 15 B–R2 P–B3!** Suddenly there is uncomfortable pressure throughout the long diagonal. **16 P–QN4 N–B5 17 B×N** 17 N×N P×N 18 B×BP P×P 19 B×QP N×B 20 P×N B×QP gives Black a beautiful game. **17 . . . P×B 18 N×BP B–B2 19 N×QP!** Not 19 P×P B×P 20 N×QP? R–Q1 winning a piece. **19 . . . B×N 20 P×P B×BP 21 Q×B B×P 22 N–R4 R–Q1 23 Q×P Q–R5 24 Q–N3 R–Q8**

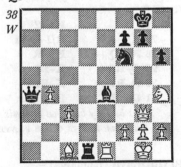

38
W

25 P–B3 Q–R2+! 26 K–R1 Not 26 K–B1?? B–Q6 mate. **26 . . . N–R4! 27 R×R N×Q+ 28 P×N B–B7 29 R–Q2** If 29 R–Q8+ K–R2 30 B–Q2 P–N4 wins the knight. **29 . . . B–N8 30 P–N4 Q–K2 31 N–B5 B×N 32 P×B Q–K8+ 33 K–R2**

Q×B 34 R–Q8+ K–R2 35 R–QB8 Q–B5+ 36 K–N1 Q×P/B4 37 R–B5 Q–K3 38 K–B2 P–B4 39 R–B7 P–B5 40 K–N1 P–R4 41 R–B5 P–R5 42 R–KN5 K–R3 43 Resigns A comical finish would be 43 R–N4 P–N4.

Analysis by Gheorghiu in THE CHESS PLAYER

39 **Ghizdavu** (Rumania) – **Shahsavar** (Iran)

Sicilian Defence

1 P–K4	P–QB4
2 N–KB3	N–QB3
3 P–Q4	P×P
4 N×P	P–KN3
5 N–QB3	B–N2
6 B–K3	N–B3
7 B–QB4	0–0
8 B–N3	P–Q3
9 P–B3	B–Q2
10 Q–Q2	R–B1
11 P–KR4	P–KR4!?

This move has been popularized recently by the US Senior Master Andrew Soltis.

12 0–0–0 N–K4 13 P–N4!?

Soltis analyses three alternatives: (i) 13 B–R6 B×B! 14 Q×B R×N! 15 P×R Q–R4 with more than sufficient compensation for the exchange;
(ii) 13 K–N1 N–B5 14 Q–Q3! N×B 15 Q×N (so far Larsen-Westerinen, Halle 1963) and now 15 . . . P–R4 and 15 . . . P–QN4 are both interesting possibilities;
(iii) 13 B–N5 N–R2! 14 B–R6 B×B 15 Q×B R×N! 16 P×R Q–R4 17 K–N2 R–B1 18 Q–K3 Q–N3 19 K–R1 Q–B4 20 P–N4!

P×P   21 P–KB4 N–B5   22 B×N
Q×B   23 R–Q3 with a slight
advantage to White. Biyiasis-Kava-
lek, Vancouver 1971. This last line
must be considered critical for Black.

13 ...	P×P
14 P–R5	N×RP
15 B–R6	P–K3!

39
W

| 16 QR–N1 | Q–B3 |

Naturally not 16 . . . B×B   17
Q×B Q–B3 18 R×N! end of game.

17 B×B	Q×B
18 P×P	N–KB3
19 R–R4	KR–Q1

19 . . . P–KN4?   20 R–R3
N/3×NP loses to 21 R/3–N3 N–KB3
22 R×P N–N3 23 N×P! etc.

| 20 R/1–R1 | N/3×NP! |
| 21 Q–N5?! | |

Stronger is 21 Q–N2! N–KB3 22
N/3–K2 followed by N–B4, though
it is still not clear how White can
break through Black's K-side defences without any pawns to help
him.

| 21 ... | P–B3?? |

A grotesque positional blunder
which is based on a false tactical
premise. Correct was 21 . . . Q–B3!
22 R–R8+ Q×R   23 R×Q+
K×R   24 Q–K7 with an unclear
position.

| 22 Q–Q2 | N–B5 |

Black must defend against the
threat to his KP. If 22 . . . R–K1 23
R–N1 P–B4   24 P×P NP×P   25
N×BP Q–N3 26 R/4×N N×R 27
R×N Q×R 28 N–R6+ ouch.

| 23 B×N | R×B |
| 24 R×N | P–K4 |

It was on this move that Black was
relying when he played 21 . . .
P–B3. But now comes the simple
refutation.

| 25 R/4–R4 | P×N |

25 . . . R×N   26 Q–R2 is quite
hopeless.

26 R–R8+!

What Black had overlooked is that
after 26 . . . Q×R   27 R×Q+
K×R, White has 28 Q–R6+ (if it
were not for this move then Black's
position would be perfectly satisfactory, even good, and his 21 . . .
P–B3 would not have been an error.)
28 . . . K–N1 29 Q×P+ K–B1 30
Q×P+ K–K1 31 N–Q5, and mate
at K7 with the queen or at QB7 with
the knight (if Black plays 31 . . .
R×KP).

26 ...	K–B2
27 R/8–R7	R/1–QB1
28 R×Q+	K×R
29 Q–R6+	K–B2
30 Q–R7+	K–B1
31 Q×P	Resigns

*Notes by Levy based on analysis by
Ghizdavu in* THE CHESS PLAYER

40 **Ghizdavu** (Rumania) –
   Tebourbi (Tunisia)

Alekhine's Defence

1 P–K4	N–KB3
2 P–K5	N–Q4
3 P–Q4	P–Q3

4 P–QB4	**N–N3**
5 P–B4	**P×P**
6 BP×P	**N–B3**
7 B–K3	**B–B4**
8 N–QB3	**P–K3**
9 N–B3	**B–K2**
10 P–Q5!	

This move has produced such good results for White in recent games that it is now surprising to find anyone who doesn't play the Four Pawns Attack.

10 . . .   **P×P**

10 . . . N–N5 11 R–B1! has been shown several times to give White a very big (probably winning) advantage. e.g. (i) 11 . . . 0–0 12 P–QR3 N–R3 13 B–Q3! with a dominating position. Parma-Mihaljcisin, Sarajevo 1969; (ii) 11 . . . P–KB3 12 P–QR3 N–R3 13 P–KN4! B×NP 14 R–KN1 P–KB4 15 P–R3 B×N 16 Q×B 0–0 17 R–B2 with a tremendous attack for the pawn. Velimirovic-Gipslis, Havana 1971; or (iii) 11 . . . P×P 12 P–QR3 P–B4 13 P×N P–Q5 14 B×P P×B 15 N×P Q–N1 16 Q–K2! B–N3 17 P–B5 N–Q2 18 P–K6! N–K4 19 Q–N5+ with a winning attack. Konikowski-Szultz, Poland 1972.

11 P×P	**N–N5**
12 N–Q4	**B–QB1**

12 . . . B–N3 has long been known to be very favourable to White, e.g. 13 B–QN5+ K–B1 14 0–0 K–N1 15 N–B5 B×N 16 R×B! N/5×QP 17 B×N! N×B 18 Q–N3 B–B4+ 19 K–R1 Q–K2 20 N–R4!! and White soon won. Stanciu-Partos, Rumania 1971.

The crucial move is 12 . . . B–Q2 which was played in Williams-Cafferty, British Championship

1971: 13 P–K6! P×P 14 P×P B–QB3 15 Q–N4! B–KR5+ 16 P–KN3! B× R 17 0–0–0! And now 17 . . . Q–B3 leads to immense complications. This line, if good for White, may well put Alekhine's defence under a thick cloud for many years to come.

13 P–Q6!

Also very strong is 13 B–QN5+ P–QB3 14 P×P 0–0 15 0–0 P–QR3 16 P×P B×P 17 B–K2 which was played in Ghizdavu-Suta, Rumania 1970. The text however, is at least as effective.

13 . . .   **B–R5+**

If 13 . . . B–N4 14 P×P Q–K2 15 B–N5+ K–B1 16 N–B3! and Black can resign; or 13 . . . P×P 14 B–QN5+ K–B1 (or 14 . . . B–Q2 15 P–K6!) 15 0–0 P×P 16 Q–B3 B–B3 17 N–B5 with an overwhelming position.

14 P–KN3   **0–0?!**

15 N–B3!	**B–N5**
16 P× B	**N–B5!?**

If 16 . . . B×N 17 Q×B N–B7+ 18 K–Q2 N×R 19 B–Q3 and as well as a winning material advantage White has a decisive attack.

17 B×N	**B×N**
18 Q×B	**Q×RP+**
19 B–B2	**Q×B/5**
20 0–0–0!	

With his king in safety White's extra piece will decide the game.

20 ...   P×P
21 P×P   N×P+
If 21 ... QR–B1 22 P–Q7.
22 K–N1   Q–N6
Threatening 23 ... QR–B1.
23 KR–N1   N×N+
Now 23 ... QR–B1 no longer works because of 24 R×P+ K×R 25 R–N1+ and mate next move. 23 ... P–KN3 allows a different mate: 24 B–Q4 N–N5 25 Q–KB6 Q–B7+ 26 K–R1 etc.

24 Q×N   Q×Q
25 P×Q   P–B3
26 P–Q7   QR–Q1
27 R–Q5   R–B2
28 R/1–Q1   P–QN3
29 B–N3   Resigns

Analysis by Ghizdavu in THE CHESS
PLAYER

41 **Kavalek** (USA) –
   Torre (Philippines)

King's Indian Defence

1 P–QB4 P–KN3 2 P–Q4 B–N2 3 N–QB3 P–Q3 4 P–K4 N–KB3 5 N–B3 0–0 6 P–KR3 Often adopted by Larsen. 6 ... P–B4 is a good reply. 6 ... P–K4 7 P–Q5 P–QR4 8 B–K3 N–R3 9 N–Q2 N×KP?! Perhaps ... N–B4 first. The text is a spirited try by the youthful Torre to unsettle the émigré Czech GM now playing top board for the USA. In view of the state of affairs in the preliminary group (this was the last round and the Philippines had to win in order to qualify for Final A) Black had to seek victory at all costs. 10 N/2×N P–KB4 11 P–KN4!

Securing a complete grip over the important K4 square, and this grants White a significant positional plus. Attempts to cling to the extra material come unstuck. e.g.: 11 B–N5 Q–K1 12 N–N3 P–B5 13 N/N3–K4 P–R3 etc ... **11 ... P×N 12 N×P P–N3 13 B–Q3 N–B4 14 P–N3 N×B+** Or 14 ... N×N 15 B×N and White is ideally placed to carry out the advance of his KRP against Black's king. **15 Q×N B–Q2 16 K–K2** 16 P–QR4 followed by 0–0–0 was safer; Black now obtains some counter-play. **16 ... P–QN4 17 P–B3 P×P 18 P×P R–N1 19 QR–QN1 R×R 20 R×R Q–R1 21 P–KR4**

41
B

Despite Black's struggles this move proves that White is still on top. **21 ... R–N1 22 P–R5 R×R 23 Q×R Q–R3 24 Q–N8+!** Forcing the exchange of queens. In the ending which follows Black's KB is no match for White's omnipotent N. One could hardly wish for a more instructive example of a recurrent King's Indian theme: N established on K4 v bad black KB. **24 ... Q–B1 25 Q×Q+ B×Q 26 P–R6!** B–B1 If 26 ... B–R1 27 B–Q2 B–R3 28 K–Q3 P–B3 29 P×P P–Q4 30 N–Q6 and wins. **27 N–B6+ K–B2**

28 N×P B–R3 29 K–Q3 P–B3 30 N–N5+ K–K2 31 P–R7 It all clicks for White now. **31 . . . B–KN2 32 N–K6 B–R1 33 B–N5+ K–Q2**

34 N–B8+ K–K1 35 N×P P×P 36 N×B B×P+ 37 K–B3 Resigns

Notes by Keene based on analysis by Gheorghiu in THE CHESS PLAYER

The Finals

FINAL GROUP A

	U	H	Y	C	W	B	R	H	U	E	S	P	D	A	S	S	Total
1 USSR	×	1½	2½	2	2½	2½	3	2½	3	3½	3½	3	3½	2	3	4	42
2 Hungary	2½	×	2½	2½	2	2½	2½	2½	2½	3½	3½	3	2	4	1½	3½	40½
3 Yugoslavia	1½	1½	×	1½	2	2	2	3	3	2½	3	3	3½	3	2½	4	38
4 Czechoslovakia	2	1½	2½	×	1½	2½	2½	2½	2	1½	1½	2½	3½	2½	4	3	35½
5 West Germany	1½	2	2	2½	×	2½	2½	2½	2½	2½	2½	2	2	3	2	3	35
6 Bulgaria	1½	1½	2	1½	1½	×	2½	3	2½	2½	2	2½	2½	2	2½	2	32
7 Rumania	1	1½	2	1½	1½	1½	×	2	2	3	2½	2½	2½	3½	2	2½	31½
8 Holland	1½	1½	1	1½	1½	1	2	×	2½	3	3	2	2½	1½	2	2½	29
9 USA	1	1½	1	2	1½	1½	2	1½	×	2½	3	3	1½	2½	2½	2	29
10 East Germany	½	½	1½	2½	1½	1½	1	1	1½	×	2½	2	2	3	4	2½	27½
11 Spain	½	½	1	2½	1½	2	1½	1	1	1½	×	2	3½	3	1½	3	26
12 Poland	1	1	1	1½	2	1½	1½	2	1	2	2	×	2	2	2	2	24½
13 Denmark	½	2	½	½	2	1½	1½	1½	2½	2	½	2	×	2	2½	1½	23
14 Argentina	2	0	1	1	1½	2	½	2½	1½	1	1	2	2	×	2½	2	22½
15 Sweden	1	2½	1½	0	2	1½	2	2	1½	0	2½	2	1½	1½	×	1	22½
16 Switzerland	0	½	0	1	1	2	1½	1	2½	1½	1	2	2½	2	3	×	21½

Holland were placed ahead of USA on their individual match result, their match records being equal (5 wins 3 draws each).

Argentina (2 wins 5 draws) were placed ahead of Sweden (2 wins 4 draws) because of their better match record.

Progressive Score Table

	R1	R2	R3	R4	R5	R6	R7	R8	R9	R10	R11	R12	R13	R14	R15
1 USSR	1½	4	6½	9	12½	15½	18½	22½	**24½**	**28**	**30½**	**33½**	**37**	**39**	**42**
2 Hungary	2½	5	8½	11½	13	16½	19	21	23½	26	29½	**33½**	36	38½	40½
3 Yugoslavia	**4**	5½	**9**	**12**	**15**	**18**	**21**	**23**	**24½**	26½	28	30	32½	35½	38
4 Czechoslovakia	3½	**6**	8	9½	12	14½	16	17½	19½	22	23½	26	30	33	35½
5 West Germany	2½	4	6½	9	11	13	16	18½	20½	22½	25	27½	30½	33	35
6 Bulgaria	2½	4	5½	7	10	12½	15	17½	19½	21	23½	25½	28	30	32
7 Rumania	1½	4½	7	9	11½	13	15½	17½	19½	22	25½	27½	29	30½	31½
8 Holland	1½	4	5½	6½	7½	10	13	16	18	19½	21½	23½	26	27½	29
9 USA	2½	4½	6½	8	9	10½	13½	16	18	19½	21	22	23½	26	29
10 East Germany	3	4	4½	6	6½	8	9	11	15	17½	20	22	23½	25	27½
11 Spain	2	3½	6½	9	12½	13½	14½	15½	18½	20	20½	22	22½	24½	26
12 Poland	2	4	5½	6½	8½	9½	11	13	15	17	19	20½	22½	23½	24½
13 Denmark	½	2	2½	5	5½	7½	9	11	13	13½	15	17	19	21½	23
14 Argentina	1	3	5½	7½	9	11	12	13½	14½	17	17½	17½	18½	20½	22½
15 Sweden	1½	4	5½	7½	10	12	13	14½	14½	16½	18½	19½	19½	21	22½
16 Swtizerland	0	2	3	5	6½	7	8	8	10	11½	13½	16½	18	19	21½

The interest in final group A always centres around two questions. Firstly: 'Will the Soviet Union win yet again?' When that question is answered in the affirmative, the natural sequitur is 'Who will be second?'

From their score during the early rounds of the finals at Skopje the Russians looked anything but gold medallists. Hampered by the absence of Boris Spassky and the presence of their champion Vladimir Savon, the Soviet team struggled through the early rounds without distinguishing themselves at all. But to those who were watching the strength of their early opponents, the writing was on the wall almost from the very start.

In the first round, the USSR lost to Hungary. Portisch has an incredibly fine (undefeated) score against Petrosian and some sources started rumours that the ex-World Champion would be 'resting' for the first round. But Petrosian did play and he came close to victory. It was Korchnoi's loss to Bilek that cost the USSR the match, but a 2½–1½ defeat is hardly a disaster when coming at the hands of the second favourites. After two 2½–1½ victories against West Germany and Holland, the Soviet Union looked like being in bad trouble against Bulgaria. Their young star Anatoly Karpov was beaten by Padevsky; Tal adjourned in what looked like a drawn ending against Radulov, and then there was the game between Korchnoi and Tringov.

The Mystery of the Disappearing Move

In the Bulgaria-USSR match from the fourth round of final group A, Tringov was playing Korchnoi at second board. After 41 moves the game was adjourned with Tringov to seal his next move. Material was even and the position appeared to be very drawish.

In international events it is usual for the player sealing the move to write down his move on his score sheet, place both his own and his opponent's score sheet in the envelope and then seal the envelope himself. At Skopje the procedure was slightly different. Instead of writing the sealed move on a score sheet, a separate piece of paper was provided. When Tringov was handed the piece of paper he queried its validity, claiming that he had always written his move on his score sheet in the past and that he saw no good reason to deviate from this practice. His attitude was quite firm. He rejected the blank slip of paper, wrote down his move and then. . . .

The following morning the adjourned position was set up.

TRINGOV (Bulgaria)

42
W

ILORCHNOY (USSR)

The envelope was opened and the score sheet removed but when the arbiter looked to find the move that Tringov had written down it was nowhere to be seen! On a closer inspection of the score sheet it was discovered that it was not even Tringov's game score but that of his opponent. The only thing that was normal about the whole situation was the envelope, clearly written in Korchnoi's hand, which was undisputedly the same one that had been handed to Tringov the previous evening.

Tringov was horrified. Where had his move gone? The first suggestion was that the arbiters were somehow at fault but the Yugoslav organizers strongly denied the accusation. With no sealed move in the envelope there was only one possible decision: Tringov must forfeit the game. The Bulgarian captain instituted formal protest proceedings but there was clearly no real hope of having the decision reversed. After a meeting of the arbitration committee (at which Tringov was unable to state with absolute certainty that he remembered putting his sealed move in the envelope) the original decision was confirmed. Instead of the result being a 2–2 tie (assuming that Tringov had drawn with Korchnoi) the match was lost by Bulgaria (Tal actually beat Radulov).

Various possible explanations were hypothesized. A few of the more evil-minded players suggested that because of their poor start in the finals, the USSR were taking steps to ensure that they did not lose any more matches. Others thought that the arbiters had lost Tringov's score sheet and didn't wish to admit to their folly. It was not until 2.00 a.m. on the morning after the closing banquet that we first learned the truth from one of Tringov's team mates: He had indeed written down his move on his score sheet but had absent-mindedly put the score sheet in his pocket. When, a few days later, he discovered what he had done he was too ashamed to admit it to the organizers. No official announcement was made and at the time of writing we believe that we are the first to put the correct facts into print.

At the end of round four the Soviet Union was still being eclipsed but then a string of good results took them into the lead. Only when playing against the weak Argentinian team in the penultimate round did the USSR look to be in difficulties again. Rubinetti was clearly winning against Korchnoi and the Russians did not seem to have anything sewn up on the other boards, but then, with nothing to lose and everything to gain by trying to cover his team with glory, the Argentinian captain agreed all four games drawn. Is this really why we come to play in the Olympiad?

In some respects it is surprising that Hungary has again taken second place. On paper, the top five Yugoslav players should have dominated the rest of the field: Gligoric, Ivkov, Ljubojevic, Matanovic, Matulovic, all are household names. But what of Ribli, Sax, Forintos and

Csom? These four Hungarians are all of good International Master standard but why should they finish 3½ points ahead of the Yugoslavs who were playing on their home ground?

In fact the Hungarian team was unlucky in more ways than one. In the early part of the finals the Soviet team had been presented with an extra half point through Tringov inadvertently misplacing his sealed move (p. 68). Later on, Portisch was more than once deprived of a half point as a result of poor analysis, by his team mates, of his adjourned positions (Portisch likes his sleep and prefers to allow his compatriots to do the work on his positions and give him the results at breakfast). The following reversal, if taken in conjunction with any of these other slips, can be held responsible for the Hungarian team taking home the silver medals instead of the gold. Played in the penultimate round when the nerves of both leading teams were on edge, the game between Forintos and Ree saw the Hungarian International Master build up a fine K-side attack.

REE (Holland)

FORINTOS (Hungary)

Forintos, to move, now missed a short, winning combination which was immediately seen by Sax, the Hungarian's sixth board: **25 Q–R4! N–K2   26 Q–B6 N–B4   27 N–N5! N×B   28 N×KP!** etc. Instead the game concluded: 25 Q–N3 N–K2 26 N–R4 R×R 27 B×R B–Q4 28 P–N3 Q–R4 29 R–K2 R–Q [fig. one] 30 R–Q2 B–N2 31 Q–N5 N–Q4 32 B–B3 B–K2 33 Q–N4 Q–B2 34 R–K2 N–B3! 35 R–B2 Q×R 36 P×N Q–N8+ 37 Resigns.

Of the remaining teams, little can be said. The biggest disappointment, after the absence of Fischer and Spassky, was that of Larsen. 'Chess as a team sport is something very difficult and there should not be done anything that makes it more difficult. I find it very strange to have Elo ratings of the results of the Olympiad and I protest against that.'

Larsen's argument is not at all unreasonable. Often it is necessary for one player to agree a draw as part of a 'package' arrangement which saves another member of his team. Sometimes a player concedes a half point so as not to prejudice his team's chances of qualifying for a particular final group or finishing in a specific place. For the masters these sacrifices are costly in terms of Elo points. For the lesser players however, and they form the vast majority of those competing in an Olympiad, there are few (or sometimes no) other opportunities to get their names added to the Elo list or to acquire a new rating.

42 **Dueball** (W. Germany) –
   Gereben (Switzerland)

Ruy Lopez

1 P–K4	P–K4
2 N–KB3	N–QB3
3 B–N5	P–QR3
4 B–R4	N–B3
5 0–0	B–K2
6 R–K1	P–QN4
7 B–N3	P–Q3
8 P–B3	0–0
9 P–KR3	N–QR4
10 B–B2	P–B4
11 P–Q4	Q–B2
12 QN–Q2	B–Q2

Black has elected to defend the Lopez in an old-fashioned manner but this does not necessarily signify that his system is a bad one.

13 N–B1	B P×P
14 P×P	KR–B1

Since Black will need a rook on the K-file it would have been more accurate to place the QR on QB1.

15 N–K3	N–B3
16 P–R3	N×QP
17 N×N	P×N
18 Q×P	B–K3
19 B–Q2	N–Q2
20 QR–B1	Q–B4

It is not good to play 20 . . . B–B3 as can be seen from: 21 P–K5! P×P 22 B×P+ K–R1 23 Q–QN4 N–B4 (thus far Shamkovich- Yudovich, Moscow 1962, but with Black's QR

on c8.) 24 B–B5! with advantage to White.

21 Q–Q3	Q–R4?

A very bad square for the queen. It was necessary to play . . . N–K4.

22 N–Q5	B×N
23 P×B	B–B3
24 P–QN3!	

Depriving Black's knight of the c4 square. Now 24 . . . B–N7 fails to win a pawn on account of 25 B–Q1! Q–N3 26 R×R+ R×R 27 Q–K3 with the powerful threat 28 B–KN4 P–B4 29 Q–K6+

24 . . .   N–B4

Since this piece is soon driven away this move merely amounts to loss of time. However, Black is already faced with severe difficulties, as can be seen from the continuation: 24 . . . N–K4 25 Q–B5! Q×Q 26 B×Q and White annexes the QB file.

25 Q–K3   QR–N1?

It is still quite impossible to play for the win of a pawn e.g. 25 . . . Q×QP 26 P–QN4 followed by B–K4, or 25 . . . B–N7 26 R–N1 B×P 27 P–QN4 N–Q2 28 B–Q1 Q×QP¦ 29 B–KB3. In view of all this Black decides to remove his vulnerable rook from its position on the long white diagonal; however, it was absolutely imperative at this point to create a haven for the king by moving one of the K-side pawns. After this omission White has available a forced winning sequence.

26 P–QN4   N–Q2

26 . . . N–R5 loses at once to 27 B×N P×B 28 R×R+ R×R 29 Q–K8+ but 26 . . . N–N2 would have rendered White's task more arduous. In that case the game would have continued: 27 B–Q1! Q–K4 28 R×R+ R×R 29 Q–N6 Q×QP 30 B–B4! when Black has no satisfactory defence to the threat of B–B3 e.g. 30 . . . R–B1 31 B–B3 Q–KB4 32 B–N3 N–Q1 33 B×P or 30 . . . B–Q5 31 Q–B7! R–B1 32 B–B3 Q–KB4 33 R–K4 N–Q1 (*33 . . . B–B3 34 Q×N P–Q4 35 P–N4*) 34 R×B N–K3 35 Q×QP N×R 36 Q×N with two bishops for a rook.

27 B–Q1!

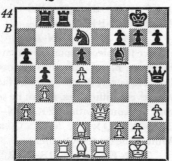

44
B

27 . . .   Q×QP

It was better to play 27 . . . Q–K4 but White still wins with 28 R×R+ R×R 29 B–N4 Q×Q 30 R×Q B–N4 31 B×N B×R 32 B×B.

28 R×R+   R×R
29 B–N4

This pin combined with the weakness of his back rank now proves fatal for Black.

29 . . .   Q–N2
30 Q–KB3!

To bring the queen to f5 with gain of tempo. After 30 . . . Q×Q 31

P×Q Black loses his knight, as is also the case after 30 . . . P–Q4 31 Q–B5 R–Q1 32 Q×N! or 31 . . . N–N3 32 Q×R+!

30 . . .   R–B3
31 R–K8+   N–B1
32 Q×B!   P–KR4

Or 32 . . . P×Q 33 B–R6 and mates.

**33 R×N+   Black
                    resigns**

*Notes contributed by J. Dueball (trans.
                    R.D.K.)*

---

43 Bilek (Hungary) –
Korchnoi (USSR)

Reti's Opening

At the Lugano Olympiad in 1968 the Soviet Union emerged victorious without the loss of a single game. At Skopje the inclusion of the Soviet Champion, Savon, seemed somewhat of a handicap, but even Petrosian (v. Hübner),* Karpov (v Padevsky) and the mighty Korchnoi could not escape defeat. Here is Korchnoi's loss.

1 N–KB3 P–Q4 2 P–B4 P–Q5 3 P–KN3 N–QB3 4 B–N2 P–K4 5 P–Q3 B–N5+ 6 QN–Q2 P–QR4 7 0–0 N–B3 8 N–K1 0–0 9 N–B2 B–K2 10 P–QR3 N–Q2 11 P–N3 N–B4 12 R–N1 B–N5 13 N–K4 N–R3 14 P–B4 P×P 15 R×P B–K3 16 Q–K1 P–B4 17 N–Q2 P–KN4?! Korchnoi's uncompromising attitude in this game recalls his handling of his 9th match game with Petrosian (Candidates' 1971) which he also lost. In both encounters Korchnoi advanced resolutely, but

* Petrosian's first loss ever in an Olympiad!!

was mown down from the edges.
**18 R–B1 N/R–N1 19 P–K3 B–B3
20 P×P N×P 21 N×N B×N+
22 K–R1 R–K1 23 N–B3 B–B3 24
Q–Q2 P–R3 25 P–Q4 P–B3 26
B–N2 B–B2 27 Q–QB2 B–K3 28
QR–Q1 N–R3 29 KR–K1 K–N2
30 P–Q5**

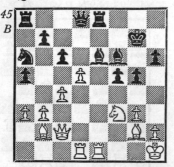

45
B

**30 . . . P×P 31 P×P B–B2 32
R×R B×R 33 N–Q4 B–Q2 34
N–K6+ B×N 35 P×B Q–QB1
Black Resigns** (36 Q×P B×B 37
R–Q7+ **is** one way).

A superb illustration of Reti's
theories concerning occupation of
the centre with pawns. For some
reason Bilek always seems to make a
special effort when he is playing
Korchnoi.

44 **Hartoch** (Holland) –
Savon (USSR)

English Opening

**1 N–KB3 P–QB4 2 P–KN3 P–KN3
3 B–N2 B–N2 4 0–0 N–QB3 5
P–B4 P–Q3** 5 . . . P–K3 followed by
. . . P–Q4 is a good method of playing
for equality. **6 N–B3 N–B3 7 P–Q4
P×P 8N ×P B–Q2** More conventional is 8 . . . N×N 9 Q×N 0–0
as in game 8 of the Fischer-Spassky
match. **9 N–B2 0–0 10 P–N3 Q–R4**

**11 B–N2 Q–R4 12 P–K4 B–N5 13
P–B3 B–R6 14 B×B Q×B 15
Q–K2** White controls slightly more
space but Black is by no means losing.
**15 . . . P–QR3 16 QR–Q1 N–Q2 17
N–R4 B×B 18 N×B Q–R3** 18 . . .
P–QN4 is more lively. The text does
little to contest the initiative. **19 N–
Q3 Q–N2** If now 19 . . . P–QN4 then
20 P×P P×P 21 N/Q3–N4 is good
for White. **20 N–B4 KR–B1 21
N–K3 QR–N1 22 Q–Q2 P–QN4 23
N/B4–Q5 P–N5?** Completely overlooking White's reply – virtually any
alternative was superior!

46
W

24 N×KP+! Winning two pawns.
**24 . . . N×N 25 Q×QP Q–B6 26
R–Q3 Q–K4 27 Q×N/Q7 R–Q1 28
Q×R R×Q 29 R×R+** With his
vast material advantage the rest is a
simple technical exercise for White.
**29 . . . K–N2 30 R–Q3 N–B3 31
KR–Q1 P–KR4 32 K–B2 P–R4 33
R–Q6 N–K2 34 P–KR4 P–R5 35
P×P Q–QR4 36 R/1–Q2 Q×P 37
P–B5 N–B3 38 P–B4 P–N6 39
P×P Q×KP 40 R×N!** Eliminat-
ing any further difficulties. The
queen cannot cope with the two
White pieces and the passed QBP.
**40 . . . Q×R 41 P–QN4 K–B1 42
R–Q8+ K–N2 43 R–Q2 K–B1 44
R–Q8+ K–N2 45 R–Q6 Q–R5 46**

R–Q2 K–B1 47 R–QB2 K–K1 48
P–B6 K–Q1 49 R–B4 Q–R7+ 50
K–B3 Q–N6 51 K–K4 Q–N8+ 52
K–Q4 K–B1 53 K–B5 Q–Q6 54
N–Q5 Q×NP 55 K–Q6 Q–Q6 56
P–N5 Q–QR6+ 57 R–B5 **Resigns**
The Russians are no longer invincible!

Notes by Keene based on analysis by
Vasyukov in THE CHESS PLAYER

The Velvet Touch

45 **Smyslov** (USSR) –
  Knaak (E. Germany)

QP, Modern Defence

1 P–QB4 P–KN3 2 N–QB3 B–N2
3 P–Q4 P–Q3 4 N–B3 B–N5?!
Not a particularly reliable version of
the 'Modern Defence'. We prefer
4 . . . N–Q2 or 4 . . . N–KB3 going
into a King's Indian. 5 **P–K3!**
Bolstering up d4 in this fashion is
White's best. In games against
Najdorf and Filip from Siegen 1970
Suttles now chose 5 . . . N–QB3.
Knaak opts for a less experimental
course and skates close to equality.
5 . . . N–KB3 6 B–K2 0–0 7 P–KR3
B×N 8 B×B N–B3 9 0–0 N–Q2 10
P–QN3 P–K4 11 B×N Preserving
a minute edge. It would be dangerous for White to hang on to his KB
e.g.: 11 P–Q5 P–K5. **11 . . . P×B**
12 P×P N×P 13 B–N2 R–N1 14
R–N1 Forestalls . . . N×BP and also
covers the QB in readiness for an
eventual exchange on the al-h8
diagonal. **14 . . . Q–K2 15 Q–B2**
N–Q2 16 N–K2 B×B 17 R×B
R–N3 This turns out to be futile.
Black should play 17 . . . P–QR4 intending to advance the pawn and
then effect an exchange on QN3.

18 N–B3 KR–N1 19 N–R4 R/3–N2
20 R/2–N1 Q–K4 21 Q–K2 N–B4
22 P–B4 Forcing a new weakness in
the opposing pawn structure. **22 . . .**
Q–K5? Better 22 . . . Q–B4. If
White wanted to inflict tripled pawns
in that case he would have to make a
slight concession himself with 23
P–KN4. **23 N×N P×N 24 P–B5**

With the subtlest and least pretentious of means Smyslov has established a winning position. Somehow,
it seems to me, it is precisely the total
unspectacularity of Smyslov's methods
that is so impressive. **24 . . . R–K1 25**
QR–K1 R/2–N1 26 P×P RP×P
27 R–B4 Q–K4 28 Q–B3 R–K2 29
R–KB1 R–KB1 30 R–B6! Threatening R×NP+ and thus forcing a
most unwelcome liquidation, at the
close of which Black's rooks are
hounded into horribly passive posts.
30 . . . Q×P+ 31 Q×Q R×Q 32
R×QBP R–K2 33 R×P/c5 R–Q1
34 R–B2 R–Q8+ 35 K–R2 P–B4
36 R–QR5 P–QB3 37 R–R6 R–QB2
38 R–K2 K–B2 39 R–K5 P–B5 40
R/K5–QR5 R/Q8–Q2 41 P–KR4
Black resigns. White wins simply
with R–QB5 followed by the advance
of the QNP.

Notes by Keene based on Vasyukov's
comments for THE CHESS PLAYER

46 Donner (Holland) –
Kavalek (USA)

King's Indian Defence

1 P–Q4	N–KB3
2 P–QB4	P–KN3
3 N–QB3	B–N2
4 P–K4	P–Q3
5 B–K2	0–0
6 N–B3	P–K4
7 P–Q5	P–KR3

A very interesting move. The idea
is that if 8 0–0 Black can play . . .
N–R4, which is very pleasant for
him. It is important that in this case
the g5 square should be under
Black's control.

8 N–Q2!

Introduced in Keene-Westerinen,
Berlin 1971, which continued: 8 . . .
QN–Q2 9 P–KN4 P–QR4 10
N–B1 N–B4 11 N–N3 P–B3 12
B–K3 B–Q2 13 P–B3 P–R5 14
Q–Q2 P×P 15 BP×P Q–R4 16
N–Q1! with advantage to White.

8 . . .	P–QR4
9 N–B1	N–R3
10 P–KN4	N–R2
11 P–KR4	P–KB4

The normal K.I.D. freeing thrust,
but it leaves White in control of
some key central squares.

12 NP×P	P×P
13 P×P	B×P
14 N–N3	Q–Q2
15 B–K3	N–N5
16 R–QB1	P–K5

It looks as if Black has organized a
dangerous offensive, but in reality it
is Black's king which is in danger.

17 R–KN1! **N–Q6+?**

This loses, but 17 . . . K–R1 also
leads to a difficult position for Black:

17 . . . K–R1 18 KN×P N×RP 19
R×B K×R 20 B–Q4+ K–N1 21
N×N B×N 22 R–B3, transferring
to the KN-file, with serious threats to
the Black king.

18 B×N	P×B
19 N–R5	R–B2
20 K–Q2!	

A neat method of bringing the QR
into play.

20 . . .	R–K1
21 N×B	

Even stronger than 21 B–Q4.

21 . . .	R×N
22 Q–R5	B–N5
23 Q×P	Q–B4
24 P–B3!	

Now 24 . . . Q×BP 25 QR–B1
Q–R6 26 B–Q4 Q–R7+ 27 R–B2 is
fatal for Black.

24 . . .	N–B3
25 QR–B1	Q–K4
26 P×B	N×NP
27 Q×R+!	

*48
B*

Breaking the back of Black's
resistance. White liquidates to an
easily winning ending.

27 . . . **Q×Q**

Also hopeless is 27 . . . K×Q 28
R×N+ and B–Q4.

28 R×N	Q×R
29 R–KN1	Q×R
30 B×Q	R–KB1

31 B–K3	R–B6
32 K×P	R–R6
33 N–N5	R–R7
34 P–N3	R×QRP
35 B–Q2	P–B3
36 P×P	P×P
37 N×P	R–R6
38 K–Q4	R×P
39 B×P	**Black**
	resigns

Notes by Keene based on a special contribution by J. H. Donner

47 **Gligoric** (Yugoslavia) – **Portisch** (Hungary)

Grünfeld Defence

A ferocious clash between two of Eastern Europe's strongest Grandmaster's.

1 P–Q4	N–KB3
2 P–QB4	P–KN3
3 N–QB3	P–Q4
4 N–B3	

Recently Gligoric has been scoring well with 4 B–N5 and, in fact, he inflicted a crushing defeat on Portisch with that move in their game from Amsterdam 1971. Since then good equalizing methods have been discovered for Black, so Gligoric switches systems. However, what he plays in this game doesn't inspire much confidence.

4 ...	B–N2
5 P–K3	0–0
6 P×P	N×P
7 B–B4	N–N3
8 B–N3	P–QB4
9 0–0	P×P
10 N×P	N–B3 *TN*

If White plays 11 N×N then P×N gives Black some play in the QN–file in conjunction with the fianchettoed KB.

11 Q–K2

A typical Gligoric pawn sacrifice. 11 . . . N×N   12 P×N B×P is dangerous after 13 R–Q1, while 11 . . . B×N   12 P×B (or 12 R–Q1) 12 . . . N×P leaves the dark squares around Black's king very exposed.

11 ...	P–QR4
12 R–Q1	N×N
13 P×N	P–R5
14 B–B2	R–R4
15 B–K4	P–R6
16 P–QN4	N–R5!
17 Q–B2	N×N
18 Q×N	R–R5
19 B–B2	

After 19 B×RP Q–N3 Black has fine compensation for the pawn.

19 ...	R–R1
20 B–N3	B–N5
21 P–B3	B–B4
22 B–N5	R–R3
23 R–Q2	P–R3
24 B–KR4	

Better B–KB4.

24 ...	R–QB3
25 Q–K3	Q–N3

Black has a substantial plus. White's position is riddled with weaknesses.

26 QR–Q1	P–K4
27 B–KB2	P×P
28 R×P	

After this White obtains desperate counterchances, but they are never sufficient.

28 ...	B×R
29 R×B	R–Q3
30 Q–K5	KR–Q1
31 B–Q5	B–K3
32 R–Q2	Q–B2
33 B–B5	

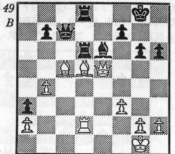

49
B

The high-point of White's counter-play – optically – but Black could win at once with 33 . . . R/3–Q2. What Portisch actually plays allows longer resistance.

33 . . .	Q–B1
34 B×P	R×R
35 B×Q	R×B
36 P–R4	B×P
37 P–R5	P–N4
38 P–N5	R–Q4
39 Q–K2	R/Q4×B
40 Q×B	R–R1
41 P–N6	R–N4
42 P–B4	P×P

White resigns

Notes by Keene based on Portisch's comments for THE CHESS PLAYER

48 **Portisch** (Hungary) – **Bobotsov** (Bulgaria)

Nimzo-Indian Defence

1 P–Q4	N–KB3
2 P–QB4	P–K3
3 N–QB3	B–N5
4 P–K3	P–B4
5 B–Q3	P–QN3

A slightly dubious move-order since White is not obliged to develop his KN on f3.

| 6 KN–K2! | B–N2 |
| 7 0–0 | P×P |

| 8 P×P | B–K2 |
| 9 P–Q5! | |

A powerful pawn-sacrifice which Black should certainly not accept.

| 9 . . . | P×P |
| 10 P×P | N×P? |

Black had to play 10 . . . 0–0 as in a game O'Kelly–Portisch, Palma 1967. Obviously Portisch learns well.

| 11 N×N | B×N |
| 12 N–B4 | B–N2 |

Or 12 . . . B–K3 13 N×B BP×N 14 Q–R5+

| 13 R–K1 | N–B3 |

13 . . . K–B1 was the wretched best. 13 . . . 0–0 is disastrous: 14 Q–R5 P–N3 15 N×P P×N 16 B×P P×B 17 Q×P+ K–R1 18 R–K5.

14 N–R5

Winning! For example: 14 . . . P–N3 15 N–B6+ and mate, or 14 . . . 0–0 15 N×P K×N 16 Q–N4+ and mate follows.

| 14 . . . | K–B1 |
| 15 N×P! | |

This blow demolishes all Black's king defences. Typically of Portisch, there is absolutely nothing speculative about this attack.

50
B

| 15 . . . | P–KR3 |

Or 15 . . . K×N 16 Q–N4+

K–B1 17 B–KR6+ K–K1 18 Q–N7

16 N–B5	**B–N4**
17 N–Q6	**Q–B2**
18 B–N6!	

The bishop is, of course, immune.

18 . . .	**N–K2**
19 B×BP	**R–R2**
20 B–N3	**Q–B3**
21 N×B	**Q×N**
22 B×B	**P×B**
23 Q–Q3	**R–N2**
24 R×N!	**K×R**

24 . . . R×R 25 B–Q5 and Q–KB3+

25 B–Q5

Black resigns. The follow up –
Q–K4+ – is lethal.

An instructive miniature.

*Notes by Keene based on comments by
Portisch for* THE CHESS PLAYER

---

49 **Martz** (USA) –
   Csom (Hungary)

Nimzo-Indian Defence

1 P–QB4 N–KB3 2 N–QB3 P–K3
3 P–Q4 B–N5 4 P–B3 P–B4 5
P–Q5 B×N+ 6 P×B N–R4 The
4 P–B3 variation of the Nimzo is
often played by the American Master
Martz, but Hungarian players gained a lot of experience in methods
against this system in the 1969
Hungarian Ch. (c.f. for example,
Portisch-Forintos, won crushingly
by Black.) Black soon gains the upper
hand in this game. 7 P–N3 P–B4 8
P–K4 P–B5 9 N–K2 P–K4 10
B–KR3 0–0 11 0–0 P–Q3 12 B–N4
P×P!! An inspired piece sacrifice,
Black has a good game in any case,
but with White's QB a spectator the
piece offer cannot be bad. 13 B×N
P×P+ 14 K–R1 Q–R5 15 B–N4

B×B 16 P×B N–Q2 17 B–N2
R×R+ 18 Q×R R–KB1 19
Q–K1 Q–R6 20 R–Q1 R–B6

51
W

21 P–N5 N–B1 22 N–B1 N–N3 23
Q–Q2 N–B5 24 P–N6. Another useless gesture – But if 24 Q×P R–B8+
25 R×R Q×R+ 26 Q–N1 Q–B6+
27 K–R2 Q–R6 mate. 24 . . . N–R4
25 P×P+ K–R1 26 N–K2 R–B7
White Resigns. A theoretically
significant encounter.

*Notes based on a contribution by
Alberic O'Kelly*

---

50 **Vogt** (E. Germany) –
   Rukavina (Yugoslavia)

Caro-Kann

1 P–K4 P–QB3 2 P–Q4 P–Q4 3
N–QB3 P×P 4 N×P B–B4 5
N–N3 B–N3 6 P–KR4 P–KR3 7
N–B3 N–Q2 8 P–R5 B–R2 9 B–Q3
B×B 10 Q×B KN–B3 11 B–B4
A little transposition. 11 . . . Q–R4+
12 B–Q2 Q–B2 13 0–0–0 P–K3 14
Q–K2

The main line with Q–K2 became
quite fashionable after the 1966
Spassky-Petrosian Match. Since then
investigation has centred on 14 . . .
0–0–0 15 N–K5 N–N3 16 B–R5
R–Q4 17 B×N P×B 18 P–QB4

R–R4 (or 18 . . . R–Q1) with a minimal positional advantage for White. A very sharp possibility is 17 P–QN4 (threatening P–QB4) which forces the unclear exchange sacrifice 17 . . . R × B. The plan chosen by Black in the present encounter is less reliable. **14 . . . P–B4 15 K–N1 0–0–0 16 P–QB4 P–R3?** Better . . . B–Q3. White's advantage is now incontestable. **17 N–K5 N × N 18 P × N N–Q2 19 P–B4 B–K2 20 N–K4 N–N1 21 B–B3 KR–N1** Protecting g7 in advance against the threat of N–Q6 + . . . B × N P × B followed by B × NP. **22 Q–K3 P–QN3 23 P–KN4 N–B3 24 P–R3 P–R4 25 K–B2 P–R5**

26 R × R+ R × R 27 R–Q1 R × R 28 K × R This ending is probably lost for Black in view of the weakness of his QRP and of his K-side pawns. **28 . . . N–Q1** Hoping to occupy the h1–a8 diagonal with his queen. No better is 28 . . . Q–Q2+ 29 K–B2 N–Q5+ 30 B × N P × B 31 Q–KB3. **29 N–Q2 K–Q2 30 Q–K4 K–K1 31 K–K2 Q–R2 32 P–B5** The avalanche starts to roll forwards. **32 . . . Q–Q2 33 P–B6 P × P 34 P × P B–B1 35 Q–R8 B–Q3 36 P–N5!** Creating a decisive passed pawn.

36 . . . P–K4 37 P × P Q–B4 38 Q–B3 Q–R2 39 Q–Q5 B–B2 40 B × P Black resigns.

Notes specially contributed by Lothar Vogt

51 **Wirthensohn** (Switzerland) – **Vogt** (E. Germany)

King's Indian Defence

1 P–QB4	P–KN3
2 P–K4	B–N2
3 P–Q4	P–Q3
4 N–QB3	N–KB3
5 B–K2	0–0
6 N–B3	P–K4
7 B–K3	

This move is less popular than 7 0–0 but it is not without sting.

    7 . . .   **Q–K2**

The main line is 7 . . . N–N5.

    8 P–Q5

In a game between Stein and Gufeld White played 8 0–0 and Black neatly equalized by means of 8 . . . N × P 9 N × N P × P.

    8 . . .   **P–QR4**

This position occurred in several other games at Skopje with the continuation: 8 . . . N–N5 9 B–N5 P–KB3 10 B–R4 and now Wirthensohn-Whiteley went 10 . . . Q–K1? 11 N–Q2 P–KB4 12 P–QN4 with advantage to White, while Ivkov-Diez del Corral saw 10 . . . P–KR4 11 N–Q2 P–R4 12 P–KR3 N–KR3 13 P–B3 N–R3 with a reasonable position for Black.

9 N–Q2	P–KR4
10 P–B3	N–R2
11 P–QR3	P–KB4
12 0–0	

After 12 P × P P × P 13 P–B4 N–KB3 there occurs a complicated

position in which Black's chances should not be worse.

12 ...	P–B5
13 B–B2	N–Q2
14 R–B1	QN–B3
15 P–QN4	P × P
16 P × P	P–KN4

The commencement of the routine Black attack in the King's Indian Defence

17 P–B5	P–N5
18 P × P/d6	BP × P
19 N–N5	

After 19 B–R4 I intended to play ... B–R3 with the possible continuation: 20 P × P P × P 21 B × P B × B 22 Q × B+ N × Q 23 B × Q P–B6 and in my opinion Black stands better.

19 ...	P × P
20 P × P?	

Better was 20 B × P N–N4. The exchange sacrifice which White is now obliged to make can hardly be sound.

20 ...	B–R6
21 R–B7	Q–Q1
22 B–N6?	

White had to play K–R1 in order to parry the threat of N–K1. However, Black retains the upper hand after 22 ... B × R 23 B × B R–B2.

22 ...	N–Q2
23 N–B4	Q–N4+
24 K–B2	

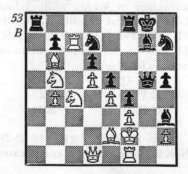

53
B

24 ...   B × R?

Black could have clinched matters logically by continuing his attack against the White king: 24 ... Q–N7+ 25 K–K1 N × B 26 N × N R–R7; after the materialistic text it is no longer clear that Black should win.

25 Q × B N × B 26 N × N QR–Q1 27 Q–R3 R–B3 28 N–B8 B–B1 29 Q–N2 Q × Q+ 30 K × Q R–B2 31 N–N6 N–B3 32 K–B2 R × R 33 N × R B–K2 34 N–K6 R–N1 35 B–N5 N–K1 36 K–N2 N–N2 37 B–Q7 K–B2 38 K–B1 B–Q1 39 N–QB8 N × N 40 B × N+?

The losing move. After 40 P × N+ K–B1 41 N– × P! I do not see how Black can win. 40 ... K–B3 41 P–N5 R–R1 42 N × P B–K2 43 N × P R–QN1 44 N–R5 R × P

Now that Black has been permitted to free his pieces his victory cannot long be postponed.

45 N–B4 R–N5 46 N–R5 R–N8+ 47 K–N2 R–N7+ 48 K–B1 R × P 49 N–N7 R–QB7 50 B–B5 R–B2 51 N–R5 R–B8+ 52 K–N2 B–N5 53 N–N7 K–K2 54 P–Q6+

Otherwise the N is trapped.

54 ... B × P 55 N × B K × N 56 B–N6 K–B4 57 B × P K–Q5 58 B–N4 K–K6 and White lays down his arms. (0–1)

Notes specially contributed by Lothar Vogt

52 **Andersson** (Sweden) – **Uhlmann** (E. Germany)

English/Neo-Grünfeld

1 N–KB3	N–KB3
2 P–B4	P–KN3

3 N–B3	P–Q4
4 P×P	N×P
5 Q–R4+	

The idea behind this move is to disrupt the normal flow of Black's development and then to transfer the White queen to KR4, whence it menaces the fortress of the black king. In the inaugural game, Gheorghiu-Olafsson, Moscow 1971, Black suffered a disastrous reverse and consequently 5 Q–R4+ grew in popularity. However, at Skopje Uhlmann had scored a zero with such an idea as White (v Korchnoi) so in this encounter he defects to the other side.

5 . . .	B–Q2
6 Q–Q4	

It would have been better to play Q–R4 at once.

6 . . .	N–KB3
7 Q–KR4	B–N2
8 P–K4	

White had to be content with equality: 8 P–Q3! P–KR3 9 B–Q2 0–0=The adventurous idea associated with the text compromises White's position more than Black's.

8 . . .	P–KR3

White's queen already begins to run short of squares.

9 P–K5	N–N5
10 Q–N3	

A sign that White's position is no longer satisfactory is that the natural 10 P–Q4 fails to . . . P–QB4 e.g.: 11 P–KR3 P×P or 11 B–QB4 Q–B1. In both cases White's centre is near collapse. But the text is very artificial and from now on Uhlmann seizes and maintains the initiative with a series of highly impressive hammer blows.

10 . . .	N–QB3
11 P–Q4	N–N5!

This bold sortie is exceedingly embarrassing for White whose queen can no longer protect the vulnerable squares on the left flank.

12 P–KR3	N–B7+
13 K–Q1	N×QP!!

Of course Black did not have in mind the petty 13 . . . N×R 14 P×N when he embarked on 11 . . . N–N5! After 13 . . . N×R White could also have good chances of catching the wandering minstrel, on a1.

14 P×N?!

The major alternative is 14 N×N with the following variations: 14 . . . B×P 15 B–KB4? B×B 16 Q×B P–K4! 17 Q–Q2 P×N 18 P×N P×N 19 Q×BP B–R5++ or 15 P–B4! B×N 16 P×N B×N 17 P×B B×P+ 18 K–B2 Q–Q2 and Black has three pawns plus a raging attack against the exposed White king as compensation for his piece. Still, this was undoubtedly White's most promising course.

14 . . .	B–R5+!

54
W

15 N×B

15 K–K1 is also miserable: 15 . . . N–B7+ 16 K–K2 Q–Q2! 17 R–QN1 0–0–0 18 N–Q2 Q–Q5! 19

N×B Q×N/a4 20 P–N3 Q×RP 21
R–N2 N–Q5+ 22 K–Q1 Q–R4 and
P–B4 can be parried by . . . P–KN4
when White's last central foothold
vanishes. White's pieces are hopelessly disjointed and Black has more
than enough for the piece. The move
chosen by the Swedish Grandmaster
sheds his queen for a certain material
compensation, but he is still plagued
by the lack of co-ordination amongst
his pieces and the want of a refuge
for his king.

15 . . .		N–B4+
16 K–B2		N×Q
17 P×N		Q–Q2
18 N–B3		0–0–0
19 B–K3		P–KN4

Black's first concern is to hem the
activity of White's numerous pieces.
Thus 19 . . . Q×P would be reveal-
ed as an error after 20 R–R4 and
White's pieces would achieve a
measure of freedom.

55
W

A picturesque situation. If White's
pawn structure was less diseased he
would stand well, but as it is he
simply has no safe squares for his
minor pieces. In this respect it is of
interest to compare the present position with the concluding phase of
Timman–Radulov (Prelim V11)
Game 34.

20 B–K2		Q×P
21 N×P		Q×P
22 N–B3		B×P
23 B×QRP		

Surely it would have been more
sensible to bring the QR into play.

23 . . .		B×N!

Removing a vital defender from
the White king's field.

24 P×B		P–K4
25 QR–KB1		R–Q4

Bringing up the heavy reserves for
the final assault.

26 B–B2		Q–N3+
27 K–B1		Q–K5

With White's entire army huddled
together in the right hand corner
there is very little he can do to ward
off the coming onslaught.

28 R–K1		Q–QR5
29 R–R4		P–K5
30 N–Q4		P–KB4?

More accurate was . . . Q–R6+!

31 N–B2?		

Better 31 K–N2 – although the
actual result of the game would
hardly be affected by this finesse.

31 . . .		Q×P
32 R/1–R1		KR–Q1
33 B–K3		Q–N6
34 R×RP		Q×P

With the unstoppable threat of . . .
R–R4.

White resigns.

*Notes by Keene based on a contribution
by Alberic O'Kelly and analysis by
Uhlmann for* THE CHESS PLAYER

53 **Kavalek** (USA) –
Bobotsov (Bulgaria)
Modern Defence

1 P–K4		P–KN3
2 P–Q4		B–N2
3 P–QB4		P–Q3

4 N–QB3   P–K4
5 P–Q5

It was finally established in Donner-Ivkov, Wijk aan Zee 1972, that 5 P×P is futile: 5 . . . P×P 6 Q×Q+ K×Q 7 P–B4 N–Q2 8 N–B3 P–QB3 9 P×P N×P 10 B–B4 N×N+ 11 P×N B–K3= However, 5 N–B3 certainly comes into consideration as a flexible alternative.

5 . . .   N–Q2
6 P–KR4?!*TN*

But probably inferior to 6 N–B3 P–QR4 7 B–K2 N–B4 8 0–0 N–B3 steering for a normal King's Indian Defence.

6 . . .   P–KR4!
7 N–B3   P–R4
8 P–QN3

Obviously White wishes to prepare P–QN4 without allowing (after 8 P–R3 for example) – . . . N–QB4 and . . . P–QR5. It seems to me, though, that this Q-side operation could have been shelved until White had developed some more pieces. In fact 8 P–N3 introduces a series of highly artificial moves by which White hands the initiative to the opposition.

8 . . .   N–B4
9 B–K2   N–KR3
10 Q–B2   B–Q2

There is no point in declaring the position of the king as yet. The text prepares to bring a rook to the 'c' file *vis à vis* White's queen.

11 P–N3

Already at this early stage, White is embarrassed for constructive moves. The manifold positional intricacies of the Modern Defence can sometimes prove too much, even for experienced Grandmasters.

11 . . .   N–N5
12 N–KN5

It's not clear what this is designed to achieve, but if White carries on with his Q-side advance he gets into trouble: 12 R–QN1 0–0 13 P–R3 P–R5!

12 . . .   P–KB3
13 N–R3   B–R3
14 P–B3?

A serious positional misconception. Mandatory was 14 B×B N×B 15 P–B3 Q–K2 restricting Black's advantage (slight pull on the dark squares) to a minimum.

14 . . .   N–K6
15 Q–N1   P–B3

Now it is apparent that White cannot trap Black's advanced knight. e.g.: 16 K–B2 Q–N3 17 B×N B×B+ 18 K×B N×KP+ 19 K×N B–B4 checkmate. In view of this White must concede the fallaciousness of his plans and expend several tempi to exchange off the frumious Bandersnatch on e3. Of course, Black can exploit the time thus gained to inaugurate a powerful attack, the more so since the White king is a permanent lodger in the middle of the board.

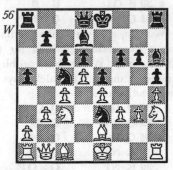

56
W

16 N–B2   P–B4

17 N/B3–Q1	N×N
18 K×N	

18 B×N is also bad for White: after 18 . . . B×B 19 Q×B P×QP 20 BP×P R–QB1 21 Q–K3 Q–B3. With the text White wanted to escape with his king to the Q-side.

18 . . .	B×B
19 Q×B	P×QP
20 BP×P	R–QB1
21 Q–K3	Q–B3
22 R–QB1	0–0
23 Q–Q2	P×P
24 N×P	N×N
25 P×N	Q–B7

White cannot stand this breakthrough. He has weak pawns everywhere and total disconnection reigns among his pieces.

26 R×R	R×R
27 Q–Q3	

Counterattack is out of the question: 27 R–B1 Q×P 28 Q–R6 B–R6 After the text Black has a neat forced win available.

27 . . .	B–N5!
28 R–K1	

If 28 B×B P×B and White cannot move at all.

28 . . .	R–B8+!
29 K×R	Q×R+
30 B–Q1	B×B
31 Q×B	Q×KP

Winning a pawn while maintaining a dominating position for the queen, and White has problems defending the QP. Kavalek plays on to the adjournment.

32 Q–Q2	Q–QN5
33 Q–N5	K–B2
34 Q–R6	Q–B4+
35 K–N2	Q–Q5+
36 K–N1	Q×QP
37 Q–R8	P–K5

38 Q–R7+	K–B3
39 Q–R8+	K–K2
40 Q–N7+	Q–B2
41 Q–B3	Q–B8+
42 K–N2	Q–B3

White resigns.

Notes by Keene based on Bobotsov's comments for THE CHESS PLAYER

54 **Bobotsov** (Bulgaria) –
Gligoric (Yugoslavia)

King's Indian Defence

1 P–Q4	N–KB3
2 P–QB4	P–KN3
3 N–QB3	B–N2
4 P–K4	P–Q3
5 P–B3	0–0
6 B–K3	P–B3
7 B–Q3	P–K4

Gligoric has a fine record against the Sämisch with the defence based on . . . P–K4 and . . . P–QB3, but only in games where White has closed the centre and then played for an attack on the K-side with P–KN4. In those encounters (and this is one of them) where White has concentrated his efforts on Q-side aggression the experiences of the Yugoslav G.M. have been less fortunate.

8 P–Q5	P×P
9 BP×P	N–R4

It is best to take immediate measures on the K-wing. 9 . . . QN–Q2 is less good: 10 KN–K2 N–B4 11 B–QB2 P–QR4 12 0–0 B–Q2 13 P–QR3 N–R4 14 P–QN4 P×P 15 P×P N–R3 16 R–N1±

10 KN–K2	P–B4
11 Q–Q2	P–B5

This traditional advance loses some of its force by virtue of the fact that White is almost certainly intending to castle on the other wing. In this case, therefore, 11 . . . P–B5 should be regarded as a space-gaining operation rather than as a declaration of hostilities towards the opposing monarch.

12 B–KB2	P–QR3
13 0–0–0	B–B3
14 K–N1	

So as to meet 14 . . . B–R5 15 B–N1 Q–N4 with 16 P–KN3 P×P 17 B–K3!

14 . . .	B–R5
15 B–N1	

The first priority is to avoid the exchange of Black's inferior bishop – for the moment at least. The incarceration of the KR is an evil of purely temporary duration.

15 . . .	N–Q2
16 N–B1	N–B4
17 B–QB2	Q–B2?

A significant error of judgement, after which Black is always struggling. It is easy for us to appreciate now that White can quite simply gain the advantage by pushing back his opponent on the Q-wing. In the heat of battle the defender always hopes for counter-chances against the opponents' king in such situations. In fact, Black had to surrender some of his light-square control in order to cement his Q-side defences. Correct was 17 . . . P–QR4! 18 N–Q3 P–N3 19 P–QR4 B–Q2 and Black is secure enough. This variation does at least lend some credence to the theoretical validity of Gligoric's opening variation.

18 P–QN4	N–Q2
19 N–N3	N–N3
20 B–Q3	N–B5

21 B×N	Q×B
22 N–R4	

The weakness of the dark squares on the Q-side is heightened by the concentrated power of White's minor pieces.

22 . . .	Q–B2

The aforementioned debility would be even more glaring after 22 . . . B–Q1 23 N–N6 B×N 24 B×B and Black's central pawns, fixed on dark squares, would be extremely vulnerable in any ending.

23 R–QB1	Q–Q1
24 N–N6	R–N1
25 B–B2	

57 B

Now that White has complete control of the Q-side dark squares it is possible to invite the exchange of bishops shunned on move 15.

25 . . .	B×B

One way to lose quickly is: 25 . . . B–Q2 26 N×B B×B 27 N×RB8 B–K6 28 N–K6! B×Q 29 N×Q B×R 30 R×B R×N 31 R–B7

26 Q×B	N–B3

For a grandmaster the rest is purely technical exploitation of a winning position. There is very little Black can do about White's domination of the 'c' file.

27 P–QR4	B–Q2
28 R–B3	P–N4

29 KR–QB1	B–K1
30 K–N2	

A dark square – just in case.

30 ...	N–Q2
31 P–R5	N–B3
32 N–B8	P–N3

The threat was Q–R7! picking up a stray dark-squared rook.

33 N × NP	B–N4
34 R–B7	N–K1
35 R–B8	R × R
36 N × R	P–N5
37 N–R7	B–Q2
38 N–B6	Q–N4
39 P–N5	RP × P
40 P–R6	N–B3
41 P–R7	R–R1
42 R–B2	Q–N2
43 Q–N6	N–K1
44 N/N3–R5	Black resigns.

Black is liable to lose at least a rook.

Notes by Keene based on Bobotsov's comments for THE CHESS PLAYER

55 **Bobotsov** (Bulgaria) – **Pomar** (Spain)

Queen's Gambit Declined. Slav Defence (by transposition)

1 P–QB4	P–QB3
2 N–KB3	P–Q4
3 P–Q4	N–B3
4 N–B3	P–K3
5 P × P	

The exciting variations commence after 5 B–N5. The exchange of the text, however, is more likely to appeal to Bobotsov's capacity for restrained power, which comes across most attractively in his best games.

5 ...	BP × P

There would be more life in Black's position after 5 ... KP × P.

6 B–B4	B–Q3
7 B–N3	N–B3
8 P–K3	0–0

8 . . . N–K5 is premature: 9 N × N P × N 10 N–Q2 P–B4 11 B–N5 B × B 12 RP × B 0–0 13 B × N P × B 14 Q–R4 and Black has many weaknesses.

9 B–Q3	P–QN3?!

This position was subjected to critical scrutiny after Portisch's famous victory against Petrosian from Moscow 1967. Then it was established that Black's best course is as follows: 9 . . . R–K1 10 N–K5 B × N 11 P × B N–Q2 12 P–B4 (thus far Portisch-Petrosian) 12 . . . N–B4! 13 B–N1 P–QN3 =

10 RQ–B1	B–N2
11 B–R4!	

If 11 0–0 B × B 12 RP × B R–B1 =

11 ...	B–K2
12 0–0	R–B1
13 B–N1	P–KR3

Rather weakening, but Black plans to offer the exchange of dark-squared bishops by means of . . . N–KR2. The immediate attempt to alleviate his cramped quarters through exchanges – 13 . . . N–K5 fails to 14 B × B N × B 15 N × N P × N 16 N–N5!

14 Q–K2

Planning a powerful central build-up based on KR–Q1 and N–K5, attacking à la Pillsbury.

14 ...	N–R2
15 B–N3	N–B3
16 N–K5	N × N
17 B × N	B–Q3?!

Allowing White to increase his advantage. Correct was 17 . . .

N–Q2 18 B–N3 B–R5 19 B–Q3±.

18 N–N5!

Knight takes dark-squares! If 18 . . . N–K1 then 19 N×B N×N 20 Q–N4 brings the game to a premature close.

18 . . .	**B×B**
19 P×B	**N–K5**
20 P–B3	

Resolutely adhering to his positional theme. 20 N×P would merely lead to unseemly adventures – e.g.: 20 . . . R×R 21 R×R Q–R1 22 N–N5 B–R3

| **20 . . .** | **N–B4** |
| **21 P–QN4** | **N–Q2** |

It was possible to lose a knight here 21 . . . N–R5 22 R×R Q×R 23 N–Q6 Q–B2 24 N×B Q×N 25 Q–B2.

22 N–Q6

58
B

Achieving a strategic decision in favour of White. It is strange that so many of Bobotsov's fine games from Skopje should have been based on a dark-square strangulation (c.f.: Bobotsov-Gligoric and Kavalek-Bobotsov).

22 . . .   **R–B2**

Sacrificing the exchange for one iota of freedom just boomerangs: 22 . . . N×P 23 N×R! B×N 24 Q–B2 P–N3 25 Q–B7 wins.

23 Q–Q3	**P–B4**
24 P–B4	**B–R1**
25 Q–Q2	**N–B3**
26 R×R	**Q×R**
27 R–B1	**Q–Q2**
28 B–Q3	**N–K5**
29 B×N	**QP×B**
30 P–N5	**B–Q4**
31 P–KR4	**R–R1**

To gain some breathing space on the QR-file.

32 P–R3	**P–R3**
33 P×P	**R×P**
34 R–B8+	**K–R2**
35 Q–B1	**P–QN4**
36 R–B7	**Q–Q1**

This permits a disaster to strike at g7. A plausible alternative was 36 . . . R–B3 heading for an ending – but White still triumphs: 37 R×Q R×Q+ 38 K–R2 R–B6 39 N×BP P×N 40 R×B R×KP 41 P–R5 R×P 42 P–K6 R–R2 43 R×BP R–K2 44 R–K5 P–N5 45 P–B5 wins. White had to find some good moves in this line so Black should have gone in for it. In the game White has no problems.

37 P–R5	**Q–R5**
38 N–K8	**R–B3**
39 N–B6+	**Q×N**
40 P×Q	**R×Q+**
41 R×R	**P×P**
42 R–B5	**B–B5**
43 P–R4	**Black resigns.**

Notes by Keene based on comments by Bobotsov for THE CHESS PLAYER

56 **Jansa** (Czechoslovakia) – **Filipowicz** (Poland)

Sicilian Defence

1 P–K4   **P–QB4**

2 N–KB3	P–K3
3 P–Q4	P×P
4 N×P	N–QB3
5 N–QB3	P–Q3
6 B–K3	P–QR3

A harmless transposition, of course, but it leaves White greater scope in selecting a continuation.

7 B–Q3	N–B3
8 0–0	B–Q2
9 N–N3	

The immediate 9 P–B4 could be answered by 9 . . . Q–N3.

9 . . .	P–QN4
10 P–B4	P–N5
11 N–N1	P–K4?!

Tempting, but nevertheless I think that the quiet 11 . . . B–K2 and then . . . 0–0 was better.

12 P–B5	P–Q4
13 N/1–Q2	B–K2
14 Q–B3	P×P?

An erroneous solution. Perhaps Black did not like the blocked position after 14 . . . P–Q5 15 B–B2 but that he should have considered before his 11th move?!

15 N×P	0–0
16 QR–Q1	Q–B2
17 N×N+	B×N
18 B–K4	QR–B1
19 R–Q5?!	

White had many good continuations at his disposal but his chosen move is not quite the best one. He could have a clear advantage after the simple 19 P–B3.

19 . . .	N–Q5!
20 N×N	P×N
21 B–B4	

White cannot play 21 B×P? because of 21 . . . B–B3! 22 B×B B×R 23 Q–N4 Q–N3+

21 . . .	Q–R2

22 R–Q6!

The only possibility of active play with the permanent threat of sacrificing on KB6.

22 . . .	B–QN4
23 B–Q3	

An interesting moment, White lost much time calculating the complications after 23 R×B?! where 23 . . . P×R? 24 B–R6 K–R1 25 Q–KN3 R–KN1 26 Q–Q6 R–N5 27 Q×BP+ K–N1 28 R–B4 'fits' but 23 . . . B×R! 24 K×B P×R 25 B–R6 K–R1 26 Q–KN3 R–N1 27 Q–Q6 R–N2 28 Q×BP R/1–KN1 29 P–KR4 Q–B2 or 29 P–N4 Q–B2 30 K–N2 Q–QB5 is far less satisfactory.

23 . . .	KR–K1?

After this move my opponent looked very content and offered me a draw. However, the exchange sacrifice has at last reached realistic proportions and naturally I did not intend to miss it. Black should have played the prophylactic 23 . . . K–R1 with chances to equalize.

24 R×B!	P×R
25 B×B	

A necessary exchange as will be seen from the continuation.

25 . . .	P×B
26 B–R6	K–R1
27 Q–KN3	R–KN1

28 Q–Q6	P–Q6+
29 K–R1	R–N5
30 Q×BP+	K–N1
31 R–B4?	

Drunken with anticipation of victory and also in time-trouble – White makes a serious mistake. The correct 31 P–KR3! Q–Q5! 32 Q–R6! R–Q1 33 P×R P–Q7 34 B×P should win.

31 ...	R×NP!
32 K×R	R×P+
33 K–B1	R–B8+
34 K–N2	R–B7+

Other checks lose easily; now White, with one minute left on his clock and naturally being sorry at spoiling the game, decided to continue fighting ...

35 K–B3!?	Q–B7+
36 K–K4	

Bad is 36 K–N4? Q–N8+ 37 K–R5 R×RP+.

36 ...	Q–K7+?

... and it has paid off. Black could force a draw with 36 ... Q–N7+! 37 K–Q4! – 37 R–B3? R–B5+ 38 K–K5 Q×NP+ and wins – 37 ... Q–N8+ 38 K–K4 Q–N7+ etc.

37 K–Q5!	Q–N7+

Too late

38 R–K4	R–B1
39 Q–N5+	Q×Q
40 B×Q	P–R3
41 B×P	P–Q7
42 R–N4+	K–R2
43 B×P	R–Q1+
44 K–K5	R×B
45 R×P	Black resigns.

There are cases where mistakes help to create interesting games.

Notes by V. Jansa specially for this volume (translation by Jana Hartston)

G

Three Games by Petrosian

In his fine volume of Mikhail Tal's best games Peter Clarke wrote: 'As long as there are players willing to run risks or to experiment there need be no fear of the game becoming reduced to an exact science. In recent years this so-called fantasy has mostly been associated with Bronstein, who on many occasions has completely confounded his opponents by the obscurity of his ideas. And there is Petrosian, who produces strategical masterpieces of a mysterious vein.' Here are three of them from Skopje.

57 Petrosian (USSR) – **Ree** (Holland)

English Opening

1 P–QB4 P–K4 2 P–KN3 N–QB3 3 B–N2 P–KN3 4 N–QB3 B–N2 5 P–Q3 P–Q3 6 B–Q2 P–KR4?! One might question the relevance of this. 6 ... P–B4 or 6 ... KN–K2 look more natural. **7 N–B3 B–Q2** And this also seems artificial. It would have been more appropriate to develop the K-side pieces. **8 P–QR3 Q–B1 9 P–R3** Petrosian wants to preserve his KB. **9 ... N–R3 10 N–Q5** From now on all White's moves emphasize his domination of the light squares. **10 ... N–Q1 11 N–N5 N–K3** It's impossible to drive away White's QN, for if 11 ... P–QB3 12 N–K4 is awfully embarrassing. **12 N×N B×N 13 B–R5!** The threat to c7 forces a further deterioration of Black's hold on the light squares. **13 ... P–N3 14 B–Q2 P–QB3 15 N–B3 0–0 16 P–QN4 P–R3 17 P–QR4** In a sense Black's whole pawn structure is now backward and White is obviously going to make progress by pressing against the most sensitive spot – c6. However, it would be an error to cash in on this factor too hastily by means of 17 P–N5? Since 17 . . . BP×P 18 P×P P–R4 19 B×R Q×B would give Black plenty of play for the exchange. Naturally Petrosian is in no hurry. Time is on his side. **17 . . . N–B4 18 R–N1** Impatience would still ruin White's entire strategic conception e.g.: 18 P–N5? RP×P 19 RP×P R×R 20 Q×R P×P 21 N×P P–K5! with complications. **18 . . . R–R2   19 P–N5** The moment of truth.

60
B

Petrosian's preparation has been superb and now Black cannot avoid crippling weaknesses on the light squares. **19 . . . RP×P   20 RP×P P–B4 21 R–R1 Q–N1 22 0–0 R–Q1 23 R×R Q×R 24 Q–R1 Q–N1 25 Q–R2 N–K2 26 R–R1** The rest is not too difficult. But how does Petrosian establish such positions after a mere 26 moves?

26 . . . N–B1 27 Q–R8 Q–B2 28 Q–B6 Q–K2 29 R–R8 K–R2 30 N–Q5 Black resigns. For example: 30 . . . B×N 31 B×B Q–B1 32 Q–B7 P–B3 33 B–K6 'It was horrible. At the end none of my pieces could do anything' (Ree).

Notes by Keene based on Vasyukov's comments for THE CHESS PLAYER

58 **Petrosian** (USSR) – **Schmidt** (Poland)

English Opening/Neo-Grünfeld

On playing over this game for the first time the following question occurred to me: to what extent is the development of new strategic ideas still possible in modern chess? Let me attempt to elaborate on this point.

A century ago the profound chess thinker Steinitz systematically collected (for the first time) a wealth of information concerning the positional and strategic elements that go up to make the game of chess. Never before had there existed information (embedded in Steinitz's own games and annotations) concerning the desirability of establishing pawn-centres; of seizing the bishop pair; of avoiding pawn weaknesses in one's own camp while inflicting such evils on the adversary's position; of creating a pawn majority on the Q-side . . . etc.

The Steinitzian theories were formulated into 'rules' by the Praeceptor Germaniae, Siegbert Tarrasch, and this massive achievement on the part of the German Grandmaster represented the close of the first major stage in the development of chess – strategic thought.

Since the time of Tarrasch there have been two more significant movements bringing with them an advance in our grasp of the strategic possibilities and limitations of the chessboard; I mean the Hypermodern revolution and the rise of the dynamic Soviet school of chess.

All three movements, the Classical, the Hypermodern and the Soviet, added something new to our thinking about chess, but, to a very large extent, the two latter movements also embodied a denial of their intellectual ancestor, the Classical school. For example: the theory of the Hypermodern masters (Reti, Grünfeld . . .) concerning the establishment of pawn centres was not so much an entirely new concept (as was the original theory concerning pawn centres) but a reversal, in certain situations, of the Classical rules.

The historical stage reached by modern chess is the eclectic.

The best of modern chess is an amalgam of all previous theories: the classical approach of Boris Spassky; the Romanticism of Tal; nowadays we see top Grandmasters gaily setting up massive pawn-centres in true classical style in some of their games while demolishing identical centres (all according to Reti) in others. Today any strategic idea will gain acceptance if it works, and it is rare that a strategic conception will be condemned on purely abstract grounds without the support of at least some analysis. Everything goes, if it is successful. The following quotation from Peter Clarke's collection of Tal's games typifies the modern approach:

'A very good rule says that one should avoid weakening one's King position by advancing pawns. However, rules are meant to guide, not to enslave. One of the blessings of present-day chess is that it is freer than ever from dogma. Many of the most valuable ideas would never have been investigated had not masters persevered with "bad" moves' (Clarke is referring to Black's 11th move in the variation: 1 P–Q4 N–KB3 2 P–QB4 P–KN3 3 N–QB3 B–N2 4 P–K4 P–Q3 5 P–B3 0–0 6 B–K3 P–K4 7 KN–K2 P–B3 8 P–Q5 P×P 9 BP×P P–QR3 10 Q–Q2 QN–Q2 11 P–KN4 P–KR4. 11 . . . P–KR4 is in fact so strong that the whole variation has now been virtually abandoned from White's side.)

So, in view of all this, can we assert that it is still possible for progress to occur in the history of chess ideas, even when we have formulated all the rules and also discovered when it is possible to violate our own formulations? In the present game Petrosian provides a possible answer to this creative dilemma. In the previous examples I quoted the Classical rules were reversed for very good and valid reasons (a further example is the good, yet backward, black Q-pawn in certain variations of the Sicilian Defence). If one accepts that chess contains an element of art in its complex make-up then one can perhaps gain some insight into Petrosian's mystical conduct of this game.

In this game he certainly reverses all Classical principles, but are the reasons ones which we can recognize as good and healthy?

It is possible to argue that the era of truly creative Western art has now passed and that all which remains for art to achieve is to parody former greatness. Does modern art have truly original statements to make or is it painfully aware of the achievements of the past, even in its very own act of 'creation?' I would be the last to deny that the work of Mahler contains elements of profound and moving beauty, but structurally this work is dominated by 'symphonies' and if one compares Mahler's 7th or 9th Symphony with any symphony by Mozart, Beethoven or Brahms one will begin to appreciate the factor of parody concealed in the artistic consciousness of the twentieth century. Examples nearer our own time are Grass, Warhol, and Shostakovich, who often creates the effect in his work of laughing at himself (e.g. the pure circus music of Shostakovich's 9th Symphony.) More extreme – approaching artistic nihilism – are Stockhausen and Cage.

In Petrosian's games this artistic crisis is sometimes translated into chess terms. If it is no longer possible to invent ideas that are truly original then it is still possible, as an act of creative defiance, to parody all the Classical rules. In this game Petrosian simply reverses all of good old Dr Tarrasch's formulations, as a sheer act of technical virtuosity. This mysterious encounter shows Petrosian mocking all the principles by which other players live, and in a sense this is chess without soul – just as so much of modern art lacks true soul. Further we might say that Petrosian's play here corresponds to that twentieth-century music

which lacks all tonal centre. I suspect that the initial impulses going to create atonal music represented just as much a negative or reversal of traditional tonality as the consciousness of being involved in the genuine process of artistic achievements.

1 P–QB4 N–KB3 2 N–QB3 P–Q4 3 P×P N×P 4 P–KN3 P–KN3 5 B–N2 N–N3 6 P–Q3 B–N2 7 B–K3 N–B3 8 B/2×N+ Giving up the B-Pair and weakening the light squares. Of course we can say that Black is saddled with doubled isolated pawns, but look at White's 13th move. **8 . . . P×B 9 Q–B1** That, at least, is comprehensible. White wants to eliminate the opposing KB, so . . . **9 . . . P–KR3** But now Black cannot castle for awhile. **10 N–B3 B–R6** Threat: . . . B–N7, destroying White's K-side. **11 R–KN1** Now White voluntarily renounces castling. **11 . . . B–N5 12 N–Q2 N–Q4 13 N×N!!** I give this move two exclamation marks to draw attention to it. On top of everything else White helps Black to straighten out his pawns. If Petrosian had lost this game I would certainly have recommended B–B5 at this point. **13 . . . P×N 14 N–N3 Q–Q3 15 P–B3 B–Q2 16 P–Q4 R–QN1 17 K–B2** Does White stand better because he has a target (c7) and Black does not? What about White's King? Note that White's best developed pieces are his N, B and King! **17 . . . P–KR4** (*61*) Black would like to castle but it's not yet possible. **18 B–B4 P–K4 19 P×P B×P 20 Q–K3 P–KB3 21 Q×P** And now he goes pawn-hunting with his queen. **21 . . . 0–0 22 QR–B1**

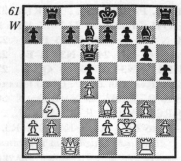

61
W

KR–K1 23 B×B Q×B 24 KR–K1
R–R1 25 Q×P Q–K6+ 26 K–N2
R–R2 27 Q–Q6 P–R5 28 P×P
B–K3 29 R–B3 Q–R3 30 P–QR3
Quietly consolidating his accumu-
lated riches. By now it's clear that
Petrosian is on top, but he has come
thus far in contradiction to a host of
established principles. For a highly
similar exploit on his part one should
examine his game v Pomar from the
previous Olympiad. **30 ... R–Q2 31
Q–N3 P–Q5 32 R–Q3 B×N 33
R×B Q–Q7 34 K–B1 K–R2 35
R–N8 R–K4** It was possible to pro-
long the game with . . . R×R. **36
Q–N4 P–B4 37 Q–N5 R–K6 38
Q–B6 Black resigns.**

59 **Petrosian** (USSR) –
Hug (Switzerland)

Dutch Defence

When Wellington thrashed Bona-
      parte,
As every child can tell
The House of Peers, throughout the
      war,
Did nothing in particular,
And did it very well.
      (Lord Mountarrarat, *Iolanthe*.)
1 N–KB3 P–K3 2 P–KN3 P–KB4
The Dutch is a strange choice against

Petrosian. **3 B–N2 N–KB3 4 0–0
B–K2 5 P–N3 0–0 6 B–N2 P–QR4
7 P–QR3 Q–K1 8 P–B4 P–Q3 9
P–Q4 Q–R4 10 N–B3 QN–Q2 11
P–K3 P–B3 12 N–K2 P–KN4** As
much a defensive measure against
N–KB4 as an attacking gesture.
Black's whole set-up is positionally
unsound and the main point of
interest is the prevaricating, cuncta-
tory, cat and mouse methods Petro-
sian uses to break down the Junior
World Champion's resistance. **13
P–QN4 P×P 14 P×P R×R 15
B×R P–Q4 16 P–B5 N–N5 17
P–R3 N–R3 18 B–B3 N–B2 19
P–N5 B–B3 20 Q–R1 P×P 21
R–N1 N–Q1 22 R×P** Real progress
at last? **22 ... N–QB3 23 Q–N2
Q–B2 24 N–K1 B–Q1 25 R–N3
B–B2 26 N–Q3 Q–N2 27 Q–R2
N–B3 28 B–K1 N–KR4 29 B–KB3
N–B3 30 B–KN2 N–KR4 31 B–Q2**
The repetition was a sham. **31 ...
K–R1 32 Q–N1 B–N1 33 R–R3
B–B2 34 R–R8 P–R3 35 Q–Q1
Q–N3 36 B–QB1 K–R2 37
N–QB3 N–B3 38 N–N5 Q–N2 39
N–Q6 Q–Q2 40 N–K5 N×N 41
P×N N–K5 42 B–R3 B×N 43
KP×B R–N1 Black resigns**
Resignation should be taken as a sign
of Black's general disillusionment
with his situation rather than as an
indication that White has an instant
bone-crusher available.
      Notes by Keene

60 **Ghizdavu** (Rumania) –
Enklaar (Holland)

Sicilian Defence

**1 P–K4 P–QB4 2 N–KB3 P–K3 3
P–Q4 P×P 4 N×P P–QR3 5**

N–QB3 Q–B2 6 B–Q3 N–QB3 7 B–K3 N–B3 8 N–N3 P–QN4 9 P–B4 P–Q3 10 0–0 B–K2 11 Q–B3 This variation has become rather popular of late, partly because it can arise in more ways than one. For an example of how the interpolation of the move P–QR3 affects White's strategy, see game 115. **11 . . . 0–0** Ghizdavu-J. Szabo, Bucharest 1970 went instead 11 . . . B–N2 12 P–QR4! P–N5 13 N–K2! N–QR4 14 N×N Q×N 15 P–KN4! with excellent attacking chances for White. **12 QR–K1 B–N2** 12 . . . R–N1 has also been tried. Nicevski-Matulovic, Skopje 1969 continued 13 P–N4 N–N5 14 P–N5 N–Q2 15 Q–R5 R–K1 16 R–B3 B–N2 17 R–R3 N–B1, and now White should have continued with 18 N–Q4! followed by P–B5. **13 P–N4 N–N5 14 P–N5 N–Q2 15 Q–R5 KR–K1 16 R–B3 N–B1** Ghizdavu-Ljubojevic, Bucharest 1970 went 16 . . . P–N3 17 Q–R6! B–KB1 18 Q–R4 B–N2 19 R–R3 N–B1 20 R–KB1! N×B 21 P×N P–N5 22 N–Q1 Q–Q1, and now 23 Q–B2! would have kept Black's K-side under severe pressure. **17 R–R3 B–Q1 18 R–KB1! N×B 19 P×N P–N5 20 N–Q1 P–N3 21 Q–R4**

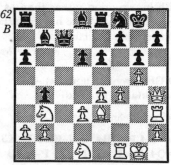

62 B

21 . . . P–K4 If 21 . . . P–KR4 22 N–Q4! threatening 23 P–B5 KP×P 24 N×P! etc. **22 P–B5 P×P 23 P×P Q–B3 24 R–N3! R–B1 25 N–B2 B–N3 26 B×B Q×B 27 P–B6 Resigns** 27 . . . Q–B3 loses to 28 N–R5 Q–B2 29 N×B Q×N 30 Q–R6 N–K3 31 R–R3, and 27 . . . R–B7 to 28 Q–R6 N–K3 29 R–R3.

Analysis by Ghizdavu in THE CHESS PLAYER

61 **Bednarski** (Poland) – **Smyslov** (USSR)

Ruy Lopez

1 P–K4	P–K4
2 N–KB3	N–QB3
3 B–N5	P–QR3
4 B×N	

The Exchange Variation is a favourite of Bednarski's – He defeated Geller with it at the last Olympiad in Siegen.

| 4 . . . | QP×B |
| 5 0–0 | Q–K2 |

A new move and a bad one. Black retards his development by shutting in his KB and thereby leaves his king embarrassingly placed on K1. 5 . . . Q–Q3 has recently come into vogue after Portisch used it successfully against Andersson at Las Palmas 1972.

| 6 P–Q4 | P×P |
| 7 Q×P! | |

After 7 N×P B–Q2 Black can castle Q-side.

| 7 . . . | B–N5 |
| 8 B–B4!? | |

Keeping Black's queen tied down to the defence of the QBP. If 8 QN–Q2 Q–B4! with equality.

8 ...	B × N
9 P × B	

The weakness in White's K-side is of no real significance. With a lead in development and Black's king still stuck in the centre, White enjoys a definite advantage.

9 ...	N–B3
10 N–B3!	

If White can bring both rooks to the central files he will be threatening to play N–Q5!

10 ...	N–R4

Not 10 ... P–KN3? 11 B × P, nor 10 ... R–Q1 11 Q–R7 Q–N5 12 B × P B–B4 13 P–QR3! when Black cannot recover his pawn.

11 B–N3	R–Q1
12 Q–R4	

12 Q–R7 does not work any longer because now Black can eliminate White's bishop and thereby remove the threat to his QBP: 12 ... N × B 13 RP × N Q–N5! 14 QR–Q1 B–K2 15 R × R+ B × R 16 R–Q1 0–0 17 Q–Q4 Q × NP! 18 Q × B Q × N and Black is better.

12 ...	N × B
13 RP × N	Q–N5
14 QR–Q1!	

Preserving his initiative.

14 ...	Q × Q

14 ... Q × NP is much too risky: 15 R × R+ K × R 16 Q–Q4+ K–B1 17 R–Q1! (17 Q–R7 Q × N 18 R–Q1 is also good for White but not so decisive) 17 ... K–N1 18 R–N1 Q–R6 19 Q–Q8+ K–R2 20 Q–B8 B–N5 21 Q × R and White should win comfortably.

15 R × R+	K × R
16 N × Q	

This is precisely the sort of ending for which White aims in the

63
B

Exchange Variation. The result now depends on how well he can utilize his 4:3 pawn majority on the K-side.

16 ...	P–KN3?!

Better is 16 ... P–QN4 17 N–B3 B–Q3 followed by ... P–B3, holding up the advance of White's pawn majority.

17 P–KB4	P–QN4
18 N–B3	B–N2
19 P–K5	

Now White has the advantage of good knight v bad bishop as well as the more active rook and his K-side majority. The ending should really only be a question of technique for Bednarski but then Smyslov *is* the world's greatest endgame player.

19 ...	K–K2
20 K–N2?!	

White had used up most of his time allocation to reach this fine position. Now he starts to let it slip away from him. Correct was 20 N–K4 and if 20 ... P–B3 then 21 R–Q1! P × P 22 N–B5! P × P 23 R–Q7+ K–B3 24 R × P and 21 P × P+ B × P 22 N × B K × N 23 R–Q1 both offer White excellent winning chances. After 20 N–K4, Black could try 20 ... R–Q1 but then White con-

tinues with R–K1, K–B1, K–K2 and
R–Q1.

20 ...	R–Q1
21 R–Q1?	

This move takes White's knight
out of play just long enough for
Black to break up the K-side.
Correct was 21 K–B3 and if 21 . . .
R–Q7 22 R–QB1 followed by 23
K–K3.

21 ...	R×R
22 N×R	K–K3
23 K–B3	P–KN4!
24 P×P	

White must play carefully – The
position could quite easily turn
against him. e.g. 24 K–K4? P×P 25
P×P P–KB4+! and Black suddenly
has the better ending because of his
outside passed pawn and the fact
that White's forward KBP is fixed on
a dark square.

24 ...	K×P
25 N–K3	P–QB4
26 P–N3	B–B1

Not 26 . . . K–Q5? 27 N–B5+
K–B6 28 N×B K×P 29 N–K8!
P–QB3 30 N–Q6, and Black's Q-
side pawns are too slow.

27 K–K2

27 P–QB3 P–N5 28 K–K2 P×P
29 K–Q3 B–N2 is good for Black.

27 ...	K–Q5
28 K–Q2	

White has held the draw! 28 . . .
P–B5? 29 P–QB3+ K–K5 30
NP×P NP×P?! 31 K–K2 offers
White some winning chances, but
after 28 . . . K–K5 White must play
29 K–K2 K–Q5 30 K–Q2 etc. And
so **Draw Agreed**

*Notes by Levy based on analysis by
Bednarski in* THE CHESS PLAYER

62 **Bednarski** (Poland) –
     Lombard (Switzerland)

Sicilian Defence

1 P–K4	P–QB4
2 N–KB3	P–K3
3 P–Q4	P×P
4 N×P	N–KB3
5 N–QB3	P–Q3
6 B–QB4	B–K2
7 B–N3	P–QR3
8 P–B4	0–0
9 Q–B3!	

9 0–0 N–B3 10 B–K3 N×N 11
B×N P–QN4! gives Black at least
equal chances.

9 ...	N–B3
10 B–K3	Q–B2?!

Better is 10 . . . N×N 11 B×N
P–QN4! 12 0-0-0 (not 12 B×N?!
B×B!! 13 P–K5 B–R5+ 14 P–N3
R–N1 15 P×B? B–N2 16 N–K4
P×P, when Black has an excellent
game for the piece because of
White's exposed king) 12 . . . B–N2
13 KR–K1 with an unclear position.
The text is unnecessary – It wastes a
tempo which can be used by White
to commence his attack.

11 P–B5!	N×N
12 B×N	P–QN4

12 . . . P–K4 13 B–B2 is clearly
better for White.

13 P–QR3

This move is possibly unnecessary,
and in any case it provides Black
with some counterplay after White
castles long. The most natural
move is 13 P–N4!? when the following possibilities arise: (i) 13 . . .
P–K4 14 B–B2 with a clear advantage to White; (ii) 13 . . . P–N5 14
P–N5 P×N 15 P×N BP×P 16
B×NP B×P 17 B×B P×B 18

R–KN1 + and mate on the KN-file;
(iii) 13 . . . P×P 14 NP×P P–N5 15
N–Q5 N×N 16 B×N B–N2 17
Q–KN3 also with mate to follow.

13 . . .   **R–N1**

Thematic. If 13 . . . P–K4 14
B–B2 B–N2 15 0–0 QR–B1 16
QR–K1 Q–N1 17 B–KR4 and
White can play on the weakness of
Black's Q4 square as well as for a
K-side attack by P–N4–N5.

14 P–N4!   **P–N5**
15 P×P?

Much stronger is 15 P–N5! when
15 . . . P×N loses to 16 P×N
BP×P 17 B×NP B–Q1 18
R–KN1 P–N3 19 Q–R5 and 20
Q–R6.

15 . . .   **R×P**
16 0–0–0

White still has the better attacking
chances but Black's position is not
entirely devoid of counterplay.

16 . . .   **P–K4!**
17 B–B2   **B–N2**
18 KR–K1   **R–N1**

Threatening 19 . . . B×P! 20
N×B N×N (or 20 . . . R×B immed-
iately) and if 21 R×N then 21 . . .
R×B.

19 R–Q3!

19 K–N1, unpinning the QBP so
that the combination mentioned in
the last note no longer works, invites
trouble of a different kind: 19 . . .
P–QR4 20 P–N5 P–R5! 21 P×N
P×B 22 P×B P×P+ 23 K×P
R×NP+!!

19 . . .   **N–Q2!**

Forestalling White's P–N5.

20 B–R7

Intending to gain a tempo so as to
move this bishop to a better square
at no extra cost.

20 . . .   **R–R1?!**

Better 20 . . . B–N4+ so that after
21 K–N1 R–R1 22 B–K3, Black can
relieve some of the pressure by exchanging bishops.

21 B–K3   **R–N1**

So White has indeed improved his
position free of charge. And now . . .

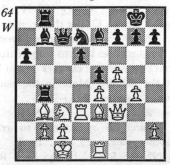

22 P–B6!!   **R×B?!**

Too slow. Black had to eliminate
White's KBP even though his condi-
tion would still have been grave:
22 . . . N×P 23 P–N5! or 22 . . .
P×P 23 P–N5 R×B 24 P×P!

Possibly Lombard's intermezzo
sacrifice was prompted by his opponent's shortage of time.

23 P×R?

23 P×B wins very quickly: 23 . . .
R–N5 24 R–B1 P–B3 25 Q–B5
(threatening 26 Q–K6+ and 27
P–K8=Q+) 25 . . . R–K1 26
Q–K6+ K–R1 27 P–N5 etc.

23 . . .   **N×P**

Now Black has one pawn for the
exchange and his position is rapidly
becoming active. Nevertheless, with
accurate play White should still
emerge on top.

24 K–N1   **Q–B3**

This shallow threat accomplishes
nothing. Better was 24 . . . R–QB1.

25 R–KB1

25 P–N5! was stronger, and if
25 . . . N×P 26 N–Q5.

25 . . .	R–KB1
26 P–N5	N–K1
27 R–B1	Q–Q2
28 N–Q5	P–B3!
29 R–B1	

29 Q–B5 is a flashy way to win a
piece: 29 . . . Q×Q 30 N×B+
K–R1 31 N×Q, but then comes 31
. . . B×P and White loses a rook.

The text does little to help White's
attack because his chances do not lie
on the KB-file. More to the point
would have been 29 Q–N2.

29 . . .   B×N?!

Missing an opportunity to grab
another pawn: 29 . . . P×P 30
Q–N2 R×R+ 31 Q×R P–R3,
when the outcome is far from clear.

30 R×B	P×P
31 Q–N2	N–B3

Now 31 . . . R×R+ 32 Q×R
P–R3 is met by 33 Q×P – Black's
29th move left the QRP unprotected.

32 R/5–Q1	P–N5
33 B–N5	R–N1
34 Q–K2	Q–K3
35 Q–B4!	K–B2
36 B×N	P×B

36 . . . Q×Q 37 P×Q P×B 38
K–B2 is hopeless for Black because
his bishop is such a useless creature.

37 R–Q5?

37 R×BP+!! B×R 38 Q–B7+
and 39 Q×R is a very easy win, but
by now the flag on White's clock
was just about ready to fall.

37 . . .	R–N3
38 Q–Q3	P–KR4
39 R–B5	K–N3
40 P–R3	R–N5 (65)
41 Q–K2??	

41 P×P P×P 42 R–B1 still leaves

65
W

White with excellent winning chances but after the text he is completely
lost. Presumably Bednarski made his
move instantaneously, unaware that
he had already reached the time
control.

41 . . .	R×KP
42 R×BP+	Q×R
43 Q×R+	Q–B4
44 Q–B2	

So that the exchange of queens
brings White's king closer to the K-
side.

44 . . .	Q×Q+
45 K×Q	P–N6
46 R–Q1	P–Q4!
47 R–KN1	

Or 47 R×P P–N7 48 R–Q1
B–B4.

47 . . .	P–R5
48 R–QR1	B–B4
49 P–N4	B–Q5
50 Resigns	

A highly entertaining struggle
despite the numerous mistakes on
both sides.

*Notes by Levy based on analysis by
Bednarski in* THE CHESS PLAYER

63 **Hamann** (Denmark) –
   Gheorghiu (Rumania)

Benko Gambit

1 P–Q4	N–KB3

2 P–QB4	P–B4
3 P–Q5	P–QN4

During the past three or four years the Benko Gambit has met with remarkable success. At Skopje, for example, the gambit was tested in some fifteen games with White failing to win a single game. When I only made a draw after employing this excellent 'defence' I was so ashamed that I felt compelled to apologize to Benko who was carefully noting down every game for his forthcoming book on the gambit.

One of the joys of playing this defence is that it is much easier for Black to find moves than for White. For the first fifteen to twenty moves, Black crudely marshalls his forces on the Q-side, taking full advantage of the QR and QN-files and the pressure exerted by his KB along the long diagonal. Then, if White has defended well, the first player may be able to salvage a draw. But often there will be some tactical resource which wins back the gambit pawn and leaves Black with the better game because of his pressure against White's remaining Q-side pawn and his own QBP which is normally a potent weapon in the endgame.

4 P×P	P–QR3
5 P–K3	

This move cannot possibly be an attempt at refuting the gambit. It is quite illogical to advance the KP to the third rank now when it will soon be forced to take up its rightful post at K4. White's idea is that Black must either exchange pawns himself (bad for Black – see the next note) or allow White to exchange on QR6

when White can then exchange the light squared bishops without losing the right to castle (compare the strategy of game 64).

5 . . .	P–N3

It is wrong for Black to exchange on QN4. e.g. 5 . . . P×P 6 B×P Q–R4+ 7 N–QB3 B–N2 8 B–Q2 P–K3 9 N–B3 Q–N3 10 P×P BP×P 11 0–0 B–K2 12 Q–K2, when Black has no compensation for the sacrificed pawn. Grigorian-Koslov, Alma Ata 1971.

6 N–QB3	B–KN2
7 P×P	0–0
8 P–K4	

So now White has given up the tempo mentioned in the note to his fifth move.

8 . . .	P–Q3
9 P–B4?	

Unthematic. Opening up his KN1–QR7 diagonal weakens White's K-side and leaves his K4 square inadequately protected. The normal continuation is 9 N–B3 Q–R4! and now: (i) 10 N–Q2 B×P 11 B×B Q×B 12 Q–K2 KN–Q2 13 P–QR4 (or 13 N–B4 P–B4 14 P–B3? P×P 15 P×P N–N3 16 N×N Q×N 17 R–B1 N–Q2 with active play for Black on both wings and in the centre. Kaufman-Benko, US Open Ch. 1968) 13 . . . Q×Q+ 14 K×Q N–R3 15 R–QN1 P–B4 Draw Agreed. Portisch-Benko, Palma de Mallorca 1971; or (ii) 10 B–Q2 B×P 11 B×B?! (11 B–K2 is met by 11 . . . Q–N5! 12 Q–B2 B×B, forcing White to recapture with his king – Benko) 11 . . . Q×B 12 Q–K2 KN–Q2 13 P–QR4 Q×Q+ 14 K×Q N–R3 15 QR–QN1 (thus far Benko-DeFotis, USA Ch. 1972)

15 . . . N–B2 (with the idea of breaking with . . . P–B4) 16 P–QN4 B×N 17 B×B R×P 18 R–R1 N–N4! (Analysis by Benko).

9 . . .   Q–R4!

After White's last, loosening move, the first player is a tempo behind in his development (compared with the games cited in the previous note) and Black's counterplay is therefore much more effective.

12 B–Q2   B×P
11 B×B   N×B

Black could also recapture with the queen, following the same strategy as in the Benko-DeFotis game mentioned above. But the text is stronger.

12 N–B3   N–QN5

Black's initiative provides ample compensation for the pawn. White's next few moves are all forced.

13 0–0   P–B5!
14 K–R1

Otherwise 14 . . . N–Q6 would be followed by 15 . . . Q–N3+ and 16 . . . N–B7+, all this a consequence of 9 P–B4.

14 . . .   N–Q6
15 Q–K2

If 15 Q–B2 Q–N3 with the double threat of 16 . . . N–B7+ and 16 . . .

Q×P. The text also sets a cheap trap.

15 . . .   KR–N1

Not 15 . . . N×NP? 16 N–Q1 Q–N4 (16 . . . Q–N3 17 B–K3) 17 R–QN1 R×P 18 N–B3 Q–R3 19 N×R Q×N 20 B–B3 and White finishes a rook ahead.

16 QR–N1

White must give back the pawn. If 16 P–QN3? N–KN5! 17 P×P N/5–B7+ 18 R×N N×R+ 19 Q×N B×N, and although White has (temporarily) two pawns for the exchange his position is in shreds.

16 . . .   R×P
17 R×R   N×R
18 N–Q4   N–Q6
19 N–B6   Q–B2
20 P–K5

White must play actively otherwise . . . P–K3 (possibly followed by . . . R–K1) will create further dynamic opportunities for Black.

20 . . .   N–K1
21 P×P   N×QP!

Offering a pawn in return for an important tempo.

22 N×P+

If 22 Q×P Q×Q 23 N×Q+ K–B1 24 N–B6 B×N 25 B×B R×P etc.

22 . . .	K–B1
23 N–B6	R–K1
24 Q–B3	Q–N3!

Threatening 25 . . . Q–N7 when White's whole position is *en prise*.

25 N–Q1	N–K5
26 B–R5	Q–N4
27 P–B5	

What else? If 27 N–K3 P–B4 followed by . . . R–R1.

27 . . .	Q×P
28 P×P	RP×P
29 N–Q8	P–B4
30 B–N6	B–B3

Naturally not 30 . . . R×N 31 B×R Q×B 32 Q×NK4.

| 31 N–K3 | Q–Q2 |

But now 32 . . . R×N is a threat (not to mention 32 . . . N–Q7).

| 32 P–N4 | P–B5! |

The most conclusive move. 32 . . . N–Q7 is also sufficient: 33 Q–Q5 Q×Q 34 N×Q R–K7.

But 32 . . . R×N 33 B×R Q×B would be much too dangerous: 34 P×P P×P 35 Q×P and Black is probably lost.

| 33 N×P | B×N |
| 34 B×B | Q×B |

Black threatens 35 . . . N/5–B7+ 36 K–N2 N×P 37 Q×N/N4 Q–Q4+ and 38 . . . Q×N.

35 K–N2	Q–Q5
36 R–Q1	N/5–B7
37 N–Q6	Q×N
38 Q×N/2	Q–QB3+
39 Resigns	

Notes by Levy

64 **Malich** (East Germany) – **Ciocaltea** (Rumania)

Benko Gambit

1 P–Q4	N–KB3
2 P–QB4	P–B4
3 P–Q5	P–QN4
4 P×P	P–QR3
5 P×P	B×P
6 N–QB3	P–N3
7 N–B3	

7 P–K4 B×B 8 K×B P–Q3 is also frequently seen. One example from the Olympiad continued 9 P–B3?! B–N2 10 KN–K2 0–0 11 B–K3 N–Q2 12 K–B2 N–K4 13 P–KN4 Q–R4 14 Q–B2 KR–N1 15 QR–N1 N–B5 with a good game for Black (Kchouk-Fuller).

In the same line, the game Malich-Ciocaltea, Vrnjacka Banja 1972 went 9 P–KN3 B–N2 10 K–N2 0–0 11 P–B4?! N–R3 12 N–B3 Q–N3 13 R–K1 N–QN5! 14 R–K2 Q–R3 15 P–QR4 KR–N1 16 R–R3 Q–B5! 17 N–Q2 Q–Q6! with equal chances.

| 7 . . . | P–Q3 |
| 8 P–K4 | |

The crucial line of the gambit now runs 8 N–Q2 B–KN2 9 P–K4 0–0 10 B×B N×B 11 0–0 N–Q2 12 N–B4 N–N3 13 N–K3 Q–Q2 14 P–QR4 KR–N1 (Vranesic-Benko, Toronto 1971) and now 15 P–R5 N–N5 16 R–R3 would have been the most precise continuation according to Benko.

8 . . .	B×B
9 K×B	B–N2
10 P–KN3	

10 P–KR3 has also been tried with the idea of removing the king to KR2 rather than KN2. The disadvantage is that the journey takes one move longer. Schaufelberger-Parma, Luxemburg 1971 continued 10 . . . 0–0 11 K–N1 N–R3 12 K–R2 Q–N3 13 N–Q2 N–Q2 14 Q–K2

N–N5 15 N–B4 Q–R3 16 R–K1
N–K4   17 N×N B×N+   18
P–KN3 KR–N1 19 Q×Q R×Q and
Black's counterplay proved more
than adequate.

10 ...	0–0
11 K–N2	QN–Q2
12 P–KR3	

It is advisable for White to prevent
Black's KN from going to KN5 (on
its way to K4). e.g. (i) 12 R–K1
N–N5! 13 R–K2 Q–R4 14 B–N5
KR–K1 15 Q–B2 P–R3 16 B–Q2
Q–R3 17 R–Q1 KR–N1 18 B–B1
R–N2 with ample counterplay for
Black. Popov-Vasyukov, Varna
1971; or (ii) 12 Q–B2 Q–N3 13
R–QN1 KR–B1 (intending . . .
P–B5) 14 P–N3?! N–N5 15 P–KR3
N/5–K4 16 N×N B×N 17 B–Q2
P–B5 18 KR–QB1 P×P 19 P×P
Q–N5   20 N–Q1 R×Q and the
players agreed to a draw even
though Black was slightly better.
Donner-Benko, Palma de Mallorca
1971.

12 ...	Q–R4
13 R–K1	

The most natural developing
move. 13 Q–B2 was tried in Popov-
Tringov, Varna 1972, but after 13
. . . N–N3 14 N–Q2 KN–Q2 15
N–N3 Q–R3 16 R–Q1 N–R5!
White's Q-side was under enormous
pressure.

With the text move White starts
his preparation for the thematic
break P–K5 and prepares to over-
protect his QNP by R–K2.

13 ...	KR–N1
14 R–K2	N–K1
15 B–N5?!	

Under the delusion that he threatens to win a pawn, White presents

his opponent with a useful tempo.
Correct was the immediate 15 B–B4.

15 ...	P–R3!
16 B–B4	

Not 16 B×KP?? P–B3 and the
bishop is trapped.

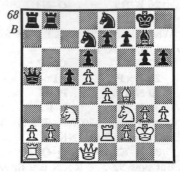

68
B

16 ...	P–N4?

Trying to extract the utmost from
White's error at move fifteen, Cio-
caltea over-extends himself on the
K-side. Natural and good would
have been 16 . . . N–B2! and if 17
P–K5 (not 17 Q–Q2? R×P!)
17 . . . P×P 18 N×P N×N 19
B×N B×B 20 R×B R×P 21
R×P Q×N 22 R×N R–R6! with a
tremendous game for Black (23
P–Q6 R–Q7).

17 B–B1	N–B2
18 P–KR4!	

Now Black's vulnerable K-side
pawn structure comes under pressure.

18 ...	P–N5
19 N–R2	N–K4
20 R–B2	P–R4
21 P–B3!	P×P+
22 N×P	N–N5

The only way to save the KRP.

23 N–KN5?!

Better would have been either 23
N–R2 N–B3 24 B–N5, or 23 Q–K2

with the same idea in mind in addition to the possibility of meeting . . . N–B3 with P–K5. Possibly White overlooked his opponent's reply.

69
B

23 . . .   **R×P!**
24 R×R

24 P–K5? is refuted by 24 . . . Q×N!

24 . . .   **B×N**
25 Q–B3

If 25 Q–B2 P–B5! so that 26 P–K5 can be met by 26 . . . Q×QP+.

25 . . .   **P–B3**
26 Q–B5!   **P×N**
27 Q×P+

27 Q–N6+ K–B1 brings White nothing.

27 . . .   **B–N2**
28 QR–N1   **R–KB1!**

If 28 . . . N–B3? 29 R–N8+ N/2–K1 30 Q–N6! Q×P+ 31 R/1–N2 Q–R2 32 R/8–N7! and Black is dead.

After the active text move Black's worries are over.

29 Q×RP   **Q–K8**
30 Q×N   **Q–B8+**
31 K–R2   **R–B7+**
32 R×R   **Q×R+**
33 K–R1   **Q–B8+**
Draw Agreed

Notes by Levy based on analysis by Ciocaltea in THE CHESS PLAYER

65 **Bednarski** (Poland) –
   Malich (East Germany)

Sicilian Defence

1 P–K4 P–QB4 2 N–KB3 P–K3 3 P–Q4 P×P 4 N×P N–KB3 5 N–QB3 P–Q3 6 B–QB4 B–K2 7 B–N3 0–0 8 P–B4 N–R3!? 9 Q–B3 N–B4 10 B–K3 P–QR3 11 P–N4?! Both 11 0–0–0!? Q–B2 12 P–B5! and 11 P–B5!? P–Q4?! 12 KP×P N×B 13 N×N P×QP 14 0–0–0! would have been in White's favour. **11 . . . P–Q4! 12 P–K5?** 12 P×P was essential, and if 12 . . . N×B 13 RP×N with an unclear position. **12 . . . N/3–K5 13 N×N P×N! 14 Q–R3 Q–R4+ 15 B–Q2?!** 15 K–K2 would have been preferable, although Black would still retain the advantage. **15 . . . Q–B2 16 P–N5 R–Q1?!** Somewhat slow. 16 . . . P–N4 would have been more active. **17 B–B3! P–N4 18 0–0–0 P–N5 19 B×NP N–Q6+ 20 R×N P×R 21 B×B P–Q7+! 22 K–Q1 R×N** After 22 . . . Q×B 23 P–B3, Black might even have been in trouble. e.g. 23 . . . Q–B2 (threatening 24 . . . R×N) 24 B–B2 P–N3 25 Q–R6 followed by P–KR4–R5 etc. **23 Q–K3** Vasyukov suggests 23 B–Q6 but then 23 . . . Q–B3 followed by 24 . . . Q–K5 seals White's fate.

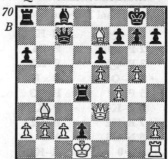

70
B

23 ... B–N2! 24 R–B1 If 24 Q×R? B–B6+ 25 K×P Q×B 26 Q–N1 Q–N2 and Black has won a rook. **24 ... R–K5 25 Q–B5 Q–Q2 26 B–Q6 R–QB1** 26 ... P–QR4 is more aggressive and to the point. Now White has an opportunity to keep Black's bishop out of play. **27 Q–B2?** But in time trouble he misses it. 27 Q–R5! makes it extremely difficult for Black to make progress. e.g. 27 ... R–Q5 28 Q–N6 or 27 ... B–B3 28 P–B4! and if then 28 ... B–N4? 29 P×B! R–B8+ 30 K×P R×R 31 P×P!! and even though he is two exchanges down White's passed pawn is so strong that Black must take a draw by 31 ... R/5×BP followed by a perpetual check employing both rooks. **27 ... P–QR4 28 P–QR4?** Losing at once. 28 P–B5 R–K8+ would have been an improvement according to Vasyukov, but after 29 R×R P×R=Q+ 30 Q×Q (or 30 K×Q) 30 ... P–R5 Black finishes a rook ahead. **28 ... B–R3 29 R–N1 B–B5 30 Q×P Q–R2! 31 Q–N2 Q–Q5+ 32 K–B1 B×B 33 Resigns**

Analysis by Vasyukov in THE CHESS
PLAYER

66 Holm (Denmark) –
Filipowicz (Poland)
Modern Benoni Defence

1 P–Q4	N–KB3
2 P–QB4	P–B4
3 P–Q5	P–K3
4 N–QB3	P×P
5 P×P	P–Q3
6 P–K4	P–KN3
7 B–K2	B–N2
8 N–B3	0–0
9 0–0	R–K1
10 N–Q2	N–R3
11 P–B3	N–B2
12 P–QR4	P–N3

The alternative is 12 ... N–Q2 when White's best course is 13 N–B4 N–K4 14 N–K3 P–B4 15 P–B4 N–B2 16 P×P P×P 17 B–Q3. e.g. 17 ... Q–B3 18 R–B3 B–Q2 19 Q–B2 N–R3 20 B–Q2 R–K2 21 R–N1! N KR3 22 B×N P×B 23 P–R3 QR–K1 24 N–K2 Q–R5 25 R–N3 with a clear advantage to White. Podgaets-Bjerre, Dresden 1969.

13 N–B4	B–QR3
14 B–N5	

Not 14 ʼN–R3? N/3×QP! 15 B×B N×N 16 Q–Q3 N×RP 17 B–QN5 P–B5! with an excellent game for Black.

14 ...	P–R3
15 B–K3	

The best retreat square. If 15 B–R4 Q–Q2 16 Q–Q2 P–KN4! 17 B–B2 B×N 18 B×B P–R3 with level chances (White cannot prevent ... P–N4).

15 B–Q2 B×N 16 B×B P–R3 is better for Black than the continuation suggested in the next note. e.g. 17 K–R1 N–Q2 18 R–QN1 R–N1 19 Q–K2 Q–B1 20 P–QN4 P–QN4 21 RP×P BP×P 22 R×P B×N 23 B×B P×P with some advantage to Black. Gligoric-Matulovic, Belgrade 1969.

15 ...	Q–Q2?!

Black mixes his moves. The correct order is 15 ... B×N 16 B×B P–QR3 17 Q–Q2 K–R2 18 QR–N1 Q–Q2, transposing to the game.

16 Q–Q2!	K–R2?

Black could have redeemed himself by 16 ... B×N 17 B×B K–R2

А. С. ПОМАР
ШПАНИЈА

A. S. POMAR
ESPAGNE

1

С. ГЛИГОРИЌ
ЈУГОСЛАВИЈА

S. GLIGORIĆ
YOUGOSLAVIE

12   A. Pomar IGM (Spain) playing S. Gligorić IGM (Yugoslavia)

13   L. Portisch IGM (Hungary) playing Junior World Champion W. Hug IM (Switzerland)

ПОРТИШ
УНГАРИЈА

L. PORTISCH
HONGRIE

1

В. ХУГ
ШВАЈЦАРИЈА

W. HUG
SUISSE

14 R. Byrne about to move against ex-World Champion v. Smyslov in the USA–USSR match

15 The Needle Match. The home team faces the USSR. National hero Svetozar Gligorić supported by vast crowd plays white against ex-World Champion Tigran Petrosian. Gligorić won a pawn but the tough struggle ended in a draw

since there is no way that Black's ... P–QR3 can be prevented.

17 QR–N1?

17 P–QN3! completely changes the picture because after . . . B×N White recaptures with the pawn creating a two pronged deterrent (QR4 and QB4) to Black's . . . P–QN4. But now things are back to normal.

17 . . .	B×N
18 B×B	P–R3
19 P–QN4	P–QN4
20 B–K2!	

If 20 RP×P RP×P 21 B–K2 P–B5 and Black is better off than in the game because of the open QR-file.

20 . . .   **P–B5**

Not 20 . . . BP×P? 21 R×P when White's forces dominate the Q-side and in particular Black will be left with a weak, isolated pawn.

21 P–R5

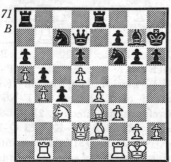

71
B

This position has occurred at least twice before in master games. (i) A passive plan: 21 . . . Q–K2 22 B–Q4 Q–B1 23 B–Q1! (so that after an eventual . . . P–B4 the K–file will not be full of white pieces. In any event, the bishop has no future on K2 whereas from Q1 it can be redeployed to QB2 from where it can

inhibit . . . P–B4) 23 . . . N–Q2 24 B×B Q×B 25 B–B2 R–K2 26 QR–K1 N–K1 27 P–B4 N/1–B3 28 R–K2 K–R1 29 R/1–K1, and while Black has been prevaricating White has steadily improved his position. Reshevsky–R. Garcia, Buenos Aires 1970; or (ii) An active plan: 21 . . . N–N1 22 B–Q4 B×B+ 23 Q×B P–B4 24 B–Q1 Q–N2 25 Q–Q2 P×P 26 N×KP R–K4 27 N–B3 QR–K1 28 B–B2 K–R1 with a balanced position. Ree–Evans, Amsterdam 1971.

Filipowicz now produces a new manoeuvre, not so active as Evans' idea in that it does not involve playing . . . P–B4 at such an early stage, but nevertheless it works out well in practice.

21 . . .   **R–K2**

22 QR–K1

22 B–Q1 followed by 23 B–B2 is more accurate, holding up Black's . . . P–B4.

| 22 . . . | Q–K1 |
| 23 B–Q4 | Q–R1! |

A novel idea. After the exchange of dark squared bishops Black's queen will be well placed on the long diagonal. The text also carries the simple threat of 24 . . . N×KP.

24 R–Q1   **N/2–K1!**

So as to be able to recapture on KN2 with the knight and thereby support the advance of the KBP.

25 Q–B2	N–Q2
26 B×B	N×B!
27 P–B4	P–B4!

Undermining the defence to White's QP – a factor which increases in significance as the endgame is reached.

28 B–B3

If 28 P–K5? P×P 29 P–Q6 R–K3 and White has nothing for the pawn.

| 28 . . . | P×P |
| 29 B×P | |

29 N×KP allows 29 . . . N–KB4 with the unpleasant threat of 30 . . . N–K6.

29 . . .	Q–K1
30 P–B5!?	P×P
31 B×P+	N×B
32 R×N	Q–N3
33 R/1–KB1?	

33 Q–B2 was essential, and after 33 . . . N–K4 34 R–KB1 Black's positional advantages (well placed knight, protected passed pawn) may be difficult to evaluate because of White's domination of the KB-file. After the text Black can force a decisive liquidation.

33 . . .	R–KB1!
34 Q–B2	R×R
35 Q×R	Q×Q
36 R×Q	K–N3
37 R–B3	N–B3
38 R–N3+	K–B2
39 R–B3	K–N3

Repeating moves just to reach the time control.

40 R–N3+	K–B2
41 R–B3	R–K4
42 Resigns	

The threat is 42 . . . K–N3, winning the QP, and if 42 R–B1 K–K2 43 R–Q1 R–K6 wins quickly.

Notes by Levy based on analysis by Filipowicz in THE CHESS PLAYER

67 Medina (Spain) –
Tringov (Bulgaria)

Sicilian Defence

1 P–K4 P–QB4 2 N–KB3 Medina for once departs from his favourite Closed Variation. **2 . . . P–K3 3 P–Q4 P×P 4 N×P N–KB3 5 N–QB3 P–Q3 6 P–KN4 P–QR3** 6 . . . P–KR3 has recently been more fashionable. **7 P–N5 KN–Q2 8 B–N_ B–K2 9 P–B4 N–QB3 10 B–K3 0–0 11 P–KR4 R–K1 12 0–0!?** If 12 Q–K2, intending to castle Q-side, Black should react vigorously with 12 . . . N×N 13 B×N P–K4! **12 . . . B–B1 13 Q–B3 Q–B2 14 QR–Q1 R–N1 15 P–R5 N×N 16 B×N P–N4** Not 16 . . . P–K4? 17 N–Q5! **17 P–B5 N–K4 18 Q–N3 P–N5 19 N–K2 N–B3**

72
W

20 B×P!? K×B 20 . . . B×B is much worse because after 21 P–B6 B–B1 Black's king is on KN1 instead of KR1 and 22 P–N6 is therefore quite effective. **21 P–B6+ K–R1 22 N–B4 N–K4 23 Q–R4 B–QN2 24 R–Q3!?** Another interesting idea. By threatening to transfer his rook to the K-side White compels his opponent to 'win' the exchange, thereby removing Black's active knight and strengthening White's hold on his K4 square. **24 . . . N×R 25 P×N P–Q4 26 K–R1 P×P 27 P×P B–Q3 28 P–N6! B×N 29 R×B R/N1–Q1 30 Q–N5!! R–Q8+ 31 K–R2 R–Q7**

32 Q–R6 BP × P 33 P × P Threatening 34 P–B7 followed by 35 P–N7 mate as well as 34 P–N7+ followed by 35 P–B7+ ! **33 . . . R × B+** 33 . . . R–KN1 allows mate in four: 34 P–N7+ R × KNP 35 P × R+ Q × P 36 R–B8+ Q × R 37 Q × Q mate. **34 K × R Q–B7+ 35 K–N3 Q–Q6+ 36 R–B3! Q–Q3+ 37 K–R3 Black Resigns** One of the finest attacking games of the Olympiad.

Notes by Levy based on analysis by Gheorghiu in THE CHESS PLAYER

68 Ciocaltea (Rumania) –
Darga (West Germany)
Sicilian Defence

1 P–K4	P–QB4
2 N–KB3	P–K3
3 N–B3	N–QB3
4 B–N5	KN–K2

Best. Other possibilities are: (i) 4 . . . N–Q5?! 5 B–Q3 N × N+ 6 Q × N B–Q3?! 7 Q–K3 P–K4 8 N–N5 Q–K2 9 P–QN4 P × P 10 Q–N3! B–N1 (10 . . . P–KN3 11 B–N2) 11 Q × NP Q–B3 12 Q × Q N × Q 13 P–QR3 P–Q4 14 P–KB3 R–N1 15 P–N3 B–R6 (15 . . . QP × P 16 BP × P P × P 17 B × P considerably improves the scope of White's pieces) 16 KP × P B–N7 17 R–KN1 B × P 18 P–Q6 with an excellent game for White. Bronstein–A. Zaitsev, Berlin 1968; or (ii) 4 . . . N–B3 5 0–0 B–K2 6 B × N NP × B?! 7 P–Q3 P–Q4 8 B–N5! 0–0 9 P–K5 with a clear advantage for White. Lein–Lengyel, Cienfuegos 1972.

5 0–0	P–QR3
6 B × N	N × B
7 P–QN3	

7 P–Q4 releases the central tension too early: 7 . . . P × P 8 N × P B–K2! (better than 8 . . . P–Q3 9 N × N P × N 10 Q–N4 Q–B3 11 B–K3 B–K2 12 P–B4 0–0 13 Q–K2, when White has a slight advantage in space and some attacking chances on the K-side, Gurgenidze–Polugayevsky, USSR Ch., Alma Ata 1969) 9 N × N NP × N 10 P–K5 Q–B2 11 B–B4 P–QB4 12 Q–Q2 B–N2 with a good game for Black. Balashov–Korchnoi, USSR 1971.

7 . . .	B–K2
8 B–N2	0–0
9 P–Q4	

An interesting alternative is 9 R–K1 P–QN4 10 P–K5. Csom–Haag, Hungary 1966 then continued 10 . . . P–B4!? 11 P–Q3 B–N2 12 P–QR4 Q–N3 with roughly equal chances.

9 . . .	P × P
10 N × P	P–Q4
11 P × P	P × P
12 R–K1	B–B3?

Black should not allow White's next move and the associated play on the dark squares. Correct was 12 . . . N × N 13 Q × N B–B3 14 Q–Q3 B–K3 with equality.

13 N–R4!	Q–Q3
14 N × N	P × N
15 B–Q4	

More accurate would have been 15 B × B Q × B 16 P–QB3! followed by Q–Q4 when, whether or not Black exchanges queens, White's knight will find a beautiful outpost on QB5.

15 . . .	B × B
16 Q × B	Q–N3!
17 R–K3!	

It is typical of Ciocaltea's enterprising style that he chooses the speculative, sacrificial continuation rather than the safe 17 Q–Q2 which would have preserved a slight positional pull. 17 P–QB3 would not be good on account of 17 . . . B–R6 18 P–N3 Q–B4 19 R–K3 QR–K1 and if 20 QR–K1?? Q–B6 forces mate. 17 R–K2 meets a similar fate: 17 . . . B–R6 18 P–KB3 QR–K1 19 QR–K1? B×P! etc.

17 . . .	**Q×BP**
18 N–B5	**B–B4**
19 QR–K1!	

19 . . .   P–QR4??

A dreadful oversight for a Grandmaster. The only sensible action was to grab a second pawn and pray: 19 . . . Q×RP 20 P–KN4 B–N3 21 P–R4 P–B3 (not 21 . . . P–R3 22 P–R5 B–R2 23 P–N5 P×P 24 P–R6 P×P 25 N–Q7 winning) 22 P–R5 B–B2 23 P–R6 with an excellent game for the pawns.

But now the game ends in a more sudden manner.

20 R/3–K2   Resigns

Analysis by Ciocaltea in THE CHESS
                                    PLAYER

69 Tringov (Bulgaria) –
   Uhlmann (East Germany)

French Defence

1 P–K4	**P–K3**

2 P–Q4	**P–Q4**
3 N–QB3	**B–N5**
4 P–K5	**N–K2**
5 B–Q2	

The start of an artificial system that promises White little hope of an advantage.

5 . . .	**P–QB4**
6 P–QR3	

6 N–N5 B×B+ 7 Q×B 0–0 8 N–KB3 P×P 9 B–Q3 is interesting but also inadequate for an advantage 9 . . . QN–B3 10 N/5×QP P–B3 11 P×P R×P 12 N×N P×N with a level game.

6 . . .	**B×N**
7 B×B	

This is the 'justification' of White's fifth move. By recapturing with the bishop White avoids the penalty of doubled pawns which is usually implied by the Winawer Variation but at the cost of putting his dark squared bishop on a useless square.

7 . . .   QN–B3

More accurate than 7 . . . P×P because then White can recapture with his queen: 8 Q×P QN–B3 9 Q–N4 and now: (i) 9 . . . N–B4 10 N–B3 P–KR4 11 Q–R3 P–Q5 12 0–0–0 Q–Q4 13 N×P N/4×N 14 B×N N×B 15 Q–QB3 Q×KP 16 R×N B–Q2 17 B–B4 Q–B3 18 KR–Q1 with an overwhelming game for White; or (ii) 9 . . . 0–0 10 N–B3 N–B4 11 B–Q3 P–Q5 12 B–Q2 when White's game is the more active and his bishop pair provides a useful long-term advantage.

8 N–B3	**P×P**
9 N×P?!	

Better is 9 B×P when 9 . . . B–Q2 produces a level position.

9 . . .   N×P!

Schwarz, in his 573 page tome *Die Französissche Verteidigung*, append a question mark to this move and claims that after Tringov's reply White has a clear advantage. But then openings books are so full of material that it is not unreasonable to assume them to contain a certain proportion of outright errors. It is just unlucky when you are the one against whom such an error is uncovered.

10 N×P	**B×N**
11 B×N	**0–0**
12 B–Q3	

If 12 B–K2 N–B3 13 B–N3 Q–B3 14 P–QB3 P–Q5! and with just three active moves Black has snatched the initiative.

12 ...	**N–B3**
13 B–N3	**Q–B3**
14 0–0!?	

14 P–QB3 P–Q5 was still the indicated continuation.

14 ...	**Q×NP**
15 R–N1	**Q×RP**
16 R×P	**KR–K1!**

Preparing to challenge White's active rook.

17 R–K1

If 17 P–KB4 Q–B4+ 18 K–R1 P–B4! and White's bishops have little scope.

17 ...	**R–K2!**
18 R–K3	**Q–R7!**

White's initiative has momentarily disappeared and he is on the defensive. In return for the sacrificed pawn he has only the two bishops to console him and some rather nebulous attacking chances against Black's K-side. Nevertheless, Tringov makes the most of these chances.

19 R–N5   **P–Q5!**

20 R–K1	**B–B5!**
21 R×R	**N×R**
22 R–QB5	**B×B**
23 P×B	**N–N3**

23 ... N–Q4 24 P–R3 N–B6 25 Q–N4 is not so good – White would still have some attacking chances and Black's knight would be somewhat out of play.

24 P–R4!	**N–B1**
25 Q–B3	**R–K1**
26 R–B7	**P–QR4**
27 R–R7	**P–R3**
28 R–R8	**Q–K3**

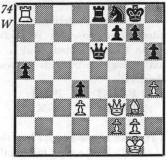

74
W

29 R×P??

Premature. White should first play 29 K–R2 when Black's extra pawn is doomed: 29 ... R×R 30 Q×R Q–QN3 31 P–B3. But after the text move Black can augment his minimal material advantage by a whole rook – noticing what he had done, **Tringov resigned** before Uhlmann had time to play 29 ... Q–K8+.

Notes by Levy based on analysis by Uhlmann in THE CHESS PLAYER

70 **Benko** (USA)
    Malich (East Germany)

English Opening

This game was played in the

penultimate round of the finals when Dr Malich needed a draw to assure himself of a Grandmaster norm. It is usual, under such circumstances, for the aspiring GM to approach his opponent before the game, inform him of the situation and hopefully come to an agreement in advance.

In this instance, Dr Malich made no overtures to Benko before the game and the American Grandmaster was therefore unaware of the importance of the half point to his opponent. But even if he had known, Benko would not have been willing to come to any agreement – he wanted to improve his individual score in the Olympiad, and '. . . What is this title business anyway? A charity!'.

1 P–KN3   P–K4
2 P–QB4   N–KB3
3 B–N2

3 N–QB3 is more usual but then 3 . . . B–N5 has become fashionable recently. But after the text maybe 3 . . . P–B3!? is a possibility.

3 . . .   N–B3
4 N–KB3   B–B4
5 N–B3

Dangerous would be 5 N×P B×P+ 6 K×B N×N 7 P–Q3 P–Q4 8 P×P N/4–N5+ 9 K–N1 N×QP 10 Q–R4+ P–B3 11 Q–Q4 Q–K2, and if 12 Q×NP then 12 . . . Q×P produces an unclear position with interesting possibilities.

5 . . .   P–Q3
6 P–Q3   P–KR3
7 0–0   0–0
8 N–QR4?!   Q–K2
9 P–K3

If 9 N×B P×N, Black gets the better game because White has no

counter-play while Black holds the centre. It is therefore necessary for White to delay the exchange until the right moment.

9 . . .   P–QR4

Better was 9 . . . P–R3 so that after the bishop retreats there may be some Q-side counterplay.

10 P–N3   R–K1
11 B–N2   B–B4
12 P–QR3   B–QR2
13 N–B3   Q–Q2
14 R–K1

Necessary, in order to keep the light squared bishops on the board and thereby to prevent his K-side from becoming weak.

14 . . .   B–R6
15 B–R1   B–N5

Here Black offered a draw.

16 Q–B2   N–R2
17 N–QN5!

Preventing Black's queen from coming into play on KB4. With this important tempo White can stop Black's K-side activity.

17 . . .   R–K2
18 P–KR4   N–B1

On this square the knight has no future. Better is 18 . . . B–N3 but then White can continue his Q-side attack with P–Q4 and P–B5. Had Black played . . . P–R3 at move nine his position now would not be so passive.

19 P–Q4   P–B3

A little passive, but 19 . . . P–K5 is dubious because of 20 N–R2 and after 20 . . . B–KB4 Black's KP loses its natural protection. In addition, 21 P–Q5 and 21 P–B5 are both very promising for White.

20 P–Q5   N–Q1
21 N–R2   P–N4?

A strategic blunder of the same magnitude as overlooking a piece. Black is hoping to occupy the KR-file for a K-side attack but actually White can take the file by force. Better would have been 21 . . . B–KB4 22 P–K4 B–R2, when Black is cramped but at least he can still play. White would then continue to play on the Q-side, commencing with 23 N×B.

22 P×P   RP×P

Had he realized his previous mistake Black would have recaptured with the BP but his game would still be very bad.

23 N×B/N4   Q×N/KN5
24 B–K4!

Taking complete control of all the important light squares. Black's game is quite hopeless.

24 . . .   N–B2
25 K–N2   Q–Q2

Black has no time for 25 . . . N–R3 26 R–R1 K–N2 because of 27 R×N K×R 28 R–R1+ followed by 29 B–B5 trapping the queen.

26 R–R1   N–R1
27 R–R6   K–N2
28 QR–R1   N–B2
29 R/6–R5   B–N3
30 B–B5

White's game plays itself.

30 . . .   Q–K1
31 Q–K4   B–B4
32 B–K6   P–B3
33 R–R7+   N×R
34 R×N+   K–B1
35 Q–N6

More aesthetically pleasing than 35 B×N which only wins the queen.

35 . . .   R×B
36 N–B7   Resigns

Notes by Benko specially for this volume

71 **Andersson** (Sweden) –
Portisch (Hungary)

Sicilian Defence

1 P–K4   P–QB4
2 N–KB3   P–Q3
3 B–N5+   N–QB3

Better is 3 . . . B–Q2 4 B×B+ Q×B 5 0–0 N–KB3 6 P–K5 P×P 7 N×P Q–B1 with equality. For 3 . . . N–Q2 see game 16.

4 0–0   B–Q2
5 R–K1   N–B3
6 P–B3   P–QR3
7 B–B1   P–K4

Possibly better would have been 7 . . . P–K3 8 P–Q4 P×P 9 P×P P–Q4 10 P–K5 N–K5 11 N–B3 N×N 12 P×N B–K2 or 7 . . . P–KN3 8 P–KR3 B–N2 9 P–Q4 P×P 10 P×P P–Q4 11 P–K5 N–K5 12 N–B3 N×N 13 P×N 0–0.

8 P–KR3   P–R3?

Correct is 8 . . . B–K2 9 P–Q4 Q–B2 10 P–QR4, when White has a slight advantage.

9 P–Q4   Q–B2
10 P–QR4   P–KN3?

The KB is needed on K2 to guard the vulnerable Q3 square as well as to protect the QBP (if White exchanges pawns in the centre). Correct was 10 . . . B–K2 11 N–R3 0–0 12

N–B4 P–QN4 13 N–K3 BP×P 14 BP×P N×QP 15 N×N P×P 16 Q×P P×P 17 N–B5 B×N 18 P×B P–Q4! 19 B–K3 when White is still slightly better. But after the text move Portisch is probably already lost.

11	N–R3	B–N2
12	P×BP	P×P
13	N B4	

Threatening to win a pawn by 14 Q–Q6!

76
B

13 ...   R–QN1

If 13 . . . 0–0 14 Q–Q6! Q×Q 15 N×Q QR–N1 (15 . . . P–N3 16 P–R5 P×P 17 N–N7 and 18 N×BP) 16 B–K3 and White wins a pawn.

14 P–QN4!

Not 14 N–Q6+? K–K2 15 N–B4 KR–Q1 when White's initiative has evaporated.

14 P–R5 would maintain White's advantage. The text increases it.

14 . . .		P×P
15 P×P		B–K3

If 15 . . . N×NP White can choose between 16 B–R3 P–QR4 17 N/4×KP (17 N×RP is unsound: 17 . . . Q×N 18 Q–Q6 N–B3 19 B–N5 B–KB1) 17 . . . 0–0 18 R–B1 with an excellent game; and 16

N/4×P! N–B7 (White was threatening 17 Q–N3 as well as 17 B–KB4) 17 B–KB4 N×R/K8 18 Q×N and White will win back the exchange with a pawn for interest.

15 . . . 0–0 would lose the exchange to 16 –N5 followed by B–R3 and B–Q6.

16 N–Q6+		K–K2
17 B–R3		

Not 17 P–N5? N–QN5 18 B–R3 P–QR4!

17 . . .		N–K1

17 . . . Q×N 18 P–N5 N–QN5 19 Q×Q+ K×Q 20 B×N+ K–B2 21 QR–B1+ is hopeless for Black.

18 N×NP!		Q×N
19 P–N5+		K–B3
20 P×N		Q–B2

If 20 . . . Q×P 21 N×P K×N 22 P–B4+ K×BP (or 22 . . . K–B3 23 Q–Q4 mate) 23 P–K5 and Black's king cannot escape.

21 N×P!		Resigns

21 . . . Q×N loses to 22 Q–B3+ B–B4 23 P×B Q×P 24 B–K7 mate and 21 . . . K×N to 22 P–B4+ as in the last note.

Notes based on analysis by Andersson specially contributed for this volume

72 **Hug** (Switzerland) –
   Hort (Czechoslovakia)

Queen's Indian Defence

This game was awarded the brilliancy prize.

1	P–QB4	N–KB3
2	N–KB3	P–K3
3	P–KN3	P–QN3
4	B–N2	B–N2
5	0–0	B–K2
6	P–Q4	0–0
7	N–B3	N–K5!

Best.

8 N×N   B×N
9 B–B4

Uhlmann's move.

9 . . .   P–Q3
10 Q–Q2   N–Q2
11 KR–Q1?!

A bad choice because it weakens the KB-file which can later become opened. Better would have been 11 QR–B1 or 11 P–QN4.

11 . . .   P–KR3

A novelty. Now White's bishop is not well placed on KB4.

12 N–K1   P–KB4!
13 B×B

If 13 P–B3 B–N2 and Black can continue with . . . P–K4 and a very good game. White's plan is now to play for control of the centre.

13 . . .   P×B
14 Q–B2   N–B3
15 P–B3

Trying to destroy Black's centre. Now 15 . . . P–Q4 is not possible because after 16 P×QP P×QP Black's QBP is left hanging.

15 . . .   P–KN4
16 B–K3

If 16 B–K5!? P×B 17 QP×P N–Q2 18 Q×P K–N2 19 Q–B6 N×P 20 Q×KP B–Q3, White does not have enough compensation for the sacrificed piece.

16 . . .   Q–K1!

A very good move, starting the attack. If now 17 P×P N–N5! with good attacking possibilities. e.g. 18 Q–Q3 Q–R4 19 N–B3 R×N!, or 18 Q–Q2 Q–N3 (attacking the KP) 19 Q–Q3 Q–R4 etc.

17 K–N2   Q–R4

If now 18 P×P N–N5 19 B–N1

R–B7+! 20 B×R Q×P+ 21 K–B3 R–KB1+ 22 K×N P–KR4 mate. Black's threat is now . . . P–N5. His game is so very good because White has absolutely no counterplay.

18 P–KR3   Q–N3
19 QR–B1

Defending the queen. If instead White plays 19 P×P, 19 . . . P–N5! is killing.

19 . . .   R–B2

With the simple threat of . . . QR–KB1 followed by . . . P–KR4 and . . . P–N5. Meanwhile, White must just wait.

20 P×P   P–N5

The most difficult move in the game. The idea is to take the KB3 square away from White's knight.

21 P–KR4

Hoping to be able to play N–Q3–B4.

21 . . .   P–K4!

A tremendous move.

22 Q–Q3

If 22 P×P P×P 23 K–R2 QR–KB1 24 N–Q3 N×P (24 . . . Q×P 25 B–N1 is not so clear) 25 N×P R–B7+ 26 B×R R×B+ 27 K–N1 Q–B4 (threatening 28 . . . Q×N or 28 . . . R–N7+ and mate in two) 28 N–Q3 B–B4 winning.

22 . . .   N×P

Allowing the self pin.

23 N–B2   QR–KB1
24 B–N1

If White has one tempo more he is saved because his KNP is now defended by his queen and he could then play R–B1 in safety. But 24 R–B1 loses to 24 . . . R×R 25 R×R R×R 26 K×R N×P+ etc.

24 ...	B×P!
25 P×B	R–B6!!
26 N–K3	R–N6+
27 K–R1	

If 27 K–R2 Q–R4.

| 27 ... | R–B7!! |
| 28 Resigns | |

Notes by Hort specially for this volume

73 **Partos** (Rumania) –
Holm (Denmark)
Modern Benoni Defence

1 P–Q4	N–KB3
2 P–QB4	P–B4
3 P–Q5	P–K3
4 N–QB3	P×P
5 P×P	P–Q3
6 P–K4	P–KN3
7 P–KB4	B–N2
8 P–K5!?	

Mikenas' line, in which White forsakes his own development in the hope that his pawn rush will flatten Black before he can organize his counter-attack.

| 8 ... | KN–Q2! |

8 . . . P×P has long been known to be a serious error. One recent example is the game Mikenas–Klyukin, USSR 1971 which went: 8 . . . P×P 9 P×P KN–Q2 10 P–K6! P×P 11 P×P Q–K2? (better is 11 . . . Q–R5+ although

White still retains some advantage after 12 P–KN3 B×N+ 13 P×B Q–K5+ 14 Q–K2 Q×Q+ 15 B×Q N–B1 16 N–B3) 12 N–Q5! Q–R5+ 13 P–KN3 Q–K5+ 14 Q–K2 Q×N 15 P×N+ K×P 16 B–N2 and Black's position was in ruins.

9 N–N5	P×P
10 N–Q6+	K–K2
11 N×B+	Q×N
12 P–Q6+	K–B1
13 N–B3	P–K5!

A new move, returning the pawn so as to gain time to recentralize the queen. The idea itself is not new however. In his monograph on the Benoni in Batsford's Contemporary Chess Openings series, Hartston gives as his main line 13 . . . N–QB3 14 B–K2 when he suggests 14 . . . P–K5 15 N–N5 P–KR3 16 N×KP B–Q5 'when it is White's king which may then become stuck in the centre'.

By playing . . . P–K5 one move earlier, Holm ensures that the White king is almost hounded to death.

14 N–N5	P–KR3
15 N×KP	Q–K1
16 Q–K2	

Forced. The threat was 16 . . . P–B4. But now White's KB is shut in and Black's attack has time to get itself moving.

| 16 ... | N–QB3 |

Threatening simply 17 . . . N–Q5, when 18 Q–K3 loses the queen and other moves allow . . . P–B4.

17 K–B2	B–Q5+
18 K–N3	K–N2
19 N–B3	

It is impossible for White to maintain his defence of the QP in view of . . . P–B4 which cannot be prevented.

19 . . .	Q–KB1
20 P–KR3	P–QR3
21 Q–B3	Q×P
22 K–R2	N–B3
23 B–Q3	KR–K1
24 R–Q1	QR–Q1!

78
W

25 K–R1?

Necessary was 25 B–B2. Now White loses more material.

25 . . .	B×N
26 P×B	P–B5!
27 B–B2	Q×R+
28 B×Q	R–K8+
29 K–R2	R/1×B
30 P–N4	R×B
31 R×R	R×R

Black has a decisive material advantage and the remainder of the game is of little interest.

32 Q–K2 R×P 33 Q–QN2 N–Q4 34 Q×P N/3–K2 35 Q×P N×P 36 Q–Q6 R×P+ 37 K–N1 N/2–Q4 38 Q–K5+ P–B3 39 Q–Q6 R–K6 40 P–R4 P–B6 41 Q–B5 R–K8× 42 K–R2 P–B7 43 Resigns

Although very one sided, this game is of considerable theoretical interest. It is the dying moans of Mikenas' pawn storm variation.

Notes by Levy

74 Radulov (Bulgaria) – **Sloth** (Denmark)

Caro Kann Defence

1 P–K4	P–QB3
2 P–Q4	P–Q4
3 N–QB3	P×P
4 N×P	N–Q2
5 B–QB4	KN–B3
6 N–N5	P–K3
7 Q–K2	N–N3
8 B–Q3	P–KR3
9 N/5–B3	P–B4
10 P×P	N/N3–Q2

This innovation of Smyslov's is very rarely seen. The normal move is 10 . . . B×P when 11 N–K5 keeps a slight edge.

11 N–K5

Against Filip at Praia da Rocha 1969, I tried an enterprising suggestion of Hartston's: 11 P–QN4!? P–QR4 12 P–B3 P×P 13 P×P P–QN3 14 P–QR4 P×P 15 P–N5 N–Q4! 16 N–R3! B–K2 17 0–0 B–B3 and the game was agreed drawn. Probably such drastic action by White is not needed – The text move seems perfectly adequate.

11 . . .	N×N
12 Q×N	Q–R4+
13 B–Q2	Q×BP
14 N–B3	B–Q3?

Correct is 14 . . . Q×Q 15 N×Q B–B4 as in Parma-Smyslov, Lugano Olympiad 1968, when 16 B–K2 N–K5 17 N–Q3 B–Q3 18 B–K3 would have kept White's advantage.

By allowing White to keep queens on the board Black exposes himself to a variety of attacking possibilities: Castling K-side for example is met by 0–0–0, KR–N1 and P–KN4.

| 15 Q–K2 | P–QN3 |

Better is 15 . . . B–Q2 so as not to allow the disrupting check on QN5.

16 0–0–0	B–N2
17 B–K3	Q–B2
18 B–QN5+!	K–K2

18 . . . N–Q2 loses to 19 R×B Q×R 20 R–Q1 etc. and 18 . . . B–B3 to 19 N–Q4 B–Q2 20 B×B+ and 21 N–N5.

19 N–Q4

Threatening 20 N–B5+ P×N 21 B×NP+ winning the queen.

19 . . .	B–K4
20 KR–K1	B×NP
21 R–N1	B–Q4

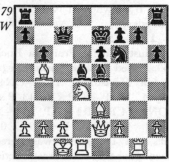

22 P–KB4!	B×BP
23 N–B5+	K–B1
24 N×NP	R–B1
25 B–Q3	B×KRP

If 25 . . . B×B+ 26 Q×B Q×RP 27 QR–B1 with a similar finish to that in the game.

By now Black was desperately short of time.

26 Q–B2!	B–K4

If 26 . . . B×R 27 R×B N–Q2 28 B–R6 R–Q1 29 Q–Q2, and the threat of 30 B×RP is most unpleasant for Black.

27 Q–R4	P–KR4
28 QR–B1	N–N1
29 B–Q4	R–R3

Or 29 . . . B×B 30 Q×B R–R3 31 Q–K3 R–KR1 32 Q–N5 with the threat of 33 N×KP+ and 34 Q–N7+.

30 N×RP	Q–K2

30 . . . B×B 31 Q×B R×N loses to 32 Q–KN4 forking rook and knight (32 . . . R–KR1 33 Q–N7+).

31 R×N+!	K×R
32 Q×Q	B–QB5
33 Q×BP+	Resigns

Notes by Levy

75 Kavalek (USA) –
Gheorghiu (Rumania)

Sicilian Defence

1 P–K4	P–QB4
2 N–KB3	P–Q3
3 P–Q4	P×P
4 N×P	N–KB3
5 N–QB3	P–QR3
6 B–KN5	P–K3
7 P–B4	QN–Q2
8 Q–B3	Q–B2
9 0–0–0	P–N4
10 B–Q3	B–N2
11 KR–K1	P–N5

The alternative, 11 . . . B–K2, is also fraught with many dangers for Black. The solid continuation, 12 Q–N3 0–0–0 13 B×N! N×B 14 Q×P, gave White a probably winning position in the fifteenth game of the Spassky-Fischer match, but the real question is whether the sacrifice (11 . . . B–K2) 12 N–Q5!? is sound:

The brilliancy prize game Velimirovic-Ljubojevic, Yugoslav Ch. 1972 went (11 . . . B–K2 12 N–Q5!?) N×N 13 P×N B×B (on 13 . . . B×P Velimirovic had intended 14 Q×B! P×Q 15 R×B+ K–B1 16

B–B5 R–Q1 17 B–K6!! winning)
14 R×P+ (according to rumours
that were circulating at Skopje,
14 N×KP is also strong) 14 . . .
P×R (better, according to Velimir-
ovic, is 14 . . . B–K2! 15 N–B5!
P×R 16 N×NP+ K–Q1! – *16 . . .
K–B2 17 N×P Q–R4 18 Q–R5+
K–N1 19 Q–N+4 K–B2 20
Q–N7+ K–K1 21 B–N6+ P×B 22
Q×P mate* – 17 N×P+ K–B1 18
N×Q K×N 19 B–B5 with an un-
clear position) 15 N×P! Q–R4 16
Q–R5+ P–N3 17 Q×B and White's
attack was decisive.

The alternative is to accept
White's sacrifice: 11 . . . B–K2 12
N–Q5 P×N 13 N–B5 and now: (i)
13 . . . B–KB1? 14 P–K5! P×P 15
P×P N×P (or 15 . . . N–K5 16
B×N P×B 17 R×P Q–B4 – *17 . . .
N–B4 18 N–Q6+* – 18 P–K6! P×P
19 N×P+! – Larsen) 16 N×P+!
B×N 17 B×N B×B 18 Q×B win-
ning. Enevoldsen-Hamann, Danish
Ch. 1972; (ii) 13 . . . P×P? 14 B×KP
B×B 15 R×B with a clear advant-
age for White – Larsen; (iii) 13 . . .
P–R3!? 14 P–K5 P×P 15 P×P
N×P 16 R×N? (16 Q–N3!) 16 . . .
Q×R 17 B–KB4 P–Q5 18 B×Q
B×Q 19 P×B K–B1 20 N×B K×N
21 B×QP KR–QB1 and Black's

material advantage is sufficient to
win. Boey-Hamann, Skopje 1972; or
(iv) 13 . . . K–B1, which is an untried
suggestion of Larsen's.

After the text move White has no
choice if he wishes to retain his
initiative.

12 N–Q5!

12 N/3–K2 N–B4 led to a roughly
equal game in Mikenas-Aronin,
USSR Ch. 1957.

12 . . .	**P×N**
13 P×P+	**K–Q1**
14 B–B5!	

An echo of one of Velimirovic's
ideas (compare the note to 13 . . .
B×B in the above mentioned Velimirovic-Ljubojevic game).

14 . . .   B–K2?

Overlooking the point of White's
last move. It was essential to move the
queen so that the white knight does
not fork king and queen if it reaches
the K6 square.

15 B–K6!

Winning an important pawn –
Important because it prevents
White's knight from jumping into K6.

15 . . .   R–KB1

Now 15 . . . Q–R4 is too late:
16 B×P Q×RP 17 N–K6+ K–B1
18 N×P Q–R8+ 19 K–Q2 Q×P
20 R×B and White will win.

16 B×P	**R×B**
17 N–K6+	**K–B1**
18 N×Q	**K×N**

The remainder of the game is
merely an efficient mopping-up
procedure.

**19 Q–K2 P–QR4 20 R–Q4 B–KB1
21 Q–N5 N–B4 22 B×N R×B 23
R–K8 R×R 24 Q×R P–N4 25
P×P R–B8+ 26 R–Q1 R–B7 27
Q–R5 K–N3 28 Q×P B–B1 29**

Q–R4 R×NP 30 Q–KB4 B–K2 31
P–KR4 B–N5 32 R–K1 B–R4 33
R×B R–N8+ 34 K–Q2 R–Q8+
35 K–K3 R–K8+ 36 K–B2
Resigns

Notes by Levy

76 **Pomar** (Spain) –
Portisch (Hungary)

Neo-Grünfeld (by transposition)

1 N–KB3	P–KN3
2 P–Q4	B–N2
3 P–KN3	P–QB4
4 P–B3	P–N3?!

Portisch had simply overlooked
the loss of a pawn after 5 P×P P×P
6 Q–Q5 N–QB3 7 Q×QBP N–B3 8
B–N2 B–QR3. Black has some compensation, but enough?

5 B–N2

Pomar evidently thought so.

5 ...	B–N2
6 Q–N3	P×P
7 N–K5	P–Q4

Black could sacrifice the exchange
here with 7 . . . B×N   8 B×B
N–QB3   9 B×R Q×B but after 10
Q–Q5 White is better.

8 P×P	P–K3
9 Q–R4+	

This results only in much loss of
time. White should continue developing, with equal chances.

9 ...	N–QB3
10 N×N	Q–Q2
11 N–B3	B×N

The pawn-structure is symme-
trical but Black's pieces are better co-
ordinated.

12 Q–N4	N–K2
13 B–B4	0–0
14 0–0	N–B4
15 KR–Q1	Q–N2

16 B–K5	P–QR4
17 Q–N3	P–R5
18 Q–B2	P–B3
19 B–B4	P–KN4
20 B–QB1	N–Q3
21 P–QR3	K–R1
22 B–Q2	B–K1

Now Black is clearly on top. White
even runs some risk of having his
queen trapped unless he acquiesces
in a weakening of his pawns.

23 P–K4	B–N3
24 P–B3	KR–B1
25 Q–Q3	N–B5
26 QR–N1	P–N4

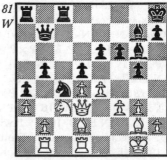

27 P–B4	NP×P
28 NP×P	N–Q3

It is inevitable that White will end
up in a position with split pawns
fixed on the same colour squares as
his QB.

29 R–K1	R–R3
30 QR–B1	P×P
31 N×P	R×R
32 B×R	N×N
33 B×N	B×B
34 R×B	P–B4
35 R–K1	Q–Q4
36 B–K3	R–R1?

Missing match point. 36 . . .
P–K4! would have been immediately decisive. Now Portisch has to
win all over again.

37 R–K2	R–Q1
38 R–Q2	B–B3
39 B–B2	R–KN1+
40 B–N3	P–R4
41 K–B1	R–N5
42 Q–K3	P–R5
43 B–B2	B–N4!
44 Q–K5+	

Not 44 P×B Q–N7+ and . . . R–K5.

44 . . .	Q×Q
45 QP×Q	B×P
46 R–Q8+	R–N1
47 R–Q6	R–N3
48 R–Q4	B×KP
49 R×KRP+	K–N2
50 R–QN4	B×RP
51 R×NP	R–N5
52 P–N3	P×P
53 R×NP	R–QR5
54 R–N7+	K–B3
55 R–QR7	R×R
56 B×R	B–B2

Despite White's gargantuan resistance Black is still winning.

57 B–Q4+	P–K4
58 B–B3	K–N4
59 P–R4	P–K5
60 P–R5	P–B5
61 K–B2	K–N5
62 B–N4	B–Q1!
63 B–B3	

Or 63 B–K1 B–K2 intending . . . B–B4+.

63 . . .	B–R5+
64 K–B1	

Some significant variations: (i) 64 K–K2 P–B6+ 65 K–Q2 B–N4+ (ii) 64 K–N1 P–K6 65 P–R6 B–B7+ 66 K–N2 P–B6+ 67 K–B1 B–N6.

64 . . .	K–B6
65 B–K1	B–K2
66 P–R6	B–B4
67 B–N4	B–R2

68 K–K1	P–K6
69 K–Q1	P–K7+
70 K–Q2	K–N7
71 Resigns	

Notes by Keene based on analysis by Portisch in THE CHESS PLAYER

77 Hamann (Denmark) – **Gligoric** (Yugoslavia)

Sicilian Defence

1 P–K4 P–QB4 2 N–KB3 N–QB3 3 P–Q4 P×P 4 N×P N–B3 5 N–QB3 P–Q3 6 B–QB4 P–K3 7 B–K3 P–QR3 8 0–0 B–K2 9 B–N3 0–0 10 P–B4 N×N 11 B×N P–QN4 12 P–K5 The fourth game of the Fischer-Spassky match went 12 P–QR3 B–N2 13 Q–Q3 P–QR4! and Spassky quickly had an overwhelming position at the cost of a pawn. **12 . . . P×P 13 P×P N–Q2 14 N–K4 B–N2 15 N–Q6 B×N! 16 P×B Q–N4** The same mate threat as was employed by Spassky in his game with Fischer. Black seizes the initiative and never lets go. **17 Q–K2 P–K4 18 B–K3 Q–N3 19 QR–Q1 K–R1 20 P–B3 B–K5 21 Q–KB2** Better would have been 21 B–Q5 to exchange Black's strong bishop. **21 . . . P–B4! 22 Q–N3 Q–K1 23 B–N5 P–B5 24 Q–B2 Q–N3 25 B–K7 R–B4!**

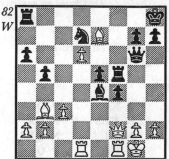

82
W

**26 KR–K1 B–B3! 27 B–B2 Q–K3
28 B–N3** White cannot afford to
capture the exchange because his
KB is needed to combat Black's control of the light squares. 28 B–K4
leaves his QRP en prise after Black
exchanges bishops. **28 . . . Q–R3 29
B–Q5 B×B 30 R×B Q–K3 31
Q–B3 R–QB1** Not 31 . . . P–K5? 32
R×R. **32 R–Q2 P–N4! 33 Q–Q5** If
33 Q–N7 R–KN1, continuing the
attack. **33 . . . Q×Q 34 R×Q** The
exchange of queens has removed the
danger of a K-side onslaught but it
has not solved the problems of
White's imprisoned bishop and
Black's passed KP. **34 . . . K–N2 35
P–QR4 P×P 36 R–R1 R–B4! 37
R×R** If 37 R–Q2 P–K5 38 R×
P P–K6 39 R–K2 R–R4. **37 . . .
N×R 38 R–Q1 N–Q2 39 R–Q5
K–N3!** Defending the rook so that
the KP may advance. **40 R–R5 P–K5
41 R×P/6 R–Q4 42 K–B1 P–K6 43
R×P** If 43 R–R7 N–K4. **43 . . . R–
Q8+ 44 K–K2 R–Q7+ 45 K–B1
R–KB7+ 46 K–N1** Or 46 K–K1
R×KNP followed by 47 . . . P–B6.
**46 . . . R×QNP 47 K–B1 P–B6! 48
P×P N–K4 49 R–K4 R–KB7+
50 K–K1** Or 50 K–N1 N×P+ 51
K–R1 R×P mate. **50 . . . N–Q6+
51 K–Q1 R–Q7 mate**

*Notes by Levy based on analysis by
Gipslis in 64*

78 Hecht (West Germany) –
Tal (USSR)

Sicilian Defence

1 P–K4	**P–QB4**
2 N–KB3	**P–K3**
3 N–B3	**N–QB3**
4 P–KN3	**P–Q4**

5 P×P	**P×P**
6 B–N2	**P–Q5**
7 N–K2	

Not 7 N–K4? P–B4! 8 N/4–N5
Q–K2+ 9 Q–K2 P–KR3 with a
clear advantage to Black.

7 . . .	**N–B3**

Already Black has an easy game
with no problems over his development and an adequate share of the
centre.

8 P–Q3	**B–Q3**
9 0–0	**0–0**
10 N–Q2!	**B–N5**
11 P–KR3	**B–Q2**
12 N–QB4	**B–B2**
13 B–B4	**R–K1**
14 R–K1	**N–KR4!**
15 B×B	**Q×B**
16 P–QB3	**QR–Q1**

Also possible is 16 . . . P×P 17
N×P R×R+ 18 Q×R R–K1 with
an unclear position. The text is more
flexible, putting White under pressure in the centre.

17 P×P	**P×P**
18 R–QB1	**Q–N1**
19 Q–Q2	**B–K3!?**
20 B–B3	

After 20 B×N?! P×B 21
N–R5 R–Q4 22 N×BP R–QB1,
Black's active position compensates
for the sacrificed pawn.

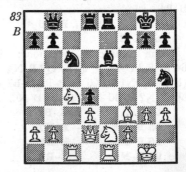

16 Viktor Korchnoi IGM (USSR) in play in the decisive last round against Rumania

17 Ex-World Champion Tigran Petrosian (USSR)

18 Ex-World Champion Mikhail Tal (USSR) won the prize for the best score on Board 4

19 V. Savon, the Soviet Champion

20   G. Kane (USA)

21   Czech émigré L. Kavalek IGM now on top board for the United States

22   A. Bisguier IGM (USA)

23   W. Martz (USA)

20 ...	B×N!
21 B×N/6	

Not 21 R×B N–K4 22 B×N N×R 23 P×N Q–K4 24 B–B3 P–Q6, nor 21 P×B when 21 . . . N–B3 leaves Black with a strong passed pawn.

21 ...	P×B
22 R×B	Q–K4
23 R/4–B1	

Better chances for a draw would be offered by 23 R×BP R–K2 24 R/6–B1 R/1–K1 25 N–B4 Q×R+ 26 R×Q R×R+ 27 K–N2.

23 ...	Q–Q3
24 N–B4	N–B3
25 Q–R5	

After 25 R×R+ R×R 26 R–K1 R×R+ 27 Q×R P–N4, Black's QP still acts as a constricting influence on White's position and White will lose much time in redeploying his knight to a useful square.

25 ...	N–Q2!?
26 R×R+	R×R
27 P–QN4?	

A time trouble error. Much better was 27 P–KR4, indirectly supporting the position of White's knight by preventing . . . P–N4. If then 27 . . . N–K4, 28 K–N2 renders Black's knight temporarily ineffectual and leaves White with a small initiative.

27 ...	N–K4
28 Q–B5	Q–B3
29 P–N5	

On 29 P–KR4 comes 29 . . . P–KR3 (not 29 . . . N–B6+ 30 K–B1 N×P because of 31 Q×BP! when White will win the ending) 30 P–R5 P–N4 31 P×P ep P×P and Black's attack is very dangerous but White is better off than in the game.

29 ...	P–N4!
30 P×P	

30 N–R5 loses to 30 . . . Q–N3 with simultaneous threats on White's knight and QP. Against other knight moves Black replies simply 30 . . . N×P.

30 ...	P×N
31 P–B7	

If 31 P×P N×P etc.

31 ...	P×P
32 P×P	N–B6+
33 K–R1	N–K8!
34 K–N1	Q–B6
35 Q–KN5+	K–R1
36 Resigns	

Notes by Levy based on analysis by Vasyukov in THE CHESS PLAYER *and Roshal in* 64

79 Tal (USSR) – Radulov (Bulgaria)

This interesting ending can only be won by White if he can force the exchange of rooks at exactly the correct moment, i.e. in a position in which the opposite coloured bishops are insufficient to save Black. Before we see what actually happened in this game let us examine an example of the sort of opposite coloured bishop ending that might arise.

White: king at K4; bishop at Q3;

pawns at QR4, QN3, QB2, KB3, KN4, KR5

Black: king at K3; bishop at QB6; pawns at QR4, QN3, K4, KN4, KR3

White wins as follows: 1 B–B4+ K–B3 (if 1 . . . K–Q3 2 K–B5 K–K2 3 K–N6 B–Q5 4 K×RP K–B3 5 K–R7 etc.) 2 K–Q5 K–K2 3 B–Q3 B–Q5 4 K–B4 K–Q3 5 P–B3 B–K6 6 P–N4 B–Q7 (6 . . . P×P 7 P×P makes no real difference) 7 P×P P×P 8 B–R7 B–K8 9 B–N8 B–Q7 10 K–Q3 B–K8 11 P–QB4 K–K2 (or 11 . . . B–B7 12 K–K4 and 13 K–B5) 12 K–K4 K–B3 13 K–Q5 and the QBP promotes.

The difference between this example and the ending that arose in the game is that Black, in the game, has a pawn at Q5 instead of K4.

42 . . .	R–Q3
43 P–KN4!	B–N7
44 R–R2	B–B8
45 P–R5	P–KN4?

After 45 . . . P×P! 46 R×P B–N4, it is not clear that White can win.

46 R–K2

For the first time White can set about exchanging rooks, now that the pawn-structure has been fixed.

46 . . .	B–N7
47 R–K3	R–Q5
48 K–B2	B–B8
49 R–K1	B–Q7
50 R–Q1	B–B6
51 K–K3	B–N5
52 B–K2	B–B4

Black can defend in other ways but in the long run he cannot avoid the exchange of rooks.

53 R×R	P×R+

We have seen from the above example how White would win after 53 . . . B×R+.

54 K–K4!

At first sight the ending looks drawn. White cannot force anything on the Q-side and Black can defend the weaknesses on the K-side. How does White win?

The position is very interesting and instructive. Black's problem is that he wants to defend the pawn at Q5 with his bishop on QB4 but then his bishop has no moves and he can only move his king. By manoeuvering his king and bishop White first forces Black's king on to the back rank.

54 . . .	K–K3
55 B–B4+	K–B3

Or 55 . . . K–K2 56 K–B5 K–K1 57 K–N6 B–B1 58 K–B6! B–K2+ 59 K–N7 B–B1+ 60 K–N8 B–B4 (or 60 . . . K–K2 61 B–B7) 61 B–N5+ followed by 62 K–N7.

56 K–Q5	K–B2

Black can only move his king and he must keep White's king out of the key square KN6.

57 K–K5+	K–N2
58 B–Q5	K–R2
59 K–B6	B–B1

Black must come back to defend the KRP.

60 B–K4+	K–N1
61 K–N6	B–N2
62 B–Q5+	K–R1
63 B–K6	

63 K–B7 is a quicker way to win.

63 . . .	B–B1
64 B–B4	B–N2
65 K–B7	K–R2
66 B–Q3+	K–R1
67 B–K4!	

The key position of the ending. Black must move his bishop off the

KB1–KR3 diagonal and it is then unable to get back to QB4 in time.

67 ...   **B–K4**
68 K–K6   **B–N2**

Or 68 ... B–B5 69 K–Q5 B–K6 70 B–Q3 and 71 K–B6.

69 K–Q5!

By attacking the QP White prevents the manoeuvre ... B–B1–B4.

69 ...   **B–B3**
70 K–B6   **B–Q1**
71 K–Q7   **B–B3**
72 K–B7

White has realized his goal and there is no defence for Black.

72 ...   **B–K2**
73 K×P   **B–N5**

Here the game was adjourned for the second time but **Black resigned** without resuming. The most precise winning line for White is 74 K–N5 K–N2 75 K–B4 B–B6 76 P–N4! B×P 77 K×P K–B3 78 P–QB4 etc.

A very interesting ending which deserves close study.

Notes by Keres in 64 translated
by A. J. Whiteley

80 **Ivkov** (Yugoslavia) –
Lombard (Switzerland)
Queen's Indian Defence (by transposition)

1 P–QB4 N–KB3 2 N–QB3 P–K3 3 N–B3 P–QN3 4 P–KN3 B–N2 5 B–N2 B–K2 6 0–0 0–0 7 P–Q4 N–K5 8 Q–B2 N×N 9 Q×N P–Q3 10 P–N3 P–QB4 Korchnoy's line. Black plays against White's QP rather than for the control of the e4 square which has been the traditional positional theme of the Q.I.D. But it's normal to introduce it via 9 ... P–QB4 10 R–Q1 and only then ...

P–Q3. Lombard's move order gives White the opportunity to put his QR on Q1 and the other rook on K1. 11 B–N2 B–KB3 12 QR–Q1 Q–K2 13 Q–Q2 R–Q1 14 KR–K1! Threatening P–K4. Filip-Korchnoi, Siegen 1970 reached an identical position, but with White's Rooks on QR1 and Q1, so in that case it was impossible for White to play 14 KR–K1. Filip continued with the feeble 14 N–K1 B×B 15 N×B but then 15 ... N–B3 was more than adequate for Black. 14 ... B–K5 Reverting to the traditional play around e4, but it does not succeed here. After his inaccurate move order in the opening Black is already in difficulties. 15 N–R4! B×B 16 N×B N–B3 17 P–Q5 B×B 18 Q×B N–Q5. If Black captures on d5 White takes back with the rook. 19 N–R4 Cutting off some squares from Black's knight. 19 ... R–K1 20 Q–N1 Q–B3 21 P×P R×P With a permanent weakness in the black pawn-structure – but 21 ... P×P 22 P–K3 N–B4 23 N×N P×N leads to similar misfortunes. 22 P–K3 N–B6+ 23 N×N Q×N 24 R–Q5 R–B3 25 R–KB1 R–K1 26 Q–Q1! R/1–K3 27 Q×Q R×Q 28 R/1–Q1 R/6–B3 Passive defence is obligatory. If 28 ... R/3–B3 29 R×QP and White threatens mate. 29 R/1–Q3 K–B1 30 P–B4 R–K1 31 K–B2 R–R3 32 P–KR4 K–K2 33 P–K4 R–Q1 34 P–B5 Squeeze. 34 ... K–Q2 35 P–K5 K–B2 36 P–B6 P–KN4 Or 36 ... NP×P 37 R×QP R×R 38 R×R winning. 37 RP×P R–R7+ 38 K–B3 R×P 39 R×QP R×R 40 R×R R–QN7 41 P–K6! Just in time for the adjournment if . . . K×R the KP promotes on f8, so **Black resigns.** A game of no great theoretical importance, but an impressive example of what a Grandmaster of Ivkov's stature can achieve after one opening slip from the opponent.

Notes by Keene based on analysis by Gheorghiu in THE CHESS PLAYER

81 **Donner** (Holland) –
 Portisch (Hungary)

Nimzo-Indian Defence

1 P–Q4 N–KB3 2 P–QB4 P–K3 3 N–QB3 B–N5 4 P–K3 P–B4 5 B–Q3 N–B3 6 N–B3 Allowing Black to play Hübner's variation. 6 KN–K2 is more frustrating for Black. 6 . . . B×N+ Very much in fashion of late, but Donner believes in the White position. 7 P×B P–Q3 8 P–K4 P–K4 9 P–Q5 N–K2 10 N–R4 P–KR3 11 P–B3 Spassky's choice in his match with Fischer was 11 P–B4 but after . . . N–N3! he could make no progress. 11 . . . Q–R4 12 Q–B2 P–KN4 13 N–B5 Donner's own special variation. In recent games he has scored well against opponents who have captured on f5 with the QB (Donner-Damjanovic, Berlin 1971, Donner-Damjanovic Cienfuegos 1972, Donner-Garcia and Donner-Andersson Palma 1971 . . .) but Portisch varies. 13 . . . N×N 14 P×N B–Q2 15 P–KR4!? Perhaps first 15 P–N4 as Donner once played in a similar position v Langeweg. 15 . . . P–N5 16 P×P? 16 P–R5 Fixing Black's KRP as a target, deserved preference. 16 . . . N×NP 17 B–K2 R–KN1 18 B×N? As usual Donner heads

straight for an absolute refutation of his opponent's ideas, but in this case he has overlooked, or underestimated, the force of Black's 19th move. Much stronger was 18 0–0, although White's king is liable to come under pressure in the KN–file after 18 . . . P–B3! followed by . . . 0–0–0. **18 . . . R×B 19 B×P** The corollary to his previous move – but it's disastrous. **19 . . . B×P! 20 Q×B Q×BP+ 21 K–B2 Q–N7+ 22 K–K3 R×NP 23 Resigns.**

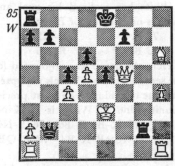

Notes by Keene based on analysis by Portisch in THE CHESS PLAYER

82 **Portisch** (Hungary) –
 Hug (Switzerland)

French Defence

1 P–Q4 P–K3 Hoping for a Dutch without wanting to risk the Staunton Gambit? 2 P–K4 P–Q4 3 N–Q2 N–KB3 4 P–K5 KN–Q2 5 P–KB4 P–QB4 6 P–B3 N–QB3 7 QN–B3 Q–R4 The latest word in this line. Black plans to rush forward his Q-side pawns to undermine the base (b2) of White's pawn-chain. 8 K–B2 P–QN4 9 B–Q3 P–N5 10 N–K2 N–N3! 11 P–KN4!?TN Portisch's improvement on the 11 B–Q2

of Matulovic-Korchnoi, Ohrid 1972.
11 . . . P–N3? Black goes astray at
once. This move creates a weakness
which White is quick to exploit. It
was better to carry on with the Q-
side offensive by means of 11 . . .
NP×P 12 NP×P N–R5! and Black
is probably no worse. **12 P–KR4
NP×P 13 NP×P P×P** Black
could try 13 . . . N–R5 here but
after 14 Q–K1 P×P 15 P×P
Q×Q+ 16 N×Q White still
retains the unpleasant threat of
P–R5. **14 P×P N–N5 15 B–N1
Q–R5 16 Q×Q+ N×Q 17 P–R3
N–B3 18 P–R5!** This ensures a
significant advantage in all lines –
e.g.: 18 . . . R–KN1 19 N–N5 or, as
played: **18 . . . P×P 19 R×P
B–QR3 20 B×P K–Q2 21 B–B2
R×R 22 P×R N–N3 23 P–B5
R–B1 24 P–B6** It's all over now.
Black must lose material to the
passed KRP. **24 . . . N–R4 25 N–K1
N–B3 26 B–Q3 B×B 27 N×B
N–R4 28 P–R6 N–N6 29 P–R7
B–R3 30 B×B N×R 31 N–B5+
Resigns.**

*Notes by Keene based on analysis by
Portisch in* THE CHESS PLAYER

83 Ghitescu (Rumania) –
Tringov (Bulgaria)

English Opening

**1 P–QB4 P–K4 2 N–QB3 N–KB3
3 N–B3 N–B3 4 P–KN3 B–N5
5 N–Q5** A good alternative is 5
B–N2 e.g: 5 . . . 0–0 6 0–0 R–K1
7 N–Q5 B–B1 8 P–Q3 P–KR3
9 N×N+ Q×N 10 N–Q2 as in
Petrosian-Gheorghiu, Moscow 1967.
**5 . . . P–K5 6 N–R4 0–0 7 B–N2
R–K1 8 0–0 B–B1 9 P–Q3 N×N**

**10 P×N P×P 11 Q×P N–K4
12 Q–B2 P–QB4 13 P–N3** with
advantage to White. Such positions
have occurred in several games
recently (Korchnoi-Ree, Wijk aan
Zee 1972; Gheorghiu-Hecht, Tees-
side 1972) and results have favoured
White, which suggests that the
system with 4 . . . B–N5 is not
entirely reliable. **13 . . . P–Q3 14
B–N2 N–N3 15 N×N RP×N
16 P–K4 P–R4 17 P–B4 P–R5
18 P–K5! B–B4 19 B–K4 RP×P
20 RP×P R×R 21 B×R Q–Q2
22 B×B Q×B 23 Q–K2 P–KN4
24 P–KN4 Q–Q2 25 BP×P P×P
26 Q–K4 P–N4** Or 26 . . . P–KN3
27 P–R4 followed by K–N2 and
P–R5. **27 P–N6 P×P 28 Q×NP
B–Q3 29 R–B6 R–Q1 30 R–K6
P–B5 31 B×P B×B 32 R×B
P×P 33 R–R5 R–KB1 34 Q–R7+
K–B2 35 R–B5+ K–K1 36 Q–R5+
R–B2 37 P–Q6 Q–R2+ 38 K–N2
P–N7 39 Q–R8+ Resigns.**

Notes by Keene

84 Gligoric (Yugoslavia) –
R. Garcia (Argentina)
King's Indian Defence (by
transposition)

1 P–Q4	**N–KB3**
2 P–QB4	**P–B4**
3 P–Q5	**P–K4**
4 N–QB3	**P–Q3**
5 P–K4	**P–KN3**

5 . . . B–K2 would stay in the
paths of the Czech Benoni.

6 B–K2	**QN–Q2**
7 N–B3	**B–N2**
8 0–0	**0–0**
9 B–N5	**P–KR3**
10 B–R4	**P–R3**

This looks dubious, since White

can now prevent . . . N–KR4.
However, it may just be playable.
Normal would be 10 . . . P–KN4
11 B–N3 N–R4 12 N–Q2 N–B5
with K-side counterplay.

11 N–Q2	Q–B2
12 P–QR3	N–R2
13 P–B3	QN–B3
14 P–QN4	P–N3
15 Q–N3	

Perhaps 15 R–N1 is better. It
looks impressive to spearhead the
attack along the 'b' file with the
queen but objectively it is more
effective to lead off with a rook.
Admittedly, White's queen does
reach QB6 by move 21 but four
moves later it is chased right back
to its starting square.

15 ...	N–R4
16 P×P	NP×P
17 KR–N1	N–N4
18 B–K1	N–B5
19 B–B1	P–B4
20 Q–N6	Q–K2

Of course, Black must retain
his queen in order to defend the
QP.

21 Q–B6	R–R2
22 R–N6	

The invasion commences in earnest
but Black is well placed to repel the
first wave.

22 ...	N–B2
23 Q–R4	N–R4
24 QR–N1	N–B3
25 Q–Q1	P–KR4
26 R/6–N2	B–R3
27 B–B2	R–QB2
28 Q–K1	P–B5?!

Was it necessary to release the
tension thus? Surely Black should
pursue a policy of enlightened in-
action. The text removes White's

worries about the K-side and permits
him to return to the charge on the
other wing.

29 N–R4	B–Q2
30 N–N6	B–K1
31 N–N3	P–N4
32 N–R5	N–Q1
33 N–R8	R–R2
34 R–N8	N–Q2
35 R–B8	B–N3

An intriguing position. White's
pieces have flooded into the vacuum
of Black's Q-flank, but it's still not
clear what targets they can assault.

36 N–N6	Q–B3
37 N–R4	

There is something quite remarkable about the whirlwind escapades
of the white knights raging in and
out of Black's Q-side – one feels,
perhaps, that Gligoric may have
been carried away by the sheer
mobility of his cavalry – rather like
a miser struck with fascination –
repeatedly running his hoard of
golden coins through his fingers.

37 ...	N–B2
38 R×R+	N×R
39 N–B6	R–R1
40 R–N7	

At last Gligoric begins to exploit
his garnered wealth for tangible
gains.

40 . . .	R–K1
41 N–N6	P–N5
42 B–K2	B–R2
43 N–Q7	N×N
44 R×N	B–N4

It was essential to play 44 . . . P×P.

45 P×P	B×P
46 P–KR4	P–B6
47 P×P	B×BP
48 P×B	N×P
49 B–K3	B×B
50 B×N	Q–B6
51 B–R4!	B×P
52 Q–B2	Resigns

Notes by Keene

85 **Bilek** (Hungary) – **Malich** (E. Germany)

King's Indian Attack

1 P–KN3 P–Q4 2 B–N2 P–QB3 3 P–Q3 N–B3 The most flexible course is 3 . . . P–KN3 followed by . . . B–N2 . . . P–K4 and the development of the KN on K2. **4 N–Q2 P–KN3 5 KN–B3 B–N2 6 0–0 0–0 7 P–K4** Reaching a Caro-Kann with 2 P–Q3 where Black has not deployed his pieces in the most effective manner. **7 . . . B–N5 8 R–K1 N–R3 9 P–K5 N–Q2 10 P–KR3 B×N 11 N×B** Threatening P–K6. **11 . . . N–B2 12 P–KR4!** Black doesn't really have much counter-play against this wing thrust since the White position does not present any tangible targets. **12 . . . P–KB4** Hoping to block the position, but White's reply leaves Black with a serious weakness on K3. **13 P×Pep P×P 14 B–B4 R–B2** Intending to cover the K3 square by means of . . . N–KB1. Gufeld prefers 14 . . . R–K1 15 B–R3

P–KB4 bringing the dormant KB to life. **15 Q–Q2 N–B1 16 B–R3 P–QR4** Looks pointless, but Black lacks squares in the centre for his pieces to undertake anything active. **17 P–R4 P–Q5** And this weakens more light squares. **18 B×N!** Exit one defender of K3. **18 . . . R×B 19 B–K6+ K–R1** 19 . . . N×B 20 R×N allows White to double on the K-file unopposed as 20 . . . R–K2 would lose the QP for nil compensation. **20 Q–B4 P–QB4 21 B–B4** Compare the respective power of the White and Black minor pieces. Black is hopelessly placed on the light squares and cannot contest the K-file. **21 . . . R–K2** . . . but he tries . . . **22 R×R Q×R 23 R–K1 Q–Q2 24 B–N5 Q–Q4 25 R–K7 R–B1 26 B–B4 Q–B3 27 N–K5! P–KN4** 27 . . . P×N 28 Q–B7 threatens 'n' different mates. **28 N–B7+ Resigns** A most attractive game by Bilek.

Notes by Keene

86 **Tal** (USSR) – **Timman** (Holland)

Modern Defence

1 N–KB3 P–KN3 2 P–K4 P–Q3 3 P–Q4 N–KB3 4 QN–Q2 B–N2 5 B–B4 0–0 6 Q–K2 P–B3 A playable alternative is 6 . . . N–B3 e.g: 7 P–Q5 N–N1 followed by . . . P–B3 or 7 . . . N–QR4 8 B–Q3 P–B4 which is unclear. After the text White can probably maintain a small plus. **7 B–N3** Forestalling . . . P–Q4. **7 . . . B–N5 8 P–K5! P×P 9 P×P N–Q4 10 0–0 N–Q2 11 P–KR3 B–B4?** After this retreat Black's QB gets in the way of his own pieces. The correct method of reducing White's advantage lay in 11 . . . B×N 12 N×B P–K3 trying to make a target of White's pawn on K5. **12 R–K1 Q–B2 13 N–B1 QR–Q1 14 N–N3 B–K3 15 Q–K4** Aiming for KR4 and KR7 – ultimately. **15 . . . KR–K1 16 Q–KR4 P–B3 17 B–R6 N×P?**

87
W

Now White strikes gold much sooner than he had expected. Black had to play 17 . . . N–B4. Incidentally, one beautiful variation concealed in this position is: 17 . . . B–R1 18 N–Q4 N–B4 19 N–K4! P–KN4 20 N×NP!+ – **18 R×N!** Indirectly smashing through to Black's KR2. **18 . . . P×R 19 N–N5 B–B3 20 N×B Resigns**

After 20 . . . B×Q 21 N×Q followed by N×R Black loses too much.

Notes by Keene based on analysis by Vasyukov in THE CHESS PLAYER

87 Knaak (E. Germany) – **Forintos** (Hungary)

Grünfeld Defence

1 P–Q4 N–KB3 2 P–QB4 P–KN3 3 N–QB3 P–Q4 4 N–B3 B–N2 5 B–N5 Nowadays it is more popular to play B–N5, if at all, on move four.

5 . . . N–K5 6 P×P N×B 7 N×N P–K3 A well known position. Normal now is 8 N–B3 P×P 9 P–QN4! with White's chances of a minority attack balancing Black's bishop pair. Instead Knaak embarks on a most perilous course which he must have examined before the game; from what follows it is clear that Forintos had examined it too! **8 Q–R4+?!** Winning a pawn at the expense of development. **8 . . . P–B3** Also playable is 8 . . . B–Q2 9 Q–N3 Q×N 10 Q×NP 0–0 with attacking prospects for the sacrificed material. **9 P×BP N×P 10 N–B3 B–Q2 11 0–0–0** This was Knaak's surprise. Previous theory (see Hartston's monograph on the Grünfeld) was 11 Q–Q1 0–0 12 P–K3 Q–N3 13 Q–Q2 P–K4 with excellent play for Black. **11 . . . 0–0!** **12 P–K3** Better is 12 Q–B2. **12 . . . N×P!**

88
W

And this was Forintos' surprise. A position is now reached by force in which White has two pieces for a rook, but the pieces are curiously cowed and the black rooks can pick off White's pawns at their leisure. Note that this combination did not work on move eleven, since Black's rooks lack co-ordination e.g: 11 . . . N×P? 12 R×N B×Q 13 R×Q+

R×R 14 N×B R–QB1+ 15 K–N1
P–QN4 16 N–B3 B×N 17 P×B
R×P 18 P–K3 K–K2 19 K–N2
P–N5 20 B–N5 KR–QB1 21 B–
R4! **13 R×N B×Q 14 R×R
KR×R 15 N×B QR–B1+ 16
N–B3 B×N 17 P×B R×P+ 18
K–N2 R1–Q/B1** winning. White
simply cannot organize his light
pieces for an adequate defence.
19 N–Q4 or 19 N–K1 R/QB6–B3
intending . . . R–QN3+. **19 . . .
P–K4 20 N–N3 R–B7+ 21 K–N1
R×BP 22 N–B1 P–K5 23 B–N5**
and **White Resigns**
There follows 23 . . . R/1–B7 24
B–R4 R–N7+ 25 K–R1 R×NP
with a Slaughter of the Innocents.
*Notes by Keene based on analysis by
Forintos in* THE CHESS PLAYER

88 **Jansa** (Czechoslovakia) –
Bisguier (USA)

English Opening

1 P–QB4	P–K4
2 N–QB3	N–KB3
3 N–B3	N–B3
4 P–KN3	B–N5

A favourite move of the American
Grandmaster. Its advantage is the
rapid development of Black's pieces,
on the other hand it somewhat
weakens the dark squares in Black's
rear.

5 B–N2

Also possible is 5 N–Q5!?, P–K5
6 N–R4. (ct. game 83)

5 . . .	0–0
6 0–0	P–Q3

After the game Petrosian -
Gheorghiu 1967 the continuation
6 . . . R–K1 7 N–Q5 B–B1 is con-

sidered as advantageous for White
because of 8 P–Q3 P–KR3 9
N×N+ Q×N 10 N–Q2! followed
by N–K4 and B3. With 6 . . . P–
K5?! my opponent had a bad
experience in his game against
Gheorghiu, Buenos Aires 1970: 7
N–KN5 B×N 8 NP×B R–K1
9 Q–B2 Q–K2 10 P–Q3! with a
better game for White

7 P–Q3	B×N
8 P×B	P–KR3?!

After the exchange of the black-
squared bishop . . . P–K5 was
necessary, now the above-mentioned
weakening of the dark squares will
prove almost the decisive factor.

9 P–K4!

White's plan is now clear: after
closing the centre an attack on the
K-side by means of P–B4.

9 . . .	N–K2
10 N–R4	P–KN4

Otherwise 11 P–B4.

11 N–B3	N–N3?

Provokes the following sacrifice;
Black could play . . . N–R2 here,
although after 12 P–B5 White has
an obvious advantage.

12 N×NP!	P×N
13 B×P	K–R2

Loses at once. 13 . . . P–B3 14
P–B4 Q–N3+ 15 P–QB5! leads to

the same result. The only defensive possibility was 13 . . . K–N2 14 P–B4 Q–K1 but even then the simple 15 P–KB5 is decisive.

14 P–B4	P×P
15 P×P	R–KN1
16 Q–K1!	

A simple decisive manoeuvre, Black has no defence against P–KB5.

16 . . .	Q K2
17 P–KB5	B–Q2
18 P×N+	R×P
19 Q–R4+	

and **Black resigned** because after 19 . . . K–N2 20 B×N+ R×B/3 21 Q–N5+ everything is dropping off. A severe defeat of the American Grandmaster who said after the game: 'This is my first loss in less than 20 moves!'

Notes by Jansa specially for this volume (Translation by Jana Hartston)

89 **Ciocaltea** (Rumania) – **Lombard** (Switzerland)

Sicilian Defence

1 P–K4	P–QB4
2 N–KB3	P–K3
3 N–B3	P–QR3
4 P–Q4	P×P
5 N×P	P–Q3
6 B–Q3	N–KB3
7 0–0	B–K2
8 P–B4	Q–B2
9 B–K3	P–QN4
10 Q–B3	B–N2
11 P–QR4	

For 11 N–N3 see game 60.

| 11 . . . | P–N5 |
| 12 N–N1 | |

Also possible is 12 N–K2 followed at some stage by N–KN3.

12 . . .	QN–Q2
13 N–Q2	0–0
14 P–N4	P–N3?!

Better is 14 . . . N–B4 15 P–N5 N/3–Q2 with chances for both sides. The text slows down White's plan of posting his queen and KR on the KR-file but it creates new weaknesses in Black's K-side.

| 15 P–N5 | N–K1 |
| 16 P–B5 | |

16 Q–R3 followed by P–B5 is possibly more accurate.

| 16 . . . | KP×P |
| 17 Q–R3 | Q–Q1! |

Not 17 . . . P×P? 18 N–K6!! P×N 19 Q×KP+ K–R1 20 Q×B winning immediately.

18 Q–R4

18 Q–R6? is answered by 18 . . . N–K4 threatening 19 . . . N–N5.

18 . . . P×P?

Inviting White's only inactive minor piece to join in the fun. 18 . . . P–B5! slows down White's attack.

| 19 N×P | P–Q4 |
| 20 N–KN3 | N–Q3 |

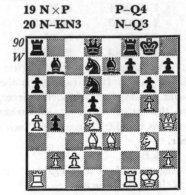

21 N/3–B5! N–K4

21 . . . P×N 22 N×P allows a quick mate (the threats include 23 Q–R6 as well as the more obvious 23 N×B+).

22 N–R6+	K–R1
23 N–K6!!	Q–Q2

If 23 . . . P×N 24 B–Q4 etc.

24 N–QB5	Q–B2
25 B–Q4	N–N4

If 25 . . . N–B4 26 R×N! B×N 27 R×N Q×R 28 B×B and White wins back the exchange to emerge a piece ahead.

26 N×BP+	K–N1

Since 26 . . . R×N 27 R×R leaves a mate *en prise* as well as the knight.

27 P×N	

27 B×P! would have won instantly. If the bishop is captured there is mate in one and if 27 . . . R×N 28 R×R the game doesn't last much longer.

But the text is good enough – Black's position is in shreds.

27 . . . R×N 28 R×R N×R 29 N×B Q×N 30 P×P Q–B1 31 R–KB1 N×P 32 Q–N3 B–B4 33 B×B Q×B+ 34 K–N2 Q–K2 35 Q–B4 N–B2 36 R–B2 R–R2 37 R–K2 Q–Q2 38 P–R3 R–B2 39 P–N3 R–R2 40 Q–N8+ K–N2 41 Q×P N–Q1 42 Q–Q4+ K–N1 43 R–K5 Resigns

Analysis by Ciocaltea in
THE CHESS PLAYER

90 **Gligoric** (Yugoslavia) –
   Kavalek (USA)

Modern Benoni

1 P–Q4	N–KB3
2 P–QB4	P–B4
3 P–Q5	P–K3
4 N–QB3	P×P
5 P×P	P–Q3
6 P–K4	P–KN3

7 N–B3	B–N2
8 B–K2	0–0
9 0–0	

The classical treatment is a great favourite with Gligoric suiting his basically sound, yet aggressive style.

9 . . .	R–K1
10 N–Q2	QN–Q2
11 P–QR4	

In the 3rd game of the Spassky–Fischer match White played 11 Q–B2 which was met by . . . N–R4!? The text move was already employed by Gligoric against Fischer at Palma 1970 with the continuation: 11 . . . N–K4 12 Q–B2 P–KN4!? Gligoric held the upper hand for some time and only lost after a gross blunder on his part.

11 . . .	N–K4
12 Q–B2	N–R4?!

Understandably Kavalek does not want to repeat 11 . . . P–KN4 which Gligoric must surely have subjected to a thorough examination in the intervening two years. However, the move of the text does not have quite the same effect as in the Fischer game, since White already has in P–QR4 which makes his 14th move possible.

13 B×N	P×B
14 N–Q1!	

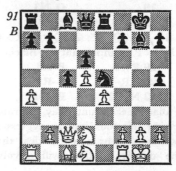

91
B

The point. As in Spassky–Fischer Black plans fluid piece play on the K-side with . . . Q–R5 . . . N–KN5 etc. – and Spassky countered this by means of (after 11 Q–B2 N–KR4 12 B×N P×B) the manoeuvre 13 N–B4 N–K4 14 N–K3 Q–R5 15 B–Q2 N–N5 16 N×N P×N when Black had a perfectly good position. Gligoric's idea is quite different. He exchanges his QN for Black's knight when it reaches g4, thus allowing his remaining KN to occupy a dominating post on c4. That is where White's P–QR4 comes in: he has already ensured control of his own QB4, so Black cannot answer 14 N–Q1 with . . . P–QN4.

14 . . .	**Q–R5**
15 N–K3	**N–N5**
16 N×N	**P×N**
17 N–B4	**Q–B3?**

Better is 17 . . . Q–K2! counter-attacking the White KP.

18 B–Q2!

Heading for QB3. As so often the exchange of dark-squared bishops in the Modern Benoni is of great benefit to White. In this case the exchange is doubly advantageous since Black's K-side pawns are rather loose and the KB is an important defensive piece.

18 . . .	**Q–N3**
19 B–B3	**B×B**

19 . . . Q×P 20 Q×Q R×Q 21 N×P is unpleasant for Black.

20 P×B	**P–N3**
21 KR–K1	**B–R3**
22 N–Q2	**R–K4**

Black seeks counterplay by transferring this rook into an aggressive position, but by now it is clear that the decisive action will revolve around White's efforts to advance his central pawn majority.

23 P–KB4	**P×P e.p.**
24 N×P	**R–R4**
25 Q–B2	**Q–B3**
26 R–K3	**R–K1**
27 QR–K1	**Q–B5**
28 P–K5!	

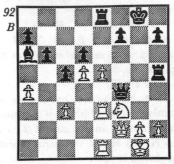

92
B

This advance not only creates a passed pawn but liberates White's pieces for a direct assault on the black king.

28 . . .	**P×P**
29 R–K4	**Q–B3**
30 Q–N3+	**K–R1**
31 N×P	

Threatening N×P+

31 . . .	**R–KN1**
32 R–KN4	

To weaken the opposition's back rank.

32 . . .	**R×R**
33 N×R	**Q–N3**
34 P–B4	

Creating the threat of Q–QB3+

34 . . .	**R–B4**
35 N–R6!	

In conjunction with R–K8+ this blow is decisive.

35 . . .	**R–B3**
36 R–K8+	**K–N2**
37 R–KN8+	**K×N**
38 Q–R4+	**Black resigns**

A theoretically important encounter.

Notes by Keene based on a contribution by Alberic O'Kelly

91 Bellon (Spain) – Padevsky (Bulgaria)

1 P–QN3

1 P–QN3 P–QB4 2 B–N2 P–Q4 3 P–K3 N–QB3 Can it be correct to permit White a Nimzo-Indian formation with colours reversed – and therefore an extra tempo? 4 B–N5 Q–N3 5 P–QR4 P–QR3 6 B–K2 A strange decision. 6 B×N+ looks more consistent with his previous moves. Now Black could have played 6 . . . P–K4 with a fine central establishment. 6 . . . N–B3?! 7 N–KB3 It is probably more accurate to preface this with P–KB4, given, that is, that White is striving for a Dutch set-up. 7 . . . P–K3 8 0–0 B–K2 9 P–Q3 0–0 10 QN–Q2 R–Q1 11 N–K5 B–Q2 12 Q–K1 Heading for KN3. White hopes to augment the pressure against Black's King along the QR1–KR8 diagonal. 12 . . . Q–B2 13 P–KB4 P–Q5 14 Q–N3! P×P 15 N×N B×N 16 B–K5 Q–N3?! Surely this leaves the queen badly stranded, but 16 . . . Q–Q2 17 N–B4 (–N6) is also unpleasant for Black. 17 N–B4 Q–R2 18 P–R5! Completing the incarceration. 18 . . . R–KB1 19 P–B5 There is really no defence to this. 19 . . . QR–K1 20 R–B4 P–KN3 21 Q–N5 KP×P Black has been reduced to such straitened circumstances that he is willing to surrender a whole piece in order to effect the exchange of White's QB – but White wants more than a piece. 22 Q–R6 B–Q1 23 B–N2 R–K3 24 R–R4 R/1–K1 25 R–KB1 B–K2 26 R×P! P×R 27 Q–N5+ K–R1 Nor is there any salvation in 27 . . . K–B1 28 R×P! 28 Q×P/f5 K–N1 29 Q–N5+ Resigns

In view of 29 . . . K–R1 30 R–N4 R–KN1 31 Q×R mate. A stunning defeat for the Bulgarian Grandmaster.

Notes by Keene

92 Uhlmann (East Germany) – Korchnoi (USSR)

English Opening

1 P–QB4 P–QB4 2 N–KB3 N–KB3 3 N–B3 P–Q4 4 P×P N×P 5 Q–R4+ N–B3 6 N–K5 Q–B2 The alternative 6 . . . B–Q2 leads to great complications. Since these complications begin as early as the sixth move it is fair to assume that Uhlmann had analysed them before the game. The analysis after 6 . . . B–Q2 might run: 7 N×P N×N 8 Q–QB4 (8 Q–KB4 is beautifully refuted by 8 . . . N–Q4 9 Q–B3 N–Q5 10 Q×N N–B7+ 11 K–Q1 N–K6+! 12 BP×N B–R5+) 8 . . . N–R4 9 Q–B4 N–Q4 10 Q–B3 Q–N3 11 N×R N–KB3 and the position is unclear. 7 N×N/5 On 7 N×N/6 N×N 8 NP×N B–Q2 with roughly equal chances. 7 . . . Q×N 8 N–N6 R–QN1 9 N×B R×N 10 P–K3 Q–Q4 Korchnoi considers 10 . . . P–KN3 stronger. It must be admitted, though, that Korchnoi often finds alternative continuations more attractive after the game. 11 Q–KN4 P–K3 12

P–QN3 P–KR4 **13 Q–R3** Usually,
when Uhlmann plays such a modest
move, it signals the beginning of an
original manoeuvre. But here 13
Q–QB4 was better. **13 . . . R–Q1
14 B–B4 Q–K4 15 R–QN1 Q–K5
16 R–N2** If 16 P–Q3 R×P! **16 . . .
B–K2 17 P–Q3 Q–N3 18 B–N5
0–0 19 B×N**

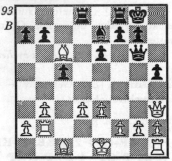

19 . . . Q×QP! 20 R–Q2 Even
more dangerous for White was 20
B–B3 P–B5 21 P×P B–N5+ 22
R×B Q–B6+ 23 K–K2 Q–B7+. **
20 . . . Q–B6 21 K–K2 P×B 22
R/1–Q1 R×R+ 23 B×R Q–B7
24 Q×RP R–Q1 25 Q–N4 Q×RP
26 Q–QR4 Q–B7 27 Q×RP B–B3
28 Q–R5 R–Q4 29 R–QB1 Q–Q6+
30 K–K1 P–B5 31 Q–N4 P–B4
32 Resigns**

*Notes by Roshal in 64 translated
specially for this volume by
Andrew Whiteley*

93 Uhlmann (East Germany) –
 Schmidt (Poland)

English Opening

1 P–QB4	**P–QB4**
2 N–KB3	**N–KB3**
3 N–B3	**P–Q4**
4 P×P	**N×P**
5 P–Q3	

This and White's next move are
not sufficiently active and they give
Black the chance to gain a strong
grip on the centre by employing a
system introduced into tournament
play by M. Botvinnik. The right
move was 5 P–KN3.

5 . . .	**N–QB3**
6 B–Q2	**P–K4**
7 P–KN3	**B–K2**
8 P–QR3	**N–B2**
9 B–N2	**P–B3**
10 R–QN1	**B–K3**
11 0–0	**Q–Q2**
12 Q–R4	**N–R3**

A better way to hold up White's
advance on the Q-side was 12 . . .
R–QN1 and if 13 P–QN4 P×P 14
P×P P–QN4 winning a pawn. Now
White could play 13 N–K4 0–0 14
KR–B1 with sufficient counterplay.
The position of Black's knight on R3
makes it more difficult for him to
strengthen his position by . . .
P–QN3.

The following manoeuvre of
White's knight to B2 is wrong. He
doesn't realize that his QB needs
protection.

13 N–K1	**R–QB1**
14 N–B2	**P–B5!**
15 B–K3	**P×P**
16 P×P	**N–B4**

16 . . . Q×P 17 B×RP 0–0 18
B–K3 N–B4 was also good for
Black.

17 B×N/5	**B×B**
18 N–K4	**B–K2**
19 P–QN4	**N–Q1**

The exchange of queens eases
White's problems. 19 . . . P–QN3
would have consolidated Black's
advantage.

20 Q×Q+	**B×Q**

21 QR–B1	N–K3
22 N–K3	N–Q5
23 R×R+	B×R
24 N–Q5	K–B2

Both of White's knights are centrally placed but Black's position is clearly preferable.

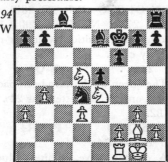

94
W

25 P–B4!

White can only save himself by active play.

25 ...	P×P

26 R–K1?

This continuation has a flaw and loses. After 26 N×P/B4 Black has nothing concrete. e.g. 26 ... R–Q1 27 N–B3 N–B7 28 N/4–Q5, and 28 ... N×RP fails to 29 R–R1.

26 ...	P–B6!

27 N×B | B–K3

28 B–R3

The last chance. If 28 ... B×B?? 29 N–Q6+ K–B1 30 N–N6+ mates. **28 ... N–K7+ 29 K–B2 B×B 30 N–Q5 R–Q1 31 N–K3 R×P 32 K×P N–Q5+ 33 K–B2 R×P 34 P–N4 P–KR4! 35 P×P N–N4 36 N–B4 R–Q6 37 N–N5+ K–B1 38 P–R6 P×P 39 N–K4 K–B2 40 R–K3 R×R 41 K×R B–N7 42 Resigns**

Notes by Boleslavsky in 64 translated specially for this volume by Andrew Whiteley

94 **Korchnoi** (USSR) – **Ciocaltea** (Rumania)

King's Indian Defence

In this Olympiad the Soviet team had its least successful result ever. Right up to the last round it was not certain that we would win. The decisive last round was played in circumstances of the utmost tension. We were only half a point ahead of the Hungarians and we had to play the powerful Rumanian team. It is true that the Hungarians were paired against the no less powerful West Germans but at the beginning of the round it was seen that the Germans had left their two Grandmasters out of the team.

(One can sympathize with the Russians for being displeased at the team fielded by the West Germans. But the Germans had their reasons. By not playing, Hübner was assured of the first board prize. By playing against Portisch, Pfleger had a chance to gain the Grandmaster title by winning – which he nearly succeeded in doing. AJW)

In this last round I was playing against the strong master Ciocaltea.

1 P–Q4	N–KB3
2 P–QB4	P–KN3
3 N–QB3	B–N2
4 P–KN3	0–0
5 B–N2	P–Q3
6 N–B3	N–B3
7 0–0	B–N5

At the Olympiad at Lugano in 1968 Ciocaltea played against me 7 ... P–QR3 8 P–KR3 R–N1 9 B–K3 P–QN4 but lost without a struggle. This time he follows a different path.

8 P–Q5   N–QR4

It is well known that after 8 . . . B×N 9 P×B White has a clear advantage.

9 P–N3   P–B4

Of course Black cannot play 9 . . . N×QP 10 N×N B×R 11 B–Q2 or 11 B–R6 with advantage to White. But 9 . . . P–B3 is interesting.

10 B–N2   P–QR3

11 N–Q2   R–N1

12 Q–B2   P–QN4

13 KR–K1

Even more energetic was 13 QR–K1.

13 . . .   Q–B2

14 N–Q1   R–N2?

The right move was 14 . . . P–K4. By playing the rook to N2 Black loses the possibility of active play in the centre and finds himself in a difficult position.

15 B–QB3   KR–N1

16 P–B4   P×P

17 P×P   N–K1

18 N–B2   B–Q2

19 N–Q3   R–R2

Black's rooks can achieve nothing on the QN-file as White's minor pieces control all points of entry.

20 B×B

After 20 P–K4 I thought 20 . . . B–Q5+ followed by 21 . . . P–K4 would be unpleasant.

20 . . .   N×B

21 Q–B3

But now 21 P–K4 was worth considering.

21 . . .   N–N2

Better was 21 . . . N–B4 22 P–K3 N–QN2, slowing down White's attack as it is no easy task to dislodge the knight from KB4.

22 P–K4   Q–R4

23 Q–N2   R/2–R1

This rook has taken four moves to return to its original square. This proves that Black's opening strategy must have been wrong!

24 N–N3

Another possibility was 24 KR–N1 N–Q1 25 Q×R R×Q 26 R×R Q×N 27 R×N+ B–K1 28 B–B1, leading to a position which is not entirely clear.

24 . . .   Q–Q1

The queen would have been badly placed on R5 but better was 24 . . . Q–B2.

25 Q–B3   P–QR4

26 P–QR4

A critical move. White reduces Black's counterplay on the Q-side at the price of putting this pawn on a square where it is weak.

26 . . .   Q–B2

After 26 . . . Q–K1 27 P–K5 B×P 28 N–Q2 N–B4 29 N–K4, White loses a pawn but gets very powerful play in the centre of the board.

27 N–Q2   N–Q1

28 P–R3!?

Black is cramped and cannot undertake anything active on either side of the board. White has no quick way of realizing his advantage. At the board I thought at first that it would be best to exchange a pair of rooks and then prepare for the advance P–K5 supported by minor pieces. Another plan, recommended by T. Petrosian, is worth considering: B–B3, B–Q1, B–B2, N–KB1, N–K3 followed by P–K5 or P–B5.

But in the heat of the last round I opted for an energetic (and premature!) advance in the centre and on the K-wing.

It is worth mentioning that after 28 B–B3 (threatening 29 P–N4) 28 . . . P–R4 29 P–B5 really would have been strong.

28 . . .	**P–R4**
29 P–B5?	**P×P**

The threat was 30 P–B6.

30 P–K5	**R–R2**
31 N–B4	**R/2–N2**

A mistake. After 31 . . . P×P 32 R×P Q–Q3 it would be very difficult for White to penetrate Black's defences and his own position would be rather precarious.

32 P–K6!	**P×P**

This time 32 . . . B–K1 was best. Now White's attack is irresistible.

33 P×P	**B–B3**
34 B–Q5	**R–N7**
35 R–KB1	**Q–N2?**

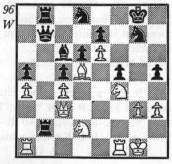

The final mistake. 35 . . . B–K1 was necessary.

36 N×P!	**N×N**
37 R×P	**N–B3**
38 R–N5+	**K–R1**

If 38 . . . K–R2 39 Q–Q3+ or 38 . . . K–B1 39 R–KB1 R×N 40 R×N+ P×R 41 Q×BP+ Q–KB2 (41 . . . N–B2 42 Q–N7+) 42 P–K7+ and mates.

39 R–KB1	**R×N**
40 Q×R	

Better than 40 R×N Q–N8+ 41 R–B1+ R–Q5 and Black is still fighting.

40 . . .	**Resigns**

Notes by Korchnoi in 64 translated specially for this volume by Andrew Whiteley

95 Olsson (Sweden) – **Smyslov** (USSR)

Sicilian Defence

1 P–K4	**P–QB4**
2 N–KB3	**P–K3**
3 P–Q4	**P×P**
4 N×P	**P–QR3**
5 P–QB4	

This move gives White a solid game and at one time seemed to be a serious threat to the Paulsen system. But a number of satisfactory ways were found to strengthen Black's defence and now the moves 5 B–Q3 and 5 N–QB3 are more common.

5 . . .	**N–KB3**
6 B–Q3	**N–B3**
7 N–B2	

Black also gets a good position after the continuation 7 N×N QP×N 8 0–0 P–K4.

7 . . .	**P–Q4!**

If Black can make this important advance safely and break the bind created by White's pawns on QB4 and K4 he can count on solving his opening problems.

8 KP×P	P×P
9 0-0	B-K2
10 B-B4	0-0
11 N-B3	B-K3
12 P×P?	

The exchange of pawns helps Black's development and gives him a dangerous initiative. White should have played 12 Q-K2.

12 ...	N×P
13 N×N	Q×N
14 Q-K2	B-B3
15 KR-Q1	Q-QR4

The only reply, but quite satisfactory. 15 . . . Q-QB4 was bad because of 16 B-Q6.

16 N-R3	KR-K1!
17 Q-K4	Q-R4

The manoeuvre of the queen from one flank to another is very effective. Now White is in serious difficulties.

97
W

18 R-Q2	B×RP

An important material gain. White loses a pawn since if 19 Q× RP+ Q×Q 20 B×Q+ K×B 21 R×B R-K8 mate.

19 Q-B5	Q×Q

20 B×Q	N-Q5
21 N-B2!	

Olsson defends himself resourcefully in a difficult position. If 21 . . . N-N6 22 R×B N×R 23 B×N QR-Q1 24 B-K1 White successfully counters Black's threats.

21 ...	N×B
22 R×B	N-Q5
23 K-B1	QR-B1

Black increases his pressure by attacking White's first rank.

24 N-K3	R-B8+
25 R-Q1	R×R+
26 N×R	N-B7

The ending is won for Black thanks to his extra pawn and active pieces. He begins to organize pressure against White's QNP.

27 N-K3	N-N5
28 R-R3	N-B3
29 B-B7	B×P
30 R-N3	B-Q5

In this way Black maintains his material advantage. If 31 R×P B×N 32 P×B R-K2 and the pin is very unpleasant. Black threatens simply to advance his passed RP.

31 N-B5	P-QN4
32 R-QR3	R-R1
33 R-Q3	B-B3
34 R-Q6	N-K4
35 N-K3	N-B5

The most accurate continuation. Black gives back one of his extra pawns but simplifies the position by the exchange of the knight.

36 N×N	P×N
37 B-R5	

37 R-B6 was no good either because of 37 . . . R-QB1 38 R×RP B-N7 39 K-K2 P-B6 40 R-B6 P-B7 41 R×P B-K4 and wins.

37 ...	R-QB1

38 R×P	P–B6
39 K–K2	P–B7
40 B–Q2	B–N7
41 Resigns	

Notes by Smyslov in 64 translated specially for this volume by Andrew Whiteley

96 Gligoric (Yugoslavia) –
Andersson (Sweden)

Slav Defence

**1 P–Q4 N–KB3 2 P–QB4 P–B3
3 N–QB3 P–Q4 4 N–B3 P×P 5
P–QR4 B–B4 6 P–K3 P–K3 7
B×P B–QN5 8 0–0 0–0 9 Q–K2
QN–Q2 10 P–K4 B–N3 11 B–Q3
R–K1 12 P–K5 N–Q4 13 B–Q2
B–K2 14 N×N!** Spassky-Petrosian, 7th match game 1969 continued 14 B×B BP×B 15 Q–K4 but the text is stronger and assures White a lasting initiative. **14 . . . BP×N 15 B×B BP×B 16 Q–N5! N–N3 17 P–QN3** If 17 P–R5 N–B5 Black has good counterplay for a pawn. **17 . . . P–QR3 18 Q–Q3 N–Q2 19 KR–B1 N–N1?!** Slightly dubious, though it is difficult to find a constructive plan for Black. **20 P–QN4 N–Q2 21 P–R5 N–B1 22 P–N5 Q–Q2 23 QR–N1 KR–B1 24 R×R Q×R 25 Q–N3 B–Q1 26 P×P R×P 26 . . . P×P 27 Q–N7!** would be worse. Even after the ensuing simplifications, Black's weaknesses at K3 and KN2 give him problems in the ending. **27 Q×NP Q×Q 28 R×Q B×P 29 B×B**

**R×B 30 P–R4 R–R5 31 P–N3
P–R3 32 K–N2 R–B5 33 K–B1
R–B1 34 N–Q2 R–Q1 35 N–N3
R–Q2 36 R–N8 K–B2 37 N–B5
R–R2 38 N–N7 K–N1 39 N–Q6
R–R5 40 R–N7 R×P 41 N–K8
R–K5 42 R×P+ K–R1 43 P–B4
R–R5 44 R–K7!** Stronger than 44 R–KB7 K–N1 45 R–K7 N–R2 and Black has some chances of hanging on. **Black resigns** White follows up with 45 N–B6 and then penetrates decisively with his king.

Notes by Gligoric

97 Liebert (E. Germany) –
Tal (USSR)

King's Indian Defence

1 N–KB3 N–KB3 2 P–B4 P–KN3
3 P–KN3 B–N2 4 B–N2 0–0 5 0–0
P–Q3 6 P–Q4 N–B3 7 N–B3 B–
N5 8 P–KR3 B×N 9 B×B N–Q2
10 P–K3 P–K4 11 P–Q5 N–K2
12 P–K4 P–KB4 13 B–N2 N–KB3
14 P×P P×P 15 P–B4 N–Q2 16
K–R2 N–KN3 17 B–K3 K–R1 18
Q–Q2 P×P 19 P×P Q–R5 20
QR–K1 R–B2 21 N–K2 R–KN1
22 N–Q4 N/Q2–K4!! 23 P×N
B×P+ 24 K–N1 Q–N6 25 N–B3
N–R5 26 N×N Q–R7+ 27 K–B2
B–N6+ 28 K–B3 B×N 29 B–Q4+
B–B3 30 Q–KB2 B–K4 31 R–KR1
Q–B5+ 32 K–K2 Q×B 33 Q×Q
B×Q 34 B–B3 R–N6 35 P–N3
B–B4 36 R/K1–KB1 R–K2+ 37
K–Q2 R–K6 38 B–Q1 R–N7+
39 K–B1 R–QB6+ 40 K–N1 B–R6
White resigns.

FUTURE WORLD CHAMPIONS?

In the Olympiad at Siegen in 1970 the participation of the then World Champion Boris Spassky plus his most likely challenger (and present champion) Bobby Fischer formed the main attraction. At Skopje neither of these two was present, and naturally this lessened the spectator appeal of the whole event to a certain extent. However, there were present three young Grandmasters whom many experts regard as potential world champions – there were the West German top board – Robert Hübner – who gained the individual gold medal on board one – the dashing Yugoslav Lubomir Ljubojevic and Anatoly Karpov of the USSR – who also made the best scores on their respective boards.

In this section we examine a selection of games played by these youthful prospects. Their games form a pleasing set of contrasts – the subtle polished power of Karpov's style; the violent invention of Ljubojevic – and the grim determination of Hübner. We have attempted to give a representative choice of games covering the highpoints and the setbacks of these various virtuosos. The only drawback to this method – Hübner did not lose a single game!

Which of this trio – if any – do you think will wrest the crown from King Bobby? Hübner – the realistic individual? Karpov – the protégé of the Soviet machine or the charismatic Ljubojevic?

98 **Ljubojevic** (Yugoslavia) –
　　Ribli (Hungary)

Sicilian Defence

98 W

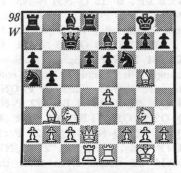

1 P–K4 P–QB4 2 N–KB3 N–QB3
3 P–Q4 P×P 4 N×P N–B3 5
N–QB3 P–Q3 6 B–QB4 Q–N3 7
N/4–K2 P–K3 8 B–N3 B–K2 9
0–0 0–0 10 B–N5 N–QR4 11 N–N3
Q–B2 12 Q–Q2 P–QR3 13 QR–
Q1 R–Q1   14 KR–K1 P–N4 (*98*)
15 N–B5! P×N 16 B×N N×B
17 RP×N B×B 18 N–Q5 Q–Q2
19 N×B+ P×N 20 Q–R6! B–N2
21 R–Q3 P–B5! 22 Q×P/B4 K–B1
23 Q×BP Q–K3 Not 23 . . . Q–
K2?? 24 Q–R8 mate. **24 Q–R8+
K–K2   25 Q×P** Restoring the
material balance at last. **25 . . .**
R–R1 26 Q–B5 Q×Q 27 P×Q+
K–Q2   28 R/3–K3 QR–K1   29
R×R R×R 30 R×R K×R 31
P–KB3 K–K2 32 K–B2 K–B3 33
P–KN4 P–Q4! 34 P–N4 If 34 P–B3
P–N5 35 P×P? P–Q5 and Black
wins with ease. **34 . . . P–Q5! 35
K–N3 K–N2   36 K–B4 P–B3!**

Draw Agreed It is impossible for White to make any progress. If 37 P–R4 B–B3 38 P–N5 B–N2.

Analysis by Gheorghiu in
THE CHESS PLAYER

99 **Schaufelberger** (Switzerland) – **Ljubojevic** (Yugoslavia)

Modern Defence

1 P–QB4 P–KN3 2 N–QB3 B–N2 3 P–Q4 P–Q3 4 P–K4 N–Q2 5 B–K2 P–K4 6 N–B3 P–B3!? Given that Black wants to play a KID without obstructing his KBP this is a very bright idea. Canadian Masters (Suttles/Day) have experimented with 6 . . . N–R3?! here, but after 7 P–KR4 Black's position looks grismold. The point of the text – which is quite useful in itself – since White's P–Q5 can always be bypassed with . . . P–QB4 – is that White has no useful waiting move which both prevents 7 . . . N–KR3 while still retaining the option of playing the embarrassing thrust P–KR4. **7 0–0** Probably best. If 7 B–K3 N–R3 8 P–KR4?! N–N5! followed by . . . P–KR4. **7 . . . N–R3 8 P–Q5?** Releasing the tension thus must be wrong. 8 R–N1 looks like an improvement which will have to be analysed. Personally, I suspect that Black's position will stand up even after this. **8 . . . P–QB4 9 R–N1 0–0 10 B–Q2 P–B3** Creating a haven for the knight on B2, whence it will discourage White from playing N–KN5 as a reply to . . . P–KB4. **11 N–K1** Now N–KN5 is no longer on, so . . . **11 . . . P–B4** and already Black is better. Amazingly the game only lasts another eleven moves! **12 N–Q3**

N–N3 13 N–B1 13 P–QN3 must be better than this. The charisma strikes again. **13 . . . P×P 14 N×P B–B4 15 P–B3 B×N!** Normally this would be considered positional treason but in this case Black is operating with tempo and the initiative is all important. **16 P×B Q–R5 17 B×N B×B 18 Q–Q3 R×R+ 19 B×R R–KB1 20 N–N3 Q–B7+ 21 K–R1 N–R5**

White's position has been surrounded. If one could legitimately compare chess games with battles this one would remind me of Napoleon's victory at Ulm where the army of the Austrian General Mack was encircled, and surrendered with hardly a shot being fired. **22 Q–K2 P–N3** and no more shots were fired. **23 Resigns** What could happen: 23 P–KR3 Q–N6 24 Q–N4 Q×Q 25 P×Q R–B7. Does it strike you that Ljubojevic's opponents often seem quite relieved to resign?

Notes by Keene

100 **Holm** (Denmark) – **Ljubojevic** (Yugoslavia)

Benoni

1 P–Q4 N–KB3 2 P–QB4 P–K3 3 N–KB3 P–B4 4 P–K3 B–K2

5 N–B3 0–0 6 P–Q5! Black's opening play is provocative and dubious too, of course, but that is all part of the charisma. **6 . . . P×P 7 P×P P–Q3 8 N–Q2 R–K1 9 B–K2 N–R3 10 0–0 N–B2 11 P–K4 B–Q2 12 P–QR4 P–QR3 13 P–B4 B–KB1 14 B–B3 R–N1 15 P–KN4 P–R3 16 P–R3** Gheorghiu recommended 16 P–N5 P×P   17 P×P N–R2   18 P–R4 as slightly better for White. Holm plays aggressively for a while, then falters, mixes his plans and succumbs. **16 . . . P–QN4 17 P×P P P×P 18 P–N4?** There is no justification for this gratuitous act of violence. **18 . . . P×P 19 N–K2 R–R1 20 B–QN2 R–R5 21 N–KN3 P–N3 22 N–N3 B–N2 23 Q–Q2 N–R1 24 P–K5 N–R2 25 KR–K1 N–N3 26 Q–B1 N–B5! 27 R×R N×B! 28 R×P N–Q6 29 Q–Q2 N×R/K8 30 Q×N P×P 31 P–B5** or 31 P×P R R×P 32 R–K4 N–N4. **31 . . . N–N4 32 B–N2 B–KB1! 33 Resigns** White's position is in total disarray.

Notes by Keene

101 **Ljubojevic** (Yugoslavia) – **Zuidema** (Holland)

1 P–QN3

1 P–QN3 P–Q4 2 B–N2 N–KB3 3 P–K3 P–K3 4 P–KB4 P–B4 5 N–KB3 N–B3 6 B–N5 B–Q2 I thought such defensive systems against the early Q-side fianchetto for White went out of fashion after Nimzowitsch's victories against Rubinstein and Spielmann. Evidently not. **7 0–0 B–K2 8 P–QR4 0–0 9 N–K5 N×N 10 P×N N–K1 11 B–Q3!** B–QB3 Black

could have played 11 . . . P–B4 since it's by no means clear that 12 P×P ep B×P 13 Q–R5 P–KN3 14 B×BP P×B 15 Q×NP+ B–N2 16 R×R+ K×R is any good for White. **12 Q–N4 P–KN3 13 N–B3 N–N2 14 R–B4 P–B5?** Losing a pawn for nothing. Black doesn't even try to make a fight of it. **15 P×P P P×P 16 R×QBP Q–R4 17 N–K4 B×N 18 Q×B N–B4** If 18 . . . Q×QP? 19 B–B3. **19 B–B3 Resigns.**

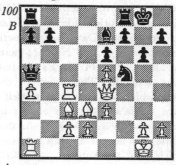

A rout.

Notes by Keene

102 **Ljubojevic** (Yugoslavia) – **Smyslov** (USSR)

Larsen's Opening

Despite the immense energy displayed by Ljubojevic in the majority of his games his play still seems to lack a certain solidity – at the highest level of course. This flaw in his style is exemplified by his bad score against the mighty Smyslov.

1 P–QN3	**N–KB3**
2 B–N2	**P–QN3!**

At Palma de Mallorca last year I (as Black) had to face Larsen who employed this very system against me. In reply I elaborated a defence based on the fianchetto of both bishops plus occupation of the centre with pawns on c5 and d5. However, at a crucial stage Larsen was able to maintain good chances by playing N-K5. (Larsen-Keene, Palma de Mallorca 1971: 1 P-QN3 P-Q4 2 B-N2 N-KB3 3 P-K3 P-KN3 4 P-KB4 B-N2 5 N-KB3 0-0 6 B-K2 P-B4 7 0-0 P-N3 8 P-QR4 N-B3 9 N-K5! B-N2 10 B-KB3 R-B1 11 P-Q3 N-Q2 12 P-Q4)

In this game Smyslov adopts essentially the same strategy as I did at Palma, but he cunningly delays ... P-Q4 thus eliminating the possibility of N-K5 by White for some time to come.

3 P-KB4

In spite of my game with Larsen I must say that I have never been able to trust such systems for White which involve an early P-KB4. To me this move seems awfully weakening.

3 ...	B-N2
4 P-K3	P-N3
5 N-KB3	B-N2
6 B-K2	P-B4
7 0-0	0-0
8 P-QR4	N-B3
9 N-R3	

Here 9 N-K5 would be pointless since Black can eject the piece with ... P-Q3.

9 ...	P-Q4

Only now. If 10 N-K5 Black has ... P-Q5 which wasn't possible in my game with Larsen.

10 Q-K1	P-K3

To parry 11 Q-R4 with ... N-K5.

11 N-K5

Maybe 11 P-Q3 is better.

11 ...	P-Q5!

(c.f: note to move 9) In principle the execution of such an advance should confer an advantage on Black. Ljubojevic now seeks for special tactical circumstances which will demonstrate the contrary.

12 B-KB3	N-Q4
13 P × P	N × QP
14 B × N/d4	P × B
15 Q-K4	

Winning Black's QP, but Black has enormous counterplay based on: (i) the bishop pair (ii) the open c file (iii) the exiled White knight at a3 (iv) the weakness of White's K-side.

15 ...	B-QR3
16 KR-K1	

Another possibility which also grants Black dynamic counterplay is 16 QN-B4 P-Q6 17 P-B3 R-B1 – a line pointed out by Vasiukov.

16 ...	Q-B2
17 Q × QP	QR-Q1
18 P-N3	KR-K1!

Not only a powerful centralization but also the prelude to a threat which Ljubojevic completely overlooks.

19 QR-Q1?

After this White is losing, but in mitigation it must be confessed that his position is already very difficult.

19 K–R1 was suggested as an improvement but it doesn't look particularly trustworthy. 19 Q–N2 – removing the queen from its exposed central position – loses to the following fine combination: 19 . . . N×P! 20 P×N Q–B4+ 21 K–R1 R×P threat . . . Q–B7; and now (i) 22 R–KN1 Q–B7 23 R–N2 (23 B–N2 B–N2!) 23 . . . Q×B! 24 N ×Q B×Q (ii) 22 KR–Q1 (22 QR–Q1? Q–B7!) 22 . . . R/1–Q1 23 R×R R×R 24 R–KN1 Q–B7 25 R–N2 R–Q8+! 26 B×R Q–B8+ 27 R–N1 B–N2+ 28 B–B3 B×B+ 29 N×B Q×N+ 30 R–N2 B×Q. (Analysis by Vasyukov)

I don't think Smyslov calculated much of this during the game. He knew 19 Q–N2 N×P! won for Black. Smyslov's own notes in *64* stop after 21 . . . R×P and state that Black wins.

19 . . .   B–KB1!

Threatening . . . B×N and . . . B–B4. The only possible resistance, pointed out by Smyslov, lay in: 20 K–N2 (20 Q–N2 Q–B4+) 20 . . . B×N 21 N–N4 B–KB1 22 B×N but then comes 22 . . . B–KN2 23 Q–K4 R×B 24 Q×R B–N2.

What follows now is slaughter.

20 P–QN4	**B×P**
21 Q–R1	**Q–B4+**
22 P–Q4	**Q–B6**
23 Q×Q	**B×Q**
24 N–N5	**B×R**
25 R×B	**B×N**
26 P×B	**N–B2**
27 B–B6	**R–K2**
28 P–B3	**P–QR3**
29 B–N7	**N×P**
30 B×P	**N–R2**
31 R–N1	**P–QN4**

32 B×P	**R–N2**
33 B–Q3	**R×R+**
34 B×R	**N–N4**
35 P–B4	**N×P**
White resigns	

Notes by Keene

103 **Hübner** (W. Germany) – **Jansson** (Sweden)

English Opening.

1 P–QB4	**P–K4**
2 N–QB3	**N–KB3**
3 P–KN3	**B–N5**
4 N–B3	**P–K5**
5 N–Q4	**0–0**

5 . . . N–B3 deserved consideration, as in the similar position (with colours reversed) from the Nimzowitsch Sicilian.

6 B–N2	**R–K1**
7 Q–B2	**B×N**
8 QP×B	

Capturing towards the centre looks more normal, but the text allows White rapid mobilization leading to increased control of the dark squares, which Black relinquished with 7 . . . B×N.

8 . . .	**P–KR3**
9 B–B4	**P–Q3**
10 0–0–0	

An unprejudiced move. White threatens P–B5.

10 . . .	**N–B3?**

Questionable, since White can now force a dark-squared blockade of the entire Black position. 10 . . . Q–K2 was preferable, avoiding the coming manoeuvre.

11 N×N	**P×N**
12 P–B5!	

Forcing Black into a rigid posture.

12 ...   P–Q4
13 Q–R4

Heading for a centralized post on d4.

13 ...   B–Q2
14 P–KR3

14 Q–R5 N–N5 would cede Black excessive counterplay.

14 ...   P–QR4
15 P–KN4   Q–K2
16 Q–Q4   R–R2
17 P–B3   R–N2
18 P–KR4   B–B1

Black is held in a dark-square vice and the factor of major significance is the mobility of White's K-side pawns. Their advance (leading to line-clearance for White's rooks) eventually decides the game.

19 P–N5   RP×P
20 RP×P

The obvious recapture, but later it was criticized by Hübner who felt that the most consistent course (and the most clear-cut) would have been: 20 B×NP Q–K4 21 Q×Q R×Q 22 B×N P×B 23 P–KB4! (23 P×P? P–B4!) 23 . . . R–K1 24 P–K3 and White has virtually an extra pawn.

20 ...   N–R2
21 P–N6

There is no point in doubling on the KR file: 21 R–R4 B–B4 22 QR–R1 KR–N1 and Black has surmounted his problems.

21 ...   N–B3!

And not 21 . . . BP×P 22 P×P P×P 23 Q–B4+ Q–K3 24 Q×Q+ B×Q 25 B×KP winning.

22 NP×P+   K×P
23 B–N5   B–B4
24 QR–B1   P–K6?

Better was 24 . . . Q–K4. The text frees White's hand for action.

25 B–R3   B–N3
26 R/B1–N1   Q–K4

Black has two major alternatives: (i) 26 . . . KR–QN1 27 P–N3 R×P? 28 P×R R×P 29 B×P and White is out of danger.
(ii) 26 . . . R–N4 27 B×N Q×B (27 . . . P×B 28 R×B! K×R 29 B–B5+!) 28 B–Q7 KR–QN1 29 P–N3 P–R5 30 Q×Q+ P×Q 31 R–R6 P×P 32 R/R×B P×P 33 R–N7+ K–B1 34 R–N8+ K–K2 35 R/1–N7 finis.

This complex variation is typical of the amount Hübner sees during a game. Note, incidentally, the significance of B–Q7 in this variation. This move serves a dual purpose: (a) restricting the movement of Black's king; (b) menacing the front doubled pawn on c6. The idea of B–Q7 recurs in the game.

27 B×N   Q×B
28 B–Q7!   KR–QN1
29 P–N3   Q×Q
30 P×Q   R–N5

If Black resorts to 30 . . . P–R5 we can see just how useful a move was 28 B–Q7: 30 . . . P–R5 31 B×P P×P 32 B×P+ K–B3 33 B×P R×B 34 P×R R×P 35 R×B+ K×R 36 K–B2 R–R6 37

R–R4 followed by R–K4 and White wins.

31 R–R4

Preparing to chop up Black's king.

31 . . .   R–B5+

This looks alarming but it achieves nothing concrete.

32 K–N2   R–B7+
33 K–R3   R–Q1

Now White no longer has any problems, but 33 . . . R × KP 34 R–B4+ K–K2 35 B × P followed by R × NP+ is equally miserable for Black.

34 R–B4+	**K–K2**
35 B × P	**B–K1**
36 R × P+	**K–K3**
37 B × B	**R × B**
38 R/N–B7	**R–K2**
39 R/4–B6+	**K–Q2**
40 P–B6+	**K–Q1**
41 R–B8+	**Resigns**

After 41 . . . R–K1 42 R × R+ K × R 43 R–K6+ White picks up the KP.

Notes by Keene based on comments by Hübner for THE CHESS PLAYER

104 Hübner (W. Germany) – **Petrosian** (USSR)

Sicilian Defence

1 P–K4	**P–QB4**
2 N–KB3	**P–K3**
3 P–Q4	**P × P**
4 N × P	**P–QR3**
5 B–Q3	**Q–B2**
6 0–0	**N–KB3**
7 K–R1	

Normal is 7 B–K3.

7 . . .	**N–B3**
8 N × N	**NP × N**
9 P–KB4	**P–Q4**

10 N–Q2	**B–K2**
11 P–QN3	

Better is 11 P–B4 when White has a slight advantage.

11 . . .   P–B4!

Attempts to take immediate advantage of White's dark squared weaknesses accomplish nothing: 11 . . . B–N5 12 B–N2 Q–R4 13 R–B2, and now both 13 . . . B × N 14 B × N and 13 . . . B–B6 14 B × B Q × B 15 R–B3 are in White's favour.

12 B–N2	**B–N2**
13 Q–K2	**0–0**
14 P–K5	**N–K1!**

Not 14 . . . N–Q2 because of 15 P–B5! when White has good attacking chances. But now 15 P–B5 can be met by 15 . . . P × P 16 R × P P–N3 17 R–B2 N–N2 followed by . . . N–K3, when White's attacking prospects have disappeared and he has no compensation for the isolation of his KP.

15 P–B4	**P–Q5**
16 N–K4	**R–N1**

16 . . . P–QR4 is also possible.

17 P–QN4   P × P

Otherwise White will establish a protected passed QNP. e.g. 17 . . . B × N 18 Q × B P–N3 19 P–N5.

18 B × P	**R–Q1**
19 B–KN1	**Q–B3**

Threatening 20 . . . R × B 21 Q × R Q × N, and thereby preventing 20 P–QB5 which would be followed by N–Q6 and an excellent game for White.

20 QR–K1	**P–B4!**
21 P × P ep	**N × P** (*103*)
22 B–N1	

Despite his passed pawn, the endgame, after 22 N × N+ R × N 23

103
W

B–K4 Q×B 24 Q×Q B×Q 25
R×B, is very bad for White: 25 . . .
R–Q7 26 P–QB5 P–QR4 27 R–B4
B–Q1 and White is reduced to
passive defence (28 R–R1).

22 . . .   **N×N**

If 22 . . . P–QR4, intending to
exchange three times on K5 followed
by . . . R–Q7, White's 23 N–N5
wins a pawn at least. So 22 . . . P–
R3 is the only alternative to the
text. Then 23 Q–QB2 forces Black
into the exchanges before he has
time for . . . P–QR4 but, as will be
seen later, . . . P–R3 would turn out
to be a useful move.

23 B×N	**Q×B**
24 Q×Q	**B×Q**
25 R×B	**P–QR4**

25 . . . K–B2 26 P–QB5 P–QR4
also leads to a draw after 27 P–QR3
P×P 28 R–R4.

26 R×P	**B–B3**
27 B–B5!	

If 27 R–R6 R–R1 28 R×R
R×R, the threat of Black's QNP
more than outweighs White's extra
pawn.

27 . . .	**R–B2?!**

27 . . . KR–K1 is without risk,
e.g. 28 R–R6 R–R1 (not 28 . . .
R–Q7 29 R×P R/1–K7 30 R–R8+
K–B2 31 P–B5 when White is two

pawns up and he has the unpleasant
threat of 32 R–KB8 mate) 29 R×R
R×R 30 R–QN1 followed by P–
QR3 and a draw.

28 B–Q6	**R–N2**
29 P–QB5	**R–QB1**
30 P–N4	**K–B2**
31 R–K4	

White still needs his rook on the
KB-file and so the text is better
than 31 R/1–K1 P–R3 when White
can no longer play P–N5. But now
31 . . . P–R3 can be met by 32 P–
N5. Had Black played 22 . . . P–R3
he would now be a tempo ahead of
the game.

31 . . .	**B–K2**
32 R/1–K1	**B×B**
33 P×B	**R–Q1**
34 R–Q4	**P–N3**

Or 34 . . . R/2–Q2 35 R/1–Q1
P–N3 36 R–Q5 K–K3 37 P–B5+
P×P 38 P×P+ K–B3 etc.

35 K–N2

35 R/1–Q1 R/2–Q2 36 R–Q5
P–R5 also draws.

35 . . .	**R/2–Q2**
36 R–K5	**R×P**
37 R×R	**R×R**

and **Black lost on time.** After 38
R×P R–N3 and 39 . . . P–N6 40
P×P R×P, the ending is totally
drawn.

Analysis by Hübner in
THE CHESS PLAYER

Immediately after the game was
awarded to Hübner on time, Petrosian tried to query the accuracy
of the clock. It seemed to him that
the flag had fallen before the hour.
For this very reason, the clocks were
all set at 3.27 instead of 3.30 at the
start of each game, thereby giving

each player three minutes longer than the statutory 150 minutes for the first 40 moves. In this way, so the theory goes, there can be no complaints of faulty clocks.

Dissatisfied with the arbiter's decision, Petrosian then walked around the playing arena, showing the clock to his friends in an attempt to extract sympathy for his plight. Even the next day he was seen to pick up the same clock and show it to one of his team.

105 Schmidt (Poland) – Hübner (W. Germany)

King's Indian Defence

The nearest thing at Skopje to a Hübner loss.

1 N–KB3	**N–KB3**
2 P–B4	**P–KN3**
3 N–B3	**B–N2**
4 P–K4	**P–Q3**
5 P–Q4	**0–0**
6 B–K2	**P–K4**
7 0–0	**N–B3**
8 P–Q5	**N–K2**
9 P–QN4	

White has various alternatives here of which 9 B–Q2 has recently become popular after the Taimanov-Fischer and Korchnoi-Geller matches in 1971. Irrespective of which move he chooses here, White's general strategy in this variation is always a swift Q-side attack while Black's play is always on the K-wing. With the text move, White's Q-side play is often combined with the manoeuvre N–KN5–K6.

9 . . .   N–R4

The most active move. Other possibilities are:

(i) 9 . . . N–Q2 10 P–QR4 P–QR4 11 B–R3 P×P 12 B×P N–QB4 13 N–Q2 B–Q2 14 P–R5 N–B1 15 N–N3, when Black's position is not entirely comfortable. Petrosian-Stein, Moscow 1969;

(ii) 9 . . . N–K1 and now: (a) 10 P–B5 K–R1 11 P–QR4 P–KB4 12 N–KN5 P–KR3 13 N–K6 B×N 14 P×B BP×P 15 P×P N×P 16 P–N5, with sufficient Q-side chances to compensate for the sacrificed pawn. Gligoric-Evans, Amsterdam 1971; or (b) 10 N–Q2! P–KB4 11 P–QR4! N–KB3 12 P–R5 P–B5 13 P–B5 P–KN4 (so far Malich-Schmitz, East Germany 1968) and now Maric suggests 14 P–R6! P–N3 15 B–N5 as being White's best way to maintain a clear advantage;

(iii) 9 . . . P–QR4? 10 P×P! R×P 11 N–Q2 N–Q2 12 N–N3 R–R1 13 P–QR4 P–KB4 14 P–B3! (otherwise 14 . . . P×P followed by . . . N–KB4 and . . . N–Q5 gives Black good counterplay) 14 . . . P–B5 15 B–R3 P–KN4 16 P–B5 N–KB3 17 P×P! P×P 18 N–Q2 N–N3 19 N–B4 with an overwhelming game for White whose Q-side attack meets almost no opposition. Gligoric-Donner, Berlin 1971.

10 P–N3

Preventing . . . N–B5. A risky continuation is 10 P–B5!? N–B5 11 B×N P×B 12 Q–Q2 which was tried in Larsen-Gligoric, Lugano 1970. After 12 . . . B–N5 13 QR–B1 B5×N 14 B×B P–KN4 15 B–N4 N–N3, Black's K-side play proved to be the decisive factor.

10 N–Q2 has not met with too much favour since the brilliancy prize game Petrosian-Gligoric,

Rovinj/Zagreb 1970: 10 . . . N–B5 11 P–QR4 P–KB4 12 B–B3 P–KN4! 13 P×P N×BP 14 P–N3 N–Q5!! and from this complicated position which objectively is probably equal, Petrosian lost his way and was strangled on the K-side.

10 . . .   **P–KB4**
11 N–KN5

White must also play actively. If 11 N–Q2?! N–KB3 12 P–B3, Black can at once take advantage of his opponent's dark squared weaknesses by 12 . . . B–R3! e.g. 13 N–N3 B×B 14 R×B P–B5 15 P–N4 P–KN4 16 P–B5 N–N3 17 P–QR4 P–KR4 and Black's attack will be the more dangerous. Yudovich-Gufeld, USSR 1966.

11 . . .   **N–KB3**
12 P–B3

White must defend his KP rather than exchange it: 12 P×P?! N×BP 13 N/5–K4 P–QR4 14 P–N5 N×N 15 N×N N–Q5 with the more active game for Black. Kuzmin-Taimanov, Harkov 1967.

12 . . .   **P–B3**

Depriving White's QN of his Q5 square after the subsequent exchange of knight for bishop.

12 . . . P–KR3 is premature: 13 N–K6 B×N 14 P×B N–B3 15 N–Q5! R–K1 16 P×P P×P 17 B–Q3, and instead of winning a pawn Black has compromised his position on the K-side.

13 P–N5!

White must continue energetically so as to extract the maximum compensation for his dying KP.

13 . . .   **P–KR3**

The only alternative is 13 . . . P–B4 14 Q–Q3 P–KR3 15 N–K6

B×N 16 P×B N–K1 (intending . . . N–B2), but then 17 P–B4 opens up the position just before Black is ready for it.

14 N–K6   **B×N**
15 P×B   **Q–B2**

Before going after the advanced KP, Black must first secure his Q-side weaknesses. The text unites the rooks and defends the squares QN2, QB3 and Q3, all of which are somewhat vulnerable.

If 15 . . . N–K1 16 NP×P NP×P 17 R–N1 N–B2 18 B–R3 P–B4 19 N–N5 with a great game for White because of his active bishop pair, his control of the light squares and the weakness of Black's backward QP.

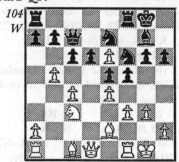

104
W

16 R–N1   **KR–Q1**
17 Q–R4

White must move his queen lest the Q-file should explode in her face. e.g. 17 B–K3 P–Q4!

17 . . .   **Q–B1**
18 NP×P   **NP×P**
19 B–K3   **Q×P**
20 R–N7

White has no difficulty in regaining the pawn.

20 . . .   **R–Q2**

Up to this point the whole game had been played before, but here

Hübner varies. Taimanov-Simagin, USSR Ch. 1960 went instead 20 . . . P–B5   21 B–B2 P×P   22 P×P K–R1   23 R×P (23 KR–N1 offers White more chances of retaining the initiative after he recaptures the pawn) 23 . . . QR–N1   24 R–N1 R×R+   25 N×R R–N1   26 R–R8 Q–B1   27 R×R Q×R   28 Q–N3 Q×Q 29 P×Q with a level position.

Hübner rejected 20 . . . P QR4 because of 21 KR–N1 K–R2   22 R–B7 R–Q2 23 R/1–N7 R×R   24 R×R, when White can pick up the QRP with ease (B–N6) and his actively posted rook seems to dominate the whole board.

21 KR–N1   K–R2

Now 21 . . . P–QR4 loses back the pawn under less favourable circumstances: 22 R–N8+ R×R   23 R×R+ K–R2   24 Q×RP.

22 Q–R6!

Tying down the QRP and maintaining his control of the seventh rank and the QN-file.

22 . . .   P–R4
23 R×R   N×R

Not 23 . . . Q×R?   24 R–N7 Q–B1   25 P–B5! winning easily.

24 Q–N7?!

Stronger would have been the more natural 24 R–N7. e.g. 24 . . . B–R3   25 B–B2 N–B4   26 B×N P×B   27 R×P R×R   28 Q×R B–K6+   29 K–N2, and White's passed QRP is a real menace.

24 . . .   R–QN1
25 Q×RP   R×R+
26 N×R (Dici. 105)
26 . . .   P–Q4?

Now Black is lost. Correct was 26 . . . P×P   27 P×P B–R3 (not 27 . . . N–B3 28 N–B3 P–Q4 29

105
B

B–B5 N–B1   30 BP×P! P×P   31 Q–R6! when White has excellent winning chances) 28 B×B (27 . . . PQ4   28 BP×P P×P   29 B–QN5 N–KB3   30 B–B5 N–B1   31 Q–R6 allows Black to hold on by 31 . . . Q–N5, taking full advantage of White's exposed king.) 28 . . . K×B   29 Q–K3+ K–N2   30 N–Q2, when White is better because of his passed pawn but Black can still fight.

27 BP×P   P×QP
28 B–QN5!   N–KB3
29 B–B5!   N/3–N1

What else? 29 . . . N–B1   30 Q–R6 Q×Q??   31 B×Q loses a knight,   29 . . . N–B3 fails to 30 Q–N6 and 29 . . . N/2–N1 to 30 B–B8.

30 N–Q2?

30 Q–Q7 is an easy win: 30 . . . Q×Q   31 B×Q QP×P   32 P×P P×P   33 P–QR4 and the QRP promotes.

30 . . .   Q–KB3
31 P×QP?

31 P–QR4 and 31 Q–Q7 were still both good enough to win.

31 . . .   N×P
32 B–B4

Here or on the next move P–QR4 was still deadly.

32 . . .   N–B6

33 Q–N6? P–K5
34 P×P P×P
35 Q×Q N×Q
36 B–Q4?

Overlooking Black's reply. 36 N–B1 or 36 P–KR3 would have retained some winning chances.

36 ... N–N5!
37 B×N B×B
38 N×P B–Q5+

Forcing the exchange of knights into an ending of opposite coloured bishops.

39 K–R1 N–B7+
40 N×N B×N
41 K–N2 B–K8
42 K–B3

Draw Agreed

Notes by Levy based on analysis by Hübner and Schmidt in THE CHESS PLAYER

106 **Hübner** (W. Germany) –
Gligoric (Yugoslavia)

Neo-Grünfeld

1 P–KN3 P–KN3 2 B–N2 B–N2
3 P–Q4 P–Q4 4 N–KB3 N–KB3
5 0–0 0–0 6 P–B4 P–B3 7 N–K5!?
B–K3 8 P×P P×P Perhaps . . .
B×P is better. 9 N–QB3 N–B3?!
What compensation does Black now obtain for his backward QBP? 10 N×N The rest of the game is an example of ruthless logic. 10 . . .
P×N 11 N–R4 N–Q2 12 P–N3
Q–R4 13 B–N2 QR–B1 14 R–B1
B–B4 15 R–K1 KR–K1 16 B–QB3 Q–N4 17 Q–Q2 Q–N1 18
B–N2 P–K4 19 P×P N×P 20
B–Q4 B–B1 21 B–B5 N–Q2 22
B×B N×B 23 N–B5 Q–K4 24
P–K4 P×P 25 B×P B×B 26
R×B Q–Q4 27 Q–K3 R×R 28

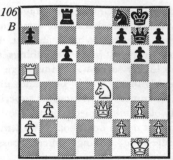

106
B

N×R Q–K4 29 R–B5 Q–N2 30 R–QR5

'The time has come, the Walrus said, To talk of many things.'

30 . . . R–Q1 31 R×P N–K3 32
K–N2 Q–K4 33 Q–KB3 P–KB4
34 N–B3 R–Q3 35 P–KR4 P–R4
36 N–K2 R–Q7 37 Q×QBP
Threatening mate with Q–K8+.
37 . . . Q–K5+ 38 Q×Q P×Q
39 R–K7 N–B4 40 N–B3 K–B1
41 R–QB7 N–K3 42 N×P R×RP
43 R–B6 K–B2 44 R–N6 R–K7
45 N–B3 R–B7 46 N–Q5 P–N4
47 P×P N×P 48 R–N7+ K–N3
49 N–B4+ **Black resigns.**

'O Oysters, said the Carpenter, You've had a pleasant run! Shall we be trotting home again? But answer came there none – And this was scarcely odd, because They'd eaten every one.'

(Which is literally true after 49 . . . K–R3 50 R–N6+ and N×P.)

107 **Hübner** (W. Germany) –
Gheorghiu (Rumania)

Neo-Grünfeld

Hübner establishes a dominating position out of the opening and then smashes Black's position with a neat manoeuvre (moves 20 and 21)

However, Gheorghiu stages an amazing comeback after some careless play by White, and at the adjournment (move 42) things are no longer so clear. At this stage we see Hübner at his best and most determined. Exploiting the superiority of his minor piece (bishop against knight on an open board) he wins a knife-edge ending where passed pawns abound on both sides.

1 P–QB4 P–KN3 2 P–Q4 N–KB3 3 P–KN3 B–N2 4 B–N2 P–Q4 5 P×P N×P 6 P–K4 N–N3 7 N–K2 N–B3 8 P–Q5 N–R4 9 0–0 P–QB3 10 QN–B3 P×P 11 P×P N/4–B5 12 P–N3 N–Q3 13 P–QR4 P–QR4 14 B–QR3 B–N5 15 R–B1 0–0 16 P–R3 B5×N 17 Q×B R–B1 18 N–N5 Q–Q2

107
W

19 B×N! The first link in a chain of moves permitting White an invasion of Black's Q-side which should prove decisive. **19 . . . P×B 20 Q–Q2 R–R1 21 Q–K3! N–B1 22 R–B7 Q–Q1 23 R×NP R–K1 24 Q–B4 R–K2 25 R×R Q×R 26 R–B1 Q–K4 27 Q×Q B×Q 28 P–R4?! N–R2 29 P–B4 N×N 30 P×B N–Q5 31 R–B7 P×P 32 P–Q6 R–Q1 33 B–Q5 R×P 34 B×P+ K–B1 35 B–B4 R–KB3 36 R×P P–K5** Now Black has real

counterplay. **37 R–Q7 N–B6+ 38 K–N2 P–K6 39 R–Q8+ K–K2 40 R–Q5 N–K8+ 41 K–R3 R–B4 42 R×R P×R 43 K–R2 K–B3 44 K–N1 N–B6+ 45 K–B1 N–Q5 46 P–QN4 P×P 47 P–QR5 P–N6 48 P–R6 P–N7 49 B–Q3 N–B3 50 B–N1 K–K4 51 P–R5 K–B3**

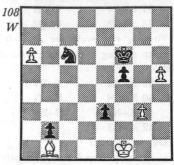

108
W

52 K–K2 K–N4 53 K×P K×P 54 K–B4 K–R3 55 K×P N–K2+ 56 K–K4 N–B3 57 K–B4 N–R2 58 P–N4 N–B3 59 P–N5+ K–R4 60 P–N6 K–R3 61 K–K3 K–N2 62 K–Q2 K–B3 63 K–B3 Black resigns.

108 Hübner (W. Germany) – **Medina** (Spain)

Catalan

1 N–KB3 P–Q4 2 P–B4 P–K3 3 P–KN3 N–KB3 4 B–N2 B–K2 5 0–0 0–0 6 P–Q4 QN–Q2 7 Q–B2 P–QN3 8 P×P N×P 9 P–K4 N–N5 10 Q–B3 B–N2 11 P–QR3 N–R3 12 Q–K3 P–QB4 13 R–Q1 Q–B2 14 N–B3 P×P 15 N×P QR–Q1 16 Q–K2 Q–N1 17 B–K3 Q–R1 18 P–B3 N–B2 19 QR–B1 P–QR3 20 B–R3 B–KB3 21 N–R4 Q–N1 22 N–N3 N–R1 23 B–N2 P–QN4?!   24 N/4–B5 N×N 25 N×N B–QB1 26 P–N3

24   R. Hübner IGM (West Germany)   25   A. Karpov IGM (USSR)

L. Ljubojević IGM (Yugoslavia) about to make his opening move against P. Benko IGM (USA)

27   Silvino Garcia I M (Cuba)

28   U. Andersson I G M (Sweden)

29   O. Rodriguez IM (Peru)

30   J. Kaplan I M (Puerto Rico)

N–N3 27 P–QR4 N–Q2 28 P×P
P×P 29 B–B1 P–N5 30 N–R4
N–K4 31 R×R R×R 32 P–B4
N–Q2 33 Q–N5 B–K2 34 Q–R5
B–N2 35 R–B7 K–B1 36 P–K5
Q–R1 37 Q–N5 B–B1 38 N–B5
Q–B6 39 B–B2 N×N 40 B×N
Resigns.

A classic example of strangulation.

109 **Karpov** (USSR) – **Dueball** (W. Germany)

Sicilian Dragon

This game witnessed an interesting move order. 1 P–K4 P–QB4 2 N–KB3 P–Q3 3 P–Q4 P×P 4 N×P N–KB3 5 N–QB3 P–KN3 6 B–K3 N–B3 7 P–B3 B–N2 8 Q–Q2 0–0 and now instead of 9 B–QB4 or 9 0–0–0 Karpov played 9 P–KN4. The idea is that after 9 . . . N×N 10 B×N B–K3 11 0–0–0 Q–R4 Black has transposed into a bad variation against 9 0–0–0 and after 12 K–N1 KR–B1 13 P–QR3 QR–N1 14 P–N5 N–R4 15 N–Q5 Q×Q 16 R×Q B×N 17 P×B White had a slight but persistent plus in the ending. The game concluded 17 . . . P–QR3 18 R–N1 P–N4 19 P–B3 P–R4 20 B–R7 R–N2 21 B–K3 B–K4 22 K–R2 R/N2–B2 23 K–N3 R–N1 24 B–Q3 N–B5 25 B–K4 P–B4 26 P×P e.p. P×P 27 R N4 P–N4 28 R–N1 N–R6 29 R–K1 B–B5 30 B–KB5 B×B 31 R×B N–B5 32 K–R2 K–B1 33 P–N4 P–R3 34 K–N2 R–K2 35 R×R K×R 36 K–N3 R–QR1 37 P–B4 RP×P 38 RP×P P×P+ 39 K×P K–Q1 40 K–N5 K–B2 41 R–QB2+ K–N2 42 B–Q7 R–R6 43 R–B6 R–Q6

44 R–N6+ K–B2 45 B–B6 N×P
46 R–N7+ K–B1 47 R–KB7 K–Q1
48 R–Q7+ K–B1 49 R–KB7 K–Q1
50 K–B4 N–B5 51 R×P P–Q4× 52
K–B5 K–K2 53 R×P R–B6+ 54
K–N6 R×P 55 P–N5 P–N5 56
R–R4 R–KR6 57 R×P N–K7 58
K–B7 R–R2 59 P–N6 K–K3+ 60
K–Q8 N–Q5 61 R×N K–Q3 62
B×P K–B4 63 R–Q2 K×P 64
R–QB2 1–0

110 **Karpov** (USSR) – **Uddenfeldt** (Sweden)

Sicilian Defence

1 P–K4 P–QB4 2 N–KB3 P–Q3 3 P–Q4 P×P 4 N×P N–KB3 5 N–QB3 P–QR3 6 P–B4 Q–B2 7 B–Q3 P–K3 A passive move. Better is . . . P–K4 either at once or after . . . QN–Q2. Even fianchettoing his KB gives Black a better defensive position than in the game. **8 0–0 B–K2 9 N–B3! QN–Q2 10 Q–K1 N–B4 11 P–K5! N/3–Q2 12 Q–N3 P–KN3 13 B–K3 P–QN4 14 B–Q4! N×B 15 P×N P–Q4** White already has a positionally won game. **16 QR–B1 Q–N2 17 P–B5! NP×P 18 Q–N7 R–B1 19 N–N5 B×N 20 Q×B Q–N1 21 N–K2 B–N2** If 21 . . . N×P? 22 R×B+. **22 N–B4 Q–Q1** Now 22 . . . N×P?

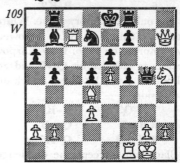

109
W

loses to 23 KR–K1 followed by 24
N×KP. **23 Q–R5** Threatening 24
N×KP. **23 . . . K–K2 24 Q×RP**
Threatening 25 N–N6+. **24 . . .
K–K1 25 N–R5 Q–N4 26 R–B7
R–QN1** (109)
27 N–N7+ Resigns Since 27 . . .
K–Q1 (or 27 . . . K–K2 28 B–B5+
K–Q1) loses the queen to 28 N×
KP+.

Notes by Nilsson in AFTONBLADET

111 **Karpov** (USSR) –
  Enevoldsen (Denmark)
French Defence

1 P–K4	P–K3
2 P–Q4	P–Q4
3 N–Q2	P–KB4

This move is rare in tournament
play. The theoretical continuation
is now 4 P×BP P×P 5 Q–R5+
P–KN3 6 Q–K2+ Q–K2 7 N/2–B3
with an advantage in the coming
endgame. 4 P–K5 also gives White
the advantage but Karpov did not
wish to play a blocked position.

4 P×BP	P×P
5 N/2–B3	N–KB3
6 B–KN5	

The characteristic move of the
variation. Of course 6 B–Q3, 7 N–
K2 and 8 0–0 also gives White a
clear advantage.

6 . . .	B–K2

The only satisfactory move. White
was threatening Q–K2+ followed
by capturing on KB6. Now Karpov
decides to sacrifice his QNP and go
all out for a win by direct attack on
the K-side.

7 B–Q3	N–K5
8 B×B	Q×B
9 N–K2	Q–N5+

Black must accept the challenge

because if White can get in 10 0–0
he will have very powerful play
against Black's weak squares on the
K-side.

10 P–B3	Q×NP
11 0–0	0–0

If Black takes the second pawn he
gets horribly crushed after (11 . . .
N×QBP 12 N×N Q×N 13 R–B1
and 14 R–K1+. The black knight
at K5 is the bulwark of his position
and cannot be exchanged for such a
small material gain.

12 P–B4	P×P

With 12 . . . P–B3 13 N–B4,
Black ties himself down to the defence
of his QP. He could still defend it by
13 . . . N–KB3 (if 13 . . . P–KN4 14
B×N BP×B 15 N×NP R×N 16
Q–R5 Q×QP – *16 . . . B–B4 17
Q–B7+ K–R1 18 Q–B8 mate* –
17 Q×RP+ K–B1 18 Q–QB7!),
but then 14 R–B1 is very strong,
giving White play on the QB-file
after the exchange of pawns on Q5.

13 B×P+	K–R1
14 R–N1	

Of course 14 N–K5 also wins but
Karpov wanted to win by forced
stages.

14 . . .	Q–R6
15 N–K5	P–KN3

The only defence against the

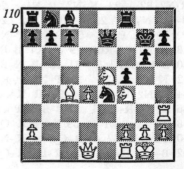

110
B

threat of N–N6+ followed by R–N3 and mate at KR3.

16 R–N3 Q–K2
17 N–B4 K–N2
18 R–KR3! (*110*)

White has two threats: 19 R×P+ and 19 N/4×P. Black can defend against both threats by 18 . . . N–N4 but after 19 R–K3 Q–Q1 20 R/1–K1 his position is hopeless.

18 . . . N–QB3
19 N/4×P

An inaccuracy. White had a beautiful way to win in 19 R×P+ K×R 20 N/4×P (20 N/5×P Q–Q3 21 N×R+ Q×N/1 22 Q–R5+ fails to mate after 22 . . . K–N2) 20 . . . Q–Q3 21 N×R+ K–N2 (or 21 . . . Q×N/1 22 Q–R5+ Q–R3 23 B–N8+ K–N2 24 Q–B7+ K–R1 25 N–N6+) 22 Q–R5 N×N 23 Q–R7+ K×N 24 P×N! (the move that Karpov missed over the board) 24 . . . Q–Q2 25 Q–N8+ K–K2 26 Q–B7+ K–Q1 27 Q–B8+ Q–K1 28 R–Q1+ B–Q2 29 Q×P followed by P–K6.

19 . . . P×N
20 N×P Q–B3!

The only way to keep control of KR1. If 20 . . . Q–N4 21 N×R K×N 22 R–R8+ K–K2 23 R–K1.

21 N×R

The quickest win. 21 N–B4 Q–N4 22 N–R5+ K–N3 23 B–Q3 (or Q5) Q–Q7 leaves White with no forced win.

21 . . . K×N
22 R–R7 N–K2?

A better try was 22 . . . N–N4 when 23 R×P does not work because of 23 . . . Q–Q3 and so Karpov had intended to play 23 R–R5 B–K3 24 B×B (Black can defend himself

after 24 R×N B×B 25 Q–R5 N–K2 or 24 P–Q5 B–B2 25 P×N B×B 26 P×P R–N1 27 Q–B1 B×R 28 Q×P R×P 29 Q×R B–K7) 24 . . . N×B 25 P–Q5 R–Q1 26 Q–N3 N/K3–Q5 27 Q×P R×P 28 Q×BP with a decisive advantage.

23 R–K1

There was no point to winning the queen by 23 R–B7+.

23 . . . Q–N3
24 R–B7+ Q×R

If 24 . . . K–K1 25 P–B3 B–K3 26 B×B Q×B 27 R–R7.

25 B×Q K×B
26 Q–R5+ K–B1
27 Q–R6+ K–B2
28 Q–R7+ Resigns

Notes based on those by Karpov in 64

112 **Karpov** (USSR) –
Ungureanu (Rumania)

Sicilian Defence

1 P–K4 P–QB4 2 N–KB3 N–QB3 3 P–Q4 P×P 4 N×P N–B3 5 N–QB3 P–Q3 6 B–KN5 P–K3 7 Q–Q2 B–K2 8 0–0–0 0–0 9 P–B4 N×N 10 Q×N Q–R4 Nowadays 10 . . . P–KR3 is considered best. **11 B–B4 B–Q2 12 P–K5 P×P 13 P×P B–B3 14 B–Q2!** During the past three years this move has taken over from 14 Q–B4 as the accepted continuation. **14 . . . N–Q2 15 N–Q5 Q–Q1 16 N×B+ Q×N 17 KR–K1! KR–B1** In Kavalek–Benko, Netanya 1969, Black tried 17 . . . Q–B4 18 Q–B4 B–N4 19 B–N3! P–QR4 but without success, White's K-side attack proving as irresistible as the one in the present game: 20

P–QR4 B–B3   21 R–K3 QR–B1
22 B–B3 P–QN4 23 R–N3 KR–K1
(if 23 . . . P×P 24 Q–R6 P–N3
25 R–R3) 24 R–B1 and Black was
given no chance. In view of these
two games, the line commencing
with 10 . . . Q–R4 will probably
disappear from master praxis in
favour of 10 . . . P–KR3. **18 Q–B4
P–QR4 19 K–N1 N–N3 20 B–Q3
N–Q4 21 Q–KN4 Q–B4 22 R–
K4! P–QN4 23 Q–R3!** Threatening
simply 24 R–KR4. **23 . . . N–N5**

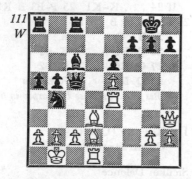

*111
W*

24 B–K3! B×R If 24 . . . Q–K2
25 R×N Q×R 26 P–R3 Q–QR5
27 Q×RP+ K–B1 28 B–KB5+ K
K1 29 Q–N8+ K–Q2 30 Q×BP+
K–Q1   31 Q–K7 mate. **25 B×B**
Stronger than 25 B×Q B×B 26
P×B. **25 . . . Q×KP 26 Q×RP+
K–B1 27 B×R K–K2** If 27 . . .
R×B 28 Q–R8+ K–K2 29 Q×R
Q×B 30 Q–Q8 mate. **28 Q–K4
Q–B2 29 Q–N7 Resigns.**

113 **Bisguier** (USA) –
Karpov (USSR)

English Opening

**1 P–QB4 P–QB4 2 N–QB3 P–KN3
3 N–B3 B–N2 4 P–K3 N–KB3 5**
**P–Q4 0–0 6 B–K2 P×P 7 P×P
P–Q4 8 0–0 N–B3 9 P–KR3 B–
B4 10 B–K3 P×P 11 B×P R–B1
12 B–K2 B–K3 13 Q–Q2 Q–R4
14 B–KR6 KR–Q1 15 B×B K×B
16 KR–Q1 R–Q3! 17 Q–K3 R/1–
Q1 18 P–R3** A conventional opening
has led to a position which I think the
readers will find interesting. A sharp
tactical struggle is just beginning.
18 . . . B–N6 19 R–Q2 19 N–QN5
failed to 19 . . . B×R   20 N×R
B×B 21 N×NP Q–N3 22 N×R
B×N. **19 . . . R–K3   20 Q–B4
N–Q4 21 N×N R×N 22 P–N4**
White defends against the threat of
23 . . . R–KB4 followed by 24 . . .
R×N and 25 . . . Q×R. If 22
B–Q3, Black gets the advantage by
22 . . . R–B3 23 Q–K3 R×N 24
P×R N×QP. This threatens 25 . . .
Q×R and 26 . . . N×P+ and if
25 B–K4 there comes the crushing
blow 25 . . . Q×R 26 B×R B×B!
27 Q–K5+ (27 Q×Q N×P+)
27 . . . K–R3. **22 . . . P–KN4 23
Q–N3 R–B3 24 B–Q1** White loses
a pawn after 24 R–Q3 B–B5   25
R–K3 B×B 26 R×B R×N! 27
Q×R N×QP followed by 28 . . .
N×R+. **24 . . . B–B5** After 24 . . .
R×N 25 B×R Q×R   26 B×B
the weakness of Black's KR2 is
fatally exposed. **25 P–N3 B–R3** Of
course I would have liked to have
taken the knight but after 25 . . .
R×N 26 Q×R Q×R, White does
not play 27 R–Q1 allowing Black to
finish him off by 27 . . . Q–B6 28
P×B R×P 29 R×R N×R 30
Q–K5+ K–R3! but instead hurries
to exchange his bishop and draws
by 27 P×B R×P 28 B×N P×B 29
Q–K5+. **26 P–N4 Q–Q1 27 B–N3**

It looks as though the American Grandmaster is winning but Black has a powerful tactical riposte.

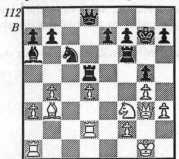

112
B

27 ... N × QP 28 R × N Bisguier does not wish to lose in a long and gruelling endgame a pawn down after 28 B × R N × N+ 29 B × N Q × R 30 R–Q1 Q–B6 and rushes precipitously to his doom. **28 ... R × R 29 N × P R–Q6 30 Q–R4 P–R3 31 N × P Q–Q5 32 R–K1 R × RP! 33 Resigns**

Notes by Karpov in 64 translated specially for this volume by Andrew Whiteley

114 **Padevsky** (Bulgaria) – **Karpov** (USSR)

French Defence (by transposition)

Karpov's only loss.
Karpov stands well from the opening and for most of the middle-game, but he starts to drift towards the end of the first session, and by move 41 it is clear that he must lose a pawn.
1 P–K4 P–QB4 2 N–KB3 P–K3 3 P–B3 P–Q4 4 P × P P × P 5 P–Q4 B–Q3 6 P × P B × BP 7 B–K2 N–QB3 8 0–0 KN–K2 9 QN–Q2 0–0 10 N–N3 B–N3 11 KN–Q4 N–N3 12 B–K3 R–K1

13 Q–B2 QN–K4 14 QR–Q1 B–Q2 15 N–Q2 N–N5 16 B × N B × B 17 QR–K1 R–QB1 18 N/2–B3 R–K5 19 Q–N3 Q–Q2 20 N–Q2 R/5–K1 21 P–B3 B–K3 22 Q–Q1 B–B2 23 R–B2 Q–Q3 24 N–B1 Q–R3 25 P–KB4 B–Q2 26 Q–N1 B–N4?! 27 N × B Q × N 28 P–KN3 R–K5 29 B–Q4 R × R 30 Q × R R–K1 31 Q–Q1 P–QR4 32 N–K3 R–K5 33 Q–N3 Q × Q 34 P × Q Now White is better since his weakness on the light squares is of little importance in the ending, while Black's isolated QP is a major factor. **34 ... N–K2 35 R–Q2 P–R4 36 K–B2 R–K3 37 K–B3 P–KN3 38 B–B5! B–N3 39 P–QN4 P × P 40 P × P**

113
B

40 ... B × B 41 P × B P–N3 42 P–QN4 P × P 43 P × P K–B1 44 N × P R–QB3 45 N × N K × N 46 R–QB2 K–Q2 47 K–K4 R–B3 48 R–R2 R–B4 49 R–R7+ K–K1 50 R–R5 K–Q1 51 K–Q4 P–R5 52 R–R8+ K–B2 53 R–R7+ K–B3 54 K–K4 R × QBP 55 R × P R–B7 56 R–B6+ K–Q2 57 R × P R × P 58 P–N4 P–R6 59 R–R6 R–R8 60 K–B5 P–R7 61 P–N5 K–K2 62 P–N6 R–R8 63 R–R7+ K–B1 64 R × P R–R4+ 65 K–B6 Black resigns.

And our predictions based on these games? David Levy believes that Karpov's all-round virtuosity backed up by the vast chess resources of the Soviet Union will one day carry him to the top, while the other 50 per cent of the editorial board, Raymond Keene, adheres to the view that Hübner is likely to be Fischer's challenger in the not too distant future.

Having committed ourselves to this Ljubojevic will probably win the World Championship!

FINAL GROUP B

		E	I	C	P	N	C	A	I	C	I	I	M	G	B	P	Total
17	England	×	2½	2	2½	3	2	2½	3½	2½	3½	3	3	3	1½	2½	37
18	Israel	1½	×	3	1½	3½	2	2½	3	2	3½	2½	3	3½	3	2	36½
19	Canada	2	1	×	1	2½	2½	2	2½	2	3	3	2½	2½	4	2½	33
20	Philippines	1½	2½	3	×	1½	2½	½	2	3½	2½	1	2	3	2½	3½	31½
21	Norway	1	½	1½	2½	×	1	1½	3	3	2	2	3½	3	3	3	30½
22	Cuba	2	2	1½	1½	3	×	3	1½	2½	2	2½	2	2	2	2½	30
23	Austria	1½	1½	2	3½	2½	1	×	2	2½	2½	1½	1	3½	2	3	30
24	Iceland	½	1	1½	2	1	2½	2	×	2	3	2½	2½	2	2½	4	29
25	Colombia	1½	2	2	½	1	1½	1½	2	×	2	3	2	2½	2½	3	27
26	Indonesia	½	½	1	1½	2	2	1½	1	2	×	3½	1½	3	4	1½	25½
27	Italy	1	1½	1	3	2	1½	2½	1½	1	½	×	1	2½	2	4	25
28	Mongolia	1	1	1½	2	½	2	3	1½	2	2½	3	×	1	2½	1	24½
29	Greece	1	½	1½	1	1	2	½	2	1½	1	1½	3	×	2½	2	21
30	Belgium	2½	1	0	1½	1	2	2	1½	1½	0	2	1½	1½	×	2½	20½
31	Peru	1½	2	1½	½	1	1½	1	0	1	2½	0	3	2	1½	×	19

Cuba (5 wins 6 draws) were placed ahead of Austria (6 wins 3 draws) because of their better match record.

Albania's score was cancelled after their withdrawal. Of the matches Albania completed they beat Italy 2½–1½, Belgium 3–1, Canada 2½–1½, Norway 3½–½, drew 2–2 with Indonesia and lost 1–3 to Austria, 1½–2½ to Colombia, 1½–2½ to Cuba, ½–3½ to Iceland and 1½–2½ to England.

Progressive Score Table

		R1	R2	R3	R4	R5	R6	R7	R8	R9	R10	R11	R12	R13	R14	R15
17	England	**3**	**5½**	**8**	**11**	**14**	**16½**	.	18	**21½**	**23½**	**25½**	**29**	**32**	34½	**37**
18	Israel	1½	4	6½	8½	12	15	**17**	.	20	**23½**	**25½**	28½	31½	**35**	36½
19	Canada	2½	5	7½	.	11½	14½	**17**	18	20½	23	25	26	29	31	33
20	Philippines	2½	5	6	8½	9	11½	15	18	21	23	25	26½	30	31½	.
21	Norway	1½	4½	7½	**11**	**14**	.	**17**	**19**	20	21½	24½	27	28	28½	30½
22	Cuba	2	4½	.	6½	8½	10	11½	13	16	18	20	22½	25½	28	30
23	Austria	2½	4	5½	7	10½	13	16½	17½	20½	.	22½	25	26	28	30
24	Iceland	2	4	6½	10½	.	13	16	18½	20	22	23	23½	24½	27	29
25	Colombia	2	3	4½	6½	9½	11	11½	14	16	19	.	21½	23½	25	27
26	Indonesia	1½	.	5½	7	9	10	11	13	13½	14	17½	19	21	24	25½
27	Italy	1	2½	5½	8	9	11½	12½	16½	.	18½	19	20½	21½	23	25
28	Mongolia	2	3½	5	5½	6½	7½	10½	13½	15½	16½	18½	19½	.	22	24½
29	Greece	1½	3½	4½	5½	6	7½	8	9½	10½	13½	15½	.	18	19	21
30	Belgium	.	1½	1½	3½	3½	5	6	8½	9½	11½	13½	15	16½	18	20½
31	Peru	2½	4	5½	5½	6½	8	10	10	11	12	14	17	17½	.	19

The struggle for first place in the B Group soon resolved itself into a race between England and Israel. Fittingly enough this contest was decided in the very last round when these two teams met for their individual match. England needed to win by a margin of 2½–1½ and this they achieved as follows:

England		Israel	
Keene	1	Kagan	0
Hartston	½	Kraidman	½
Wade	½	Kaldor	½
Markland	½	Balshan	½

The Israelis handicapped themselves psychologically from the beginning of the match since three of the four games commenced with the English Opening! By drawing his game with Kraidman Hartston fulfilled the norm for the International Master title. Since this was his second performance, and a total of 25 games only is now required, he should be awarded the title at the next FIDE congress. On the Israeli side Kaldor also made a master norm, but this has to be repeated.

It was expected at the commencement of the Finals that the Canadians would be the chief contenders for top place, but their Grandmaster, Abe Yanofsky, was not in his best form and although the ingenious Canadian secret weapon, Duncan Suttles, started off like a tornado he faded badly at the close.

A major point of interest in the B Final was the weird behaviour of the Albanian contingent, and this is examined in detail in the article which follows.

The Albania Incident
What follows is a translation of the official account of the withdrawal of the Albanian team from the Olympiad.

'As we know, the Albanian team failed to appear for their match with Israel in the eighth round of the B-final (see photograph 39). The match Israel–Albania did not take place and the arbiters announced a result of 4–0 by forfeit in favour of Israel. At the start of this round the President of FIDE Dr Max Euwe received a written protest from the captains of the following teams: Canada, Belgium, England, Norway, Iceland, Italy, the Philippines, Greece, and Austria, whereby they expressed their revulsion at the intervention of politics in chess. The captains of these teams from the B-Group regarded the gesture of the Albanian team as a protest of a political nature. In their opinion it was necessary to annul the results of the Albanian team in the final and to modify the FIDE regulations by making provision for fixed and rigorous sanctions if such a case should arise again.

'This protest was followed by a decision from the supreme arbiter, Dr Max Euwe, according to which all the matches of the Albanian team in the final would be considered as "friendly" encounters. Dr

Euwe then summoned the Albanian captain who declared that the action of his team in failing to appear for the match with Israel was due to certain "technical" reasons and had nothing at all to do with politics. The Albanian captain, Mitat Luci, further declared that en route to their match with Israel the car containing their team had broken down and since this accident meant that they would be very late for the start of the round they considered it futile to appear in the playing hall.

'When he was informed of the protest by the nine B-Group captains the Albanian captain requested a meeting with them where he confirmed that the action of his team was by no means a political one. This meeting lasted about three hours and involved a general discussion on the nature of the Albanian gesture: could it or could it not be construed as a political protest?

'After receiving the official decision that the Albanian results were to be regarded as friendly matches the Albanian team delivered the following written protest: "For certain technical reasons we were not in a position to play our match with Israel and therefore lost it by a score of 4-0. We would like to explain that this problem is not due to a secret agreement with the Israeli team in order to make them a present of four points, nor do we desire to damage the chances of other teams. Such affirmations represent a false accusation and we consider them an intrusion into our personal affairs. In acting thus certain elements wish to make a political problem with disagreeable consequences out of a problem which is purely technical. We regard the decision of the supreme arbiter as unilateral, for the blame which has been attributed to the Albanian team is unjustifiable and we cannot accept it. We request the appeals commission to reconsider this irregular decision". This protest was signed by the Albanian captain Mitat Luci.

'The appeals commission, elected before the beginning of the Olympiad, at a meeting of all the team captains, as a supreme democratic organ for this competition, then examined this request by the Albanian team. The commission unanimously modified the decision of the supreme arbiter by accepting the Albanian plea that they had been unable to play the match with Israel for technical reasons. It was decided that the match Israel-Albania should be replayed on 13 October at 10 a.m.

'On 9 October the Albanian captain addressed a letter to the organising committee of the Olympiad in the course of which he said (inter alia): "This is not the first time that our team refuses to play with that of Israel, a country which practises a policy of expansion and aggression. In view of this we regard the decision of the appeals commission as entirely unjustifiable and that is why our team is unfortunately obliged to withdraw from this Olympiad."

'A written declaration of similar content was handed to the Press centre on the evening of 9 October. On the afternoon of the same day Mitat Luci informed the chief director, Jordan Ivanofski, and the supreme arbiter and President of FIDE, Dr Max Euwe, of the Albanian decision to retire from the Olympiad.'

Editorial comment: A clairvoyant who had miraculously predicted the breakdown of the Albanian vehicle had made known the supernatural information that the Israel-Albania match would not take place several days beforehand and this was common knowledge amongst the competitors at least two days before round eight of the final. In fact the protest of nine was prepared (in three different languages) before the commencement of round eight.

The Albanian hand was forced by virtue of the fact that a few rounds later they had to meet Greece (another team unacceptable to the Albanian polit-commissars) and it was implausible that their car should fall victim to another breakdown. Thus the whole Albanian fraud was exposed. It seems to us quite correct that a country should not be allowed to play on its own terms. The FIDE motto is 'Gens Una Sumus' and the Albanian action was in total violation of this.

115 **Uitumen** (Mongolia) –
 W. Hartston (England)
Sicilian Defence
1 P–K4 P–QB4 2 N–KB3 P–K3
3 N–B3 P–QR3 4 P–Q4 P×P 5
N×P N–QB3 6 B–K3 Q–B2 7
P–QR3?! P–QN4 8 N–N3 B–N2
Also possible is 8 . . . N–K4 followed by . . . N–B5. 9 P–B4 P–Q3 Interesting is 9 . . . P–N5. 10 B–Q3 N–B3
11 0–0 B–K2 12 Q–B3 0–0 13
Q–R3 P–N5! 14 N–R4 If 14 P×P
N×NP 15 N–R5 N×B 16 P×N
and Black is slightly better. 14 . . .
P×P 15 P×P N–Q2 16 R–B3
KR–K1 17 R–N3 B–KB1 18 R–KB1 P–N3! 19 N–N2 Probably White should have tried 19 P–B5 KP×P 20 P×P though after 20 . . . N/3–K4 Black has a good grip on the centre, his K-side is quite secure and his forces well placed for a counter attack. 19 . . . B–N2 20 N–Q1 N–K2! Not 20 . . . P–B4?

because of 21 P×P KP×P 22 B–B4+ K–R1 23 B–B7 and 24 B×P.
21 P–B5 Otherwise Black can play 21 . . . P–B4 with impunity. **21 . . . KP×P 22 P×P N–Q4 23 P×P?** Stronger is 23 B–R6. **23 . . . BP×P 24 B–Q4** 24 Q×P+ is unsound: 24 . . . K×Q 25 B×NP+ K–N1 26 B–B7+ K–B1! and White can do nothing useful with his discovered check. **24 . . . N–K4**

Black's position is so beautiful that this diagram should be hung in some art gallery. The black knights, both adequately supported, occupy two of the central squares from where they can exert their influence over much of the board. The remainder of Black's army is equally well placed. His king is perfectly safe, guarded by an unassailable fianchettoed bishop. His queen simultaneously defends the second rank and lies in wait until she can enter White's position at some point on the QB-file. The QB is lurking, pointing towards White's K-side as a constant reminder that the counter-attack is coming.

Meanwhile, White has taken great care to post his queen and rooks far from the centre so that they can cause Black the least possible trouble. White's bishops are impotent; his knights are laughable. Ten moves ago White thought that he was attacking. Now his position is little more than a shambles. **25 Q–R4 R–KB1 26 R–R3 R×R+ 27 B×R Q×P!** 28 N–R5 After 28 Q×P+ K–B2 29 B×N P×B 30 R–KB3+ N–B3 Black is threatening both 31 . . . Q×N/Q8 and 31 . . . R–R1 winning the queen. **28 . . . Q×N 29 B×N?** Better is 29 N×B N–KB6+ 30 R×N B×B+ when Black should still win but with more difficulty than in the game. **29 . . . P×B 30 Q×P+** If 30 N×B P–K5! 31 Q×P+ K–B1! and Black threatens 32 . . . B–Q5+ followed by mate. **30 . . . K–B2 31 R–Q3** If 31 R–KB3+ N–B3 threatening both 32 . . . B×R and 32 . . . Q×R. **31 . . . Q–N8 32 N×B** Or 32 R–QN3 Q×R 33 N×Q R–R1. **32 . . . Q×N 33 R–KB3+ N–B5 34 B–**

B4+ K–B3 35 Q–R4+ P–N4 36 Q–N4 Q–B1 37 R×N+ KP×R 38 Q–K2 Q–QB4+ 39 K–B1 Q–K4 40 Q–Q1 K–K2 41 Q–R4 Q–R8+ 42 K–K2 Q–N7+ 43 K–B3 P–N5+ **44 Resigns** Throughout the game Black's extra rook did not move!

Notes by Levy based on analysis by Hartston in THE CHESS PLAYER

116 Tatai (Italy) – **Keene** (England)

Pirc Defence

1 P–K4	P–KN3
2 P–Q4	P–Q3
3 N–QB3	B–N2
4 P–B4	N–KB3
5 N–B3	O–O
6 P–K5	P×P
7 QP×P	Q×Q+
8 K×Q	R–Q1+

Of late this has become a popular line for White against the Pirc. Some years ago a lot of attention was directed to lines arising from 6 P–K5 KN–Q2 7 P–KR4, but I think everyone agrees now that this is good for a draw at best as White. Recently attention has shifted to 6 P–K5 KN–Q2 7 B–B4 which is probably sufficient for a small plus. Personally I am always prepared to play the queenless middle-game after 6 P–K5 P×P and I firmly believe that this holds no terrors for Black.

9 K–K1

Tatai's attempt at improving on the 9 B–Q3 N–K1 10 K–K2 N–QB3 11 B–K4 B–N5 12 B–K3 P–B3 13 B–Q5+ K–R1 = of Gligoric-Keene, Hastings 1971/72.

9 ...	N–K1
10 B–B4	B–B4
11 B–K3	

It could be dangerous now to play 11 . . . B×BP 12 N–Q4 B–B4 13 N×B followed by P–K6!

11 ...	N–QB3
12 R–QB1	N–R4
13 B–K2	P–KB3
14 P–KR3	P×P?

A careless move. 14 . . . B–K3! is quite good for Black. The text gives away the g5 square to a White knight.

15 P×P	B–K3
16 B–KB4?	

An automatic reaction which allows Black to escape unscathed after his error on move 14. 16 B–B5! is very unpleasant for Black.

16 ...	P–KR3!

Now everything is under control

17 K–B2	P–B4
18 N–K4	P–N3
19 P–B4	N–B2
20 K–K3?	

This loses a pawn to a neat combinative sequence, but in my opinion Black already stands well (not yet winning of course) in view of White's slight weakness on e5 and Black's potential grip on d4.

20 ...	B×BP!
21 B×B	N×B+
22 R×N	N–Q4+
23 K–B2	N×B
24 N×P	P–KN4!

Without this resource Black could gain nothing from his combination.

25 P–KN3	N×P+
26 R×N	P×N

and White cannot capture on c5 in view of . . . P–N5. So Black keeps his precious booty.

27 R–R1	R–Q4
28 R/1–QB1	R–N1
29 P–N3	R–N4
30 K–K3	P–K3
31 R–K4	P–QR4
32 P–KN4	R–N5
33 R×R	RP×R
34 K–K4	K–B2
35 R–KR1	K–N3
36 R–KN1	B–B1
37 R KR1	B–K2
38 K–K3	B–Q1
39 K–K4	B–B2
40 R–QB1	B–N3
41 R–KR1	R–Q2

The sealed move

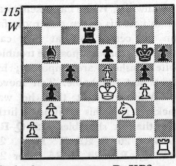

115
W

Black threatens . . . R–KB2, . . . P–B5 and . . . R–B5+, to which there are two defences – (a) the text (b) 42 R–QB1 R–KB2 43 R–B4 R–B5+ 44 K–K3 R×R 45 P×R but then 45 . . . P–R4 wins.

42 R–KB1

Meeting . . . R–KB2 with 43 N–Q2!

42 ...	K–N2!

Zugzwang number 1! White literally has no move apart from 43 R–B1 when 43 . . . R–KB2 44 R–B4 R–B5+ 45 K–K3 R×R 46 P×R is no longer so good for Black since he must waste a move before he can play . . . P–R4. So:

43 R–B1	R–KB2
44 R–B4	K–N3!!

Zugzwang number 2! There really are no moves left now, e.g: 45 K–K3 R–QR2 46 R–B2 P–B5+ or 45 R–B1 P–B5!

45 N–K1

This allows decisive penetration by Black's rook.

45 . . .	R–B7
46 N–Q3	

Or 46 R–B2 R–B5+ and if 46 N–B2 R–K7+

46 . . .	R×P
47 R–B1	

Also hopeless is 47 N×BP B×N 48 R×B R–KN7 49 K–B3 R–N7.

47 . . .	P–B5!
48 N×P	R–K7+
49 K–B3	R–K6+
50 K–N2	P×P
	White resigns

Notes by Keene

117 **W. Hartston** (England) – **Mariotti** (Italy)

Vienna Game

1 P–K4 N–QB3 2 N–QB3 I occasionally play the Vienna on the spur of the moment; in retrospect, this was not one of the more auspicious moments. **2 . . . P–K4 3 P–KN3** Next time I get this position I will play 3 B–B4. **3 . . . B–B4 4 B–N2 P–KR4 5 N–B3** Probably White should play 5 P–KR4 or 5 N–QR4 but I felt it my duty to test the correctness of Black's idea. **5 . . . P–R5 6 N×RP R×N 7 P×R Q×P 8 P–Q4?!** After 8 0–0 N–B3 9 Q–B3 N–Q5 10 Q–N3 Q×Q 11 RP×Q N×BP 12 R–N1 Black has more than enough for the exchange,

but this was probably better than what I played. **8 . . . B×P 9 Q–K2 B×N+! 10 P×B P–Q3** Black now has a wonderful game for his sacrificed exchange. All White's pawns are immobile and he can just wait for rigor mortis to set in. I should have played 11 Q–K3 here to prevent . . . P–KN4 and maintain chances of P–KB4. After the move chosen the game deteriorates into a hopeless struggle to create active play at the cost of hundreds of pawns. **11 0–0 P–KN4! 12 Q–K3** Too late. **12 . . . P–B3 13 Q–KN3 Q–R2 14 B–B3 KN–K2 15 R–K1 N–N3 16 B–K3 K–K2 17 P–QB4 P–N3 18 P–B5 NP×P 19 P–B3 N–B5 20 B–N4 B×B 21 Q×B R–R1 22 P–KR4 Q–N1 23 B×N R×P 24 Q–N2 KP×B 25 P–K5 N×P 26 Q–N7 R–N5+ 27 K–B1 Q–B5+ 28 R–K2 K–Q2 29 Q–K4 P–B6 30 Q×Q N×Q 31 R–QB2 R–N7 32 R–K1 P–B4 33 R/B–K2 K–B3 34 Resigns**

Notes by W. Hartston specially for this volume

118 **Whiteley** (England) – **Skalkotas** (Greece)

King's Indian Defence

1 P–Q4	N–KB3
2 P–QB4	P–KN3
3 P–KN3	B–N2
4 B–N2	0–0
5 N–QB3	P–Q3
6 N–B3	P–B3
7 0–0	Q–R4

The Kavalek Variation.

8 P–KR3

This cuts across Black's plan of

transferring the queen to the K-side since 8 . . . Q–R4 is met by 9 P–KN4. The game now transposes into a well-known variation more often reached by the move order 6 . . . QN–Q2 7 0–0 P–K4 8 P–K4 P–B3 9 P–KR3 Q–R4.

8 . . .	QN–Q2
9 P–K4	P–K4
10 B–K3	R–K1

10 . . . P×P used to be popular but recent games have shown that 11 N×P N–N3 12 N–N3! followed by 13 P–B5 is very strong.

| 11 R–K1 | P–QN4 |

If now 11 . . . P×P 12 N×P N–N3 13 P–B5!

12 QP×P

12 P–B5 was tempting but Black can equalize by 12 . . . P–N5 13 N–QR4 P–Q4!

| 12 . . . | QP×P |
| 13 N–Q2 | P–QR3 |

13 . . . P–N5 was slightly better though White retains a slight advantage after 14 Q–R4.

| 14 P–R3 | N–B1 |
| 15 N–N3 | Q–B2 |

Better 15 . . . Q–Q1.

| 16 P×P | RP×P |

After 16 . . . BP×P 17 R–QB1, Black's queen would be exposed but this was the lesser evil since now

116
B

Black's QB3 and QB4 squares are very weak.

17 R–QB1	Q–N1
18 N–R2	B–N2
19 N–N4	R–Q1
20 Q–B2	R–B1
21 N–B5 (*116*)	
21 . . .	N/3–Q2
22 N×N	N×N
23 KR–Q1	N–B1

The attempt to lift the blockade by 23 . . . P–QB4 fails to 24 R×N P×N 25 Q–N3!

Now White cannot prevent the freeing 24 . . . P–QB4 without reducing his pressure on QB6 by 24 N–Q3 or 24 B–B5 and so chooses to convert his advantage into another form.

24 P–KR4	P–QB4
25 N–Q5	B×N
26 R×B	P–B5
27 B–R3	N–K3
28 B×N	P×B
29 R–Q7	

White's better bishop and pawn formation guarantee him a lasting advantage.

29 . . .	R–Q1
30 R/1–Q1	R×R
31 R×R	Q–QB1
32 Q–Q2	Q–B3
33 B–N5	

If 33 Q–Q6 Q×Q 34 R×Q P–B6! gives Black counterchances. Now Black is in a sort of *zugzwang* since the natural 33 . . . R–KB1 fails to 34 Q–Q6! when Black is a tempo behind the previous variation. Black's position was probably lost anyway but he shortens the struggle with a blunder.

| 33 . . . | Q×P?? |
| 34 R×B+ | Resigns |

After 34 . . . K×R   35 Q–Q7+
and 36 B–R6 forces mate.

*Notes by Whiteley specially for
this volume*

119 **Tatai** (Italy) –
    Rodrigues (Peru)

Blumenfeld Gambit

1 P–Q4	N–KB3
2 P–QB4	P–K3
3 N–KB3	P–B4
4 P–Q5	P–QN4?!

Theory considers this dubious, and
rightly so. Black wants to establish
a dominating central pawn majority
after 5 QP×P BP×P 6 P×P P–
Q4, but this is rather unrealistic.
The only gambit of this type considered playable at the moment is
Benkö's speciality: 1 P–Q4 N–KB3
2 P–QB4 P–B4 3 P–Q5 P–QN4,
the rationale of which is purely
positional.

5 **B–N5!**   KP×P

It looks more logical to play 5 . . .
NP×P, nibbling at White's centre,
but then 6 P–K4 Q–R4+ 7 B–Q2
Q–N3 8 N–B3 B–R3 9 N–K5 is
good for White according to Tai-
manov.

6 P×QP	P–KR3
7 B×N	Q×B
8 Q–B2	P–Q3
9 P–K4	P–QR3
10 P–QR4	

In exchange for the surrender of
the bishop pair White has annexed
the light-square complex on the
Q-side and also leads in development.

10 . . .	P–N5
11 B–Q3	

Also not bad is 11 KN–Q2 followed

by N–B4 and QN–Q2 reinforcing
the light square grip.

11 . . .	N–Q2
12 QN–Q2	P–N4?!

Very loosening, but Black is seeking dark-square compensation – e.g:
by hindering a possible P–KB4 from
White.

13 N–B4	B–N2
14 0–0	0–0
15 QR–K1	

This declares White's intention of
organizing a massive central push
against Black's weakened K-side.

15 . . .	Q–K2
16 P–K5!	

Now 16 . . . P×P 17 P–Q6 is
ruinous for Black.

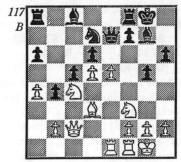

117
B

16 . . .	N×P
17 KN×N	B×N

Or 17 . . . P×N 18 P–Q6 Q–Q1
19 N×P.

18 N×B	P×N
19 P–B4	

At the cost of one pawn White
has reduced Black's position to a
complete shambles. It's quite surprising that Black can actually avoid
checkmate.

19 . . .	NP×P
20 R×BP	B–Q2
21 B–B5	

The technical solution. White

plays on Black's shattered pawns. Alternatively White could have continued more ambitiously, though less securely, with 21 R–K3, transferring this piece to the vicinity of Black's king.

21 ...	B×B
22 Q×B	QR–K1
23 R/4–K4	Q–Q3
24 R/1–K3	

Now threatening R–KN3+ followed by R/4–KN4 and R–N7.

24 ...	K–R1
25 R–KN3	R–KN1
26 Q×BP	

Black has been obliged to return the pawn in order to ward off White's threats but this sop has failed to placate the opponent's wrath.

26 ...	R/K1–KB1
27 R×R+	R×R
28 Q–K6	

White's conduct of this game has been marked throughout by its prediliction for solutions of a simple and logical nature. The triumph of this method over Black's frenzied efforts provides one of the game's main attractions.

28 ...	Q×Q
29 P×Q	R–QB1

The only plausible alternative is 29 ... R–K1 but this loses: 30 R×KP K–N2 31 K–B2 K–B3 32 R×P R×P 33 R–B4 R–QN3 34 P–R5!

30 R×KP	K–N2
31 P–K7	K–B2
32 K–B2	P–B5
33 P–K8 = Q+	

A final neat simplification.

33 ...	R×Q
34 R×R	K×R

35 K–K3	P–QR4
36 K–Q4	Resigns

Notes by Keene based on analysis by Tatai in THE CHESS PLAYER

120 **Rodrigues** (Peru) –
Suttles (Canada)

Modern Defence

1 P–K4 P–KN3 2 P–Q4 P–Q3 3 P–QB3 N–KB3 Avoiding 3 ... B–N2 **4 P–KB4. 4 B–Q3 P–K4 5 P×P** Playing safe. Spassky likes P–KB4. **5 ... P×P 6 N–B3 QN– Q2 7 Q–K2 B–N2 8 N–R3 0–0 N–B4** This is too ambitious. White is trying to prevent ... N–QB4 and ... P–QR4, but it puts too great a strain on his own position. **9 ... R–K1 10 P–QN4** Questionable. Better 10 0–0 P–QR4 approximately =. **10 ... N–Q4! 11 P×N P–K5 12 0–0 B×P! 13 R–N1 P×B 14 Q×P B–N2** White has been chopped on the long diagonal but is well centralized in compensation. **15 B– N5 N–B3 16 N–K3 Q–Q3!** Escaping from the pin and preparing a little combination. **17 B–R4 N–K5 18 KR–K1 B–Q2** Meeting 19 N–B4? with ... Q–R3 20 R×N? R×R 21 Q×R B–B4. **19 N–Q2 N–B6** (White's inability to shift this beast gives Black the advantage.–Eds) **20**

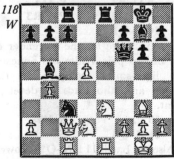

118
W

31 R. D. Keene I M on top board for
England

32 R. G. Wade I M (England), General
Editor of the Batsford Opening Series

33 A. Whiteley (England)

34 P. Markland (England)

E. U. ВИТЛ

35   D. Suttles I M (Canada)

36   D. A. Yanofsky I G M (Canada)

38   W. Browne IGM (Australia) tries a spot of hypnotism against Sarapu (New Zealand)

37   B. Amos I M (Canada)

B–N3 Q–KB3 21 QR–B1 B–N4
22 Q–B2 QR–B1! (*118*)

Accepting White's offer of the exchange would cede White a powerful QP after White had captured on c7. After the text White's Q-side is very weak. **23 N–B3 Q–R3 24 K–R1 N×RP** If 25 R–R1 N×P wins. **25 R–N1 N–B6 26 R–R1 Q–N3 27 R–R5?** On this square the rook is badly exposed. **27 . . . P–QR3 28 R–QB1 P–QB4!** **29 R/5–R1 P×P 30 P–Q6 B–Q2 31 N–N5 P–N6 32 Q–N2 Q–N4 White resigns.**

Notes specially contributed by Suttles

121 **Siaperas** (Greece) –
Suttles (Canada)

Closed Sicilian

1 P–K4	P–QB4
2 N–QB3	N–QB3
3 P–KN3	P–KN3
4 B–N2	B–N2
5 P–B4	

In my opinion not good.

5 . . .	P–Q3
6 P–Q3	R–N1

Waiting a move to play . . . N–R3 to avoid the possibility: 6 . . . N–R3 7 P–B5!? P×P 8 Q–R5 with some open lines for the pawn.

7 N–B3	N–R3
8 0–0	P–B4

If 8 . . . 0–0 9 P–B5 is again reasonable.

9 R–N1	0–0
10 K–R1	K–R1

Avoiding checks.

11 B–K3

This idea (looking at Black's QBP) does not work because Black has not weakened his supporting

QP by playing . . . P–K3. So P–K5 is never a threat from White.

11 . . .	P–QN4

12 B–N1?

A mistake which loses the QRP. 12 P–QR3 was necessary.

12 . . .	P–N5

13 N–Q5

The other possibility is very passive: 13 N–K2 Q–R4 14 N–B1

13 . . .	Q–R4!

The only logical way for Black to capitalize on his Q-side plus. Pushing the QRP wastes several tempi to accomplish the same goal.

14 R–K1	Q×P
15 P×P	N×P

15 . . . Q×N allows White's KN to move, discovering an attack on c6.

16 N–N5

A clever idea to bring the White queen to the K-side. However, a knight at KR3 (remember, this is a Suttles game! Eds.) can block the attack adequately.

16 . . .	B×P

119
W

17 Q–N4	B–KN2
18 Q–R3	N–R3
19 Q–R4	R–N2?!
20 N–K3?	

Not best. This allows the Black queen to return to the centre and then White must lose. White could

maintain practical chances with 20
R–R1! and if 20 . . . Q×P 21 N–
K3 Q×P 22 B×N R–QB2 with a
difficult position for both.

20 . . .	N–Q5
21 B×R	

Or 21 B–Q5 P–N6!

21 . . .	B×B+
22 N–K4	N/R–B4
23 Q–R3	N–B6

Wins something.

24 Q–N2	N×R
25 R×N	N×N
26 B×N	P–QR4
27 P–N4	Q–Q4
28 R–KN1	P–B5
29 R–QB1	P–N6

Destroying the base of the pawn
chain, therefore **White resigns.**

Notes specially contributed by
Duncan Suttles

122 **Capece** (Italy) –
Friedman (Israel)

English Opening

1 P–QB4	P–KN3
2 N–QB3	B–N2
3 P–KN3	P–K4
4 B–N2	P–KB4
5 P–Q3	N–K2
6 B–N5	P–KR3
7 B–Q2	0–0
8 P–KR4	P–Q3
9 N–R3	N–Q2

Preparing to bring the knight to
KB3 to help in the defence of his
K-side against White's attack.

10 Q–B1	K–R2
11 P–R5?!	P×P!

11 . . . P–KN4? allows 12 B×
KNP P×B 13 N×P+ followed by
14 N–K6 Q–K1 15 N×P.

12 N–N5+?!	P×N
13 R×P+	K–N1

Also possible is 13 . . . K–N3 14
R×P+ K–B2 15 N–Q5 with an
unclear position.

14 B×KNP	N–KB3!?

The natural move, but simpler was
14 . . . P–B3 15 B–R6 R–B3.

15 N–Q5!	N×R

If 15 . . . P–B3? 16 B×N! B×B
(or 16 . . . P×N 17 B×QP+ R–B2
18 B×B winning) 17 Q–R6 B–N2
18 R–N5 R–B2 19 N–B6+ K–B1
20 R×B R×R 21 N–R5 and
White wins. Unclear was 15 . . .
N/2×N 16 B2×N+ R–B2.

16 B×N	Q–Q2
17 Q–N5?	

White had overlooked Black's
22nd move. Better was 17 B×R
K×B 18 Q–N5 P–B3 19 Q×N
P×N 20 B×P Q–K1 followed by
21 . . . B–K3, when Black is still well
on top. Now White's position collapses.

17 . . .	R–B2!
18 0–0–0!?	P–B3
19 R–R1	P–K5!!

The only move. If 19 . . . P×N
20 B2×P Q–K1 (or 20 . . . P–N3
21 R×N B–N2 22 R–R8+ K×R
23 B×R) 21 R×N B–Q2 22 R–
R2! B–QB3 23 B–K6 B–Q2 24
Q–R4 winning for White. Also bad
would have been 19 . . . R×B 20

N×R+ K–B2 21 N–Q5! P×N
22 B×P+ K–K1 (or K–B1) 23
R×N P–K5 24 P–Q4! B–B1 25
Q–N6+ K–Q1 26 R–R8 Q–K2
27 R–R7 Q–K1 28 Q–B6+ B–K2
29 Q–N7 and White wins.

| 20 Q×N | R×B |
| 21 N×R+ | |

Or 21 N–B4 P–Q4!

21 ...	Q×N
22 P×P	Q–K4!
23 Q–N6	B–K3
24 R–R5	Q×NP+

The rest is easy.

**25 K–Q1 Q–N8+ 26 K–Q2 Q×
RP+ 27 K–K3 Q×BP 28 R–N5
Q–B8+ 29 K–B3 P×P+ 30
Q×P R–KB1+ 31 Q–KB4 Q–B6+
32 P–K3 B–Q4+ 33 R×B P×R
34 B–R3 R×Q+ 35 NP×R P–Q5
36 B–K6+ K–B1 37 Resigns**
*Notes by Friedman specially for
this volume*

123 **Tatai** (Italy) –
    Torre (Philippines)
King's Indian Defence (by
transposition)

1 P–Q4	N–KB3
2 P–QB4	P–Q3
3 N–KB3	P–KN3
4 N–B3	B–N2
5 P–KN3	0–0
6 B–N2	N–B3
7 0–0	P–QR3

7 ... P–K4 – Uhlmann's Variation – is the major alternative.

8 P–Q5
Korchnoi's 8 P–KR3 coupled with
B–K3 has become popular recently,
but the text is probably White's best
try for an enduring initiative.

| 8 ... | N–QR4 |
| 9 P–N3 | P–B4 |

Of course not 9 ... N–K5?? 10
N×N B×R 11 B–Q2 wins.

10 B–N2	R–N1
11 N–Q2	P–QN4
12 Q–B2	

White's move order (delaying
Q–B2) has some important points
in its favour. In particular, the fact
that White's queen is still on Q1
makes it difficult for Black to play
... P–K4 (or P–K3) at any stage
earlier than he actually does.

| 12 ... | P–K4 |

If this does not work Black will
have to go back to Donner's idea of
12 ... P×P followed by 13 ...
B–R3. 12 ... P×P 13 P×P P–K4
14 QR–N1 – intending B–QR1 –
is good for White, it should be noted.

| 13 QP×P ep! | B×P?! |

This has never been considered
adequate by theory. Crucial is 13 ...
BP×P 14 P×P P×P 15 QR–Q1
with a complex struggle between
White's pieces and Black's central
pawns. The latest word on this position is 15 ... B–N2 16 QN–K4
Q–K2 17 N×N+ B×N 18 QB×B
R×B 19 B×B! (not 19 N–K4?)
19 ... N×B 20 Q–Q3! with some
advantage to White.

| 14 P×P | P×P |
| 15 QR–Q1 | |

15 QN–K4 is also strong.

| 15 ... | B–B4 |
| 16 N/2–K4 | |

Speculative, but not unpromising
for White, is 16 P–K4 B–N5 17
P–B3 B–K3 18 P–K5! P×P 19
N/2–K4 with good play for the
pawn; Patterson-Heyns, Siegen 1970.

| 16 ... | P–N5 |
| 17 N–Q5 | |

The pieces are clearly in the

ascendant. Black's pawn centre is a
severe liability.

17 . . .   **N×N/K5**
18 B×B

Once the dark squared bishops
are exchanged Black's king becomes
acutely exposed along the al-h8
diagonal.

18 . . .   **K×B**

18 . . . N–B6 19 P–K4 is unpleasant for Black, but 18 . . . N–B6
19 Q×N?! P×Q 20 B–B6 Q×B
21 N×Q+ K–N2 22 R×P KR–Q1
does not look wholly clear.

19 B×N	**B×B**
20 Q×B	**R–K1**
21 Q–B2	**N–B3**
22 P–K3	**P–B4**

Very loosening, but if 22 . . .
N–K4 there comes 23 Q–N2 P–B3
24 P–B4 N–N5 25 QR–K1 followed
by P–KR3, P–KN4 and P–N5.

23 P–KR4!	**N–K4**
24 K–N2	**Q–Q2**
25 Q–N2	**K–B2**
26 P–R5	**Q–B3**
27 P×P+	**P×P**
28 R–KR1	

A decisive penetration.

28 . . .	**R–KR1**
29 R×R	**R×R**
30 P–B4	**R–K1**

On 30 . . . N–N5 there is a pleasant
variation for White 31 Q×R N×P+
32 K–N1 N×N 33 Q–KR1 K–K3
34 R–K1+ K–B3 35 P–N4! and
wins.

31 P×N	**R×P**
32 P–K4	**P–QB5**
33 NP×P	**Q×P**
34 R–Q4	**Q–B4**
35 Q×P	**Q–B7+**
36 R–Q2	**Q×KP+**
37 Q×Q	**R×Q**

and Black resigns

Notes by Keene based on analysis by
Tatai in THE CHESS PLAYER

124 **Quinones** (Peru) –
W. Hartston (England)

Czech Benoni

1 P–Q4	**N–KB3**
2 P–QB4	**P–B4**
3 P–Q5	**P–K4**
4 N–QB3	**P–Q3**
5 P–K4	**QN–Q2**

At the time this was my favourite
move order, I did not like 5 . . .
B–K2 after 6 P–KN3 and wanted
to retain the option of a king's side
fianchetto. Since this game I have
been forced to realize the strength
after 6 P–KN3 P–KN3 7 B–N2
B–N2 of 8 N–R3! (Kushnir-J.
Hartston, Skopje 1972) when Whte
is well-prepared for P–B4. The Old
Benoni needs a re-think.

6 N–B3	**B–K2**
7 B–K2	**0–0**
8 0–0	**P–QR3**
9 Q–B2?!	

White plans to hold up . . . P–B4.
Usual is 9 P–QR3 N–K1 10 P–QN4
P–QN3 11 R–N1 P–N3 12 B–R6
N–N2 13 Q–Q2, though I expect I
would have played 9 or 10 . . . K–R1

here to keep White guessing (cf. next note).

9 ...	N–K1
10 P–QR3	K–R1

Good psychology! Usually Black plays 10 ... P–KN3 11 B–R6 N–N2 followed by ... N–B3, ... K–R1 and ... N–N1 to chase away the bishop. Playing ... K–R1 first looks eccentric but can hardly be worse.

11 R–N1	P–KN3
12 B–Q3	N–N2
13 B–R6	N–B3
14 P–QN4	P–N3
15 P×P	

Probably premature. In such positions it is usually best to maintain the tension until White is ready to exploit the opening of the QN-file.

15 ...	NP×P
16 N–QR4	B–N5!
17 N–Q2	N/B3–R4

It no longer seemed necessary to play ... N–N1 so I decided to move all my pieces nearer his king to see what would happen.

18 KR–K1?

It must be better to play 18 P–B3 B–Q2 19 N–N6 followed by N×B, though Black is still a little better.

18 ...	B–N4
19 B×N+	K×B
20 N–B1	R–R2
21 N–K3	B×N!

Naturally! Now Black has the better minor pieces and a promising attacking position.

22 R×B	B–Q2
23 N–B3	P–B4 (*122*)
24 Q–N2?	

24 P×P was essential.

24 ...	P–B5
25 R/3–K1	P–B6!
26 P–N3?	

I thought it was all over now; Black's attack must mate. I expected 26 Q–N6 Q×Q 27 R×Q N–B5 with a clear advantage to Black.

26 ...	B–R6
27 Q–N6	Q–K2
28 B–B2	N–B5!
29 B–R4	

29 P×N R×P 30 K–R1 Q–N4 31 Q×R+ K–R3 is too easy.

29 ...   **R–KB2**

There are many ways to win now. I thought I might as well strengthen my position before closing in for the kill – it saves the energy of working out complications.

30 R–N3   **Q–B3**

Objectively 30 ... Q–N4 immediately is better, but I hoped for the continuation 31 KR–N1 N–K7+! 32 N×N P×N 33 P–B3 Q×P! 34 R×Q R×R 35 Q×R+ K–R3 and White's extra queen doesn't help.

31 B–B6	Q–N4
32 Q–N8	B–N7

This could have been played earlier, but now it requires no calculation.

33 P–KR4

Or 33 P×N Q–N5 34 N–K2 B–R8+ 35 N–N3 Q–R6

33 ...   **Q–N5**

Also 33 ... N–R6+ 34 K–R2

N×P 35 P×Q N–N5+ 36 K–N1
P–B7+ 37 K×B P×R = Q wins,
but the text is simpler and quicker.

34 Q×QP   Q–R6
35 Q×KP+   R–B3
36 Resigns

*Notes by W. R. Hartston specially
for this volume*

125 **Kagan** (Israel) –
Tatai (Italy)

Sicilian Defence

1 P–K4 P–QB4 2 N–KB3 P–Q3
3 P–Q4 P×P 4 N×P N–KB3 5
N–QB3 P–QR3 6 P–KN3 Kagan
is fond of this rather innocuous
system against the Najdorf. 6 . . .
P–K4 7 N/4–K2 B–K2 8 B–N2
QN–Q2 9 0–0 P–QN4 10 P–
QR4?! The theme of precipitating
the advance of Black's QNP and
then exchanging it for White's QBP
is rarely seen because the resulting
positions usually favour Black. Here,
for instance, White is slightly embarrassed by the attack on his QN. The
ensuing pawnstructure on the Q, K
and KB-files is soon seen to favour
Black, and White's 'compensation'
(the 2:1 Q-side pawn majority) is of
no value. 10 . . . P–N5 11 N–Q5
N×N 12 P×N If 12 Q×N R–QN1
13 B–K3 Q–B2 followed by 14 . . .
N–B3 when Black's game is the more
active. 12 . . . P–QR4 13 P–QB4
P×P ep 14 N×P B–R3 15 R–K1
R–QN1 16 B–B1 Essential so as to
be able to occupy QN5 with his
knight at a later stage. 16 . . . B×B
17 K×B? White's rook is of no use
on the K-file and a better continuation would therefore have been 17
R×B followed by N–N5 and P–B4.

17 . . . 0–0 18 N–N5 R–N2! Black
is thinking in terms of a K-side
attack, not a normal idea in the
Najdorf but then this is not a normal
Najdorf. 19 P–N3 N–B3 20 B–N5
N–K1 21 B×B R×B 22 R–B1
P–B4 23 R–B6 The advance of
Black's KB-pawn cannot be stopped.
e.g. 23 P–B4 P×P 24 P×P R–K5!
and White's king is exposed to all
the elements. 23 . . . P–B5 24 P–
KN4? An alternative would have
been 24 Q–N4!? N–B3 25 Q–R3
N×P 26 R×QP Q–R1 27 K–N1
(not 27 R–K6? N–K6+ 28 R×N –
*28 P×N Q–B1 29 N–B7 R×N
winning* – 28 . . . P×R 29 R×R
Q–R8+ 30 K–K2 R×P+ 31
K–Q3 Q–Q4+ 32 K–B3 Q–B4+
33 K–Q3 R–Q7 mate) when White
has better chances of surviving the
attack. Now Tatai takes immediate
advantage of the self-inflicted wound
on White's K-side. 24 . . . P–B6
25 K–N1 R/2–KB2 26 R–K4 If 26
K–R1 Q–R5 is even more deadly
(if that is possible). 26 . . . Q–R5
27 N×P N×N 28 R×N R–B5
29 R×R R×R 30 K–R1 Q–R6
31 R–Q8+ K–B2 32 Resigns

*Notes by Levy based on analysis by
Tatai in* THE CHESS PLAYER

126 **Wibe** (Norway) –
Kristinsson (Iceland)

Ruy Lopez

1 P–K4 P–K4 2 N–KB3 N–QB3
3 B–N5 P–QR3 4 B–R4 N–B3 5
0–0 N×P 6 P–Q4 P–QN4 7
B–N3 P–Q4 8 P×P B–K3 9
P–B3 B–QB4 10 QN–Q2 0–0 11
Q–K2? More usual and correct is
11 B–B2. 11 . . . B–B4 12 P–K6!?

Enterprising but incorrect. White should now satisfy himself with a level game: 12 N×N P×N 13 N–N5 N×P 14 N×KP B–KN5 (or 14 . . . Q–Q6) with equality in each case – Larsen. **12 . . . N–R4!** 12 . . . B×KP offers no more than equal chances after 13 N×N P×N 14 Q×KP B×B 15 P×B (not 15 N–N5 P–B4 16 Q×N Q–Q4 17 Q×BP when the complications probably favour Black) 15 . . . Q–B3. 12 . . . P×P, on the other hand, fully justifies White's twelfth move: 13 N×N B×N 14 N–N5 and Black is possibly even lost. **13 P×P+ K–R1** White's initiative is evaporating. Black's king is off the dangerous KN1–QR7 diagonal and his control of the centre and active piece play combine to give him the better chances. **14 B–Q1** Not 14 N×N P×N 15 N–N5 N×B 16 P×N Q–Q6! **14 . . . B–QN3** Black must keep some control over his Q5 square. If 14 . . . B–K2 15 N–Q4! **15 N×N P×N 16 N–N5 Q–Q4!**

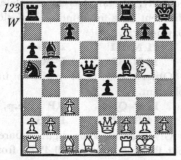

123
W

17 B–B4 Not 17 B–B2 P–K6! **17 . . . P–R3 18 Q–R5 N–B5** Intending to come to Q6 via QN7. **19 P–QN4** If 19 B–QN3 B–KR2 and the white knight is pinned against the undefended queen. **19 . . . QR–Q1**

20 B–N4 N–N7! 21 Q–R3 B×B 22 Q×B R–Q2 23 QR–K1 R–K2 24 B–K3 N–Q6 25 B×B Q×N 26 Q×Q P×Q 27 B–Q4 N×R 28 B–B5 R/2×P! Not 28 . . . R/1× P? 29 B×R N–Q6 30 B×P when Black loses the ending. But now, after capturing Black's rook, White's bishop has no good means of escape. **29 B×R N–Q6 30 B–B5 N×B 31 P×N R–B4** The point. Black has a winning rook and pawn ending. **32 P–QB4 R×QBP 33 P×P P×P 34 P–B3 P×P 35 R×P R–B8+ 36 K–B2 R–B7+ 37 K–N3 R×RP 38 R–QB3 R–R2 39 K–B3 P–QN5 40 R–N3 and White resigned** because of 40 . . . R–R6.

Notes by Sigurjonsson specially for this volume

127 **Uitumen** (Mongolia) – **Sigurjonsson** (Iceland)

Alekhine's Defence

1 P–K4 N–KB3 2 P–K5 N–Q4 3 P–Q4 P–Q3 4 P–QB4 N–N3 5 P–B4 P×P 6 BP×P B–B4 7 N–QB3 P–K3 8 B–K3 B–QN5! This innovation, first suggested by Keene and Williams a little over a year ago, is still catching some masters by surprise. **9 P–QR3?** Better is 9 N–B3 when great complications ensue. **9 . . . B×N+ 10 P×B Q–R5+!** The point of Keene's idea. **11 K–Q2!?** The alternatives are no more appetizing: (i) 11 B–B2 Q–K5+ 12 Q–K2 (or 12 B–K2 Q×NP 13 B–B3 Q–N3 14 B×P B–K5! winning) 12 . . . N×P 13 Q×Q B×Q 14 B×N? B×P and Black wins; or (ii) 11

P–N3 Q–K5 12 Q–B3 P–B4 with a
tremendous game for Black. 11 . . .
P–B4 12 N–B3 Q–K5 12 . . . Q–Q1
is also possible. 13 P–QR4! The
only chance. 13 . . . P–QR4 14
Q–N3 N/1–Q2 15 N–K1 R–Q1
16 Q–N5 0–0 17 B–Q3 Q–R5 18
B–K2 R–B1! Now Black threatens
simply . . . Q–Q1 followed by . . .
P–B3, smashing open White's king
position. 19 R–QB1 Q–Q1 20 B–
Q3 P–B3 21 KP×P N×KBP 22
R–B1 B×B 23 N×B N–K5+ 24
K–B2 R×R   25 R×R N–Q3
Forcing the decisive liquidation.
26 B–N5 N×Q 27 B×Q N–R6+
28 K–N3 R×B 29 K×N N×BP+
30 K–R2 P×P 31 P×P R×P
32 N–B5 R–Q3 33 N×NP R–Q7+
34 K–N3 R–N7+ 35 K×N R×N
36 K–B5 R–N7 37 R–KN1 K–B2
38 P–R3 R–N5 39 R–QR1 R–N7
40 R–KB1+ K–K2 41 R–KN1
R–N5 42 R–QR1 P–R4 43 P–N3
P–N4 44 R–R3 K–B3 45 R–R1
P–K4 46 K–Q5 R–Q5+ 47 K–B5
K–K3 48 K–N6 R–Q4 49 R–K1
P–N5 50 P×P P×P 51 R–K3
K–B4 52 K–B6 K–K3 53 K–N6
K–B4 54 K–B6 R–Q8 55 K–N6
P–K5 56 K×P R–Q6 57 R–K1
P–K6 58 R–KB1+ K–K5 59
R–B4+ K–Q4 60 R–B5+ K–B5
61 K–N6 R–Q3+ 62 **Resigns**

*Notes by Sigurjonsson specially
for this volume*

128 **Keene** (England) –
Kagan (Israel)

English Opening

Played on top board of the last
round clash between the two leading
teams.

1 N–KB3	P–QB4
2 P–KN3	P–KN3
3 B–N2	B–N2
4 0–0	P–K4

I once considered this Botvinnik
system rather dubious in view of the
hole on d5, but now I regard it as a
perfectly viable equalizing method
for Black.

5 P–B4	N–K2
6 N–B3	QN–B3
7 P–Q3	0–0
8 R–N1	P–Q3
9 P–QR3	P–QR4!

White must not be allowed to
expand unchallenged on the Q-side.

10 B–Q2   P–KR3?!

Leads to a sharp struggle, which
was what I wanted as well, in view
of the situation in the group. A few
weeks after this game I reached the
same position against Hartoch
(Anglo-Dutch Match, Flushing
1972) and the Dutch master continued with 10 . . . R–N1! 11 N–K1
B–K3 12 N–B2 (12 N–Q5 P–QN4)
12 . . . P–Q4 and Black has absolute
equality. Kagan has a completely
different idea in mind – a K-side
pawn-storm.

11 N–K1	P–B4
12 N–B2	P–R5

Otherwise P–QN4 really is unpleasant.

13 P–QN4	RP×P e.p.
14 R×P	P–B5

Gives away some light squares,
but Black must forestall P–B4 from
White, which would stifle his attack.

15 P–K3   P–KN4
16 N–Q5?!

This could be wrong. Possibly 16
Q–K2 at once followed by KR–N1
is most accurate.

16 ...	N×N
17 B×N+	K-R1
18 Q-K2	Q-B3
19 KR-N1	

Perhaps the exchange sacrifice R×NP will be on one day?

| 19 ... | P-B6 |

Definitely best. Black cannot strengthen his attack without this move.

| 20 Q-Q1 | P-R4?! |

But this is dubious. I suspect Black overlooked White's next move. Correct was 20 ... P-N5 and only the ... P-R4.

21 P-Q4!

Exploiting the temporary under protection of Black's KBP. If Black captures on d4 the 'f3' point falls into White's hands (don't forget White's rook on QN3 can move sideways too) and Black's K-side falls apart. So, Black ignores this demonstration, but with White's QB on c3 the diagonals to Black's own king become severely exposed.

21 ...	P-R5
22 P×BP	QP×P
23 B-B3	P×P
24 RP×P	P-N5
25 R-N5	Q-R3

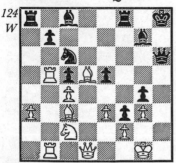

124
W

The threat of ... Q-R6 can be held by Q-KB1 and at the moment

endings favour White in view of his domination of the Q-side, but Black has something far more loathsome in mind: ... R-KB4 —KR4-KR8. Measures must be taken to stop this.

26 P-K4

A concession in as much as Black now creates a passed pawn.

| 26 ... | N-Q5 |
| 27 N×N | BP×N?! |

Black has an idée fixe that he should deliver mate, but this is too simple an assessment of the position. In my opinion Black should play here 27 ... KP×N 28 B-Q2 Q-R6! 29 Q-KB1 R×P going into a double rook and bishop ending that is totally unclear. Note that the mating call 27 ... KP×N 28 B-Q2 Q-R2 29 R×BP B-K4 is rejected after 30 R-N6! R-R3 31 R×R P×R 32 R-N6 and Black is in trouble.

| 28 B-Q2 | Q-R2 |

28 ... Q-R6 29 Q-KB1 R×P is now a complete flop in view of B-N4!

29 R-N6

Now White even begins to think of a mating attack by turning his advanced columns sharp right along the sixth rank.

| 29 ... | R-Q1? |

Planning an exchange sacrifice which wins for White. I expected 29 ... R-B3 30 B-B1 and thought White stood a little better.

30 B-N5!

Black's last chance now is 30 ... Q-R6 to force off queens before White plays B-R4, when White's own king would be perfectly secure while Black's monarch would find himself on a blasted heath (protected, admittedly, by a fool on g7).

   30 . . .   **R × B**

The point of his previous move. Black obtains a mass of central pawns for the sacrifice but he has overlooked one factor, to wit: White can now launch a mating attack! Black has so long regarded this sort of thing as his own perogative that he has been blind to the possibility of a White counteraction.

   31 BP × R   **Q × P**

   32 B–R6!

Decisive.

   32 . . .   **Q–R2**

The best defence. 32 . . . Q × P 33 B × B+ K × B 34 Q–QB1! is even more horrible.

   33 Q–QB1   **P–K5**

The stiffest line was: 33 . . . B–Q2 34 Q–N5 R–KN1 35 Q–R5 B–

KB3! but after 36 R × B! Q × R+ 37 K–R2 Q–R2 38 R–B7 White wins easily.

   34 Q–N5!

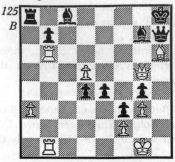

Black could resign now.

   34 . . .   **R–R3**

   35 R × R   **P × R**

   36 R–N6!

Wins Black's queen. **Black lost on time.**

Notes by Keene

FINAL GROUP C

		A	F	S	I	B	P	T	I	P	M	T	W	N	D	B	J	Total
32	Australia	×	3	2	3	2	3½	3½	3	3	4	3	2½	3	3	2½	4	45
33	Finland	1	×	3	2	2	3½	2½	3	2	3½	2½	3½	2½	3	4	4	42
34	Scotland	2	1	×	2	2½	2½	2½	1½	3	2½	2	2½	3½	3½	4	4	39
35	Iran	1	2	2	×	3½	3	1	1½	2½	3	3	3	3	3½	3	2½	37½
36	Brazil	2	2	1½	½	×	1½	2	2½	3	2½	2	2	3½	3	4	3½	35½
37	Portugal	½	½	1½	1	2½	×	1½	3½	2	2½	2	2½	2	4	3	3½	32½
38	Turkey	½	1½	1½	3	2	2½	×	1½	3½	4	1	2	1½	2	2	2½	31
39	Ireland	1	1	2½	2½	1½	½	2½	×	2½	1	2	2	2	1½	3½	2½	28½
40	Puerto Rico	1	2	1	1½	1	2	½	1½	×	2½	4	2½	2	3½	2	1½	28½
41	Mexico	0	½	1½	1	1½	1½	0	3	1½	×	3	3	2	3	2	3	26½
42	Tunisia	1	1½	2	1	2	2	3	2	0	1	×	2	1½	2	2½	3	26½
43	Wales	1½	½	1½	1	2	1½	2	2	1½	1	2	×	2	2½	2	3½	26½
44	New Zealand	1	1½	½	1	½	2	2½	2	2	2	2½	2	×	1	2	2½	25
45	Dominican Rep.	1	1	½	½	1	0	2	2½	½	1	2	1½	3	×	2½	2½	21½
46	Bolivia	1½	0	0	1	0	1	2	½	2	2	1½	2	2	1½	×	2	19
47	Japan	0	0	0	1½	½	½	1½	1½	2½	1	1	½	1½	1½	2	×	15½

Ireland (6 wins 3 draws) were placed ahead of Puerto Rico (4 wins 4 draws) because of their better match record.

Mexico (5 wins 2 draws) and Tunisia (3 wins 6 draws) were placed ahead of Wales on their better match records and Mexico headed Tunisia on the result of their individual match.

Portugal beat Dominican Rep. 4–0 by default in the last round.

Progressive Score Table

		R1	R2	R3	R4	R5	R6	R7	R8	R9	R10	R11	R12	R13	R14	R15
32	Australia	3½	**6½**	**8½**	10½	13½	**17½**	**20**	**22½**	**25½**	**29½**	**32½**	**35½**	**39**	**42**	**45**
33	Finland	3½	5½	8	10½	12½	15½	17½	20½	24	28	31½	32½	36½	39½	42
34	Scotland	**4**	**6½**	**8½**	**12½**	**16**	17	19½	21½	25	27½	30½	32½	35	36½	39
35	Iran	3½	5½	**8½**	11½	14½	15½	18	20	23½	25	28	31	34	35	37½
36	Brazil	2½	**6½**	**8½**	10½	14	17	19	20½	21	24½	26½	29½	31	33	35½
37	Portugal	½	2½	3½	5½	7	9	10½	13	16½	19	22	24½	25	28½	32½
38	Turkey	½	3	5	6½	9	12	13½	14½	18	19½	21½	23	27	29	31
39	Ireland	2	3	6½	8½	9½	12	13½	14½	15	17½	19½	22	24½	27	28½
40	Puerto Rico	2½	3½	5	8½	10½	12½	14	16	16½	20½	21½	22½	24	26½	28½
41	Mexico	1½	4½	7½	9½	12½	12½	15½	18½	19	20½	21½	23½	23½	25	26½
42	Tunisia	2	4	5	6	8½	10	12	15	16	16	19	21	23	25	26½
43	Wales	1½	3	5	7	8	10	12	13½	17	19½	20	21½	22½	24½	26½
44	New Zealand	2½	3½	5	6	8	10½	13	15	15½	16	18	20	22	24	25
45	Dominican Rep.	½	3½	5½	6	6½	7½	10	11	13½	15	16	18½	20½	21½	21½
46	Bolivia	0	0	½	2½	4	6	7½	9½	11	11	12	13	15	17	19
47	Japan	1½	3	5½	5½	6	7	8½	10½	11	11	12	13½	13½	14	15½

Scotland was leading group C for the first half of the finals thanks to their position in the draw which gave them the majority of the weakest teams as their early opponents. It was in the eighth round that Australia overhauled Scotland. After their bad luck in the preliminaries it was only just that Australia should win the C-final convincingly. Led by twenty-three-year-old Grandmaster Walter Browne, their young team produced some lively chess and played with great determination throughout. Browne might have been expected to carry off the first board prize but his ambition was foiled when he met his bogey opponent Heikki Westerinen, the Finnish International Master who seems to find Browne a friendly opponent (Westerinen won their encounters at Siegen 1970 and again at the annual Netanya tournament in 1971).

Towards the end of the finals Finland too overtook Scotland. Japan did well to qualify for this group at only their second Olympiad. Chess is not at all popular in their country and its geographical remoteness makes it almost impossible for its leading players to find any real competition in the two years that separate the Olympiads. There were no big surprises in final-C. No tension in the final rounds. No disputes; no drama. Until the last day that is . . .

Another Forfeit
In the last round of final group C, the tables of the Portugal-Dominican Republic match were empty from the start. After the fuss over the Albania-Israel question it was natural to assume that the absence of the Dominican team was connected in some way with Portugal's foreign policies. In fact, nothing could have been further from the truth. The Dominican team had arrived in Skopje three days early, and when paying for the 'extras' on their hotel bill (laundry, drinks, telephone calls, etc.) they discovered that they had been charged a total of 300 dollars for the extra days. Thinking the amount to be excessive they had refused to pay with the result that their passports had been seized by the local police. The Dominican captain protested but to no avail. The organisers were well within their rights to charge for the extra days and the standard rate for the Dominicans' accommodation was 100 dollars per day for the whole team.

The Dominicans felt that their complaint was handled rather brusquely. They apologised in advance to their Portuguese opponents for any embarrassment that they might be caused, paid the 300 dollars under protest and caught the first available 'plane out of Skopje.

129 **Williams** (Wales) –
    German (Brazil)

Queen's Indian Defence

1 P–Q4 N–KB3 2 P–QB4 P–K3
3 N–KB3 P–QN3 4 P–KN3 B–N2

5 B–N2 B–K2 6 0–0 0–0 7 N–B3
N–K5 8 B–Q2 A relatively new move in this notoriously drawish variation, giving White some surprisingly dynamic possibilities. If Black exchanges his advanced knight

White is well placed to attempt a central advance, while maintaining it on K5 is not without problems as the sequel shows. **8 . . . B–KB3** Unusual but probably not bad. The pressure on White's Q4 is irritating. Also, 9 P–Q5 is prevented for the time being on account of 9 . . . N×N and 10 . . . B×B doubling the QBP's. **9 R–B1 P–Q4** 10 P–Q5 was threatened. **10 P×P P P×P** Both 10 . . . N×N and 10 . . . N×B leave White with pressure.

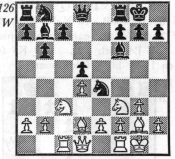

11 B–B4! P–B4? Black is probably lost after this move, though even after the superior 11 . . . N×N and 12 . . . P–QB3 White retains some advantage. **12 N×N P×N 13 N–Q2 B×P** If 13 . . . Q×P simply 14 N×P!, or if Black defends the KP then 14 P×P and 15 Q–B2. **14 N×P K–R1** Objectively better may be 14 . . . B×NP, but after 15 R–N1 White is winning at least the exchange (the threat is N–B6+). **15 P–K3!** More accurate than 15 Q–B2 when Black can try 15 . . . P–B4. If now 15 . . . B×NP, 16 N–Q6, threatening both 17 N×B and 17 N×P+, is terminal. **15 . . . B–KB3 16 Q–B2 B–B3** 17 N×B was threatened. **17 KR–Q1 Q–B1** Or 17 . . . Q–K2 18 B–Q6. **18 N×B**

P×N 19 Q–B3 Q–B4 20 R–Q6 Resigns If 20 . . . B×B 21 R×BP and White's next is going to be quite strong.

Notes by Williams specially for this volume

130 **Kaplan** (Puerto Rico) – **Pritchett** (Scotland)

Bird's Opening (by transposition)

1 N–KB3	P–QB4
2 P–QN3	P–Q4
3 P–K3	N–KB3
4 B–N2	P–K3
5 N–K5	

An interesting move. It hampers Black's normal development (. . . N–QB3) since after the exchange of knights Black would have no compensation for the doubled QBP's.

5 . . .	B–K2
6 P–KB4	

The opening now becomes a reversed Dutch Defence in which Black has adopted the passive development . . . P–K3 and . . . B–K2 instead of . . . P–KN3 and . . . B–N2. The long diagonal is now a powerful trump in White's hand; Black must play very carefully.

6 . . .	0–0
7 B–Q3!?	

The same development of the bishop occurred in a famous game Lasker–Bauer, Amsterdam 1889, in which Lasker offered both bishops for a mating attack: 1 P–KB4 P–Q4 2 N–KB3 P–K3 3 P–K3 N–KB3 4 P–QN3 B–K2 5 B–N2 P–QN3 6 B–Q3 B–N2 7 N–B3 0–0 8 0–0 QN–Q2 9 N–K2 P–B4 10 N–N3

Q–B2 11 N–K5 N×N 12 B×N
Q–B3 13 Q–K2 P–QR3 14 N–R5!
N×N 15 B×KRP+! K×B 16 Q×
N+ K–N1   17 B×P! K×B 18
Q–N4+ K–R2   19 R–B3 P–K4
20 R–R3+ Q–R3   21 R×Q+
K×R 22 Q–Q7 B–KB3 23 Q×B
K–N2 24 R–KB1 QR–N1 25 Q–
Q7 KR–Q1 26 Q–N4+ K–B1 27
P×P B–N2   28 P–K6 R–N2   29
Q–N6 P–B3 30 R×P+ B×R 31
Q×B+ K–K1 32 Q–R8+ K–K2
33 Q–N7+ K×P   34 Q×R and
White won.

In addition to the tactical threats,
the move has a sound positional idea
as we shall soon see.

7 . . .   P–QN3?

Too slow. Correct was 7 . . . N–
K5 in order to secure the K-side
with . . . P–B4. During the game I
was considering (7 . . . N–K5) 8
B×N P×B 9 N–QB3 P–B3 10
N–B4 P–B4 11 Q–K2, and now
the main idea behind 7 B–Q3
becomes evident: the exchange on
his K5 square leaves Black with a
rigid pawn formation that gives
White's minor pieces excellent scope.
White's position is very flexible – he
can castle on either wing and can
start operations on the Q-side with
P–QR4–5; on the K-side with P–
KN4; and even in the centre with
P–Q3, exposing the opponent's weak
Q3 square.

8 P–KN4!

Now, in addition to Black's other
problems, he has to face a powerful
K-side attack.

8 . . .   B–N2

Better is 8 . . . N–K5 9 P–N5
P–B3, although after 10 B×N P×B
(10 . . . P×N?? 11 B×RP+) 11

P×P B×P 12 Q–N4 B–R5+ 13
K–Q1, White has the better pawn
structure and attacking chances.

9 P–N5   N–K5
10 B×N   P×B
11 Q–R5!

It is doubtful that Black can hold
the game any longer. If now 11 . . .
N–Q2 (to control the KB3 square
with another piece) then 12 N–N4,
threatening R–N1 followed by N–
R6+ or R–N3–R3, and Black
cannot play 12 . . . P–B4? because
of 13 P–N6! P×P 14 Q×NP B–KB3
15 B×B N×B 16 N–R6+ K–R1
17 N–B7+; nor can Black prepare
. . . P–B4 with 12 . . . Q–K1 for
then 13 N–B6+ forces mate.

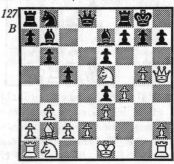

127
B

11 . . .   N–B3
12 N–N4   P–K4!?

Black tries to save his king by
giving up a pawn. Instead of taking
it with 13 N×P, White makes a
very questionable decision: he tries
to maintain his attack.

13 P×P?!   B×P

An interesting possibility is 13 . . .
P–N3 14 Q–R3! B×P 15 N–B6+
B×N 16 P×B P–KR4 17 R–N1
K–R2 18 Q–R4 or 18 N–B3, and
here the bad position of the black
king is a decisive factor. Notice that
White cannot play 14 Q–R6? B×P

15 N–B6+?? Q×N, or 15 P–K6 N–Q5! with unclear complications.

14 P–KR4   B–K2
15 N–B3

Not 15 N–B6+ P×N   16 Q–R6 N×P!   17 B×N K–R1 and Black can hold.

15 . . .   P–B4?
16 P×P e.p.   B×P
17 N×P!

This pseudo sacrifice decides the game very quickly. But White was beginning to get short of time and Black finds a way to play on.

17 . . .   N–Q5!
18 N/N4×B+   R×N?

This makes it easy. But even after 18 . . . P×N   19 R–KN1+ K–R1   20 P×N B×N   21 0–0–0 (threatening 22 Q–N4) Black is lost.

19 N×R+   Q×N
20 B×N   P×B
21 R–KB1   Q–K2
22 0–0–0   P–R4
23 Q–QN5   P×P?
24 P×P   Q×KP+
25 K–N1   P–R3
26 Q–B4+   K–R2
27 QR–K1   Q–R6
28 R–N1   R–QB1
29 R×P+!   K×R
30 R–K7+   K–B3
31 Q–KB7 mate

Notes by Kaplan specially for this volume

131 **Westerinen** (Finland) – **Miyasaka** (Japan)

Hara Kiri!

13 . . . P–K4?   14 N–B5 P–K5??   15 N–R6+ Resigns 15 . . . K–R1 allows 16 Q×N! P×Q 17 QB×P mate

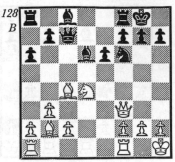

132 **Ribeiro** (Portugal) – **Levy** (Scotland)

Sicilian Defence

1 P–K4 P–QB4   2 N–KB3 P–Q3   3 P–Q4 P×P   4 N×P N–KB3   5 N–QB3 P–KN3   6 B–QB4 B–N2   7 B–N3 0–0   8 P–B3 N–B3   9 B–K3 B–Q2   10 Q–Q2 R–B1   11 P–N4!? Not usually seen at this juncture but of course there are transpositional possibilities after 11 . . . N–K4 12 0–0–0 N–B5   13 B×N R×B   14 K–N1 or 14 P–KR4. **11 . . . N–K4 12 B–R6?!** Premature. **12 . . . B×B 13 Q×B   R×N!** Thematic. In return for the exchange Black gets one pawn and oodles of play. **14 P×R Q–R4   15 0–0** If 15 Q–K3 R–B1 16 K–Q2 (16 N–K2? B–N4) 16 . . . N×BP+! 17 N×N (or 17 Q×N) R×P and Black emerges with queen and three pawns for two rooks. **15 . . . Q×BP 16 QR–Q1 P–R4 17 P–QR4 N–B5!** Threatening 18 . . . Q–K6+ winning the exchange, and starting to surround White's isolated QRP. **18 K–R1** After 18 B×N Q×B, Black wins the QRP at once. But probably better than the text is 18 R–Q3. (*129*) **18 . . . Q–K6! 19 Q–R4 N–N7!** Winning back the exchange. Not,

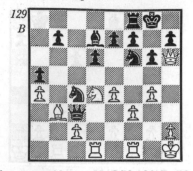

129
B

however, 19 . . . N–Q7? 20 R–B2.
**20 KR–K1 Q–B6 21 Q–N5 N×R
22 R×N R–B1 23 K–N2** Relieving
the knight from the defence of the
KBP. **23 . . . K–N2?** With the idea
that after an eventual N–B5 B×N;
NP×B, White will no longer be
threatening P×NP RP×P; Q×
NP+. But instead of being afraid
of such ghosts Black should have
continued 23 . . . Q–B4 24 Q–B4
Q–K4. **24 P–K5! P×P 25 Q×KP**
Now White reaches a drawn ending
by force. **25 . . . Q–B4 26 R–K1
P–K3 27 P–N5 Q×Q 28 R×Q
N–Q4 29 B×N P×B 30 R–K7!**
30 R×P B×P   31 R×P B×P
would still leave Black winning. But
now White's rook and knight work
together very well, harassing the
black king which is being kept a
prisoner by White's pawn at KN5.
30 . . . B×P 31 R×NP K–B1
If 31 . . . B×P 32 R–Q7 P–R5 33
R×QP P–R6 34 R–R5 drawing.
**32 R–R7 R–B5   33 P–B3 R–B4
34 K–N3 B–K1   35 K–B4 P–R5
36 K–K5 R×P   37 K×P R–Q6
38 K–K5 R–Q7 39 P–R4 R–KR7
40 R–R8 R×P   41 N–N5! Draw
Agreed** Black is forced to simplify
by 41 . . . R–R8 42 N–B7 R–K8+
43 K–B6 R–K2 44 N×B R×N 45

R×P. The winning try 41 . . . K–
K2 42 R–R7+ B–Q2 rebounds
unpleasantly after 43 N–B7 and 44
N–Q5+.
Notes by Levy

133 **Browne** (Australia) –
  Harandi (Iran)
Ruy Lopez

1 P–K4	**P–K4**
2 N–KB3	**N–QB3**
3 B–N5	**P–QR3**
4 B–R4	**N–B3**
5 0–0	**P–QN4**
6 B–N3	**B–N2**
7 P–Q4	

For 7 R–K1 see game 38.

7 . . .	**N×QP**
8 B×P+	

When I played at Venice in 1971
Cosulich tried the alternative 8
N×N against Radulov but got a
bad game after 8 . . . P×N 9 P–
QB3 (9 P–K5 N–K5 10 P–QB3!
is correct) 9 . . . N×P 10 R–K1
B–K2 11 Q–N4 0–0!

8 . . .	**K×B**
9 N×P+	**K–N1**
10 Q×N	**P–B4**
11 Q–Q1	

Best. If 11 Q–K3 Q–K1!

11 . . .	**P–Q3**

The theoretical continuation is
11 . . . Q–K1 12 N–KB3 Q×P 13
N–B3 (not 13 B–N5?! N–Q4! with
a slight advantage to Black. But also
possible is 13 R–K5 Q–Q4   14
QN–Q2 P–B5 15 R–K1 Q–B3
with an unclear position. Hasin-
Nezhmetdinov, USSR 1962.) 13 . . .
Q–B3!

12 N–N4! N×P	

Of course I would have preferred
him to play 12 . . . B×P 13 N×N+
Q×N 14 N–B3 when I gain control

39 The match that never was. Four Israelis stare at empty Albanian boards. Behind Friedman is Kraidman talking to (left) Anderton, English Captain and Gurevich, Israeli Captain.

40 Kraidman (Israel) playing Hartston (England) in the final round of Group B

41   D. Levy I M on top board for Scotland against Japan

42   The top and bottom teams of Final D: Haik (France) in play against the Virgin Islands captain, Edwards

of Q5. Then I would have been very happy.

13 P–KB3	**N–N4**
14 N–B3	**P–Q4**
15 Q–K1	**N–B2**
16 B–B4	

Intending N–K5.

16 . . .	**P–KR4!**
17 N–K5	**Q–B3**
18 N × N	**Q × N/2**
19 Q–Q2	**P–R5!**

Planning to bring the KR into play via KR4 to KB4.

20 QR–K1	**R–R4**
21 N–K2	**B–K2**
22 N–B1	

With the idea of N–Q3 followed by N–K5, and if . . . P–B5 then the knight can return to K2 on its way to Q4.

22 . . .	**R–B4**
23 N–Q3	**P–N4**
24 B–K5	**P–R6**
25 B–N3!	

Even though it looks as though White's K-side is under pressure Black has weakened his own K-side even more.

25 . . .	**P × P**
26 Q × P/N2	**P–Q5**
27 N–K5	**Q–R2**
28 N–N4	**QR–KB1**
29 R–K6!	

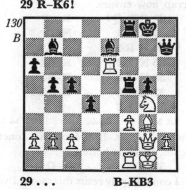

130
B

29 . . .   B–KB3

29 . . . R × P loses to 30 N–R6+ K–R1 31 B–K5+ etc. and 29 . . . B × P to 30 R × B R × R 31 N–R6+ K–R1 32 B–K5+ R/6–B3 33 Q × P (33 . . . Q–KN2 34 Q × Q+ K × Q 35 N–B5+!)

30 B–Q6	**B–N2**

30 . . . R/1–B2 would also have led to a very bleary finish: 31 R–K8+ K–N2 32 N–K5! winning the exchange (32 . . . B × N 33 B × B+ K–N3 34 R–K6+)

31 B × R	**R × B**
32 P–N3	**P–B5**
33 P × P	**P × P**
34 R–K7	**P–Q6**
35 N–K5!	

A sharp move in a tricky position.

35 . . .	**Q–B4**
36 R × B/QN7	**Q × N**
37 P × P	**P × P**
38 K–R1	**Q–B5**
39 R–Q7	

The rest is history.

39 . . . Q–B4 40 R–Q6 R–N1 41 Q–N4 Q–K4 42 Q–QB4+ K–B1 43 R–Q5 Q–K7 44 R–KB5+ Resigns

Notes by Browne specially for this volume

134 Ojanen (Finland) – **Pritchett** (Scotland)

Modern Benoni

1 P–Q4	**N–KB3**
2 P–QB4	**P–B4**
3 P–Q5	**P–K3**
4 N–QB3	**P × P**
5 P × P	**P–Q3**
6 P–K4	**P–KN3**
7 B–Q3	**B–N2**
8 KN–K2	

Ojanen's own system with which he won a well-known game against

Keres in 1960 and which was responsible for Penrose's victory over Tal later in that same year.

| 8 ... | 0–0 |
| 9 0–0 | P–N3 |

Also possible are 9 . . . P–QR3, 9 . . . N–R3 and 9 . . . R–K1. The text move seeks an easy development after the exchange of light squared bishops.

10 P KR3	B–R3
11 N–N3	B×B
12 Q×B	P–QR3
13 P–QR4	QN–Q2
14 B–K3	P–KR4!?

Since White has a resilient position on the Q-side it seems logical to probe for play on the K-side and in the centre.

15 KR–B1

15 KR–K1 is possibly better.

15 ...	P–R5
16 N–B1	N–R4
17 Q–Q2	

Better than 17 P–B4 P–B4, after which White's bishop is shut in by its own pawns and Black has fine prospects.

17 ...	P–B4
18 B–N5	B–B3
19 B×B	Q×B
20 P×P	P×P
21 R–K1	N–K4

131 W

A delicate position. Black has pawn weaknesses but active pieces and more space on the K-side. White's next move came as a shock. Plausible and perhaps better moves were 22 R–K2, 22, N–KR2 and 22 K–R1. I felt that Black must stand better after the violent text move.

22 P–B4?!	N–B5
23 Q–KB2	Q–Q5
24 Q×Q	

If 24 P–QN3 N–R4 with some advantage to Black.

24 ...	P×Q
25 N–K2	P–Q6
26 N–Q4	N×BP
27 P–QN3	N–K4
28 N–K3	QR–B1?!

After this move however, the pendulum swings the other way. Better was 28 . . . R–B3! 29 N/3× BP QR–KB1 30 N×RP N×QP 31 N/R4–B3 N×N+ 32 N×N N–B5 with a clear advantage to Black.

29 N/3×P	R–B4
30 N×RP	KR–B1
31 N/R4–B5	R/1–B2!

The only good move. 31 . . . P–Q7? is an hallucination: 32 KR–Q1 R–B8? 33 N–K7+ etc. A real scrap now ensues.

32 QR–Q1	R×P
33 R–K4	N/5–N3
34 P–R4	N–K2
35 N–K3	R–R4
36 N–N4	R–B6
37 K–B2	R/4–B4
38 N–K3	

38 K–K3? allows 38 . . . N–Q4+ 39 K–Q2 R–B7+! when, once again, Black is better.

| 38 ... | N–Q4! |

I could hardly resist this move. I've

never seen a centre in such a terrible mess!

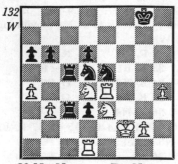

132
W

39 N×N	R×N
40 P–KN4	N–Q2
41 N–B5	R–K4
42 R–K3	

The sealed move. 42 K–K3 and 42 N×P were plausible alternatives.

42 ...	R×R
43 K×R	R×P
44 P–N5!?	

After this move I felt relieved. White must have thought that 44 R×P R×R+ 45 K×R N–B4+ 46 K–Q4 N×P 47 K–Q5 was only drawn. This may be so but, after the text, the draw is easier.

44 ...	N–K4
45 P–KR5	P–Q7+!
46 K×P	R–KR6
47 N×P	R×P

Draw Agreed
Notes by Pritchett specially for this volume

135 Browne (Australia) –
Westerinen (Finland)

Ruy Lopez

1 P–K4	P–K4
2 N–KB3	N–QB3
3 B–N5	P–QR3
4 B–R4	P–Q3
5 0–0	B–Q2

Better than 5 ... B–N5. e.g. 6 P–KR3 P–KR4 7 P–B4 Q–B3 8 Q–N3 0–0–0 9 B×N P×B 10 N–R2 (10 P×B P×P 11 N–R2 Q–N3! was seen to be good for Black in the game Faibisovich-Vorotnikov, USSR 1972) 10 ... B–K3 11 P–Q4 P×P 12 N–KB3 with a clear advantage for White.

6 P–Q4	N–B3

Also possible is 6 ... P–QN4 7 B–N3 P×P 8 P–QR4!? B–K2.

7 P–B3	B–K2
8 R–K1	0–0
9 QN–Q2	R–K1
10 P–QR3	B–KB1

10 ... P–QR4 is also possible so as to prevent White's Q-side expansion.

11 P–QN4	P–KN3

11 ... P–Q4 is an interesting alternative.

12 B–N2	B–N2
13 P–Q5	N–K2
14 P–B4	P–QN4!
15 B–N3	P×P
16 N×BP	N–R4
17 R–QB1	N–B5

133
W

18 N/3×P	

'I was trying for the brilliancy prize' – Browne.

Correct is 18 Q–Q2! P–R3 (18 ... P–KB3 19 N–Q4 N×NP is

unclear) 19 N/3×P P×N 20 N×P
N/2×QP! 21 B×N (Not 21 N×BP
Q–K2 when Black is clearly better)
21 . . . Q–N4 22 B×P+ K–R2 23
B×P+ N×B 24 Q×Q P×Q 25
R×P N×N 26 B×N R×B 27
R×B P–R4 when the game should
probably be drawn.

| 18 . . . | P×N |
| 19 N×P | N–B1 |

19 . . . R–KB1 is also a possible
consolidating idea. If then 20 Q–Q2
N/2×P, or 20 Q–B3 P–N4.

20 N×BP

20 Q–B3 does not work because
of 20 . . . B×N 21 B×B N–R6+
winning.

| 20 . . . | K×N |
| 21 P–Q6+ | K–B1 |

21 . . . B–K3 22 R×P+ Q×R
23 P×Q B/2×B 24 Q–B3 and
21 . . . N–K3 22 P×P Q–K2 23
P–K5 K–N1 24 Q–Q5 are unclear
alternatives. 21 . . . R–K3! however,
ought to prove as decisive as the
text.

22 B×B+

If 22 P×P Q–N4! 23 B×B+
K×B 24 Q×B+ R–K2! 25 Q–
Q4+ K–R3 26 P–N3 N–K7+ 27
R×N Q×R+ etc.

22 . . .	K×B
23 R×P	K–R3
24 R×B	Q×R
25 B–R4	Q–Q1!
26 B×R	N×QP
27 Q–B3	Q–N4
28 B–B6	R–QB1
29 P–K5	N–B4

As well as a terribly lost position
Browne is hampered by his usual
bad time trouble.

30 B–Q7

Or 30 B–N7 N–R5 etc.

| 30 . . . | R–B6 |
| 31 Q–R8 | R–B8! |

And not 31 . . . N–R5 32 Q–
KB8+ K–R4 33 P–N4+ winning
for White.

32 R×R	N–R6+
33 K–B1	Q×R+
34 K–K2	Q–B7+
35 K–B3	Q×P+
36 K–N4	

Or 36 K–K4 Q–Q5+ 37 K–B3
N–N8 mate!

| 36 . . . | Q–B5+ |
| 37 K×N/R3 | Q–R5 mate |

*Notes by Westerinen for Informator
and for this volume*

136 **Rantanen** (Finland) –
    Denman (Scotland)

Sicilian Defence

**1 P–K4 P–QB4   2 N–KB3 P–Q3
3 P–Q4 P×P   4 N×P N–KB3   5
N–QB3 P–QR3   6 B–KN5 P–K3
7 P–B4 B–K2   8 Q–B3 Q–B2   9
0–0–0 QN–Q2   10 B–K2 P–N4   11
B×N N×B** If 11 . . . P×B 12 Q–
R5 N–B4 13 B–B3 B–N2 14 P–B5
with a clear advantage to White.
12 P–K5 B–N2   13 P×N Not 13
Q–N3 P×P 14 P×P N–Q2 15
Q×P Q×P when Black stands better
– Fischer. **13 . . . B×Q   14 B×B
R–QB1!?** The normal continuation
is 14 . . . B×P 15 B×R P–Q4 16
B×P B×N 17 R×B P×B, when
White's best is probably 18 R–K1+
with an unclear position. **15 P×B
Q–N3?** 15 . . . Q×P loses at once
to 16 N–B5! An interesting alterna-
tive is 15 . . . P–N5 16 N–Q5!?
P×N 17 KR–K1 (threat 18 B×P)
17 . . . Q–B5, when White seems to
have no real compensation for the

sacrificed material. On 15 . . . P–N5, White must therefore find some alternative knight move and the outcome is not clear. **16 KR–K1 P–KR4 17 P–B5 P–K4 18 P–B6!** Now Black is lost. **18 . . . P–N3** If 18 . . . P×N 19 P×P R–KN1 20 N–Q5, or 18 . . . R×N 19 P×P R–N1 20 N–B5 etc. **19 R×P! P×R 20 B–B6+ Resigns**

Notes by Rantanen specially for this volume

FINAL GROUP D

		F	S	M	H	L	L	F	S	C	M	A	M	G	I	v	Total
48	France	×	2	3	4	3	4	1½	2½	3½	3	4	4	4	4	4	46½
49	Singapore	2	×	3½	3	3½	3	2½	3½	2½	3	3½	2½	4	3	3	42½
50	Malta	1	½	×	2½	3	1	3½	2½	2	2½	2½	2	3½	3	2½	32
51	Hong Kong	0	1	1½	×	1½	2½	3½	1½	2	2½	3	3	3½	2½	2½	30½
52	Lebanon	1	½	1	2½	×	2	2½	2½	2	2	2	3	2½	3	3½	30
53	Luxemburg	0	1	3	1½	2	×	2	3	2½	3½	2	3	½	2½	3	29½
54	Faroe Isl.	2½	1½	½	½	1½	2	×	1½	3½	2½	2½	2½	2	2½	3½	29
55	Syria	1½	½	1½	2½	1½	1	2½	×	2	1	1½	2½	3½	3½	3	28
56	Cyprus	½	1½	2	2	2	1½	½	2	×	2½	2	2½	3	2½	3	27½
57	Morocco	1	1	1½	1½	2	½	1½	3	1½	×	2½	2½	1½	2	4	26
58	Andorra	0	½	1½	1	2	2	1½	2½	2	1½	×	2½	1	2½	3½	24
59	Malaysia	0	1½	2	1	1	1	1½	1½	1½	1½	1½	×	2½	2½	4	23
60	Guernsey	0	0	½	½	1½	3½	2	½	1	2½	3	1½	×	1½	2½	20½
61	Iraq	0	1	1	1½	1	1½	1½	½	1½	2	1½	1½	2½	×	3½	20½
62	Virgin Isl.	0	1	1½	1½	½	1	½	1	1	0	½	0	1½	½	×	10½

Guernsey (4 wins 1 draw) were placed ahead of Iraq (2 wins 1 draw) because of their better match record.

Progressive Score Table

		R1	R2	R3	R4	R5	R6	R7	R8	R9	R10	R11	R12	R13	R14	R15
48	France	4	5½	8½	12½	15½	19½	.	22½	26½	30½	34	38	40	42½	46½
49	Singapore	4	6½	9½	.	13	16	19½	22	25	28	31½	34½	36½	40	42½
50	Malta	2½	5	8½	11	12	15	17½	18½	.	20½	24	26	29	29½	32
51	Hong Kong	1½	4½	8	10	12½	13½	15	.	18	21½	24	26½	28	30½	30½
52	Lebanon	2	4	.	7½	8½	9½	12½	15	17	20	20½	23	25½	27½	30
53	Luxemburg	.	2	5	5	8	11	11½	14½	16½	17½	20½	22	24	26	29½
54	Faroe Isl.	3½	6	6½	9	11	14½	17	18½	20	20½	23	.	25½	27½	29
55	Syria	2½	6	8	11½	12	.	14½	16	18½	19½	20½	22	25	26½	28
56	Cyprus	2½	4	6	8	10	10½	13	14½	16½	19½	20	22	24½	27½	.
57	Morocco	2	6	7	8½	11	12½	14	16	17	20	21½	24	25½	.	26
58	Andorra	0	1½	4	5	7	9½	10	12½	13½	.	15	16½	18½	20½	24
59	Malaysia	1½	2½	4	5½	7	8	9	13	13	15	.	17½	19	21½	23
60	Guernsey	0	½	1	4	6	8½	12	13½	16	16	16½	18	.	19	20½
61	Iraq	1½	.	2	3	4½	6	7½	9½	11	12	15½	15½	16½	18	20½
62	Virgin Isl.	½	½	1½	2	.	2	3½	3½	5	6	6½	7½	8½	10	10½

After their miserable showing in the Preliminaries the French pulled themselves together to dominate Final D. From round 8 to round 15 they were never out of the lead, nor did they share it at all. One member of the victorious team who covered himself with glory was the second reserve, Haik, who made the fine total score of 11/12.

The French and the men of Singapore were clearly in a class by themselves, as were the Virgin Islanders. A full 10½ point margin separated Singapore from Malta, while, at the other end of the scale, Guernsey and Iraq beat the Virgin Islands to the line by 10 lengths.

137 **Vassiades** (Cyprus) –
   Maalouf (Lebanon)

Sicilian Defence

1 P–K4 P–QB4 2 N–KB3 N–QB3
3 P–Q4 P×P 4 N×P P–Q3 5
N–QB3 P–QR3 6 B–QB4 P–K3
7 B–N3 N–B3 8 B–K3 B–K2 9
0–0 0–0 0–0 10 P–B4 B–Q2 One wonders why Maalouf did not follow the 10
. . . N×N 11 B×N P–QN4 of Fischer-Spassky, 4th match game. Possibly he had in mind some improvement on Fischer-Larsen, 3rd match game 1971 which continued 11 P–B5! Q–B1? 12 P×P B×P 13 N×B P×N 14 N–R4! **11 Q–B3**

But Vassiades smells a rat and varies from Fischer's play. **11 . . . Q–B2?** Too slow. Better 11 . . . N×N and 12 . . . P–QN4. **12 P–B5 N×N 13 B×N P–QN4?** Too slow. 13 . . . P×P 14 P×P B–B3 was a little better, or 13 . . . P–K4 14 B–K3 P–QN4. But White's attack is very strong in any case. **14 P–N4! P–R3 15 P–KR4 P×P 16 KP×P B–B3 17 Q–N3 P–N5 18 P–N5 K–R1 19 N–Q5 N×N 20 P×P R–KN1 21 P×P+ K–R2 22 B×N B×B 23 Q–N4 P–B3 24 Q–N6 mate** A fitting end to a collection of men's Olympiad games.

Notes by Levy

The Ladies' Olympiad

THE PRELIMINARIES

PRELIMINARY GROUP I

	U	E	H	A	I	Total	Final Group
USSR	×	2	2	2	1½	7½	A
East Germany	0	×	1½	1½	2	5	A
Holland	0	½	×	1½	2	4	B
Australia	0	½	½	×	2	3	B
Ireland	½	0	0	0	×	½	C

PRELIMINARY GROUP II

	E	C	Y	A	S	J	Total	Final Group
England	×	1	1½	2	2	2	8½	A
Czechoslovakia	1	×	1	2	2	2	8	A
Yugoslavia	½	1	×	2	2	2	7½	B
Austria	0	0	0	×	1½	2	3½	B
Scotland	0	0	0	½	×	1½	2	C
Japan	0	0	0	0	½	×	½	C

PRELIMINARY GROUP III

	R	B	M	B	I	S	Total	Final Group
Rumania	×	1	2	2	1½	1½	8	A
Bulgaria	1	×	1½	1½	2	2	8	A
Mongolia	0	½	×	1	1	2	4½	B
Brazil	0	½	1	×	1½	1	4	B
Israel	½	0	1	½	×	1	3	C
Switzerland	½	0	0	1	1	×	2½	C

PRELIMINARY GROUP IV

	H	WG	P	S	F	S	Total	Final Group
Hungary	×	1	1	2	2	2	8	A
West Germany	1	×	1	2	1½	2	7½	A
Poland	1	1	×	1	2	2	7	B
Sweden	0	0	1	×	1	2	4	B
Finland	0	½	0	1	×	1	2½	C
Singapore	0	0	0	0	1	×	1	C

'Gens Una Sumus' is the motto of FIDE, but only in the Skopje Olympiad was the motto properly fulfilled by the combination, under one roof,* as it were, of the male and female Olympiads. This arrangement met with general approval and hopes were expressed on all sides that the Olympics would continue to be 'Co-ed'.

It has been a noticeable feature of the recent athletic Olympic Games that the best women's performances are now overtaking the male records of previous events. At Skopje too one could not fail to be impressed by the rising standards of the Lady players. Their best games, of which we give a selection here, were certainly comparable in terms of toughness, ideas and power of execution with games by male masters.

There follows tables of results plus commentaries on the preliminaries and finals.

Preliminary Results

Preliminary Group 1:

As was to be expected the USSR, led by the two claimants for the World title (Nona Gaprindashvili and Alla Kushnir), qualified with the minimum of effort for the top final group. Nona experienced some difficulties in an exciting struggle against her Australian opponent (see game) while Levitina dropped a ½ point v Ireland; but these were the only mishaps. E. Germany defeated Holland by 1½/½ in the final round, which decided the second qualifying place.

138 **Kellner** (Australia) –
　　Gaprindashvili (USSR)

Modern Defence

1 P–K4 P–KN3 2 P–Q4 B–N2 3 N–KB3 P–Q3 4 B–KN5 P–QB3 5 N–B3 Q–N3 6 Q–Q2 Q×NP 7 R–QN1 Q–R6 8 B–QB4 N–Q2 9 0–0 KN–B3 10 P–K5 P×P 11 P×P N–N5 12 R–N3 Q–B4 13 B×BP+ K×B 14 Q–B4+ K–N1 15 N–K4 Q×QBP 16 B×P QN×P 17 N×N N×N 18 B–B6! Q×N 19 Q×Q B×B 20 Q–QN4?! K–N2 21 R–K1 P–QR4 22 Q–B5 R–Q1 23 R/3–K3 R–Q4 24 Q–R3 B–K3 25 R×N? B×R 26 Q–K7+ B–B2

27 Q×NP QR–Q1 28 P–N3 R–Q8 29 K–B1 B–B6 30 R×R R×R+ 31 K–N2 R–Q7 32 P–KR4 B–Q5 33 P–N4 R×BP+ 34 K–N3 P–B4 35 P–R4 R–QN7 36 Q–Q7 B–K4+ 37 K–B3 R–N6+ 38 K–N2 P–KR3 39 Q–K7 B–Q5 40 Q–Q7 R–Q6
White resigns

Preliminary Group 2:

A great triumph for the English Ladies who qualified for the A Group above the favourites Czechoslovakia and Yugoslavia. This was almost entirely due to Jana Hartston's superbly polished positional victory over Lazarevic in the first round (see

* Actually, the Ladies' Tournament was situated in an elegant and spacious hall adjacent to the two buildings housing the larger men's event.

game). After this set-back the host team could not avoid relegation to Final B.

139 **Lazarevic** (Yugoslavia) – **J. Hartston** (England)

Bird's Opening

1 P–KB4 N–KB3 2 N–KB3 P–KN3 3 P–KN3 B–N2 4 B–N2 0–0 5 0–0 P–B4 6 P–Q3 P–Q4 7 N–B3 P–Q5 8 N–K4 QN–Q2! 9 N–R4 P–K3 10 P–B4 Q–K2 11 R–N1 N–N5 12 Q–K1 P–B4 13 N–B2 N×N 14 R×N P–K4 15 P×P N×P 16 B–Q5+ B–K3 17 B×B+ Q×B 18 N–N2 N–N5 19 N–B4 Q–R3 20 R–KB1 Q×RP 21 B–Q2 Q–R3 22 N–Q5 Q–Q3 23 P–QN4 P–N3 24 P–R3 N–B3 25 P×P P×P 26 B–B4 Q–Q2 27 N–B7 QR–B1 28 Q–R5 N–R4 29 R–N7 N×B 30 P×N R–B2 31 R×P R×N 32 R–R8+ R–KB1 33 R–N1 R×R 34 Q×R+ R–B1 35 Q–R6 Q–K1 36 K–B1 Q–B3 37 R–N6 Q–R8+ 38 K–B2 R–R1 **White resigns**

Mrs Hartston had been held up by unco-operative border guards at the Yugoslav frontier for three days on her way to Skopje. Far from exhausting her this experience seemed to lend her play a further dimension of determination.

Preliminary Group 3

The clearest of the preliminary sections. It was obvious from an early stage that Rumania and Bulgaria would qualify, and in fact both teams achieved this with one round to spare.

Preliminary Group 4

The most bitterly contested of the Preliminaries. Hungary and Poland were the clear candidates, but the West German Ladies performed magnificently and squeezed in ahead of their E. European rivals. Interestingly all the matches between the top teams here ended 1–1.

THE FINALS

FINAL GROUP A

		U	R	H	B	C	W	E	E	Total
1	USSR	×	2	1½	1½	1	2	1½	2	11½
2	Rumania	0	×	2	1	1	2	1	1	8
3	Hungary	½	0	×	1	1½	1	2	2	8
4	Bulgaria	½	1	1	×	1	½	2	1½	7½
5	Czechoslovakia	1	1	½	1	×	1	1	1½	7
6	West Germany	0	0	1	1½	1	×	½	1½	5½
7	East Germany	½	1	0	0	1	1½	×	½	4½
8	England	0	1	0	½	½	½	1½	×	4

Rumania were placed ahead of Hungary on the result of their individual match since their match records were equal (Rumania 2 wins 4 draws, Hungary 3 wins 2 draws).

FINAL GROUP B

		P	Y	A	H	S	B	M	A	Total
9	Poland	×	1½	1½	2	1	1½	1½	1½	10½
10	Yugoslavia	½	×	1	½	1½	2	1½	1½	8½
11	Austria	½	1	×	1½	2	1	0	1	7
12	Holland	0	1½	½	×	1	1	2	1	7
13	Sweden	1	½	0	1	×	1	1	2	6½
14	Brazil	½	0	1	1	1	×	1½	1	6
15	Mongolia	½	½	2	0	1	½	×	1	5½
16	Australia	½	½	1	1	0	1	1	×	5

Austria were placed ahead of Holland on the result of their individual match since their match records were equal (2 wins and 3 draws each).

FINAL GROUP C

		S	I	S	I	F	S	J	Total
17	Switzerland	×	1	2	1½	2	½	2	9
18	Israel	1	×	1	1½	1½	1½	2	8½
19	Singapore	0	1	×	1	1½	1½	1	6
20	Ireland	½	½	1	×	1½	1½	½	5½
21	Finland	0	½	½	½	×	2	2	5½
22	Scotland	1½	½	½	½	0	×	1½	4½
23	Japan	0	0	1	1½	0	½	×	3

Ireland were placed ahead of Finland because of their better match record (Ireland 2 wins 1 draw; Finland 2 wins)

Final A

Eastern European domination of the Final was complete. The USSR won by a huge margin, conceding only one drawn match. West Germany and England could only manage places 6 and 8 and it is obvious that a lot of improvement is needed before Western Ladies can catch up with Eastern training methods. Strangely, there was no team competing in the Olympiad from the USA which somewhat weakened the Western challenge.

One curious point: Mrs Hartston scored singlehanded 3 of England's 4 points (75 per cent)!

The Other Final Groups

As was to be expected the two Eastern European teams who found themselves in the B-final proved themselves clearly superior.

Final C contained a depressingly high percentage of teams from the British Isles.

140 **Levitina** (USSR) –
  Shikova (Bulgaria)

Philidor's Defence

1 P–K4 P–K4 2 N–KB3 P–Q3 3 N–B3 3 P–Q4 is more common **3 . . . N–KB3 4 P–Q4 QN–Q2 5 B–QB4 B–K2 6 0–0 0–0 7 Q–K2 P–B3 8 P–QR4 P–QR4** Theory recommends 8 . . . Q–B2 9 P–R3 P–QN3 10 R–Q1 B–N2. **9 P–R3 Q–B2 10 R–K1 N–N3** More logical is 10 . . . P–QN3 followed by . . . B–N2, maintaining control of the square K4. **11 B–N3 B–Q2 12 B–K3 N–B1** If 12 . . . QR–Q1 13 P×P P×P 14 N×P Q×N 15 B×N. **13 QR–Q1 R–N1** The attempt to switch the field of combat to the Q-side fails. White's threats in the centre are too powerful. **14 Q–Q2 P–QN4 15 QP×P P–N5** Alas 15 . . . QP×P fails to 16 N×KP Q×N 17 B–KB4. **16 P×N P×N 17 Q× BP B×BP 18 B–Q4 B×B 19 N×B P–QB4 20 N–B5!** White exploits her material and positional

advantages by a direct K-side attack. **20 . . . B×N 21 P×B R–N5 22 P–B6 P–N3** If 22 . . . P–B5 White would have continued 23 P×P. **23 Q–K3 Q–Q1** White would still have a few technical problems in realizing her advantage after 23 . . . R–R5. **24 Q–N5 P–B5 25 R–K7!!**

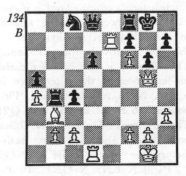
134
B

This powerful sacrifice is decisive. Black has to lose a piece to avoid the threat of 26 Q–R6. **25 . . . N×R 26 P×N Q–N1 27 P×R=/Q+ K×Q 28 B–R2 R×RP 29 Q–B6! Q–B2 30 R×P** More accurate was 30 Q–R8+ K–K2 31 R–K1+ K–

Q2   32 Q–K8 mate. **30 . . . K–K1
31 R–Q1 R × B 32 R–K1+ Resigns**
[Levitina, playing in her first
tournament outside the Soviet
Union, scored 5½ out of 6 and could
soon be a serious threat to the
Gaprindashvili/Kushnir hegemony
in women's chess – AJW]

*Notes by Gipslis in 64 translated
specially for this volume by
Andrew Whiteley*

141 **J. Hartston** (England) –
Polihroniade (Rumania)

Modern/Pirc Defence

**1 P–Q4 P–KN3 2 P–K4 B–N2 3
N–QB3 P–Q3 4 P–B4 N–QB3 5
B–K3 N–R3** A very dubious line,
although my opponent had a few
recent successes with it, as we quite
accidentally discovered a couple of
days before this game. So naturally
I was well prepared beforehand by
the appropriate experts in the
English men's team. (That is if you
can call a twenty minute session
over lunch a preparation, but in
this case it proved quite sufficient.)
Thus Black's 5 . . . N–R3 pleased
me enormously; the alternative is
5 . . . N–B3 with a normal 'Pirc
position'. **6 N–B3 B–N5 7 Q–Q2!**
The key move. **7 . . . B × N** Other
possibilities, also not very satis-
factory, are: 7 . . . P–B4 8 P–Q5
P × P 9 N–KN5 N–QN1 10 P–
KR3 B–QB1 11 P–KN4± or 7 . . .
P–Q4 8 P × P! B × N 9 P × B
N–QN5 10 B–B4±. **8 P × B P–K3?**
Alternatively 8 . . . P–K4 9 BP × P
P × P 10 0–0–0 (not 10 B × N?
Q–R5+) N–KN1 11 P–Q5 QN–
K2 12 B–QN5+ also with a very

bad position. **9 0–0–0 N–K2** Loses
by force. Black must try to struggle
on with 9 . . . P–KB4 or 9 . . .
Q–R5, though P–Q5 is strong after
either. The rest of the game is easily
comprehensible and very enjoyable
for White. **10 P–B5 KN–N1 11
P × KP P × P 12 B–R3 P–K4 13
P × P B × P 14 P–B4 B–N2 15
P–K5 N–B4 16 B × N P × B 17
Q N2 B–R3 18 P × P P–B3 19
P–Q7+ K–B2 20 Q–R3 Q–R4**
A good alternative here was 'resigns'.
21 KR–K1 K–N3 22 R–Q6+

135
B

**22 . . . K–B2 23 Q–R5+ K–B1
24 R × B N × R 25 Q × N+ K–B2
26 B–Q4 Resigns**
Notes by Jana Hartston

142 **Kushnir** (USSR) –
J. Hartston (England)

Czech Benoni

1 P–Q4	**N–KB3**
2 P–QB4	**P–B4**
3 P–Q5	**P–K4**
4 N–QB3	**P–Q3**
5 P–K4	**QN–Q2**

Trying to avoid lines commencing
5 . . . B–K2 6 P–KN3 which Kushnir
plays consistently against the Czech
Benoni. Now after 6 P–KN3 Black

43 Ladies' World Champion Nona Gaprindashvili

44 Jana Hartston (England) in determined mood against Japan. In the background, Mary McGinn (Scotland) playing white against Katerina Jovanović (Yugoslavia)

45 White: Milunka Lazarević (Yugoslavia), Black: Nancy Elder (Scotland)

46 Freda Rabinovitch (Israel)

can fianchetto the dark-squared bishop transposing into the King's Indian Defence.

6 P–KN3	P–KN3
7 B–N2	B–N2
8 N–R3!	

Probably an important contribution to the theory of this Benoni/King's Indian position. Normally White would play 8 KN–K2, to retain the option of advancing the KBP, or 8 N–B3, so as to answer Black's intended . . . P–KB4 with N–KN5. The text keeps open all of these possibilities.

8 . . .	0–0
9 0–0	P–QR3
10 P–R4	R–N1

Perhaps it would be an improvement to omit this and continue at once with 10 . . . N–K1, so as to have some sort of defence against White's projected P–KB4.

11 Q–Q3

Controlling QN5 and KB5.

11 . . .	N–K1
12 B–Q2	N–B2
13 R–R2	

Rather too cautious. White should proceed immediately with P–KB4, when Black is in danger of being squashed.

13 . . .	Q–K1
14 P–N3	P–B4
15 P–B4	KP×P
16 NP×P	B–Q5+
17 K–R1	N–B3

Gipslis recommended 17 . . . P–QN4 at this stage, but I didn't like the look of 18 RP×P RP×P 19 R–R7.

18 P–K5!

This thrust exploits the somewhat disconnected state of Black's pieces.

| 18 . . . | P×P |
| 19 P×P | B×P |

The Polish master Sobkowski suggested 18 . . . Q×KP, but this fails to 20 B–B4 Q–K2 21 P–Q6 and Black's position disintegrates.

20 B–R6

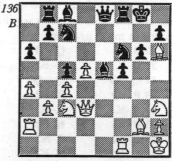

136
B

| 20 . . . | R–B2 |

After this Black is in deep trouble. 20 . . . N–K5 was variously suggested, as an improvement and this sharp attempt does seem to be the last genuine opportunity for Black to infuse some life into the position—e.g: 21 B×R N×N 22 R–QB2 Q×B 23 R×N B×R 24 Q×B with some positional advantage for White, but a pawn less. Probably best is the highly unclear 21 P–Q6 N–K3! 22 N–Q5

21 R–K2	N–K5
22 N×N	P×N
23 Q×P	R×R+

Korchnoi thought 23 . . . B×N was the most accurate.

24 B×R	B×N
25 B×B	B–Q3
26 Q–N2?	

Much stronger was 26 Q×Q+ R×Q 27 R×R+ N×R 28 B–QB8 winning a pawn or if then 26 . . . N×Q 27 B–K6+ K–R1 28 R–KB2 with a decisive penetra-

o

tion. This explains the relevance of 23 . . . B×N!

26 . . .	Q–B2
27 R–KB2	Q–K2
28 R–K2	Q–B2
29 R–K6	B–B5?

29 . . . R–K1! was now best, exploiting White's back row weakness. It's not clear in this case that White can make progress.

30 B×B	Q×B
31 R–K7	R–KB1
32 Q–N3	Q×Q
33 P×Q	R–B2
34 R–K3	R–B3
35 P–R5	K–B1
36 B–B8	P–N3
37 R–Q3	N–K1

37 . . . K–K2 looks better but fails to 38 P–Q6+ R×P 39 R×R K×R 40 P×P N–K1 41 B×P

| 38 P–Q6 | N×P |
| 39 P×P | N×B?? |

Throwing away the game. Admittedly, it wasn't possible to play 39 . . . N–K1 on account of 40 P–N7 R–N3 41 R–Q5 R×P/6 42 R×P N–Q3 43 R–QN5!! but with 39 . . . N–K5 40 P–N7 R–N3 Black would still have chances to resist.

| 40 P–N7 | Black resigns |

Notes specially contributed by Jana Hartston

143 **Gaprindashvili** (USSR) – **Laakman** (W. Germany)

French Defence – Tarrasch Variation

1 P–K4	P–K3
2 P–Q4	P–Q4
3 N–Q2	N–KB3
4 P–K5	KN–Q2
5 P–KB4	P–QB4

| 6 P–B3 | N–QB3 |
| 7 QN–B3 | P×P |

A bit old-fashioned and static. With this manoeuvre White is obliged to displace her king but Black obtains no real chances to undermine White's pawn chain Modern praxis prefers the more. fluid 7 . . . Q–R4 followed by . . . P–QN4 and . . . P–QN5.

| 8 P×P | B–N5+ |
| 9 K–B2 | |

9 B–Q2 Q–N3 is not bad for Black.

| 9 . . . | P–B3 |
| 10 P–KN3 | |

White must remove the king from the potentially open KB file with the utmost speed.

10 . . .	P×P
11 BP×P	0–0
12 K–N2!	B–K2

Black doesn't really have a constructive plan available since she lacks any useful pawn-levers. The text tries to minimize White's obvious spatial plus on the K-side, but White's next move reasserts this salient feature of the position.

| 13 P–KR4 | Q–N3 |

Black embarks on a tortuous regrouping designed to liberate her Q-side pieces. Actually Black is ahead in development quantitatively and optically, but qualitatively Black has been left standing. White's pieces have something to do – Black's simply do not.

14 N–K2	R–B2
15 N–B4	N–B1
16 B–Q3	B–Q2
17 P–R3	

The Ladies' World Champion certainly understands the strategic requirements of the situation. Before passing to the decisive assault against Black's king she minimizes her opponent's chances on the opposite wing.

17 ...	R–B1
18 P–QN4	P–QR3
19 B–Q2	P–R3
20 R–QN1	Q–R2
21 B–K3	P–QN4
22 N–N6	B–Q1
23 N–N5	

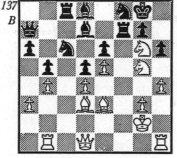

137
B

A neat conclusion. If 23 ... P×N 24 P×P N×N 25 B×N R–K2 26 Q–R5 mates.

23 ...	N×N
24 B×N	R–B1
25 Q–Q3	B–N3
26 QR–KB1	R×R
27 R×R	P×N
28 B–B7+	Resigns

After 28 ... K–B1 29 B×NP Black's king has no flight square and execution by discovered check is imminent.

Notes by Keene

144 **Eretova** (Czechoslovakia) – **Nicolau** (Rumania)

Alekhine's Defence

1 P–K4 N–KB3 2 P–K5 N–Q4 3 P–Q4 P–Q3 4 N–KB3 P–KN3 5 B–QB4 N–N3 6 B–N3 B–N2 7 P–QR4 Karpov has played 7 N–N5 here with the continuation 7 . . . P–Q4 8 P–KB4 and White has a useful space advantage. The text move has been favoured by Keres. 7 . . . P–QR4 8 P×P This release of the tension looks wrong, 8 Q–K2 is probably better. 8 . . . BP×P 9 0–0 0–0 10 P–R3 P–Q4 11 N–B3 N–B3 12 N–QN5 N–R2 13 N×N R×N 14 R–K1 R–R3 15 Q–K2 It looks more natural to play 15 P–B3 and follow up with B–KB4– K5 to expose Black's dark squares. 15 . . . B–K3 16 P–B3 N–B1 17 B–B2 B–Q2 18 B–B4 R–K3 19 Q–Q2 N–Q3 20 P–QN3 R×R+ 21 R×R N–B1 22 N–K5 22 B–K5 is more to the point. 22 . . . B–K3 23 B–R6 N–Q3 24 B×B K×B 25 Q–B4 B–B4 Once Black has this bishop off her chances are certainly no worse. 26 B×B N×B 27 P–KN4

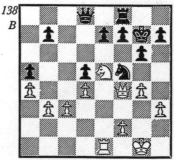

138
B

Much too ambitious. This weakens White's position rather than inflicting damage on Black. 27 . . . N–Q3 28 R–K3 N–K5 29 P–B4 P–K3 30 N–Q3 P–KN4 31 Q–K5+ Q–B3 32 P×Q Q×Q 33 N×Q P×P Now Black has an advantage in the ending, because it is much easier for

her rook to come to the QB file.
**34 N–Q7 R–B1   35 N–N6 R–B8+
36 K–N2 R–B7   37 R–KB3 R–Q7
38 N×P R×QP   39 N–K7 R–N5
40 N–B5+ K–B1   41 R–Q3 K–K1
42 R–Q5** White can attempt to such
salvation in the rook ending with
42 N–Q6+ N×N   43 R×N R×
QNP   44 R–Q5 P–N3   45 R×NP
and after . . . R–N5 Black is bound
to obtain united passed pawns on
the Q-side. **42 . . . P–N3   43 P–B3
N–B4   44 N–Q6+ K–K2   45 N–
B8+ K–K3   46 R×P N×NP   47
R–R5 P–N4!   48 R–R6+ K–K4
49 P×P P–R5   50 R–R6 N–B4**

51 R–R5 K–B5 Black is playing
the ending with immense precision.
The creation of a passed QRP has
lured White's pieces into a corner to
prevent its advance. Meanwhile
Black can start a K-attack in an
ending with only three pieces! **52
P–N6 R–N7+   53 K–B1 K×BP   54
K–N1 K–N6   55 K–B1 N–K5   56
R×P** Loses the rook, but if 56 K–
K1 K–B6   57 K–Q1 N–B7+   58
K–B1 N–Q6+   59 K–Q1 K–K6
mates. **56 . . . R–N8+   White
resigns.**

Notes by Jana Hartston

THE FIDE CONGRESS

Each year, FIDE (Fédération International des Échecs) holds its congress, or annual general meeting. It is traditional that in even years the congress meetings take place alongside the Olympiad and this was the case at Skopje.

Many matters were discussed. Seven new Grandmasters were added to the lists, twelve International Masters, five lady International Masters (surely this title ought to be International Mistress) and twenty-seven International Arbiters. From the dozens of pages of congress minutes we have extracted a few items for inclusion in this summary:

Syria, Iraq, The Dutch Antilles, Jamaica and Trinidad and Tobago were admitted as new member nations.

Dr Schudel, Vice President of Zone 1, protested at the exclusion of South Africa and Rhodesia from the Olympiad. (These two teams had been refused visas by the Yugoslav Government). The assembly decided that future Olympiads may only be organised by member federations who guarantee, well in advance, that every member can participate.

Editorial note: At the nineteenth Olympiad in Siegen, 1970, when the venue of the 1972 Olympiad was discussed the Yugoslav delegate announced that no guarantee could be given that South Africa and Rhodesia would be granted visas. Since they did not wish the issue to cause the collapse of arrangements for the Skopje event they extracted promises from the delegates of these two countries that if visas were refused, no issue would be made of it.

It was decided that the participation of Albania in future Olympiad, would only be considered if the Albanian federation gives an unqualified guarantee that they are prepared to play against all other nations.

With the recent increase in the number of chess publications it was deemed appropriate to discuss the possibility of copyrighting game scores. The Swedish delegate, Rolf Littorin, a copyright expert, explained that this would be impossible for three different reasons:

(1) There are two players and therefore two authors. How should the profits be split?

(2) Many games have substantial parts which have been played before. They are not, therefore, original works of art.

(3) Roughly half of the world's governments have not ratified the existing copyright conventions (this includes the USSR) and so any agreement pertaining to game scores would not be fully enforceable.

MEN'S OLYMPIAD

Individual Results

1 USSR

	Preliminaries				Finals				Total				%
	P	W	D	L	P	W	D	L	P	W	D	L	
Petrosian	4	3	1	0	12	3	8	1	16	6	9	1	65·6
Korchnoi	4	4	0	0	11	4	6	1	15	8	6	1	73·3
Smyslov	4	4	0	0	10	4	6	0	14	8	6	0	78·6
Tal	4	4	0	0	12	8	4	0	16	12	4	0	87·5
Karpov	4	4	0	0	11	8	2	1	15	12	2	1	86·7
Savon	4	2	1	1	4	1	2	1	8	3	3	2	56·3
TC Keres													

2 Hungary

	Preliminaries				Finals				Total				%
	P	W	D	L	P	W	D	L	P	W	D	L	
Portisch	3	1	2	0	14	7	6	1	17	8	8	1	70·6
Bilek	5	4	1	0	10	3	7	0	15	7	8	0	73·3
Forintos	4	2	1	1	10	2	7	1	14	4	8	2	57·1
Ribli	6	5	1	0	11	4	7	0	17	9	8	0	76·5
Csom	4	3	1	0	11	6	4	1	15	9	5	1	76·7
Sax	6	5	1	0	4	3	0	1	10	8	1	1	85·0
TC Florian													

3 Yugoslavia

	Preliminaries				Finals				Total				%
	P	W	D	L	P	W	D	L	P	W	D	L	
Gligoric	3	3	0	0	12	5	3	4	15	8	3	4	63·3
Ivkov	5	3	2	0	13	3	10	0	18	6	12	0	66·7
Ljubojevic	5	5	0	0	14	8	5	1	19	13	5	1	81·6
Matanovic	5	2	2	1	7	1	6	0	12	3	8	1	58·3
Matulovic	6	4	2	0	12	5	7	0	18	9	9	0	75·0
Rukavina	4	2	1	1	2	0	1	1	6	2	2	2	50·0
TC Smederevac													

4 Czechoslovakia

	Preliminaries				Finals				Total				%
	P	W	D	L	P	W	D	L	P	W	D	L	
Hort	5	5	0	0	13	6	7	0	18	11	7	0	80·6
Smejkal	6	4	1	1	13	3	10	0	19	7	11	1	65·8
Filip	5	2	3	0	12	2	9	1	17	4	12	1	58·8
Jansa	6	4	2	0	12	5	6	1	18	9	8	1	72·2
Pribyl	3	2	1	0	5	0	1	4	8	2	2	4	37·5
Trapl	3	3	0	0	5	1	4	0	8	4	4	0	75·0
TC Fichtl													

5 West Germany

	Preliminaries				Finals				Total				%
	P	W	D	L	P	W	D	L	P	W	D	L	
Hübner	5	5	0	0	13	7	6	0	18	12	6	0	83·3
Darga	4	2	2	0	9	1	6	2	13	3	8	2	53·8
Pfleger	5	4	1	0	10	1	9	0	15	5	10	0	66·7
Hecht	5	5	0	0	9	0	6	3	14	5	6	3	57·1

5 West	Preliminaries				Finals				Total				
Germany—cont.	P	W	D	L	P	W	D	L	P	W	D	L	%
Kestler	5	4	0	1	10	5	4	1	15	9	4	2	**73·3**
Dueball	4	3	1	0	9	3	5	1	13	6	6	1	**69·2**
TC Kinzel													

6 **Bulgaria**	Preliminaries				Finals				Total				
	P	W	D	L	P	W	D	L	P	W	D	L	%
Bobotsov	7	2	5	0	12	3	8	1	19	5	13	1	**60·5**
Tringov	5	2	3	0	13	1	5	7	18	3	8	7	**38·9**
Radulov	6	5	0	1	15	5	9	1	21	10	9	2	**69·0**
Padevsky	5	1	4	0	13	5	7	1	18	6	11	1	**63·9**
Peev	5	4	1	0	7	2	3	2	12	6	4	2	**66·7**
Bohosian	0	0	0	0	0	0	0	0	0	0	0	0	—
TC Neikirch													

7 **Rumania**	Preliminaries				Finals				Total				
	P	W	D	L	P	W	D	L	P	W	D	L	%
Gheorghin	5	2	2	1	15	3	10	2	20	5	12	3	**55·0**
Ciocaltea	5	3	2	0	14	4	7	3	19	7	9	3	**60·5**
Ghitescu	6	3	2	1	8	3	3	2	14	6	5	3	**60·7**
Ungureanu	5	2	3	0	8	1	4	3	13	3	7	3	**50·0**
Ghizdavu	4	3	1	0	8	3	3	2	12	6	4	2	**66·7**
Partos	3	2	1	0	7	3	2	2	10	5	3	2	**65·0**
TC Troianescu													

8 **Holland**	Preliminaries				Finals				Total				
	P	W	D	L	P	W	D	L	P	W	D	L	%
Donner	4	0	4	0	11	1	7	3	15	1	11	3	**43·3**
Ree	5	2	3	0	11	5	3	3	16	7	6	3	**62·5**
Zuidema	5	3	1	1	9	1	6	2	14	4	7	3	**53·6**
Timman	7	5	2	0	10	1	5	4	17	6	7	4	**55·9**
Hartoch	3	1	2	0	11	4	5	2	14	5	7	2	**60·7**
Enklaar	4	2	2	0	8	3	2	3	12	5	4	3	**58·3**
TC Bouwmeester													

9 **USA**	Preliminaries				Finals				Total				
	P	W	D	L	P	W	D	L	P	W	D	L	%
Kavalek	5	3	2	0	13	5	5	3	18	8	7	3	**63·9**
R. Byrne	4	3	1	0	10	3	6	1	14	6	7	1	**67·9**
Benkö	5	2	3	0	11	4	4	3	16	6	7	3	**59·4**
Bisguier	6	3	3	0	10	0	7	3	16	3	10	3	**50·0**
Martz	4	3	1	0	8	1	6	1	12	4	7	1	**62·5**
Kane	4	2	1	1	8	0	4	4	12	2	5	5	**37·5**
TC D. Byrne													

10 **East Germany**	Preliminaries				Finals				Total				
	P	W	D	L	P	W	D	L	P	W	D	L	%
Uhlmann	4	3	1	0	14	3	7	4	18	6	8	4	**55·6**
Malich	5	4	1	0	13	4	6	3	18	8	7	3	**63·9**
Knaak	5	4	1	0	6	1	1	4	11	5	2	4	**54·5**
Liebert	4	2	2	0	7	1	3	3	11	3	5	3	**50·0**
Schöneberg	5	4	0	1	8	0	5	3	13	4	5	4	**50·0**
Vogt	5	3	2	0	12	5	5	2	17	8	7	2	**67·6**
TC Platz													

11 Spain

	Preliminaries				Finals				Total				
	P	W	D	L	P	W	D	L	P	W	D	L	%
Pomar	5	3	1	1	12	2	6	4	17	5	7	5	50·0
Diez del Corral	6	4	1	1	10	4	4	2	16	8	5	3	65·6
TC Medina	6	3	2	1	12	1	5	6	18	4	7	7	41·7
Toran	4	2	2	0	11	2	6	3	15	4	8	3	53·3
Bellon	4	2	1	1	9	5	2	2	13	7	3	3	65·4
Visier	3	1	2	0	6	0	1	5	9	1	3	5	27·8

12 Poland

	Preliminaries				Finals				Total				
	P	W	D	L	P	W	D	L	P	W	D	L	%
Schmidt	6	3	3	0	13	2	8	3	19	5	11	3	55·3
Bednarski	5	4	1	0	12	1	7	4	17	5	8	4	52·9
Pytel	3	2	0	1	12	0	10	2	15	2	10	3	46·7
Sznapik	4	2	2	0	5	0	1	4	9	2	3	4	38·9
Filipowicz	6	5	1	0	10	2	6	2	16	7	7	2	65·6
Sydor	4	1	3	0	8	1	5	2	12	2	8	2	50·0
TC Vasyukov													

13 Denmark

	Preliminaries				Finals				Total				
	P	W	D	L	P	W	D	L	P	W	D	L	%
TC Hamann	6	3	2	1	13	1	7	5	19	4	9	6	44·7
Jakobsen	6	2	3	1	11	1	5	5	17	3	8	6	41·2
Sloth	5	2	2	1	12	3	5	4	17	5	7	5	50·0
Holm	5	1	4	0	10	1	7	2	15	2	11	2	50·0
Enevoldsen	0	0	0	0	1	0	0	1	1	0	0	1	0·0
Pedersen	2	1	1	0	13	5	5	3	15	6	6	3	60·0

14 Argentina

	Preliminaries				Finals				Total				
	P	W	D	L	P	W	D	L	P	W	D	L	%
TC Rossetto	5	2	1	2	4	0	1	3	9	2	2	5	33·3
R. Garcia	6	3	1	2	15	2	8	5	21	5	9	7	45·2
Rubinetti	5	3	0	2	9	1	4	4	14	4	4	6	42·9
Emma	5	4	0	1	9	1	2	6	14	5	2	7	42·9
Debarnot	3	2	1	0	12	2	7	3	15	4	8	3	53·3
Hase	4	3	0	1	11	3	5	3	15	6	5	4	56·7

15 Sweden

	Preliminaries				Finals				Total				
	P	W	D	L	P	W	D	L	P	W	D	L	%
Andersson	6	3	2	1	12	1	7	4	18	4	9	5	47·2
Jansson	6	4	1	1	10	0	7	3	16	4	8	4	50·0
Ornstein	5	3	1	1	10	1	5	4	15	4	6	5	46·7
Liljedahl	5	2	3	0	10	2	5	3	15	4	8	3	53·3
Olsson	3	1	2	0	10	2	3	5	13	3	5	5	42·3
Uddenfeldt	3	2	1	0	8	1	4	3	11	3	5	3	50·0
TC Nilsson													

16 Switzerland

	Preliminaries				Finals				Total				
	P	W	D	L	P	W	D	L	P	W	D	L	%
Hug	5	1	3	1	14	1	8	5	19	2	11	6	39·5
Lombard	6	3	2	1	14	3	6	5	20	6	8	6	50·0
TC Bhend	2	0	1	1	2	0	1	1	4	0	2	2	25·0
Schaufelberger	6	3	3	0	9	2	3	4	15	5	6	4	53·3
Wirthensohn	6	4	2	0	11	3	1	7	17	7	3	7	50·0
Gereben	3	2	1	0	10	1	4	5	13	3	5	5	42·3

17 England

	Preliminaries					Finals				Total				%
	P	W	D	L		P	W	D	L	P	W	D	L	
Keene	6	2	3	1	(½)	13	3	9	1	19	5	12	2	57·9
Hartston	6	4	1	1	(½)	11	5	5	1	17	9	6	2	70·6
Wade	5	1	3	1		9	3	4	2	14	4	7	3	53·6
Markland	5	2	3	0	(1)	10	4	6	0	15	6	9	0	70·0
Whiteley	4	3	0	1		8	5	3	0	12	8	3	1	79·2
Littlewood	2	1	1	0	(½)	5	2	3	0	7	3	4	0	71·4
TC Anderton														

18 Israel

	Preliminaries				Finals				Total				%
	P	W	D	L	P	W	D	L	P	W	D	L	
Kagan	6	2	2	2	11	3	3	5	17	5	5	7	44·1
Kraidman	6	2	3	1	12	5	6	1	18	7	9	2	63·9
Geller	3	0	0	3	4	1	1	2	7	1	1	5	21·4
Kaldor	5	4	0	1	11	6	5	0	16	10	5	1	78·1
Balshan	6	4	2	0	10	6	4	0	16	10	6	0	81·3
Friedman	2	1	1	0	8	5	2	1	10	6	3	1	75·0
TC Gurewtz													

19 Canada

	Preliminaries					Finals				Total				%
	P	W	D	L		P	W	D	L	P	W	D	L	
Suttles	6	2	3	1	(1)	11	4	4	3	17	6	7	4	55·9
Yanofsky	4	1	1	2		9	3	3	3	13	4	4	5	46·2
Vranesic	5	1	4	0	(0)	9	3	6	0	14	4	10	0	64·3
Biyiasis	4	3	1	0		11	5	6	0	15	8	7	0	76·7
Amos	5	3	2	0	(½)	10	3	7	0	15	6	9	0	70·0
Day	4	2	1	1	(0)	6	0	4	2	10	2	5	3	45·0
TC Prentice														

20 Philippines

	Preliminaries				Finals				Total				%
	P	W	D	L	P	W	D	L	P	W	D	L	
Torre	6	4	0	2	11	5	4	2	17	9	4	4	64·7
Cardoso	5	3	0	2	12	7	3	2	17	10	3	4	67·6
R. Rodriguez	6	3	2	1	10	5	2	3	16	8	4	4	62·5
de Castro	5	3	1	1	9	2	2	5	14	5	3	6	46·4
Badilles	4	3	0	1	6	2	2	2	10	5	2	3	60·0
Lobigas	2	2	0	0	8	3	2	3	10	5	2	3	60·0
TC Guerrero													

21 Norway

	Preliminaries					Finals				Total				%
	P	W	D	L		P	W	D	L	P	W	D	L	
Kristiansen	6	4	1	1	(½)	9	2	4	3	15	6	5	4	56·7
Wibe	5	3	0	2	(0)	8	3	2	3	13	6	2	5	53·8
TC Johanessen	3	0	2	1	(0)	11	7	2	2	14	7	4	3	64·3
Hoen	5	3	2	0	(½)	6	3	1	2	11	6	3	2	68·2
Ogaard	5	4	0	1		11	3	5	3	16	7	5	4	59·4
Zwaig	4	3	1	0		11	2	7	2	15	5	8	2	60·0

22 Cuba

	Preliminaries					Finals				Total				9
	P	W	D	L		P	W	D	L	P	W	D	L	%
J. Rodriguez	6	1	3	2	(1)	8	0	7	1	14	1	10	3	42·9
S. Garcia	5	0	3	2	(½)	12	5	4	3	17	5	7	5	50·0
Cobo	5	2	2	1		10	1	6	3	15	3	8	4	46·7

22 Cuba—cont.

	Preliminaries				Finals				Total				%
	P	W	D	L		P	W	D	L	P	W	D	L	
Hernandez	4	3	0	1		11	3	7	1	15	6	7	2	63·3
Estevez	2	1	1	0	(½)	7	1	4	2	9	2	5	2	50·0
Diaz	2	1	1	0	(½)	8	4	4	0	10	5	5	0	75·0
TC Vega														

23 Austria

	Preliminaries					Finals				Total				%
	P	W	D	L		P	W	D	L	P	W	D	L	
Robatsch	0	0	0	0	(1)	8	2	5	1	8	2	5	1	56·2
Röhrl	5	0	3	2	(½)	9	1	7	1	14	1	10	3	42·9
Janetschek	7	3	2	2	(1)	11	4	6	1	18	7	8	3	61·1
Watzka	5	2	2	1	(½)	10	3	3	4	15	5	5	5	50·0
Strobel	7	4	3	0		10	3	4	3	17	7	7	3	61·8
Holaszek	4	2	1	1		8	3	3	2	12	5	4	3	58·3
TC Kinzel														

24 Iceland

	Preliminaries					Finals				Total				%
	P	W	D	L		P	W	D	L	P	W	D	L	
TC Sigurjonsson	7	2	3	2		8	2	5	1	15	4	8	3	53·3
Kristinsson	6	2	4	0	(½)	9	4	4	1	15	6	8	1	66·7
Thorsteinsson	6	4	0	2	(1)	11	2	4	5	17	6	4	7	47·1
Solmundarson	6	3	1	2		11	5	3	3	17	8	4	5	58·8
Thorvaldsson	1	1	0	0	(1)	8	1	3	4	9	2	3	4	38·9
Magnusson	2	1	1	0	(1)	9	4	3	2	11	5	4	2	63·6

25 Colombia

	Preliminaries					Finals				Total				%
	P	W	D	L		P	W	D	L	P	W	D	L	
TC Cuellar	6	1	4	1	(1)	13	6	5	2	19	7	9	3	60·5
Gutierrez	6	1	2	3	(1)	11	0	3	8	17	1	5	11	20·6
Cuartas	7	4	3	0	(0)	11	5	5	1	18	9	8	1	72·2
de Grieff	6	2	2	2	(½)	10	2	6	2	16	4	8	4	50·0
Minaya	3	2	1	0		10	2	5	3	13	4	6	3	53·8
Castro	0	0	0	0		1	0	0	1	1	0	0	1	0·0

26 Indonesia

	Preliminaries					Finals				Total				%
	P	W	D	L		P	W	D	L	P	W	D	L	
Wotulo	5	3	1	1	(½)	4	1	1	2	9	4	2	3	55·6
Ardiansjah	7	4	2	1	(½)	12	4	3	5	19	8	5	6	55·3
Bachtiar	7	3	2	2	(½)	10	2	2	6	17	5	4	8	41·2
Sampouw	5	1	2	2		14	5	3	6	19	6	5	8	44·7
Suradiredja	2	1	0	1		8	2	4	2	10	3	4	3	50·0
Turalakey	2	0	0	2	(½)	8	3	4	1	10	3	4	3	50·0
TC Sumanti														

27 Italy

	Preliminaries					Finals				Total				%
	P	W	D	L		P	W	D	L	P	W	D	L	
Tatai	6	2	4	0	(0)	12	5	4	3	18	7	8	3	61·1
Mariotti	5	3	2	0	(1)	10	3	5	2	15	6	7	2	63·3
TC Paoli	4	0	3	1	(0)	11	3	5	3	15	3	8	4	46·7
Micheli	5	1	2	2		7	1	1	5	12	2	3	7	29·2
Capello	5	1	3	1	(½)	8	2	3	3	13	3	6	4	46·2
Capece	3	3	0	0		8	1	2	5	11	4	2	5	45·5

28 Mongolia

	Preliminaries				Finals				Total				
	P	W	D	L	P	W	D	L	P	W	D	L	%
Uitumen	7	2	3	2	12	2	5	5	19	4	8	7	42·1
Miagmasuren	7	3	3	1	10	2	4	4	17	5	7	5	50·0
Tumurbator	6	2	2	2	11	2	6	3	17	4	8	5	47·1
Dzigzidsuren	3	1	1	1	9	3	3	3	12	4	4	4	50·0
Niamdorzi	4	4	0	0	8	4	1	3	12	8	1	3	70·8
Zorigt	1	1	0	0	6	1	2	3	7	2	2	3	42·8
TC Purevzhav													

29 Greece

	Preliminaries				Finals				Total				
	P	W	D	L	P	W	D	L	P	W	D	L	%
Siaperas	5	3	0	2	10	1	4	5	15	4	4	7	40·0
Vizantiadis	5	2	1	2	11	2	4	5	16	4	5	7	40·6
Skalkotas	5	1	1	3	9	1	4	4	14	2	5	7	32·1
Trikaliotis	6	2	1	3	10	2	4	4	16	4	5	7	40·6
Makropoulos	5	2	3	0	9	2	5	2	14	4	8	2	57·1
Balascas	2	1	0	1	7	2	1	4	9	3	1	5	38·9
TC Mastichiadis													

30 Belgium

	Preliminaries					Finals				Total				
	P	W	D	L		P	W	D	L	P	W	D	L	%
Boey	6	4	0	2	(½)	6	1	5	0	12	5	5	2	62·5
Van Seters	3	0	1	2	(0)	12	5	2	5	15	5	3	7	43·3
Cornelis	5	2	2	1	(0)	6	1	1	4	11	3	3	5	40·9
Beyen	5	2	2	1	(½)	10	1	4	5	15	3	6	6	40·0
Verstraeten	3	1	1	1		11	1	3	7	14	2	4	8	28·6
Wostyn	2	2	0	0		11	2	4	5	13	4	4	5	46·2
TC Douha														

31 Peru

	Preliminaries				Finals				Total				
	P	W	D	L	P	W	D	L	P	W	D	L	%
O. Rodriguez	7	3	3	1	11	3	3	5	18	6	6	6	50·0
Quinones	7	4	3	0	10	2	3	5	17	6	6	5	52·9
Vasquez	7	3	2	2	10	1	5	4	17	4	7	6	44·1
Pesantes	5	2	2	1	12	3	3	6	17	5	5	7	44·1
Villasante	2	2	0	0	8	0	5	3	10	2	5	3	45·0
P. Garcia	0	0	0	0	5	0	1	4	5	0	1	4	10·0
TC Zapata													

32 Australia

	Preliminaries				Finals				Total				
	P	W	D	L	P	W	D	L	P	W	D	L	%
Browne	7	3	3	1	15	12	2	1	22	15	5	2	79·5
Fuller	5	1	2	2	9	5	4	0	14	6	6	2	64·3
Hay	3	2	0	1	8	6	1	1	11	8	1	2	77·2
Flatow	4	2	0	2	7	1	5	1	11	3	5	3	50·0
Hamilton	5	3	1	1	10	5	2	3	15	8	3	4	63·3
Shaw	4	1	2	1	11	8	2	1	15	9	4	2	73·3
TC Koshnitsky													

33 Finland

	Preliminaries				Finals				Total				
	P	W	D	L	P	W	D	L	P	W	D	L	%
TC Westerinen	5	1	2	2	12	7	2	3	17	8	4	5	58·8
Ojanen	5	2	2	1	8	2	6	0	13	4	8	1	61·5

33 Finland—cont.

		Preliminaries				Finals				Total				%
		P	W	D	L	P	W	D	L	P	W	D	L	
	Saren	5	1	2	2	10	4	5	1	15	5	7	3	56·7
	Sorri	4	1	2	1	10	6	3	1	14	7	5	2	67·9
	Rantanen	3	1	0	2	12	10	2	0	15	11	2	2	80·0
	Kanko	2	1	1	0	8	2	4	2	10	3	5	2	55·0

34 Scotland

		Preliminaries				Finals				Total				%
		P	W	D	L	P	W	D	L	P	W	D	L	
	Levy	6	2	1	3	12	4	4	4	18	6	5	7	47·2
	Pritchett	5	3	1	1	13	6	6	1	18	9	7	2	69·4
TC	Bonner	6	2	1	3	11	6	3	2	17	8	4	5	58·8
	Jamieson	5	0	3	2	11	7	3	1	16	7	6	3	62·5
	Denman	2	0	1	1	8	5	1	2	10	5	2	3	60·0
	Aitken	4	1	0	3	5	0	5	0	9	1	5	3	38·9

35 Iran

		Preliminaries				Finals				Total				%
		P	W	D	L	P	W	D	L	P	W	D	L	
	Harandi	7	2	3	2	15	6	8	1	22	8	11	3	61·4
	Shirazi	7	4	1	2	7	2	3	2	14	6	4	4	57·1
	Shahsavar	6	2	0	4	10	2	4	4	16	4	4	8	37·5
	Sharif	7	2	2	3	14	6	4	4	21	8	6	7	52·4
	Savadkoohi	1	0	0	1	14	11	2	1	15	11	2	2	80·0
TC	Saloor													

36 Brazil

		Preliminaries				Finals				Total				%
		P	W	D	L	P	W	D	L	P	W	D	L	
	German	7	3	3	1	13	5	5	3	20	8	8	4	60·0
	Trois	7	2	2	3	14	4	8	2	21	6	10	5	52·4
	Nobrega	6	2	2	2	11	7	1	3	17	9	3	5	61·8
	Toth	6	3	2	1	9	5	3	1	15	8	5	2	70·0
	van Riemsdyk	2	1	0	1	10	3	5	2	12	4	5	3	54·2
	Santos	0	0	0	0	3	0	1	2	3	0	1	2	16·7
TC	Camara													

37 Portugal

		Preliminaries				Finals				Total				%
		P	W	D	L	P	W	D	L	P	W	D	L	
	Ribeiro	6	1	4	1	14	2	7	5	20	3	11	6	42·5
	Durao	7	4	0	3	13	6	7	0	20	10	7	3	67·5
	Silva	7	2	2	3	13	6	6	1	20	8	8	4	60·0
	Santos	3	1	2	0	8	5	1	2	11	6	3	2	68·2
	Cardoso	1	0	0	1	5	0	1	4	6	0	1	5	8·3
	Figueiredo	4	1	1	2	7	1	3	3	11	2	4	5	36·4

38 Turkey

		Preliminaries				Finals				Total				%
		P	W	D	L	P	W	D	L	P	W	D	L	
	Suer	6	1	1	4	10	2	4	4	16	3	5	8	34·4
	Külür	2	0	1	1	9	0	7	2	11	0	8	3	36·4
	Onat	6	1	3	2	11	6	5	0	17	7	8	2	64·7
	Erözbek	6	0	3	3	9	1	5	3	15	1	8	6	33·3
	Uzman	1	0	0	1	12	5	1	6	13	5	1	7	42·3
	Bilyap	7	3	2	2	9	5	2	2	16	8	4	4	62·5
TC	Günsav													

39 Ireland

	Preliminaries				Finals				Total				%
	P	W	D	L	P	W	D	L	P	W	D	L	
Moles	6	1	3	2	13	4	6	3	19	5	9	5	**50·0**
McGrillen	6	0	2	4	13	4	8	1	19	4	10	5	**47·4**
TC Littleton	5	3	2	0	13	4	8	1	18	7	10	1	**66·7**
Cassidy	4	1	0	3	6	0	2	4	10	1	2	7	**20·0**
Coldrick	3	1	1	1	10	1	6	3	13	2	7	4	**42·3**
Keeshan	4	2	1	1	5	0	1	4	9	2	2	5	**33·3**

40 Puerto Rico

	Preliminaries				Finals				Total				%
	P	W	D	L	P	W	D	L	P	W	D	L	
Kaplan	7	2	4	1	10	4	6	0	17	6	10	1	**64·7**
Martinez	6	1	1	4	14	4	3	7	20	5	4	11	**35·0**
Berrios	6	0	2	4	9	2	3	4	15	2	5	8	**30·0**
Benitez	3	0	0	3	13	1	9	3	16	1	9	6	**34·4**
TC Sacarello	2	0	1	1	10	3	4	3	12	3	5	4	**45·8**
Colon	4	2	1	1	4	1	2	1	8	3	3	2	**56·2**

41 Mexico

	Preliminaries				Finals				Total				%
	P	W	D	L	P	W	D	L	P	W	D	L	
Campos	6	3	2	1	9	4	4	1	15	7	6	2	**66·7**
Frey	6	1	3	2	13	5	4	4	19	6	7	6	**50·0**
Escondrillas	6	1	1	4	8	2	5	1	14	3	6	5	**42·9**
de la Cruz	5	2	0	3	9	0	3	6	14	2	3	9	**25·0**
Padilla	4	1	0	3	11	2	1	8	15	3	1	11	**23·3**
Barrientos	1	0	0	1	10	3	4	3	11	3	4	4	**45·5**
TC Reza													

42 Tunisia

	Preliminaries				Finals				Total				%
	P	W	D	L	P	W	D	L	P	W	D	L	
Belkadi	7	3	2	2	14	3	8	3	21	6	10	5	**52·4**
Kchouk	5	2	2	1	11	1	4	6	16	3	6	7	**37·5**
Drira	7	3	1	3	13	2	7	4	20	5	8	7	**45·0**
Tebourbi	3	0	0	3	8	3	2	3	11	3	2	6	**36·4**
Najar	4	2	1	1	6	1	0	5	10	3	1	6	**35·0**
Lagha	2	0	1	1	8	5	2	1	10	5	3	2	**65·0**
TC Mohsen													

43 Wales

	Preliminaries				Finals				Total				%
	P	W	D	L	P	W	D	L	P	W	D	L	
Williams	6	3	1	2	11	3	7	1	17	6	8	3	**58·8**
Hutchings	7	1	5	1	12	4	5	3	19	5	10	4	**52·6**
Gavrilovic	5	0	3	2	9	0	5	4	14	0	8	6	**28·6**
Jones	6	2	2	2	12	3	6	3	18	5	8	5	**50·0**
Haigh	3	0	0	3	7	3	0	4	10	3	0	7	**30·0**
James	1	0	0	1	9	0	4	5	10	0	4	6	**20·0**
TC Mills													

44 New Zealand

	Preliminaries				Finals				Total				%
	P	W	D	L	P	W	D	L	P	W	D	L	
Sarapu	6	2	4	0	10	1	4	5	16	3	8	5	**43·7**
Sutton	7	3	3	1	10	1	6	3	17	4	9	4	**50·0**
Stuart	7	2	1	4	10	0	6	4	17	2	7	8	**32·3**
Carpinter	2	0	0	2	11	5	4	2	13	5	4	4	**53·8**

44 New Zealand—cont.

	Preliminaries				Finals				Total				%
	P	W	D	L	P	W	D	L	P	W	D	L	
Van Dijk	3	1	0	2	8	2	3	3	11	3	3	5	40·9
Kerr	3	1	1	1	11	3	3	5	14	4	4	6	42·9
TC Hollander													

45 Dominican Rep.

	Preliminaries				Finals				Total				%
	P	W	D	L	P	W	D	L	P	W	D	L	
Belliard	5	2	0	3	11	4	1	6	16	6	1	9	40·6
Delgado	5	1	0	4	11	1	6	4	16	2	6	8	37·5
Gonzalez	5	0	3	2	11	1	4	6	16	1	7	8	28·1
Pena	4	0	1	3	9	1	2	6	13	1	3	9	19·2
Malagon	3	1	0	2	9	3	2	4	12	4	2	6	41·7
Alvarez	2	0	0	2	9	3	2	4	11	3	2	6	36·4
TC Damiron													

46 Bolivia

	Preliminaries				Finals				Total				%
	P	W	D	L	P	W	D	L	P	W	D	L	
Vaca	6	1	0	5	9	0	2	7	15	1	2	12	13·3
Chavez	7	2	0	5	13	1	5	7	20	3	5	12	27·5
Alvarez	7	2	1	4	13	3	2	8	20	5	3	12	32·5
Aliaga	7	2	1	4	13	4	4	5	20	6	5	9	42·5
Salinas	1	0	0	1	12	2	5	5	13	2	5	6	34·6

47 Japan

	Preliminaries				Finals				Total				%
	P	W	D	L	P	W	D	L	P	W	D	L	
Miyasaka	6	2	0	4	14	5	3	6	20	7	3	10	42·5
TC Matsumoto	6	1	0	5	11	1	1	9	17	2	1	14	14·7
Honda	6	0	3	3	12	0	8	4	18	0	11	7	30·6
Takahashi	6	2	1	3	6	1	3	2	12	3	4	5	41·7
Otani	0	0	0	0	8	0	0	8	8	0	0	8	0·0
Nakamori	4	0	2	2	9	0	2	7	13	0	4	9	15·4

48 France

	Preliminaries				Finals				Total				%
	P	W	D	L	P	W	D	L	P	W	D	L	
Rossolimo	6	1	1	4	11	6	3	2	17	7	4	6	52·9
Todorcevic	6	1	1	4	8	7	1	0	14	8	2	4	64·3
Letzelter	4	1	1	2	11	7	2	2	15	8	3	4	63·3
Huguet	5	0	2	3	11	9	0	2	16	9	2	5	62·5
Raizman	3	2	0	1	7	6	1	0	10	8	1	1	85·0
Haik	4	3	0	1	8	8	0	0	12	11	0	1	91·7
TC O'Kelly													

49 Singapore

	Preliminaries				Finals				Total				%
	P	W	D	L	P	W	D	L	P	W	D	L	
Tan	7	2	2	3	12	9	3	0	19	11	5	3	71·1
Lim	7	0	3	4	11	3	5	3	18	3	8	7	38·9
Giam	7	1	3	3	14	11	2	1	21	12	5	4	69·0
Choong	4	1	0	3	7	5	0	2	11	6	0	5	54·5
Pang	1	0	0	1	5	4	1	0	6	4	1	1	75·0
Ee	2	1	0	1	7	4	2	1	9	5	2	2	66·7
TC Karaklaic													

50 Malta	Preliminaries				Finals				Total				
	P	W	D	L	P	W	D	L	P	W	D	L	%
Camilleri	7	0	0	7	13	5	6	2	20	5	6	9	40·0
Gouder	6	0	2	4	11	2	6	3	17	2	8	7	35·3
Attard	1	0	0	1	13	6	2	5	14	6	2	6	50·0
Saliba	5	0	2	3	8	5	1	2	13	5	3	5	50·0
Vincenti	6	0	2	4	6	2	4	0	12	2	6	4	41·7
Casha	3	0	0	3	5	2	1	2	8	2	1	5	31·3
TC Floridia													

51 Hong Kong	Preliminaries				Finals				Total				
	P	W	D	L	P	W	D	L	P	W	D	L	%
Krstic	6	1	3	2	14	4	7	3	20	5	10	5	50·0
Hasan	6	0	1	5	6	2	3	1	12	2	4	6	33·3
Kwan	5	1	0	4	13	6	5	2	18	7	5	6	52·8
TC Hobson	3	1	0	2	3	0	1	2	6	1	1	4	25·0
Kong	5	0	0	5	11	6	1	4	16	6	1	9	40·6
Krouk	3	0	1	2	9	2	4	3	12	2	5	5	37·5

52 Lebanon	Preliminaries				Finals				Total				
	P	W	D	L	P	W	D	L	P	W	D	L	%
Tarazi	1	0	0	1	0	0	0	0	1	0	0	1	0·0
Sursock	6	0	2	4	6	2	3	1	12	2	5	5	37·5
Loheac-Ammoun	7	1	1	5	13	7	5	1	20	8	6	6	55·0
Maalouf	4	0	0	4	13	4	4	5	17	4	4	9	35·3
Bedros	6	1	1	4	13	2	8	3	19	3	9	7	39·5
TC Galeb	4	0	2	2	11	1	8	2	15	1	10	4	40·0

53 Luxemburg	Preliminaries				Finals				Total				
	P	W	D	L	P	W	D	L	P	W	D	L	%
TC Philippe	4	0	0	4	8	2	3	3	12	2	3	7	29·2
Weber	4	0	0	4	10	4	5	1	14	4	5	5	46·4
Stull	4	1	1	2	10	4	4	2	14	5	5	4	53·6
Schammo	4	0	1	3	10	2	4	4	14	2	5	7	32·2
Simon	4	0	1	3	10	4	5	1	14	4	6	4	50·0
Kirsch	4	0	0	4	8	2	2	4	12	2	2	8	25·0

54 Faroe Islands	Preliminaries				Finals				Total				
	P	W	D	L	P	W	D	L	P	W	D	L	%
Petersen	5	1	1	3	12	6	2	4	17	7	3	7	50·0
Joensen	5	1	1	3	7	0	3	4	12	1	4	7	25·0
Midjord	6	1	0	5	10	6	2	2	16	7	2	7	50·0
Mikkelsen	5	1	0	4	8	1	4	3	13	2	4	7	30·7
TC Thomsen	3	0	0	3	10	4	4	2	13	4	4	5	46·2
Olsen	4	1	1	2	9	2	5	2	13	3	6	4	46·2

55 Syria	Preliminaries				Finals				Total				
	P	W	D	L	P	W	D	L	P	W	D	L	%
Shorbagey	7	1	0	6	12	3	5	4	19	4	5	10	34·2
Katlan	4	1	1	2	13	6	4	3	17	7	5	5	55·9
Nashed	7	1	1	5	12	2	4	6	19	3	5	11	28·9
Asfary	5	0	2	3	6	2	2	2	11	2	4	5	36·4
Sayed	3	0	0	3	4	1	1	2	7	1	1	5	21·4
Tabba	2	0	0	2	9	4	4	1	11	4	4	3	54·5

56 Cyprus

	Preliminaries				Finals				Total				
	P	W	D	L	P	W	D	L	P	W	D	L	%
Kleopas	5	0	0	5	8	1	2	5	13	1	2	10	15·4
Constantinou	0	0	0	0	7	3	3	1	7	3	3	1	64·3
Avgousti	6	1	0	5	12	5	5	2	18	6	5	7	47·2
Martides	6	1	1	4	10	4	1	5	16	5	2	9	37·5
Vassiades	5	1	0	4	9	4	1	4	14	5	1	8	39·3
Hadjitofi	6	0	2	4	10	2	5	3	16	2	7	7	34·4
TC Lantsias													

57 Morocco

	Preliminaries				Finals				Total				
	P	W	D	L	P	W	D	L	P	W	D	L	%
Ben Larbi	7	2	1	4	10	3	5	2	17	5	6	6	47·1
Kadri	7	0	1	6	14	5	8	1	21	5	9	7	45·2
Abbou	7	2	0	5	13	3	3	7	20	5	3	12	32·5
TC Chami	5	1	1	3	10	3	3	4	15	4	4	7	40·0
Sbia	2	0	0	2	9	1	3	5	11	1	3	7	22·7
Abdelmalek	—				—				—				

58 Andorra

	Preliminaries				Finals				Total				
	P	W	D	L	P	W	D	L	P	W	D	L	%
Clua	5	2	0	3	10	3	4	3	15	5	4	6	46·7
Calderon	5	1	0	4	10	2	4	4	15	3	4	8	33·3
TC de la Casa	5	0	1	4	12	3	6	3	17	3	7	7	38·2
Gomez	5	0	1	4	11	4	4	3	16	4	5	7	40·6
Pantebre	4	0	0	4	7	1	2	4	11	1	2	8	18·2
Iglesias	4	0	0	4	6	0	2	4	10	0	2	8	10·0

59 Malaysia

	Preliminaries				Finals				Total				
	P	W	D	L	P	W	D	L	P	W	D	L	%
Foo	7	0	0	7	14	2	7	5	21	2	7	12	26·2
Chan	7	2	2	3	13	4	5	4	20	6	7	7	47·5
Kao	5	0	0	5	12	5	0	7	17	5	0	12	29·4
TC Fang	2	0	0	2	3	0	0	3	5	0	0	5	0·0
Chee Loh	5	0	0	5	13	2	8	3	18	2	8	8	33·3
Ariff	2	0	0	2	1	0	0	1	3	0	0	3	0·0

60 Guernsey

	Preliminaries				Finals				Total				
	P	W	D	L	P	W	D	L	P	W	D	L	%
Palmer	7	0	0	7	14	3	6	5	21	3	6	12	28·6
Le Marquand	5	1	2	2	13	4	5	4	18	5	7	6	47·2
TC Bisson	4	0	0	4	7	0	2	5	11	0	2	9	9·1
Moriarty	4	0	0	4	8	1	3	4	12	1	3	8	20·8
Wallbridge	4	0	0	4	7	0	3	4	11	0	3	8	13·6
Gavey	4	0	0	4	7	1	4	2	11	1	4	6	27·3

61 Iraq

	Preliminaries				Finals				Total				
	P	W	D	L	P	W	D	L	P	W	D	L	%
Taha	6	1	0	5	11	3	4	4	17	4	4	9	35·3
al Hamami	6	1	0	5	10	1	2	7	16	2	2	12	18·7
al Jasani	5	1	0	4	8	1	0	7	13	2	0	11	15·4
Ahmed	4	2	0	2	9	2	3	4	13	4	3	6	42·3
al Mawla	3	0	0	3	9	2	5	2	12	2	5	5	37·5
Saleem	4	1	1	2	9	2	5	2	13	3	6	4	46·2

62 Virgin Islands

		Preliminaries				Finals				Total			
		P	W	D	L	P	W	D	L	P	W	D	L	%
	Abraham	7	0	2	5	14	0	2	12	21	0	4	17	**9·5**
	E. Grumer	7	0	0	7	14	1	1	12	21	1	1	19	**7·1**
	Hamilton	2	0	0	2	14	4	6	4	16	4	6	6	**43·7**
TC	Francis-Edwards	7	0	0	7	14	1	0	13	21	1	0	20	**4·8**
	Hoyt	—				—				—				—
	S. Grumer	5	0	0	5	0	0	0	0	5	0	0	5	**0·0**

The figures in brackets before the final scores of some of the teams placed 17–31 are the individual results against Albania which were later cancelled.

Albania played 10 matches in Final B before their withdrawal with the following results:

Albania

		Preliminaries				Finals				Total			
		P	W	D	L	P	W	D	L	P	W	D	L	%
	Pustina	7	2	5	0	9	1	4	4	16	3	9	4	**46·9**
	Vila	6	3	2	1	9	2	4	3	15	5	6	4	**53·3**
	Adhami	6	3	3	0	8	2	3	3	14	5	6	3	**57·1**
	Muco	7	5	1	1	8	4	4	0	15	9	5	1	**76·7**
	Omari	1	1	0	0	2	0	1	1	3	1	1	1	**50·0**
	Zadrima	0	0	0	0	4	0	4	0	4	0	4	0	**50·0**
TC	Luci													

LADIES' OLYMPIAD

Individual Results

1 USSR	Preliminaries				Finals				Total				
	P	W	D	L	P	W	D	L	P	W	D	L	%
N. Gaprindashvili	3	3	0	0	5	2	3	0	8	5	3	0	81·3
A. Kushnir	3	3	0	0	5	3	2	0	8	6	2	0	87·5
I. Levitina	2	1	1	0	4	4	0	0	6	5	1	0	91·7
TC A. Gipslis													

2 Rumania	Preliminaries				Finals				Total				
	P	W	D	L	P	W	D	L	P	W	D	L	%
E. Polihroniade	3	2	1	0	7	3	1	3	10	5	2	3	60·0
A. Nicolau	4	2	2	0	5	4	0	1	9	6	2	1	77·8
G. Baumstark	3	2	1	0	2	0	1	1	5	2	2	1	60·0
TC S. Samarian													

3 Hungary	Preliminaries				Finals				Total				
	P	W	D	L	P	W	D	L	P	W	D	L	%
M. Ivanka	4	3	1	0	6	3	2	1	10	6	3	1	75·0
Z. Veröci	4	2	1	1	6	3	1	2	10	5	2	3	60·0
E. Krizsan	2	2	0	0	2	0	1	1	4	2	1	1	62·5
TC F. Jenei													

4 Bulgaria	Preliminaries				Finals				Total				
	P	W	D	L	P	W	D	L	P	W	D	L	%
A. Georgieva	4	2	2	0	7	1	5	1	11	3	7	1	59·1
V. Assenova	5	3	2	0	6	2	4	0	11	5	6	0	72·7
V. Shikova	1	1	0	0	1	0	0	1	2	1	0	1	50·0
TC P. Ivanov													

5 Czechoslovakia	Preliminaries				Finals				Total				
	P	W	D	L	P	W	D	L	P	W	D	L	%
S. Vokralova	5	3	2	0	6	2	3	1	11	5	5	1	68·2
K. Eretova	4	2	2	0	4	0	3	1	8	2	5	1	56·3
E. Hojdarova	1	1	0	0	4	1	2	1	5	2	2	1	60·0
TC J. Podgorny													

6 West Germany	Preliminaries				Finals				Total				
	P	W	D	L	P	W	D	L	P	W	D	L	%
A. Laakmann	4	2	2	0	6	1	2	3	10	3	4	3	50·0
I. Karner	4	3	1	0	4	1	1	2	8	4	2	2	62·5
U. Wasnetsky	2	0	2	0	4	1	2	1	6	1	4	1	50·0
TC M. Grzeskowiak													

7 East Germany	Preliminaries				Finals				Total				
	P	W	D	L	P	W	D	L	P	W	D	L	%
W. Nowarra	3	2	0	1	3	0	0	3	6	2	0	4	33·3
Dr G. Just	4	2	1	1	6	2	2	2	10	4	3	3	55·0

7 East Germany—cont.

	Preliminaries				Finals				Total				
	P	W	D	L	P	W	D	L	P	W	D	L	%
C. Hölzlein	1	0	1	0	5	1	1	3	6	1	2	3	33·3
TC E. Bonsch													

8 England

	Preliminaries				Finals				Total				
	P	W	D	L	P	W	D	L	P	W	D	L	%
J. Hartston	4	4	0	0	7	1	4	2	11	5	4	2	63·6
E. Pritchard	3	1	2	0	4	0	0	4	7	1	2	4	28·6
A. Sunnucks	3	2	1	0	3	1	0	2	6	3	1	2	58·3
TC H. Golombek													

9 Poland

	Preliminaries				Finals				Total				
	P	W	D	L	P	W	D	L	P	W	D	L	%
K. Radzikowska	4	2	1	1	5	3	2	0	9	5	3	1	72·2
H. Erenska	3	2	1	0	6	4	2	0	9	6	3	0	83·3
M. Litmanowicz	3	2	0	1	3	1	1	1	6	3	1	2	58·3
TC S. Witkowski													

10 Yugoslavia

	Preliminaries				Finals				Total				
	P	W	D	L	P	W	D	L	P	W	D	L	%
M. Lazarević	3	1	1	1	1	1	0	0	4	2	1	1	62·5
K. Jovanović	5	3	2	0	6	2	2	2	11	5	4	2	63·6
H. Konarkovska	2	2	0	0	7	2	5	0	9	4	5	0	72·2
TC M. Petronić													

11 Austria

	Preliminaries				Finals				Total				
	P	W	D	L	P	W	D	L	P	W	D	L	%
TC Dr I. Kattinger	4	1	1	2	5	1	1	3	9	2	2	5	33·3
M. Hausner	4	2	0	2	4	1	3	0	8	3	3	2	56·3
W. Samt	2	0	0	2	5	2	2	1	7	2	2	3	42·8

12 Holland

	Preliminaries				Finals				Total				
	P	W	D	L	P	W	D	L	P	W	D	L	%
H. Timmer	3	2	0	1	6	3	1	2	9	5	1	3	61·1
I. Jansen	3	0	2	1	2	0	0	2	5	0	2	3	20·0
A. v. d. Giessen	2	1	0	1	6	3	1	2	8	4	1	3	56·3
TC van Scheltinga													

13 Sweden

	Preliminaries				Finals				Total				
	P	W	D	L	P	W	D	L	P	W	D	L	%
S. Haraldsson	4	1	0	3	4	1	1	2	8	2	1	5	31·3
I. Kemenyova-Svenson	3	2	0	1	5	1	1	3	8	3	1	4	43·8
U. Bohmgren	3	1	0	2	5	3	1	1	8	4	1	3	56·3
TC A. Hildebrand													

14 Brazil

	Preliminaries				Finals				Total				
	P	W	D	L	P	W	D	L	P	W	D	L	%
R. Cardoso	4	1	2	1	5	5	0	0	9	6	2	1	77·8
R. Fontanelli	2	0	0	2	5	0	1	4	7	0	1	6	7·1
I. Moises	4	2	0	2	4	0	1	3	8	2	1	5	31·3
TC Camara													

15 Mongolia

	Preliminaries				Finals				Total				
	P	W	D	L	P	W	D	L	P	W	D	L	%
Khulgana	5	2	1	2	6	1	2	3	11	3	3	5	40·8
TC Khandsuren	3	1	0	2	6	1	3	2	9	2	3	4	38·9
Biamba	2	1	0	1	2	0	2	0	4	1	2	1	50·0

16 Australia

	Preliminaries				Finals				Total				
	P	W	D	L	P	W	D	L	P	W	D	L	%
N. Kellner	3	1	0	2	5	0	3	2	8	1	3	4	31·3
M. McGrath	3	1	0	2	5	1	3	1	8	2	3	3	43·8
L. Maddern	2	0	2	0	4	1	0	3	6	1	2	3	33·3
TC A. Pope													

17 Switzerland

	Preliminaries				Finals				Total				
	P	W	D	L	P	W	D	L	P	W	D	L	%
TC A. Näpeer	5	2	0	3	4	2	2	0	9	4	2	3	55·6
E. Lüssy	3	0	0	3	4	2	1	1	7	2	1	4	35·7
J. Fässler	2	0	1	1	4	3	1	0	6	3	2	1	66·7

18 Israel

	Preliminaries				Finals				Total				
	P	W	D	L	P	W	D	L	P	W	D	L	%
F. Rabinovitch	3	0	0	3	6	2	4	0	9	2	4	3	44·4
L. Gal	3	1	2	0	5	3	2	0	8	4	4	0	75·0
S. Klugas	4	1	0	3	1	0	1	0	5	1	1	3	30·0
TC A. Burstein													

19 Singapore

	Preliminaries				Finals				Total				
	P	W	D	L	P	W	D	L	P	W	D	L	%
P. Mok	4	0	0	4	4	0	2	2	8	0	2	6	12·5
Y. Giam	3	0	0	3	4	0	2	2	7	0	2	5	14·3
J. Tan	3	1	0	2	4	4	0	0	7	5	0	2	71·4
TC N. Karaklaić													

20 Ireland

	Preliminaries				Finals				Total				
	P	W	D	L	P	W	D	L	P	W	D	L	%
D. O'Siochru	3	0	0	3	5	1	4	0	8	1	4	3	37·5
A. Noonan	3	0	0	3	4	2	0	2	7	2	0	5	28·6
A. O'Clery	2	0	1	1	3	0	1	2	5	0	2	3	20·0
TC O. O'Siochru													

21 Finland

	Preliminaries				Finals				Total				
	P	W	D	L	P	W	D	L	P	W	D	L	%
TC S. Vuorenpaa	5	2	0	3	6	2	3	1	11	4	3	4	50·0
J. Tuomainen	4	0	1	3	3	1	0	2	7	1	1	5	21·4
M. Palasto	1	0	0	1	3	1	0	2	4	1	0	3	25·0

22 Scotland

	Preliminaries				Finals				Total				
	P	W	D	L	P	W	D	L	P	W	D	L	%
TC N. Elder	4	0	1	3	4	2	1	1	8	2	2	4	37·5
M. McGinn	4	1	0	3	4	0	2	2	8	1	2	5	25·0
M. Little	2	0	1	1	4	0	2	2	6	0	3	3	25·0

23 Japan

		Preliminaries				Finals				Total				
		P	W	D	L	P	W	D	L	P	W	D	L	%
	M. Watai	5	0	0	5	3	0	1	2	8	0	1	7	6·3
TC	K. Otani	3	0	1	2	6	2	1	3	9	2	2	5	33·3
	K. Watanabe	2	0	0	2	3	0	0	3	5	0	0	5	0·0

PREVIOUS OLYMPIADS

I London 1927
1 Hungary 40
(Maroczy, Nagy, Vajda
Steiner, Havasi)
2 Denmark 38½
3 England 36½
4 Holland 35
5 Czechoslovakia 34½
6 Germany 34
7 Austria 34
8 Switzerland 32
9 Yugoslavia 30½
10 Italy 28
11 Sweden 28
12 Argentina 27
13 France 24½
14 Belgium 21½
15 Finland 21½
16 Spain 14½

II The Hague 1928
1 Hungary 44
(Nagy, Steiner, Vajda,
Havasi)
2 U.S.A. 39½
3 Poland 37
4 Austria 36½
5 Denmark 34
6 Switzerland 34
7 Czechoslovakia 34
8 Argentina 33½
9 Germany 31½
10 Holland 31½
11 France 31
12 Belgium 31
13 Sweden 31
14 Latvia 30
15 Italy 26½
16 Rumania 25½
17 Spain 13½

III Hamburg 1930
1 Poland 48½
(Rubinstein, Tarta-
kower, Przepiorka,
Makarczyk, Frydman)
2 Hungary 47
3 Germany 44½
4 Austria 43½

5 Czechoslovakia 42½
6 U.S.A. 41½
7 Holland 41
8 England 40½
9 Sweden 40
10 Latvia 35
11 Denmark 31
12 France 28½
13 Rumania 28½
14 Lithuania 22½
15 Iceland 22
16 Spain 21½
17 Finland 18
18 Norway 16

IV Prague 1931
1 U.S.A. 48
(Kashdan, Marshall,
Dake, Horowitz,
Steiner)
2 Poland 47
3 Czechoslovakia 46½
4 Yugoslavia 46
5 Germany 45½
6 Latvia 45½
7 Sweden 45½
8 Austria 45
9 England 44
10 Hungary 39½
11 Holland 35
12 Switzerland 34
13 Lithuania 30½
14 France 29½
15 Rumania 28
16 Italy 24
17 Denmark 19½
18 Norway 15½
19 Spain 15½

V Folkestone 1933
1 U.S.A. 39
(Kashdan, Marshall,
Dake, Horowitz,
Steiner)
2 Czechoslovakia 37½
3 Poland 34
4 Sweden 34
5 Hungary 34
6 Austria 33½

7 Lithuania 30½
8 France 28
9 Latvia 27½
10 England 27
11 Italy 24½
12 Denmark 22½
13 Belgium 17
14 Iceland 17
15 Scotland 14

VI Warsaw 1935
1 U.S.A. 54
(Fine, Marshall, Kup-
chik, Dake, Horowitz)
2 Sweden 52½
3 Poland 52
4 Hungary 51
5 Czechoslovakia 49
6 Yugoslavia 45½
7 Austria 43½
8 Argentina 42
9 Latvia 41
10 France 38
11 Estonia 37½
12 England 37
13 Finland 35
14 Lithuania 34
15 Palestine 32
16 Denmark 31½
17 Rumania 27½
18 Italy 24
19 Switzerland 21
20 Ireland 12

VII Stockholm 1937
1 U.S.A. 54½
(Reshevsky, Fine Kash-
dan, Marshall, Horo-
witz)
2 Hungary 48½
3 Poland 47
4 Argentina 47
5 Czechoslovakia 45
6 Holland 44
7 Lithuania 41½
8 Estonia 41½
9 Yugoslavia 40
10 Sweden 38½
11 Latvia 37½

12 Finland	34
13 England	34
14 Italy	26½
15 Denmark	25½
16 Iceland	23
17 Belgium	22½
18 Norway	19½
19 Scotland	14

VIII Buenos Aires 1939
Group A

1 Germany	36
(Eliskases, Michel, Engels, Becker, Reinhardt)	
2 Poland	35½
3 Estonia	33½
4 Sweden	33
5 Argentina	32½
6 Czechoslovakia	32
7 Latvia	31½
8 Holland	30½
9 Palestine	26
10 France	24½
11 Cuba	22½
12 Chile	22
13 Lithuania	22
14 Brazil	21
15 Denmark	17½

Group B

16 Iceland	28
17 Canada	28
18 Norway	27
19 Uruguay	26
20 Bulgaria	25½
21 Equador	21
22 Guatemala	15½
23 Ireland	15½
24 Peru	14
25 Bolivia	10
26 Paraguay	9½

IX Dubrovnik 1950

1 Yugoslavia	45½
(Gligoric, Pirc, Trifunovic, Rabar, Vidmar, Puc)	
2 Argentina	43½
3 West Germany	40½
4 U.S.A.	40
5 Holland	37
6 Belgium	32
7 Austria	31½

8 Chile	30½
9 France	28½
10 Finland	28
11 Sweden	27½
12 Italy	25
13 Denmark	22
14 Peru	21½
15 Norway	15
16 Greece	12

X Helsinki 1952
Group A

1 U.S.S.R.	21
(Keres, Smyslov, Bronstein, Geller, Boleslavsky, Kotov)	
2 Argentina	19½
3 Yugoslavia	19
4 Czechoslovakia	18
5 U.S.A.	17
6 Hungary	16
7 Sweden	13
8 West Germany	10½
9 Finland	10

Group B

10 Holland	21
11 Israel	19½
12 Poland	16½
13 East Germany	16½
14 Denmark	16
15 Cuba	15
16 England	14
17 Austria	13
18 Italy	12½

Group C

19 Brazil	18½
20 Greece	13½
21 Norway	13
22 Switzerland	13
23 Iceland	12½
24 The Saar	12½
25 Luxembourg	1

XI Amsterdam 1954
Group A

1 U.S.S.R.	34
(Botvinnik, Smyslov, Bronstein, Keres, Geller, Kotov)	
2 Argentina	27
3 Yugoslavia	26½
4 Czechoslovakia	24½

5 West Germany	23½
6 Hungary	23
7 Israel	22
8 Holland	21
9 England	17
10 Bulgaria	17
11 Sweden	15
12 Iceland	13½

Group B

13 Switzerland	37
13 Canada	36
15 Austria	36
16 Denmark	34½
17 Italy	28½
18 Columbia	27½
19 Belgium	27
20 Finland	26½
21 France	26
22 The Saar	24
23 Norway	22
24 Greece	21
25 Ireland	11
26 Luxembourg	7

XII Moscow 1956
Group A

1 U.S.S.R.	31
(Botvinnik, Smyslov, Keres, Bronstein, Taimanov, Geller)	
2 Yugoslavia	26½
3 Hungary	26½
4 Argentina	23
5 West Germany	22
6 Bulgaria	22
7 Czechoslovakia	20½
8 England	20
9 Switzerland	19
10 Denmark	19
11 Roumania	19
12 Israel	15½

Group B

13 Austria	28
14 Iceland	27
15 Sweden	26½
16 Belgium	23½
17 Finland	22½
18 Columbia	21
19 Holland	21
20 East Germany	20½
21 France	19½
22 Chile	19

23	Poland	19
24	Norway	16½

Group C

25	Philippines	24
26	The Saar	23
27	India	20½
28	Iran	19
29	Puerto Rico	18½
30	Mongolia	18½
31	Scotland	17½
32	Greece	17
33	Ireland	13
34	Luxembourg	9

XIII Munich 1958
Group A

1	U.S.S.R.	34½
	(Botvinnik, Smyslov, Keres, Bronstein, Petrosian, Tal)	
2	Yugoslavia	29
3	Argentina	25½
4	U.S.A.	24
5	Czechoslovakia	22
6	East Germany	22
7	West Germany	22
8	Switzerland	19
9	Spain	17½
10	Bulgaria	17
11	England	16
12	Austria	15½

Group B

13	Hungary	31
14	Holland	28½
15	Canada	24½
16	Columbia	24½
17	Israel	23½
18	Denmark	23
19	Poland	22½
20	Sweden	21
21	Finland	19
22	Iceland	18
23	France	15
24	Belgium	13½

Group C

25	Norway	30
26	Philippines	29½
27	South Africa	28
28	Italy	26½
29	Scotland	25½

30	Greece	25
31	Portugal	23
32	Iran	20
33	Puerto Rico	14½
34	Ireland	14½
35	Tunisia	14
36	Lebanon	13½

XIV Leipzig 1960
Group A

1	U.S.S.R.	34
	(Tal, Botvinnik, Keres, Korchnoi, Smyslov, Petrosian)	
2	U.S.A.	29
3	Yugoslavia	27
4	Hungary	22½
5	Czechoslovakia	21½
6	Bulgaria	21
7	Argentina	20½
8	West Germany	19½
9	East Germany	19
10	Holland	17
11	Rumania	16½
12	England	16½

Group B

13	Sweden	27½
14	Israel	26½
15	Austria	24½
16	Denmark	23½
17	Finland	23½
18	Cuba	23
19	Norway	23
20	Spain	22½
21	Poland	22
22	Chile	19½
23	Iceland	16½
24	India	12

Group C

25	Philippines	28½
26	Indonesia	27½
27	Mongolia	27½
28	Albania	26½
29	Equador	26
30	Portugal	26
31	France	25
32	Italy	24
33	Belgium	23½
34	Tunisia	21½
35	Greece	20½
36	Bolivia	19½
37	Monaco	17½

38	Ireland	17
39	Malta	14
40	Lebanon	8½

XV Varna 1962
Group A

1	U.S.S.R.	31½
	(Botvinnik, Petrosian, Spassky, Keres, Geller, Tal)	
2	Yugoslavia	28
3	Argentina	26
4	U.S.A.	25
5	Hungary	23
6	Bulgaria	21½
7	West Germany	21
8	East Germany	20½
9	Rumania	20½
10	Czechoslovakia	18½
11	Holland	18
12	Austria	10½

Group B

13	Spain	26½
14	England	26½
15	Israel	25
16	Cuba	22½
17	Sweden	22½
18	Poland	22½
19	Belgium	22
20	Finland	20½
21	Mongolia	20
22	Switzerland	20
23	Iceland	19
24	Denmark	17

Group C

25	Norway	32½
26	Albania	28½
27	Tunisia	28½
28	India	26½
29	Iran	25
30	France	23½
31	Puerto Rico	22½
32	Uruguay	22
33	Greece	18½
34	Luxembourg	18
35	Turkey	17
36	Ireland	14½
37	Cyprus	1½

XVI Tel Aviv 1964
Group A
1	U.S.S.R.	36½
	(Petrosian, Botvinnik,	
	Smyslov, Keres, Stein,	
	Spassky)	
2	Yugoslavia	32
3	West Germany	30½
4	Hungary	30
5	Czechoslovakia	28½
6	U.S.A.	27½
7	Rumania	27
8	Bulgaria	26½
9	Argentina	26
10	Poland	24
11	Holland	21½
12	Canada	19
13	Israel	17½
14	Spain	17½

Group B
15	East Germany	38½
16	Sweden	32
17	Denmark	31½
18	England	31
19	Austria	27½
20	Peru	27½
21	Cuba	26
22	Mongolia	25½
23	Norway	25½
24	Chile	24
25	Philippines	22½
26	Equador	18
27	Paraguay	17½
28	Scotland	17

Group C
29	Iceland	37½
30	Switzerland	36½
31	Columbia	35
32	Finland	35
33	Venezuela	30½
34	France	29½
35	Greece	27½
36	Iran	23½
37	India	22
38	Puerto Rico	21½
39	Turkey	20½
40	Mexico	20
41	Ireland	13
42	Monaco	12

Group D
43	Australia	22½
44	South Africa	18
45	Bolivia	15½
46	Uruguay	14½
47	Portugal	14
48	Luxembourg	12
49	Dominican Rep.	10½
50	Cyprus	5

XVII Havana 1966
Group A
1	U.S.S.R.	39½
	(Petrosian, Spassky,	
	Tal, Stein, Korchnoi,	
	Polugayevsky)	
2	U.S.A.	34½
3	Hungary	33½
4	Yugoslavia	33½
5	Argentina	30
6	Czechoslovakia	29½
7	Bulgaria	28½
8	Rumania	26½
9	East Germany	25½
10	Denmark	20
11	Iceland	19
12	Spain	18
13	Norway	14
14	Cuba	12

Group B
15	Holland	37
16	Poland	31½
17	Austria	30
18	Switzerland	28½
19	Israel	28½
20	Finland	28
21	England	27½
22	Columbia	26½
23	Canada	25½
24	Sweden	24½
25	Belgium	23
26	France	20
27	Indonesia	18
28	Scotland	15½

Group C
29	Italy	38
30	Mongolia	33½
31	Philippines	31
32	Greece	29
33	Uruguay	28
34	Tunisia	26½
35	Turkey	25½
36	Venezuela	25
37	Chile	25
38	Portugal	23½
39	Equador	23½
40	Ireland	21
41	Puerto Rico	18½
42	Luxembourg	16

Group D
43	South Africa	28
44	Mexico	24½
45	Bolivia	22
46	Monaco	20
47	Morocco	19½
48	Nicaragua	17
49	Panama	16½
50	Lebanon	11
51	Cyprus	11
52	Hong Kong	10½

XVIII Lugano 1968
Group A
1	U.S.S.R.	
	(Petrosian, Spassky,	
	Korchnoi, Geller,	
	Polugayevsky, Smyslov)	
2	Yugoslavia	31
3	Bulgaria	30
4	U.S.A.	29½
5	West Germany	29
6	Hungary	27½
7	Argentina	26
8	Rumania	26
9	Czechoslovakia	24½
10	East Germany	24½
11	Poland	23
12	Denmark	21
13	Canada	19
14	Philippines	13½

Group B
15	Holland	33½
16	England	33
17	Austria	30½
18	Israel	30
19	Spain	28½
20	Cuba	27
21	Switzerland	27
22	Iceland	26
23	Finland	24½
24	Sweden	22½
25	Brazil	21½
26	Belgium	20½
27	Mongolia	20
28	Scotland	19½

Group C

29	Australia	38
30	Norway	36
31	Italy	31½
32	Venezuela	30
33	Turkey	29½
34	Greece	28½
35	Portugal	27½
36	South Africa	27½
37	Tunisia	26
38	Ireland	21
39	Luxembourg	20½
40	Puerto Rico	19½
41	Morocco	16
42	Monaco	12½

Group D

43	Singapore	32
44	France	30
45	Paraguay	27½
46	Mexico	23½
47	Dominican Rep.	23½
48	Hong Kong	22½
49	Costa Rica	14½
50	Lebanon	13½
51	Cyprus	13
52	Virgin Islands	11
53	Andorra	9

XIX Siegen 1970

Group A

1	U.S.S.R.	27½

(Spassky Petrosian, Korchnoi Polugayevsky, Smysov, Geller)

2	Hungary	26½
3	Yugoslavia	26
4	U.S.A.	24½
5	Czechoslovakia	23½
6	West Germany	22
7	Bulgaria	21½
8	Argentina	21½
9	East Germany	19
10	Rumania	18½
11	Canada	17½
12	Spain	16

Group B

13	Israel	27½
14	Poland	25
15	Australia	24
16	Mongolia	23½
17	Sweden	23½
18	Holland	23
19	Denmark	22
20	Finland	21
21	Cuba	20
22	Austria	19½
23	Colombia	18
24	Indonesia	17

Group C

25	England	30
26	Philippines	27½
27	Iceland	26
28	Brazil	25½
29	Norway	24
30	Italy	22½

31	Greece	20½
32	Iran	19
33	Belgium	18½
34	Scotland	18½
35	Tunisia	17½
36	Puerto Rico	14½

Group D

37	Switzerland	29½
38	Albania	28
39	Peru	27½
40	Singapore	26½
41	Portugal	24½
42	Ireland	23½
43	South Africa	22½
44	Mexico	21
45	Lebanon	17
46	Luxembourg	15½
47	Japan	15
48	Dominican Rep.	13½

Group E

49	New Zealand	36
50	Rhodesia	28
51	Turkey	28
52	Malta	27½
53	Hong Kong	26
54	Morocco	25
55	Faroe Islands	19
56	Andorra	18
57	Cyprus	16
58	Virgin Islands	15
59	Guernsey	13
60	Monaco	12½

LADIES' OLYMPIADS

I Emmen 1957

Group A

1	U.S.S.R.	10½
2	Rumania	10½
3	East Germany	10
4	Hungary	8½
5	Bulgaria	8
6	Yugoslavia	7½
7	England	7
8	West Germany	6
9	Holland	4

Group B

10	U.S.A.	8
11	Czechoslovakia	8
12	Poland	7½
13	Denmark	4½
14	Ireland	1
15	Scotland	1

Group C

16	France	8½
17	Austria	7½
18	Finland	6
19	Norway	4½
20	Belgium	2½
21	Luxemburg	1

II Split 1963

1	U.S.S.R.	25
2	Yugoslavia	24½
3	East Germany	21
4	Rumania	18½
5	Bulgaria	17½
6	Hungary	17
7	Holland	15½
8	Poland	15
9	U.S.A.	12½
10	West Germany	10½
11	Mongolia	10½
12	Austria	8
13	Belgium	5

14 Monaco	5		
15 Scotland	4½		

III Oberhausen 1966

1 U.S.S.R.	22
2 Rumania	20½
3 East Germany	17
4 Yugoslavia	16½
5 Holland	16
6 Hungary	15
7 Czechoslovakia	15
8 Bulgaria	14

9 England	12
10 U.S.A.	9½
11 Poland	9
12 West Germany	6½
13 Denmark	5
14 Austria	4

IV Lublin 1969

1 U.S.S.R.	26
2 Hungary	20½
3 Czechoslovakia	19

4 Yugoslavia	18½
5 Bulgaria	17½
6 East Germany	17
7 Poland	16½
8 Rumania	16½
9 Holland	13
10 England	12½
11 West Germany	10
12 Denmark	10
13 Austria	6
14 Belgium	4½
15 Ireland	2½

THE OPENINGS AT SKOPJE

L. S. Blackstock

To do justice to a tournament of nearly 2800 games would require an immense amount of space so I have limited myself to the more important theoretical contributions. Despite the regrettable absence of both Fischer and Spassky their influence was clearly present as several games followed variations which had been played in the recent World Championship match.

Ruy Lopez

1 P–K4 P–K4   2 N–KB3 N–QB3 3 B–N5 P–QR3   4 B–R4 N–B3   5 0–0 B–K2   6 R–K1 P–QN4   7 B–N3 P–Q3   8 P–B3 0–0   9 P–KR3 N–N1   10 P–Q4 (Matanovic was successful against Hecht with 10 P–QR4 B–N2   11 P–Q3 QN–Q2 12 P×P P×P   13 R×R B×R   14 N–R3) 10 . . . QN–Q2 11 QN–Q2 B–N2   12 B–B2 R–K1   13 P–QN4 B–KB1   14 P–QR4 N–N3   15 P–R5 QN–Q2.

139 W

This position arose in the 10th game at Reykjavik and Fischer played 16 B–N2 Q–N1 17 R–N1! with a complicated position. After 16 B–N2, Tringov-Ree continued 16 . . . P–N3 17 P–B4 NP×P 18 P–Q5 P–B3 19 P×P B×P 20 N× BP with a minute advantage to

White but 17 Q–N1! followed by Q–R2 is thought to be stronger. Instead of 16 B–N2, Savon played immediately 16 R–N1 against Vogt, allowing Black to equalize with 16 . . . P–Q4!   17 KP×P KP×P 18 N×P B×QP. It is not clear why nobody played 14 . . . P–QR4! in this variation which seems to guarantee immediate equality.

Pirc/Modern Defence

Fischer's only experience with the Pirc was in the 17th game at Reykjavik which opened 1 P–K4 P–Q3 2 P–Q4 P–KN3   3 N–QB3 N–KB3 4 P–B4 B–N2   5 N–B3 P–B4   6 P×P Q–R4   7 B–Q3 Q×BP   8 Q–K2 0–0   9 B–K3 Q–QR4   10 0–0 B–N5 11 QR–Q1 (Tatai-Suttles continued 11 P–KR3 B×N   12 Q×B N–B3 13 P–R3 as Korchnoi recommended after the match and after 13 . . . N–Q2   14 B–Q2 Q–N3   15 K–R1 N–B4   16 QR–N1 was eventually drawn) 11 . . . N–B3   12 B–B4 N–R4   13 B–N3 B/N2×N   14 P×B Q×BP   15 P–B5 N–B3. A suggested alternative was 15 . . . N–K4 to answer 16 B–Q4 with 16 . . . N–KB5. Instead, Gligoric-Hort continued 15 . . . N–R4   16 B–Q4!

Q–B2 17 P–KR3 (17 Q–Q2 was probably stronger) 17 . . . N×B 18 BP×N B×N 19 Q×B N–B3 20 Q–B4 and White has active play for his pawn.

Ljubojevic has been successful in the past with 1 P–K4 P–Q3 2 P–Q4 N–KB3 3 N–QB3 P–KN3 4 P–B4 B–N2 5 B–B4 e.g: 5 . . . N×P?! (better is 5 . . . P–Q4 6 P×P QN–Q2 7 N–B3 0–0 8 N–K5 N–N3 9 B–N3 P–QR4 Ljubojevic-Keene, Palma 1971) 6 B×P+ K×B 7 N×N R–K1 8 N–KB3 K–N1 9 0–0 N–Q2 10 P–B3 N–B3 11 Q–N3+ P–Q4 12 N–B2 with advantage Ljubojevic - Donner, Palma 1971. However, Jansa has now found a more than satisfactory reply: 5 . . . P–B4! 6 P–K5 KN–Q2 7 N–B3 BP×P 8 Q×P 0–0 9 Q–K4 N–QB3 10 P–K6 P×P 11 B×P+ K–R1 12 Q–K2 N–B4 and Black already stands much better.

Rodriguez-Keene opened 1 P–K4 P–KN3 2 P–Q4 P–Q3 3 P–QB3 B–N2 4 P–B4 N–KB3 5 B–Q3 0–0 6 N–B3. At this point theory mentions only 6 . . . QN–Q2 7 0–0 P–B4 8 P–K5!± but Keene found 6 . . . P–B4! 7 P×P QN–Q2! 8 P×P P×P 9 B–K3 R–K1 10 0–0 N×P 11 B×N R×B 12 B–Q4 N–B3 13 N–N5 R–K2 and Black has recovered his pawn with much the better game.

Sicilian Defence

1 P–K4 P–QB4 2 N–KB3 P–Q3 3 P–Q4 P×P 4 N×P N–KB3 5 N–QB3 P–QR3 6 B–KN5 P–K3 7 P–B4 B–K2 8 Q–B3 Q–B2 9 0–0–0 QN–Q2 10 B–Q3 P–QN4 11 KR–K1 B–N2.

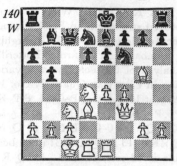

Surprisingly there were no further tests of 12 Q–N3 which Spassky played in the 15th match game, but two games continued with Velimirovic's speculative 12 N–Q5. After 12 N–Q5 N×N 13 P×N Wibe-Alvarez continued 13 . . . N–B3 (instead of 13 . . . B×B 14 R×P+ Velimirovic - Ljubojevic Yugoslav Ch. 1972 which remains unclear) but after 14 B×N B×B 15 B–K4 P–K4 16 N–B6 White had a clear positional advantage.

Boey-Hamann went 12 N–Q5 P×N 13 N–B5 P–R3! (a prepared improvement on 13 . . . B–KB1 14 P–K5! Enevoldsen-Hamann, Denmark 1972 which Black lost disastrously) and after 14 P–K5 P×P 15 P×P N×P 16 R×N Q×R 17 B–KB4 P–Q5! 18 B×Q B×Q 19 P×B K–B1 20 N×B K×N 21 B×QP KR–QB1 White had insufficient compensation for the exchange.

The sacrifice also occurred in a different form when Black had omitted B–K2. 7 . . . QN–Q2 8 Q–B3 Q–B2 9 0–0–0 P–QN4 10 B–Q3 B–N2 11 KR–K1 P–N5 (11 . . . B–K2 would transpose to the previous line) 12 N–Q5! P×N 13 P×P+ K–Q1 14 B–B5! B–K2 15 B–K6! R–KB1 16 B×P R×B

17 N–K6+ and White's queen proved stronger than Black's assortment of pieces in Kavalek-Gheorghiu.

Dueball-Kerr confirmed Botterill's analysis of the Polugayevsky variation in Chessman Quarterly No. 13, August 1970. 7 . . . P–QN4 8 P–K5 P×P 9 P×P Q–B2 10 Q–K2 KN–Q2 11 0–0–0 B–N2 12 Q–N4 Q×KP 13 B–Q3 P–R3! (The book line is 13 . . . N–KB3 14 Q–R4! with advantage) 14 B–R4 P–N4!! (not 14 . . . P–KR4 15 Q×KP+!) 15 N×KP (Botterill also mentions 15 KR–K1 P–KR4 16 Q–R3 Q–B5+!) 15 . . . P–KR4! and now Dueball sacrificed his queen unsoundly by 16 Q×NP B–R3 but no better are 16 Q–R3 B–R3! or 16 N–B7+ Q×N2 17 KR–K1+ N–K4 18 B×QNP+ P×B 19 N×P P×Q 20 N×Q+ K–K2 21 B×P+P–B3 22 R×N+ K–B2 23 N×R P×R.

Hamann-Gligoric confirmed the opinion from the World Championship match that K-side castling for White is innocuous in the Sozin. 1 P–K4 P–QB4 2 N–KB3 N–QB3 3 P–Q4 P×P 4 N×P N–KB3 5 N–QB3 P–Q3 6 B–QB4 P–K3 7 B–K3 P–QR3 8 0–0 B–K2 9 B–N3 0–0 10 P–B4 N×N 11 B×N P–QN4.

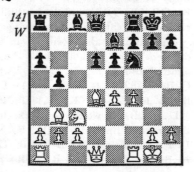

141
W

In this position Fischer played 12 P–QR3 and had the worst of it after 12 . . . B–N2 13 Q–Q3 P–QR4! Hamann tried 12 P–K5 P×P 13 P×P N–Q2 14 N–K4 B–N2 15 N–Q6 but after 15 . . . B×N 16 P×B Q–N4 17 Q–K2 P–K4 Black's central pawns gave him the better chances.

The game Karpov-Dueball witnessed an interesting move order in the Dragon. (For whole game see No. 109, p. 153).

A drastic improvement occurred in the game Hort-Jansson. 1 P–K4 P–QB4 2 N–KB3 P–Q3 3 B–N5+ B–Q2 4 B×B+ Q×B 5 P–B4 N–QB3 6 N–QB3 P–KN3 7 P–Q4 P×P 8 N×P B–N2 9 B–K3 N–R3 10 P–B3 P–B4 11 Q–Q2 N–B2 12 P×P P×P 13 P–B4 B×N 14 B×B Q–K3+. All this had happened in Minic-Stein, Zagreb 1972. Minic played 15 K–B2 R–KN1 16 P–QN3 and lost 4 moves later. Hort, who had played in that tournament, continued 15 K–Q1 R–KN1 16 N–Q5 K–Q2 17 R–K1 and won in another 7 moves!

Queen's Gambit Declined

1 N–KB3 P–Q4 2 P–B4 P–B3 3 P–Q4 P–K3 4 N–B3 N–B3 5 P–K3 QN–Q2 6 B–Q3 P×P 7 B×BP P–QN4 8 B–Q3 P–N5 9 N–QR4 P–B4. Toran-Filip continued 10 N×P though 10 P–K4 is usually considered stronger. Black tried to play as in the Larsen variation (8 . . . B–N2) by giving up the two bishops. The result was an instructive miniature. 10 . . . B×N 11 P×B N×P 12 B–N5+ K–K2 13 N–Q4 B–N2

14 0–0 Q–N3 15 P–QR3! P×P
16 P–QN3! P–QR3 17 B–B4 KR–
Q1 18 B/1×RP K–K1 19 Q–K2
N/B4–Q2 20 P–B4 P–N3 21 Q–K1
B–Q4 22 Q–R4 Q–B2 23 Q–R6
N–KN1 24 Q×RP N–K2 25 N×P
1–0.

English

1 P–QB4 N–KB3 2 N–KB3 P–KN3
3 N–B3 P–Q4 4 P×P N×P 5
Q–R4+ B–Q2 6 Q–KR4. Schmidt-
Portisch continued 6 . . . B–B3! 7
P–KN3? (better is 7 Q–Q4) 7 . . .
B–N2 8 B–N2 0–0 9 0–0 P–K4
and Black is already slightly better.
This is an improvement on
Gheorghiu-Olafsson, Moscow 1971
which went 6 . . . N–KB3 7 P–
KN3 P–B4 8 B–N2 N–B3 9 0–0
B–N2 10 P–Q4! with a clear
advantage to White.

King's Indian Defence

1 P–Q4 N–KB3 2 P–QB4 P–KN3
3 N–QB3 B–N2 4 P–K4 P–Q3 5
N–B3 0–0 6 B–K2 P–K4 7 P–Q5
QN–Q2 8 B–N5 P–KR3 9 B–R4
P–KN4 10 B–N3 N–R4 11 P–KR4
P–N5 12 N–R2 N×B 13 P×N
P–KB4 14 P×P N–B4 15 N×P
B×P 16 0–0 P–K5 17 Q–Q2 B×N
18 B×B Q–K2.

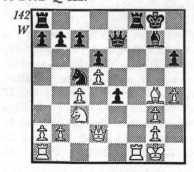

This critical position in the Petrosian system now seems quite satisfactory for Black as was shown by
Rodriguez-Gligoric which is worth
quoting in full.

19 Q–K3 (Bukic-Gligoric, Budva
1967 went 19 R×R+ R×R 20
R–K1 Q–K4 21 K–R2 R–B3 22
Q–K2 R–N3 23 R–KB1 and White
won but 21 . . . N–Q6 22 R–K2
P–N3 was better) 19 . . . Q–K4
20 R×R+ R×R 21 R–KB1
(O'Kelly-Gligoric, Havana 1967
went 21 R–Q1 N–Q6 22 N×P
N×P 23 R–QB1 N–R5 with
equality) 21 . . . Q–Q5 22 R×R+
K×R 23 Q×Q B×Q+ 24 K–B1
B×N 25 P×B N–R5 26 K–B2
N×P 27 P–R3 P–N4! 28 P×P
N×NP 29 K–K3 N×P 30 K×P
N–B5 31 B–Q1 P–QR4 32 P–N4
K–N2 33 B–B2 N–N3 34 B–N3
K–B3 35 B–R2 P–R5 36 K–B4
P–R6 37 K–K4 N–Q2 38 K–B4
N–K4 39 P–N5+ P×P+ 40
P×P+ K–N2 41 K–B5 N–Q6
42 K–K6 N–N5 43 B–N3 P–R7
44 B×P N×B 45 K–Q7 N–B6
46 K×P N–K5 0–1.

Modern Benoni

1 P–Q4 N–KB3 2 P–QB4 P–B4
3 P–Q5 P–K3 4 N–QB3 P×P 5
P×P P–Q3 6 P–K4 P–KN3 7
N–B3 B–N2 8 B–K2 0–0 9 0–0
R–K1 10 N–Q2 QN–Q2 11 P–
QR4 (Spassky played 11 Q–B2 in
the 3rd match game which seems
to be less accurate on account of
11 . . . N–R4 12 B×N P×B 13
N–B4 N–K4 14 N–K3 Q–R5).
Gligoric-Kavalek now continued 11
. . . N–K4 12 Q–B2 N–R4 with the

same idea as Fischer but in a slightly different situation. Fischer did well with 12 . . . P–KN4 13 N–B3 N×N+ against Gligoric at Palma 1970 but better was 13 N–B4 N×N 14 B×N N–N5 15 N–K2! P–QR3 16 R–R3 Q–K2 17 R–KN3!± Najdorf-Ree, Wijk aan Zee 1971. After Kavalek's 12 . . . N–R4, 13 B×N P×B 14 N–Q1 Q–R5 15 N–K3 N–N5 16 N×N P×N 17 N- B4 proved to be good for White.

Nimzo-Indian Defence

1 P–Q4 N–KB3 2 P–QB4 P–K3 3 N–QB3 B–N5 4 P–K3 P–B4 5 B–Q3 N–B3 6 N–B3 B×N+ 7 P×B P–Q3 8 P–K4 P–K4 9 P–Q5 N–K2 10 N–R4 P–KR3 11 P–B3 (Spassky played 11 P–B4 in game 5 without much success). Some previous examples of this position are 11 . . . P–KN4 12 N–B5 B×N 13 P×B Q–R4 14 Q–B2 0–0–0 15 P–KR4 P–K5 with a sharp position, Donner - Damjanovic, Cienguegos 1972, or 11 . . . P–KN4 12 N–B5 N×N 13 P×N N–R4 14 P–N3 N–N2 15 Q–B2 B–Q2 16 K–B2 Q–B3 with approximate equality, Donner-Langeweg, Wijk aan Zee 1971. Donner-Portisch continued 11 . . . Q–R4 12 Q–B2 P–KN4 13 N–B5 N×N 14 P×N B–Q2 15 P–KR4 P–N5 with an excellent position for Black.
1 P–Q4 N–KB3 2 P–QB4 P–K3 3 N–QB3 B–N5 4 P–K3 0–0 5 B–Q3 P–B4 6 N–B3 P–Q4 7 0–0 QP×P 8 B×BP QN–Q2 9 Q–K2 P–QR3 10 P–QR4 Q–B2 11 N–R2! P–QN4! 12 B–Q3! The only previous record of this position is

Antoshin-Keres, Moscow 1963 which continued 12 . . . B–R4 13 P–K4 P–B5 14 B–N1 P–K4 15 RP×P KP×P 16 N×P B–N3 with a complicated position. Portisch-Ardiansjah varied with 12 . . . NP×P 13 N×B P×N 14 R×P P–QR4 15 P–K4 Q–B3! 16 R–R1 B–R3 and Black has a comfortable equality.
1 P–Q4 N–KB3 2 P–QB4 P–K3 3 N–QB3 B–N5 4 P–K3 P–B4 5 B–Q3 P–QN3 6 KN–K2 B–N2 7 0–0 P×P 8 P×P B–K2 9 P–Q5. Old theory gives 9 . . . N–R3 10 N–N3 0–0 11 R–K1 N–B2 12 B–B4 with advantage to White, O'Kelly - Portisch, Palma 1967. Portisch-Bobotsov continued with a losing innovation 9 . . . P×P 10 P×P N×P? 11 N×N B×N 12 N–B4! B–N2 13 R–K1 N–B3 14 N–R5! and White has a crushing attack.

Grünfeld Defence

1 P–Q4 N–KB3 2 P–QB4 P–KN3 3 N–QB3 P–Q4 4 N–B3 B–N2 5 P–K3 0–0 6 P×P N×P 7 B–B4 N–N3 8 B–N3 P–QB4 9 0–0 P×P 10 N×P. Now Gligoric-Portisch continued 10 . . . N–B3 which is a new move and after 11 Q–K2 P–QR4 12 R–Q1 N×N 13 P×N P–R5 14 B–B2 R–R4 15 B–K4 P–R6 Black had good chances in the middle-game. This is probably stronger than the old lines which were also sufficient for equality: 10 . . . B–Q2 11 Q–K2 N–B3 12 N×N QB×N 13 R–Q1 Q–B2= Minev-Malich, Varna 1962 or 10 . . . N–R3 11 Q–K2 N–B4 12 B–B2 B–Q2 13 P–QR4 P–K4 14

N–B3 B–K3=Najdorf-Benkö, Los Angeles 1963.

1 P–Q4 N–KB3 2 P–QB4 P–KN3 3 N–QB3 P–Q4 4 N–B3 B–N2 5 B–N5 N–K5 6 P×P N×B 7 N×N P–K3 8 Q–R4+. A risky and old-fashioned line with which Knaak has been successful against 8 . . . B–Q2. The game Knaak-Forintos continued 8 . . . P–QB3! 9 P×BP N×P 10 N–B3 B–Q2 and now instead of 11 Q–Q1 0–0 12 P–K3 Q–N3 13 Q–Q2 P–K4 14 P–Q5 N–Q5! with a good game for Black, Blagidze - Gurgenidze, Tiflis 1959, Knaak tried the new move 11 0–0–0, only to be swept aside after 11 . . . 0–0 12 P–K3 N×P 13 R×N B×Q 14 R×Q KR×R 15 N×B QR–B1+ 16 N–B3 B×N 17 P×B R×P+ 18 K–N2 R/Q1–QB1!

1 P–Q4 N–KB3 2 P–QB4 P–KN3 3 N–QB3 P–Q4 4 B–N5 N–K5 5 B–R4 P–QB4 6 P–K3 N×N 7 P×N B–N2 8 BP×P P×P 9 KP×P Q×P 10 N–B3 N–B3 11 B–K2. This line has been very popular recently and the best buy up to now has been 11 . . . 0–0 12 0–0 P–K4 13 P–B4 Q–K5 14 P–Q5 N–Q5! Bukic-Smejkal, Vrnjacka Banja 1972. Ungureanu-Ribli further refined the variation with 11 . . . P–K4! 12 P×P Q–R4 13 0–0 0–0 14 B–B6 B×B 15 P×B Q–KB4! (if 15 . . . Q×BP 16 Q–Q6! followed by 17 Q–KB4) 16 Q–Q6 R–Q1 17 Q–B7 R–Q2 18 Q–N3 Q×KBP and Black's superior pawn-structure assure him better chances.

1 P–Q4 N–KB3 2 P–QB4 P–KN3 3 N–QB3 P–Q4 4 B–B4

B–N2 5 R–B1 0–0 6 P–K3 P–B4 7 QP×P B–K3 8 N–B3 N–B3 9 B–K2 N–K5. This position has been known for over thirty years and has always been thought quite promising for Black, e.g: 10 Q–R4 B×N+ 11 P×B P×P 12 N–Q4 B–Q4 13 B–R6 KR–K1 14 0–0 P–K4 15 N–B3 N×P/B4 with good play for Black, Ragozin-Botvinnik, match 1940 or 10 P×P N×N 11 P×N B×QP 12 Q–R4 Q–R4 13 Q×Q N×Q 14 P–B4 B–K5 with a strong initiative for the pawn, Lyublinsky-Smyslov, Moscow Ch. 1944.

However, Portisch introduced the simple 10 0–0 which still seems to set Black some problems;

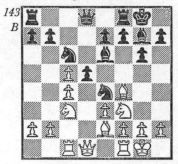

Portisch-Schmidt continued (after 10 0–0) 10 . . . B×N 11 P×B P×P 12 N–Q4 N×P/B4 13 B–R6 R–K1 14 N×B N×N 15 B×P N–B4 16 Q–K2 Q–R4 17 P–B4 N–K5 18 B×P+ K×B 19 Q–B4+ P–K3 20 Q×NK4 Q×RP 21 QR–Q1 QR–Q1 22 B–N5 R–Q7 23 P–B4 Q–R4 24 Q–N1 R×R 25 R×R Q–B2 26 P–R4 N–R4 27 Q–N5 N–B3 28 Q–N2 P–K4 29 R–Q5 P×P 30 P×P K–N1 31 Q–Q2 N–N1 32 B–R6 Q×QBP 33 P–R5 K–B2 34 R–KN5 R–K7 35 P×P+ P×P 36 Q–Q6 1–0.

In a later round Schmidt sought to improve by retaining the bishop-pair but this proved to involve some difficulties in regaining the bishop's pawn.

Hamann-Schmidt went 10 . . .
N×N   11 P×N P×P   12 N-N5
B-Q2   13 B×P N-R4   14 B-K2
R-B1   15 P-K4! R×P   16 B-K3
R-B1   17 B×P N-B5   18 N-B3
P-K4   19 Q-N3 P-QN4   20 KR-Q1 R-B2   21 B×N R×B   22 B-K3
Q-K2   23 N-Q2 R-R5   24 P-QB4
R-R6   25 Q-N1 P-N5   26 P-B5
B-R5   27 R-K1 B-QB3   28 Q×P
R×P   29 R-R1 R×R   30 R×R
R-B1   31 N-B4 B-B1   32 P-B3
Q-K3   33 R-R6 R-R1   34 R×R
B×R   35 N-R5 Q-R3   36 P-R3
Q-Q6   37 B-B2 Q-Q1   38 Q-N6
Q-Q8+   39 K-R2 Q-Q7   40 P-B6
1-0.

Index of Games

(The numbers refer to games. Bold type indicates that the first named player has White, p following the number indicates a a game position.)

Index of Openings

No's are game numbers. Brackets indicate transposition.